THE METAPHYSICAL POETS

THE MACMILLAN COMPANY
NEW YORK · BOSTON · CHICAGO · DALLAS
ATLANTA · SAN FRANCISCO

MACMILLAN & CO., Limited
LONDON · BOMBAY · CALCUTTA
MELBOURNE

THE MACMILLAN COMPANY
OF CANADA, Limited
TORONTO

THE
METAPHYSICAL POETS

A STUDY IN RELIGIOUS EXPERIENCE

BY

HELEN C. WHITE

NEW YORK
THE MACMILLAN COMPANY
1936

To

Frederick A. Manchester
who encouraged my first critical studies

ACKNOWLEDGMENTS

My thanks are due, first of all, to the John Simon Guggenheim Memorial Foundation and to the Research Committee of the Graduate School of the University of Wisconsin for the generous grants of funds that made possible the research on which this study is based and the writing of the book. For help with the preparation of bibliography I am indebted to Miss Leslie Spence and Miss Ada I. Thompson of the University of Wisconsin. For valuable suggestions and aid received at various stages of my work I should like to express my appreciation to Professor H. J. C. Grierson of Edinburgh University, to Miss Edith C. Batho of University College, London, to Miss Julia Grace Wales of the University of Wisconsin, to Miss Kathleen I. Barratt of King's College, London, who put at my disposal her master's thesis on Herbert and gave me the benefit of her textual knowledge, to Mr. P. J. Dobell of Tunbridge Wells, who allowed me to examine his Traherne manuscripts, to Father David Mathew of London, and especially to my colleagues, Miss Ruth C. Wallerstein and Mr. Mark Schorer, who read the book through in manuscript and gave me the benefit of their criticism. Finally, I wish to thank the authorities of the British Museum, the Bodleian Library, Dr. William's Library, the Library of the University of London, Harvard College Library, and the Library of the University of Wisconsin for their unfailing help and courtesy.

H. C. W.

Madison, Wisconsin,
June 1, 1936

CONTENTS

THE METAPHYSICAL POETS

MYSTICISM AND POETRY

POETRY and mysticism have, to begin with, this in common, that both alike belong to the field of contemplation rather than of action. Both are concerned primarily with the recognition of pattern, of significance, ultimately of value, in the world about them and within them. As distinguished from the man of action, say, the contemplative is concerned not with the conquest of the external world but with the understanding of it. Not possession but appreciation is his goal. The poet does not wish to carry the sunset home in his hat but with the eyes of his body and his mind to seize upon it so that the memory of it will abide with him. The mystic does not think of his God as a faithful genie to answer the rubbing of some Aladdin's lamp of prayer. He does not pray that his God will do his will, but only that He will give him Himself that he may behold Him face to face. The hunger for God is the basic human hunger, so every mystic of every tradition agrees. "Thou madest us for Thyself, and our heart is restless, until it repose in Thee," is the way Saint Augustine puts it.[1] "Beauty is its own excuse for being," said the poet Emerson as he looked upon the woodland flower.[2] But in each case the satisfaction of the hunger, the final justification of the experience, is to be found in the experience itself.

Once aboard ship I heard a spiritual globe-trotter, famous for the catholicity and zest of his religious appreciation, tell a curious audience of American tourists about the almost miraculous energy and accomplishments of an Oriental mystic. It

1

was at the height of our late prosperity when anything seemed possible to the aggressive disciple of the strenuous life, and it was frightening to see the intentness with which that audience listened to the speaker's suggestion of undreamed-of energies to be discovered in the mystic's contact with God. One of that audience at least was reminded of the enthusiasm with which Milton's fallen angels set about prospecting the burning fields of hell for gold and silver and precious stones. So the dupes of a power-maddened age listened with bated breath to this news of a super-source of power waiting to be tapped and exploited. Damming Niagara Falls to turn a wheel seemed a puny thing to the possibilities of this super-dynamo of God, and focussing the rays of the universal sun to roast an egg a triumph of the fitness of things. But eight centuries ago the Moslem woman Rabi'a had prayed, "O God! if I worship Thee for fear of Hell, send me to Hell; and if I worship Thee in hopes of Paradise, withhold Paradise from me; but if I worship Thee for Thine own sake, then withhold not from me the Eternal Beauty." [3] And the story is told of the mystic, Thomas Aquinas, that, as he knelt in the Church of Saint Dominic in Naples, weary from the labor of his great defence of the Real Presence in the Sacrament, he heard the voice of his Master speak from the crucifix before him. And the Voice asked him what reward he would have for the work he had done so well. The answer which the great theologian is said to have returned on that occasion is the one answer of which the mystic could approve, "I will have Thyself." [4]

In other words, for poet and mystic alike, it is the contemplation of the object, and not its conquest or its use toward some other end, that is the purpose of their being. The triumph of utilitarianism in the last century set up a final criterion for all human activity, "What use is it?" The humanitarianism of the Victorians gave that standard some elements of breadth and generosity. But the scepticism of altruism that is so widespread today has made of it something narrower and harder. The man in the street in a certain light-hearted revue of a summer or two ago in London expressed a common attitude when he confronted a lively travesty of the glories of the national history with the persistent challenge, "What good did it do me?" It is significant of their basic relation that poetry and mysticism alike suffer in an age that glorifies action at the expense of contemplation, utility at the expense of understanding or delight, and material achievement at the cost of worship. For in their essence both poetry and mysticism are contemplative activities, finding in the attainment of their object their own excuse for being.

The mystic and the poet are alike, also, in that neither is willing to remain passive. So often unresisting submission to the flood of experience seems the sole alternative to the aggressive conquest of one's environment, to the imposition of one's own mood upon the offerings of the day, to the bending of one's surroundings, animate and inanimate, to one's private purpose, that it is worthwhile remembering that there is another way in which the opportunities of experience may be even more richly fulfilled. The contemplative does not remain helpless before the impact of experience. True, he does not repel it, but neither does he fall bewildered before it. He receives it, with a thousand tentacles of awareness taking possession of what cannot be possessed in any other way. In a certain sense, perhaps, he surrenders to the fullness of the moment, but it is a selective surrender. What he gives up is no jot of his own identity or of his own integrity but only those preoccupations, those reserves, those impediments of appetite and passion, that insulate the private spirit. To the contemplation of a beautiful sunset, for instance, I bring myself, together with those misgivings, those anxieties, those irritations, perhaps those greeds or resentments, that clog and imprison and heat the potential self. These I surrender, or rather am relieved of, in a sudden

inrush of sense and feeling that takes possession of the re-
leased spirit. The word that bruised, the thought that fettered,
are forgotten in the light of color, the spacious freedom of the
effortless clouds, the coolness of the vast and unbroken air.
But I am there still, in a thousand suggestions and recollections
of other sunsets seen, far perhaps from this inland prairie, at
sea, or from foreign hill-tops, or behind dimly glimpsed and
still alien mountains. There are memories of paintings which
have hinted of things to look for in color and the stratification
of the clouds. There are the words of poets—it was Coleridge
who first in "This Lime Tree Bower" opened to me the cool
delight of that greenish yellow that comes only when the first
glory of the sunset is spent. There are the fantasies of childhood when the eyes of unspoiled wonder beheld the souls of
the day's dead go riding joyously through the light-foaming
gates of heaven, or in the remoter swirls of orchid and topaz
saw the Valkyries of the singers and the Aurora of the sculptors
urging unimagined steeds and chariots through the melting
distance. Then there are those deeper thoughts of light fading
here to shine on other worlds—and with these delight and release pass into awe and that simple lifting of the heart that is
perhaps the most universal and the most basic of the forms of
worship of the race.

All of this is, of course, highly selective. Past experience,
taste, ignorance even, play their part in the choice of im-
pressions to be received and still more to be registered. In that
sense even the fullest surrender to the moment is imperfect.
For in the very act of selection experience is shaped by the
patterning habits of the mind that receives it. And still more
when the individual consciousness takes possession of the im-
pressions of the moment, registering them and, as it were,
naturalizing them in its own contexts of association, then
obviously the role of the contemplative consciousness assumes
a character far from passive. Finally, when the contemplative,

so to speak, assimilates the experience, or at least that portion of it which he is capable of assimilating, the active element in the process of contemplation becomes quite obvious. For, the very delight of the artist in the materials of beauty, like the awe of the worshipper, involves a process of identification, of reference, of determination of context. In other words, the poet and the mystic find in the experience its pattern, its value, its significance. "What a beautiful sunset!" "The heavens declare the glory of God." [5] Each in its degree is a conclusion of meaning, of value. In reaching such a conclusion, the mind and the heart of the contemplative act upon the materials of the experience, and to that extent elements of aggression do enter into the act of contemplation. But it is upon the materials of the experience as they exist within himself and not upon the source of those materials that the poet or the mystic works. And in that sense the operations of the contemplative differ fundamentally from those of the man of action.

In other words, contemplation belongs to the realm of the mind and the spirit. But what one may call the process of contemplation is still essentially different from the usual working of the mind in two very important respects. The first is that character of total-working that is perhaps the most striking element in contemplation whether it be the contemplation of the mystic or the contemplation of the poet. No one who has ever tried to analyze a poem as one must, say, when one is trying to help an inexperienced reader to get hold of it, can fail to appreciate the indissoluble integrity of the poet's experience. He did, it is true, see certain things, and feel certain things, and think certain things, but he did not first see and then feel and then think, but he did these things all at once. Nothing makes a teacher of poetry feel so helpless when, for instance, he is trying to share with a novice even his partial understanding of the poet's experience as this overwhelming sense of the integrity of the experience. And still more is this true when the expression of experience with which he is dealing is the report of a mystical experience. Even something so matter-of-fact, so humbly point-by-point, as the account which Bernard of Clairvaux in one of his sermons on the Canticle of Canticles gave to his brethren of what seems to have happened when he was at the height of contemplation, leaves the reader who has caught a glimpse of what Bernard is talking about overpowered with the sense of something beyond the ordinary faculties of the mind.[6] For the mind of man like his body can operate upon the facts of experience only piecemeal. All human action is by very necessity of the basic limitations of human capacity partial and exclusive. We take up one thing at a time, and the rest we do not take up. We look at one thing, and to do so look away from the rest. As Henri Bergson so shrewdly pointed out to the bafflement of all of us who wrestle with the demon of absent-mindedness, we forget in order to think.[6a]

Now the common man, who is neither poet nor mystic but who by virtue of the fact that he is the common man often shows surprising evidence of having the roots of many of these more ambitious trees in his own low ground, has some vague sense of this state of affairs. For instance, nothing is more frequent in the experience of the teacher of literature than the student who objects, "But it spoils the poetry to analyze it." To a certain extent he is right. The process of analysis does do violence to the essential nature of the experience involved. And it is always a good deal of a question whether the student who has been forced to inquire into the grounds of his elementary and hazy reaction to the totality of a poem will be able to reconstitute that integrity of experience on the higher level of awareness to which the teacher is endeavoring to lead him. Similarly, every lover of the mystics who has tried to share his degree of understanding of their value with his non-mystical brother is familiar with the repeated gibe of the sceptic that mysticism is essentially a surrender of thought to emotion.

Indeed, this latter misapprehension is so widespread, the misuse of the term "mystical" as a stick with which to belabor whichever of the "isms" of the present day the speaker most emotionally dislikes, so common, that sometimes it seems as if it might be wiser to give up the term "mysticism" altogether and fall back upon the less inclusive and less misunderstood term, "contemplation." But, however annoying, both misunderstandings, like so many of the philosophic misapprehensions of the common man, rest on a very just, if hazy, perception of a fact, namely, that both the experience of the poet and that of the mystic have an integrity of character that eludes the process of analysis. So it is not surprising that the sentimental uninstructed lover of poetry assumes that the integrity will be damaged by that process of analysis, nor that the sceptic of rationalistic prejudices takes it for granted that what will not survive it never existed anyway.

In this both the student and the sceptic pay homage, even if unconsciously, to the totality of an experience which neither understands, and both recognize the presence of something that is not entirely accounted for or taken possession of by our ordinary analytic methods of point-by-point dissection and diagrammatic summation. Nevertheless both of them mistake the essential nature of the experience of the poet and the mystic in that they assume that its totality of character is identical with and restricted to the unanalyzed continuity of that succession of sensations and perceptions which constitutes the raw-material of experience. In other words, neither recognizes that out of the process of taking possession of that material with all the capacities of the human personality operating at once, there results a new totality, a reintegration of the elements of experience on a higher level, the level of the poet and the mystic.

Now, it is true that in trying to follow that process of reintegration the student of either poetry or mysticism is forced, at least at the beginning, to take up its elements one at a time. And it is probably true that whenever he is trying to explain or to give an account of a piece of poetic or mystical expression, he will be forced to take up one aspect of the activity of the human personality at a time and carry through his exposition more or less in terms of a point-by-point analysis. For instance, in discussing a poem he will be forced to consider imagery before he takes up implied meanings, or vice versa. He cannot discuss both at once without risk of confusion. That is one reason why the critic and the expositor in either field must so often feel himself an obstruction rather than a bridge in this process of communication between the two levels of experience, that of the poet and mystic and that of the common man. For the human personality in either the mature poetic or the mature mystical experience acts as a living unit, and the result is a single and, in the degree of its realization, a whole experience. In spite of the misgivings of the sceptic, the keen and logically alert mind with which Saint Augustine listened to the arguments of the Manichaeans was not put to sleep that wonderful day in the house at Ostia when talking with his mother Monica "of what sort the eternal life of the saints was to be," he seemed to himself to have risen to the very gates of heaven.[7] Nor did Plato lay aside that gift of his for catching the movement of truth in the flash of something seen in a moment's image when he discoursed of the ideal beauty at that immortal banquet which has ever since haunted alike the dreams of poet and mystic. For both of these are whole men, possessed of an uncommon capacity for integrating the energies of the human personality.

No less baffling to the common man than this totality and integrity of contemplative experience is a certain character of "otherness," of something from without and beyond at least the everyday range of either poet or mystic. It is very difficult to find neutral terms to describe an element which depends to so large an extent for its definition upon the psychology, to say nothing of the metaphysics, of the critic. But of the presence of the element, however one may choose to identify it, there can be no question. [Everyone who writes discovers now and then that he has written something so much better than the habitual product of his mind or imagination that not even literary vanity can forbear asking whether this be really he who has written so well. And the same holds true of the mystic. Bernard of Clairvaux, seeking to find words for what happens within his own soul in moments of mystical experience, is finally driven to offer as his final bit of evidence the greater purity and peace that he discovers within himself at such times. "Yet it has not come from within me, for it is good, and I know that in me dwelleth no good thing," he says, drawing upon St. Paul in his extremity.[8] Many terms have been used to describe this feeling of inspiration or possession from the daemon of Socrates to the unconscious of Dr. Freud, but the experience itself is almost universally acknowledged whenever the deeper levels of mind or imagination or feeling are involved in the creation of a work of art.

For the writer or the mystic the predominating mood in the presence of this phenomenon would seem to be one mainly of wonder, the essential character of the experience, surprise. It is not just that the candid spirit knows that nothing so good or great can come out of his normal and habitual self. It is rather that when he was seeking something different, perhaps even something inferior, this happened. There has been a good deal of quite reasonable laughter over the tales of Tennyson, for instance, reading his own verse with obvious delight and even admiration. But we may be sure that there is something more involved in such situations than the obvious vanity. Indeed, probably vanity, however omnipresent, is quite the least of it. We may be sure that just as important for the poet is the surprise at what has suddenly come into his work, beyond his shrewdest calculation, beyond, probably, even his wildest hope. Something of astonishment is, we may be certain, the essential character of all inspiration, and I am not sure but that in the poet's delight in his own work there may not be quite as much of the humility of surprise as of any other emotional or spiritual ingredient.

One of the particular grounds of this astonishment is to be found in the element of sudden fulfilment of hope deferred, of which so many of the mystics speak and which is so familiar in the experience of the creative imagination in any field. One of the best descriptions of the phenomenon, indeed, is to be found in the account which the great French mathematician, Poincaré, gives of his struggles with difficult problems in mathematical creation.[9] The main lines of the experience are widely familiar. The scholar wrestles with a problem in mathematics, the writer tries to bring a situation alive in a story, to round out the beginning of an image, to follow through the curve of a feeling in a poem, or the mystic strives to rise from one level of prayer to another, say from that which finds its expression in words to that in which the aspiration soars fully and warmly without the intervention of words into a closer communion with the Object of all prayer. It does not matter what the field of endeavor is, the process seems to be much the same. The weary and defeated and overlabored spirit confesses its bafflement and for the time being gives over the struggle. Empty, in despair or in acquiescence, it just waits. Perhaps even it turns to other matters, trivial and irrelevant to the essential purpose. And then the wonderful thing happens. Suddenly, the answer to the problem flashes across the seemingly empty mind, and it is as if the sand of the desert had bloomed in a moment with a thousand undreamed-of flowers. Or the scene that had stopped still and turned to stone before one's frantic eyes but a few hours back is suddenly struck to life, and the story out of the imageless air unfolds its seemingly predestinate course. Or the poet with heart bursting from the pressure of feelings but half uttered and then frozen into silence hears the rest of his music, as sudden, as surprising as that first music when the morning stars sang together. Or the contemplative, knocking in vain on the doors of divine indifference suddenly finds that lo, He whom he sought to soar to is here beside him in his own spirit, answering the prayer which mortal frailty had given up all hope of ever being able to frame. It is no wonder that the poet swears that he has caught the music of the spheres, and the mystic is sure that his God has come down from his heaven and entered beneath his low roof, and that even the positivist marvels a little at the mysteries of the mind of man. In such moments the meanest of us is a little more than himself, and the proudest is awed by the sudden inrush of a power beyond the most arrogant of his dreams.

In these things, poetry and mysticism belong to the same world and are subject to much the same processes. No wonder, then, that a man like the late Abbé Brémond, richly in possession of both the fields of poetry and mysticism, should have been so much impressed by their points of likeness that in *Prière et Poésie* he develops them almost at the expense of their points of difference. But those differences are no less important. However similar the experiences of the poet and the mystic may be in the groundwork, the moment we begin to examine them in their peculiar contexts, certain no less striking differences become apparent.

To begin with, the processes of mysticism involve more of the direct application of the will than do those of poetry. There are on record some dramatic cases of sudden illumination, seemingly striking without warning or any apparent preparation on the part of the recipient. One case above all others will occur to anyone familiar with Christian tradition, that of Saul of Tarsus on the road to Damascus. But in the great majority of instances we find that the mystic has been striving for some time to focus all his resources upon his main purpose of coming into direct contact with his God. Usually, he has been preparing himself by penitence and disciplining himself by mortification for this supreme effort. And usually before he is ready to make any very distinct advance on that long and difficult road, he has worked arduously on the lower levels of the spiritual life. In a certain sense he is prepared. And this is true in spite of the fact that most schools of mystical thought, within the bounds of Christianity at least, have held that the more advanced stages of contemplation are not to be compassed by human effort but are the free gift of God.

But with poetry the situation is very different. It is true that certain experiments that have been made in the encouragement of children to write verse would suggest that some at least of the elements of poetic feeling and poetic expression are more widely distributed than is commonly assumed. And, of course, only the incurable romantic would insist that mature poetic achievement is pure genius, untarnished by effort. But most observers would still agree that however much the gifts of nature may be spoiled or improved, poets are still born, not made. By taking thought one may make himself a better poet, but not even the most confident of the devotees of education would claim, I think, that any man may make himself a poet.

When all allowance has been made, then, for the fact that any very developed degree of mystical experience has a very large element of the purely given, and that, on the other hand, a very large part of poetic experience is unquestionably to be credited to cultivation and preparation of mind and senses, it still remains true, I think, that the will plays a larger part in the background of mystical experience than of poetic. The difference is, as here suggested, not easy to determine and still less easy to measure, but significant for the character it imparts to the whole field of contemplative experience.

The same is true of the no less important question of reference. No experience means very much to us unless it finds some context in the environment of our minds, unless it in some way relates to the rest of what we know about the world in which we live. In that sense the most fragmentary and casual appreciation of the loveliness of nature, for instance, involves some finding of context, however limited, some reference to a center of significance, even if that be nothing more than an implied standard of the delight of vivid sense-stimulus. But that degree of reference may be, indeed in much poetry is, very tenuous, compared with the concentration of value implied in the reference of mystical experience to God. Even the faintest glimpse of the possibility of coming into contact with God involves such a range of suggestions, opens up such vast possibilities of implication, that the point of reference takes the center of the stage as it cannot in any experience mainly esthetic or intellectual. In other words, reference to God in any degree involves at once a concentration, a focus of attention, that transcends any other reference in its magnetism and in the range of possible relations it opens to heart and mind. It is something of that sort that Catherine of Siena must have had in mind when in *A Treatise of Obedience* she cried, "Thou, oh eternal Trinity, art a deep Sea, into which the deeper I enter the more I find, and the more I find the more I seek." [10] Such an experience as this implies, of course, a very lively awareness of the meaning of the concept of God. No mere abstraction will have such an effect. But we must not forget that such a liveliness of awareness is indispensable to any developed mystical experience, and even the faint adumbrations of such experience will in some degree, however slight, partake of this character. The defining quality is, then, a much sharper concentration, a much wider range of implication, in the process of mystical than in that of poetical reference.

It is in this reference that the source is to be sought, I

think, for that attraction which even the beginnings of mystical experience hold for the sensitive spirit. Mystics of all traditions have testified to the compulsive power of that attraction to God. That is why it is not easy for the mystic to content himself with flashes and glimpses of his goal. The perennial delight of the poet in the fragments of natural beauty which the day-to-day experience of life affords, the discursive and fugitive pleasures of the incidentals of the life of the senses that constitute so much of the wonder of lyric poetry, are not possible to the mystic. He may take delight, indeed, often does take delight in the elementary and incidental openings of insight that relieve the strenuous labors of his way, but such delight is in no way satisfying to that yearning which is but the more intensified by such fragmentary insights. For the fragmentary and the casual are relevant to the more discursive purposes of the poet. There is no poetic theory so exclusive that the incidental loveliness of the natural world cannot find its own excuse for being as the theme of poetry if not of the highest kind, perhaps, yet still of value for the essential purposes of poetic delight. In other words, while it is unquestionably true that the great poets have all in some degree and on some occasions wrestled with the problem of the sorry scheme of things and by implication, if not explicitly, suggested some theory of relation of part to whole, it still remains true that poetic expression of a good deal of power and value is possible when seemingly autonomous segments of experience are treated for their own sake alone. But in the case of mystical experience this is hardly true, for the mystical character of experience lies precisely in its power to relate the fragments of awareness to the center of spiritual reality, God himself, in whatever terms conceived. In other words, the essential nature of mystical experience is to be found in its active reference to a center. This is not true, certainly to anything like the same degree, of poetical experience.

Further evidence to support this suggestion that poetic experience may be, as it were, autonomous, and mystical experience not, will be found when we turn to the question of consequences or results. What are the impulses to which these two types of experience give rise in the inner being of the man capable of feeling the full force of their effect? That is not an easy question to answer if we keep in mind the possibility, indeed, the certainty, that some at least of the elementary types of poetical experience befall people who have not only no capacity but, indeed, no desire to express that experience by poetic utterance. On the other hand, no one would dream of calling such a tongueless genius a poet except by a sort of romantic courtesy. The impulse to express the poetic experience in poetic terms seems an essential to the qualification of the poet as poet, and the carrying out of that impulse with some degree of success, however modest, even more indispensable. It would seem fair, therefore, to say that for the poet the impulse to express such experience in terms of poetry is the first consequence of the experience itself.

But that is not the necessary or defining consequence of mystical experience. "Thee when I first knew, Thou liftedst me up, that I might see there was what I might see, and that I was not yet such as to see," said Saint Augustine.[11] Here the peculiar magnetism of the center of mystical experience becomes the essential fact. The mystic cannot rest in his fragment of insight but must press on to the fullness of the mystical union, at least as far toward that fullness as is possible to one of his capacities and his calling. In other words, the expression of experience is essential to the poet and not to the mystic. The making of the work of art that in another medium will reproduce the effects or communicate the effects of the experience is the outcome of the poetic experience, and the essential and defining consequence.[12] But that is not true of mystical experience. The goal of the mystic is not the expression of his experience in words or in any other medium, but the carrying on, the carrying through, of that seeking of God which he has begun.

This does not mean that the mystic may not be moved to the expression of his experience. He often is and to impressive effect. The considerable body of mystical poetry that is recognized to be of distinguished rank in English, Latin, Persian literature, to take a few notable examples, is sufficient witness to the fact. But even so impressive a result as the poetry of Bernard of Clairvaux or Jalalu'd-Din-Rumi is recognized to be a by-product or an incidental of the poet's mystical experience rather than its main excuse for being or its distinctive triumph. For there have been great mystics whose mysticism has found but scant literary expression. Of these Saint Francis of Assisi is perhaps the best-known. Such men remind us that the expression of mystical experience in verse or prose, for that matter, is an accident, in no way essential to mystical greatness.

Furthermore, even where the mystic does write poetry, one soon finds that the finished expression of the experience, the re-creation in art of what has been discovered in living, does not occupy the same position in the process as does the poem in the process of general poetic experience. The poem is the end of the process for the poet. It is its own excuse for being. There is nothing more to be done in that series—at least so far as the poet is concerned. Where the poet undertakes to be the teacher of his own poetry, as some poets have done, another factor enters into the situation of course, but one that passes out of the poetic process into another one, that of teacher or prophet. One may say that as life-process, that of poetic experience finds its close in the creation of the poem. Most of us at some time or other have had the experience of finding at the conclusion of a piece of poetic expression that suddenly we are at rest, free, at peace. But for the mystic that final satisfaction comes not through any expression of the fragments or stages of his experience but only through the completion of it, in the fullness of the experience of union, of direct and immediate contact in his spirit with the spirit toward which he has been struggling, his God. In other words, the fragmentary mystical experience drives the mystic on. Only the final fullness of experience, according to all the great traditions of mysticism, rare and brief and infrequent as it is, can give the mystic the satisfaction of complete fulfilment.

What, then, is the significance of the expression which the mystic sometimes gives to his experience? The expression of mystical experience usually does one of three things. At its simplest, it may bear witness to the goodness of God, taking *1.* the form of a narrative or account of God's graciousness. To no small extent, Saint Teresa of Avila's *Interior Castle* is of this character. Closely associated with this type is the narrative of the mystic's experiences, delivered from motives of *2.* brotherly charity that others may be moved to embark upon the same undertaking and may be guided and helped by the mystic's account of his experience. Bernard of Clairvaux' great series of sermons on the Canticle of Canticles is preëminently of this type. There is a third possible type, in which the expression becomes an instrument of mystical effort, a prayer for *3. This* help in the way to God, an act of worship in itself designed to bring the spirit nearer to its goal, to promote that assimilation of spirit that is the objective of the mystic. In such a case, the expression may take on a ritualistic character, though, I think, the social implications of ritual are on the whole foreign to the essentially interior and highly personal enterprise of the mystic. To say this is in no sense to compromise the social implications of mysticism, which are very great but are important at another point of the mystical process and not relevant to this discussion.

But even in the three types of literary expression of mystical experience enumerated above, it is clear that something more than mysticism is involved. Indeed, some element has come into the situation that carries us quite out of the mystical process so that we are face to face with something that is not exclusively mystical. The mystic's poem, for instance, is a work of art, a piece of poetry quite as much as a piece of mystical expression. It is, in other words, mystical poetry. It is the work of the mystic and the poet at once, or perhaps, to be more precise, of a man who is at once both mystic and poet.

Such a work of art must be approached, therefore, from two points of view. It must be approached as poetry and as mysticism. And it must be judged accordingly. For there are from the point of view of the critic two sets of standards involved. The first concerns the mystical character of the piece of verse. Does this particular poem give the reader in any fashion and in any degree a glimpse of the reality behind the appearance of the world? Does it share with the reader the writer's sense of the presence of that mystery and his relation to it? Does it bring the reader closer to that reality? The character and the degree of the mystical experience involved, in other words, is the first element to be appreciated by the student or the critic. And these questions are by no means easy to answer, for in a matter that so engages the deepest convictions and the profoundest feelings of the reader, it is very difficult to be dispassionate. For, obviously, we all read in the light of our experience. And those forms of religious experience that are most intelligible to us because of our religious capacity or environment will naturally be those to which we are most sympathetic. This is probably the reason why so many barren and stilted expressions of religious sentiment are to be found current in all religious groups. The feeling which the faithful bring to the theme invests it with the meaning which the actual expression but hints at or at most releases.

On the other hand, the feeling may be of a very profound

character, and yet the poem may fail for want of the other set of values involved in mystical poetry, for want of the distinctively expressive gifts of the poet. The verse of the great Cambridge Platonist, Henry More, is a case in point. There can be no question of the reality of his mystical experience in its kind and its degree. But the bulk of his work remains amorphous as poetry, lacking, it would seem, that mediative and communicating power which is essential to its genre. There are any number of possible reasons why a specific poem might be rich in its adumbrations of mystical experience and yet dry and inert as poetry. But of these possible reasons, the most obvious, obscurity or difficulty of communication, is probably the least important. The recent success of the poetry of Gerard Manley Hopkins, though belated and heavily indebted to certain contemporary critical fashions, is a case in point. Hopkins is not easy. But however involved his thought, however complicated and intertwined the processes of his imagination, what he writes has that effect on the nerves that is essential to poetry. He may try to say too many things at once, he may demand a wider span of application than the usual reader is accustomed to give, but he has the gift of projecting his state of mind to the point where it stirs all the sensibilities of his reader. Much of this power of his is probably due not so much to any logical resolution of the persistent complexities of his state of mind as to his command of the emotional possibilities of image and sound.

For, in the last analysis, the mystic like the poet is dependent for expression upon the resources of communication between men. Like the poet he deals in states of mind and in states of feeling. Like the poet, in his effort to communicate these intangibles he must appeal to material things, to those common counters of experience that lie between the speaker and the spoken-to in the sources of sense stimuli in the world about us, and through them to those common reactions that we all de-

pend upon for communication. And yet in that very appeal he
is drawing the reader's attention away from what he is primarily interested in to what is at best subsidiary and, more
often, distracting. His other resource is the perilous resource
of magic. He may suggest by the indescribable total of images,
he may induce the state of feeling he wishes by the spell of the
sound of the verse. "The wind bloweth where it listeth, and
thou hearest the sound thereof, but canst not tell whence it
cometh, and whither it goeth: so is every one that is born of
the Spirit." [13] To the present writer that is one of the most
magical of passages in English literature, and magical in the
mystical direction. But it would be a very delicate matter of
literary assessment to determine how much of the effect of
that sentence is due to the sound of the words, to the suggestions of the image, to the appositeness of the image to the
idea, and how much to the deep feeling of mystery which
so many generations have discovered in the sound of the wind.

The problem of excellence in mystical poetry is therefore
a double one, involving both poetic and mystical value. And it
is not easy to achieve that double excellence, for as the foregoing pages have tried to make clear, the direction of expression in these two genres is not the same. The tendency of mystical endeavor is toward concentration, toward absorption.
That of poetic expression is more diffusive. Its tendency is
by no means wholly centrifugal even in the most fugitive, say,
of imagist verse. But in much of poetic expression there is a
definite tendency toward autonomy of the various elements of
experience. It is often a matter of degree rather than of kind,
but there can, I think, be no question that, on the whole, the
direction of poetry is first out from the centre, then in, and
of mystical expression, first in, then out. In other words, the
mystic drives to his God, and then in his God he finds all
things. That certainly is the method of classic Christian mysticism. And by inversion it is the method of the great nega-

tive way of the Buddhists. But for the poet the particular fragment of experience that comes under his eye at that moment takes possession of him, and then by implication it may or may not bring to his mind larger contexts and more significant references.

There is a profound difference, also, between the position of the poet and that of the mystic as regards the problem of mediation. As we have seen, both must use sense imagery for the expression of the non-sensual elements of experience. But for the poet these sense elements are of great service not only for the purpose of communication but for the creation of the work of art as such. On the other hand, for the mystic their very potency may be, as we have seen, centrifugal, may actually lead the mind away from the objective of the mystic. Here, however, we might remind ourselves that in the spiritual world any particular good enriches the whole. In that sense the mystic may rejoice at any fragmentary appreciation of God's world, so long as that partiality does not mean a loss of the context that gives it life and value. The love of beauty may even coexist with great intellectual and moral corruption, and yet for the areas where it operates, it may in itself effect in some degree that broadening of vision and that opening of heart that make it easier for the presence of God to be felt.[14] In that sense the mystical poet may rejoice in the purely poetic excellences of his own work and of other men's work. But with these, of course, he cannot in the end be content. For the creation of the work of art must ever seem to him of less consequence than the expression of the experience. It would probably seem at first sight to the critic who does not share the preoccupations of the mystical poet that such a point of view must involve the principle of sacrifice of art to morality. But actually the age-old controversy as to the relations of art and religion is not relevant to a situation in which the double jurisdiction is implicit by definition. The mystical poem must be viewed as both poetry and mysticism. Of neither can the rights be sacrificed. The poem must be genuinely and significantly mystical, or it is shallow. It must be poetical, or it is not a poem at all. As for the relative values, obviously the poet who exploits mystical feeling for the sake of a poem will not look like much but a charlatan beside a real mystic, and the poem as a poem will suffer from the lack of reality. On the other hand, no degree of mystical insight or ecstasy will make a stiff and wooden poem a thing of beauty and a joy forever.

But the dichotomy upon which the preceding paragraphs rest is not a dichotomy of fact, but a tool of the critic for the purposes of analysis. It is not a strange hybrid of poet and mystic who writes a mystical poem. It is not a man who writes first as a mystic and then as a poet. It is not even a mystic who turns over to the poet who happens to dwell within the same brain and body the materials of his insight to be made into a work of art by the competent craftsman. It is rather that the same human being is at once poet and mystic, at one and the same time, from the beginning of the process to the end. Obviously, there are not very many such. As Mr. T. S. Eliot has very shrewdly pointed out, "The capacity for writing poetry is rare; the capacity for religious emotion of the first intensity is rare; and it is to be expected that the existence of both capacities in the same individual should be rarer still." [15]

In those very rare cases, the resultant poetry will be found, as a rule, to owe its power to the fact that it does one of two things. Either it sweeps us out of our ordinary world into one freer, purer, more beautiful, more widely significant, or it throws a bridge between our world of the everyday and the realm of the spirit. In the case of the first, we of this earth, caught here and now but not unvisited by intimations of another world, are for an instant swept beyond the dikes of the immediately present into a larger and freer realm. And for a moment we are made free of that world, not as aliens and as transients but as exiles who for a little have come home. The poet who can do that to the ordinary child of earth has not only the power of rising, himself, above this low-lying ground of ours but the still more miraculous power of carrying us heavier-witted ones with him. Such power as his is properly to be described as transcendental. There are probably fewer of this type of poet than of any other. Shelley, with all his emotional restrictions, to an extraordinary degree was one. So was Dante, though those passages of the *Paradise* that best reveal his genius in this field are probably among the least-appreciated portions of his work.

More common, I suspect, and incomparably more accessible is the second type of poet, the one who having sure intuitions of this other world, can yet descry intimations of it in the materials of this earth. He is the poet who with William Blake can see "a World in a grain of sand," [16] and with Francis Thompson behold Jacob's ladder stretching from the prosy pavements of Charing Cross to the heights of heaven.[17] If we can call mystical poetry of the first type the poetry of transcendence, then surely this we may call the poetry of immanence. For it is the presence of the indwelling divinity in the world of the temporal and the material that such a poet discovers, and in his sharing of his discovery with us, he throws a bridge between the two. There is something even of the sacramental in such poetry as this, for the things of the senses become the occasions, the humble instruments and vehicles of the divine grace, forever seeking even on the lowest levels of human experience to reach its wayfallen but not estranged children. Hence the peculiar wistfulness and magnetism to be found in the homeliness that so often characterizes the poetry of immanence. There is ever in it something of the breath-taking tenderness of the Creator who became even as the creation of his hands and subject to the bondage of the creature that He might rescue that creature from the isolation of his own selfhood.

There is, of course, another view of the poetry of immanence, a view that has found perhaps its fullest occidental development in some of the contemporary forms of pantheism. To this approach the important thing about the poetry of immanence is that it discovers in the material forms about us the shaping principles, the animating forces that we share in with the rest of nature. In the east, in the poetry of Buddhism and Hinduism, similar views have led to a suppression of the world of nature. But in the western world this pantheism has tended rather to the suppression of the supernatural in the interest of the natural, and the "Hertha" of Swinburne, though obviously an extreme example, is yet significant of a movement that, though probably past its high tide, has yet by no means entirely spent its force.

But it is unwise to insist too much upon absolutes in the definition of poetic types, for the full and complete realizations of any type are few. Here, as in every field, the partial and the approximate are far more common and even more significant. For what we miss in our successes, we sometimes take in our failures. A good many men have shared in the aspiration of the mystic, without even in their yearning passing the level of mere wistfulness. Something of inability to believe, something of fear of the not quite reconciled portions of their own nature, something of coldness in the surrounding air, something of impediment or reserve in the fullness of their surrender, who shall say why some of the tenderest of religious spirits have never gone beyond that first stage of undifferentiated longing? Some of these men even seem to find a sort of equilibrium in this half-world of abortive flight and diffused sensibility, so that their contribution to this varied field is one of dim insights and of vague suffusions of emotion. Others there are, like John Donne, who by the very warmth and violence of their longing would seem able to take heaven by storm, and yet though their thoughts fly up, something holds their hearts below, like an aeroplane that with straining wings and throbbing engines cannot quite lift its load from the too tenacious earth. And at the other extreme there are those whose imaginations venture where neither feeling nor thought would perhaps carry the whole man. And we have all those anthropomorphisms that are the stock of the verse of divine whimsy, like Herrick's "To His Saviour, a Child" or some of the verses of Coventry Patmore. There are many poems of this type that without question make good their claim to inclusion in the anthology of religious poetry, and not a few of them deserve respectful attention as minor varieties of the great type of mystical verse. For poetry is like a tree in the wind. Many tiny leaves make a great rustling, and no twig is so small or leaf frond so tight but it may help to syllable that earth-roaming music.

Indeed, not the least of the claims of this minor poetry is that it helps to develop the mediating material of the great mystical poetry. However humble, it has an especial grace with the abundant suggestions of nature. It is at home with legend and tradition, with those materials that employ the aura of the ancient and the supernatural to float the becalmed spirit out of its too matter-locked harborage. It knows how to invoke the angel and the saint, who help to make the children of earth feel a little more at home in the perhaps too free air of heaven. Finally, in its delight in ritual and in liturgy it reminds the austerer religious spirit that we are body and soul and not disembodied mind and spirit. These services are not indispensable to mystical poetry, but they afford subsidiary agencies which the great mystic might not scorn to use, and in general has not, within the limits or the extent of his tradition. They may do much to invest the austerer framework of theology with the intermedial grace of poetry. And they wing the spiritual challenge of the mystic to the laziness and the stodginess of the rest of us with the humane appeal to the sense of beauty. On the other hand, the debt of the ordinary man to these minor mystics who write so much of the world's mystical verse is very great, for they intercede for us in the less compliant tribunals of mystic understanding and mystic appreciation.

As for the great mystical poet, he will be at once a great mystic and a great poet. That means that he will have to be a person of rare complexity and of rare unity of consciousness. For the poet cannot rest until he has found the words and the music that will ease the pressure of his feeling, that with the presentment of a new creation will satisfy the craving of his imagination. On the other hand, the mystic is forever thrusting beyond the hungers and the achings of experience to the peace that is behind them all. It is told of Thomas Aquinas that a little before he came to die, he said to his friend Reginald, "I can write no more. I have seen things which make all my writings like straw." [18] That does not mean, I think, that the confidence of that great intellect in the operations by which it had taken possession of and brought into order the wisdom of its day was broken. Rather, I should say, the Thomas who had written so beautifully of the mystery of the Eucharist, Thomas the mystic, had caught sight of that prospect of contemplation before which the mighty labors of the *Summa* sank to their proper place, work of this life, done out of love and the inescapable compulsion of charity, but no longer to be remembered on the threshold of that vision of God for the enjoyment of which he knew himself to have been created.

In that sense, the end of the mystical poet is silence, the silence of contemplation before which beauty even is a little thing. But until that end, the mystical poet is a poet, and the more poet for his mysticism. For the essential paradox of all mystical activity obtains here as in all other things, learning, bodily works of mercy, art even. The end of the mystic is contemplation. The things of this world are but shadows, however dear, upon the supreme light to which they owe their being. And the pursuit of a partial and single thing when one might have all things in One seems from any scheme of reckoning a poor business. But seen in the light of its end, even the least of the things of this world takes on a compulsion that its own autonomous value would never command. It is Teresa of Avila who returned the classic answer to the classic question that the man of action asks of the mystic, "If a beggar should knock at the door when you are absorbed in contemplation, what then would you do?" when she said to her Lord: "How great is the love you bear the children of men: the worthiest service we can give you is to leave you for love of them and for their greater good." [19] For the great master of the interior life there was really no question as to the answer. She would go at once to the door because not only her needy neighbor was waiting there but in him, her God, Himself. That is the ultimate answer to the question of the relation between the values of poetry and the values of mysticism. In great mystical poetry they are one.

Chapter I

THE INTELLECTUAL CLIMATE [1]

ALL human history is an unquiet thing. Whatever visions of peace the restless fancies of men have succeeded in conjuring up have been born of no established and known gentleness of life but of the bitter need for what the troubled and actual world about them could not yield. There are a few exceptions, times like that of Virgil and the young Shakespeare when a new order has but recently impressed itself upon an exhausted and defeated confusion, and the ambitious intellectual sees in the accomplished fact an opportunity for self-realization hitherto impossible. Then men may sing with hope and conviction of old dreams come to pass. But more commonly the treasure of a quiet life has been sought by men disillusioned by the contentions for power of a turbulent world and unsatisfied by the meager spiritual yieldings of greed and violence. Only rarely do we find spirits at once gentle and hardy confronting the arrogance of the times with a passion that transcends their turmoil and an energy too positive for flight or resignation. Perhaps an alchemy capable of so distilling from its opposites the nourishment of its own critical enthusiasm is possible only to the mystic or the artist with their capacity for drawing upon realms beyond the literal consciousness, their certainty of an ultimate appeal from the success or failure of the narrow moment. Yet even for them, the possibility of strength and truth is to no small extent dependent upon their capacity for penetrating sympathetically to the grounds of dissension, for appreciating those diverse and hardly reconcilable facets of reality to which even the passionate segmentation of controversy ultimately bears witness.

There is a famous passage in the second book of *Paradise Lost* in which aboriginal Chaos and "eldest Night" are discovered holding "Eternal Anarchie" amid the warring elements of the universe.[2] To more than one reader that passage has seemed a fit description of the intellectual climate of the seventeenth century, just as the poet's obvious horror has seemed the natural reaction of a civilized imagination to such confusion. But there is another side to that war of the elements. The very turmoil itself bears witness to the presence of more of the conflicting forces of human experience than are commonly to be found in the provisional truces of quieter times. For if anarchy is fatal to the range and sweetness of life, the freedom of the spirit is no less endangered by facile simplifications and premature unities. As we shall see, many of the same forces with which we wrestle today were at work then through the confusion, slowly moving in the direction of those achievements to which we of today, however disillusioned, are still so profundly indebted. But their victory was not yet accomplished, and the values they were to trample upon and stifle were yet present in the midst of the undoubted evils and weaknesses they were to overcome, and the happier possibilities they were to make certain.

When, in the nineteenth century, the early seventeenth century writers began again to be studied after more than a hundred years of neglect, it was for their difference from the prevailing fashions that they were first valued, for their quaintness, for their freshness in the dust of ancient libraries. For some years they continued to enjoy the pleasant immunities of the remote and happily irrelevant. But in the first decades of our century some of them were discovered to be more relevant than had been supposed, and changing tastes seized upon them with avidity for the sudden comfort they yielded to the pre-dilections of a newer time. So we find the strange vogue of John Donne as a "modern," an interpretation of that most elusive of mentalities, that is likely to prove congenial enough to a time of confusion to last for some few years more. But the meaning of "modern" is one of the most transient and chameleon-like of all meanings. At the present moment there seems to be a very considerable tendency among critical moderns to find in the seventeenth century the beginning of the world against which, at least so far as certain aspects of life are concerned, they are coming more and more to rebel.

One claim, certainly, the seventeenth century may have upon the admiration of such moderns. It was a time of great con-fusion, as we shall see, of mingled disillusion and exhilaration, but it was also a time of resolution, of conscious determination to do something about the confusion. It was a highly critical, intensely self-aware age, but it had within itself nothing of the passivity, the fugitiveness, the carelessness, the despond-ency, so often found in such times. In spite of the delicacy of the seventeenth-century analysis of mood and feeling, the center of seventeenth-century psychology was the will. It was not for nothing that the greatest scientist of the century, as Mr. Edwin A. Burtt has pointed out, in the definition of his highly mathematical God tended to subordinate the intellect to the will, wisdom to dominion,[3] or that the greatest poet of the time devoted the carefully garnered spiritual and intellectual re-sources of a lifetime to the extended consideration of the nature and scope of man's will. And while the tight-clenched pur-posiveness of the Puritan was in theory and fact repudiated by a large majority of his less narrow and less strenuous breth-ren, nevertheless Puritan absolutism was but an extreme de-velopment of something to be found everywhere in the seven-teenth-century temperament. To this temperament the issues of life were of immediate and critical importance, their solution something to be passionately sought and no less passionately propounded. The cruelty and fanaticism of the time are but the darker expression of the serious-mindedness and sincerity of an age in which as yet the sense of obligation and of confidence in the power of the human will and human mind has hardly begun to yield to the disintegrating influences of growing scepticism.

There is still in the seventeenth century, even in that world of intellect and fashion which, in the satire of the time, we see yielding to bitter disillusionment, something of the memory of the hope for a renewal of life that was so marked a feature of the spiritual orientation of the preceding period. The hope that suddenly the sluggish will of man might be awakened and the institutions of his life cleansed and renewed and the world brought closer to its Maker's intention, is nothing new or peculiar to the sixteenth and seventeeth centuries. It is a hope indigenous to Christianity; indeed, it is one of the mainsprings of the Christian life. The spiritual history of the Middle Ages is to no small extent the story of the successes and failures of that hope. But the peculiar dynamic of that approach is to be discerned in the period of the Renaissance and the Reformation operating on a larger scale and with the reënforcement of more manifold forces than probably ever before. And, naturally, in a time of centrifugal action and of radical segmentation, its manifestations are more dramatic than they were in a period of greater centralization and of larger and looser harmonies, like that of the thirteenth century. Something has happened to that hope in the England of the seventeenth century; it is already grown sectarian and fanatic. But it is still the old hope, and it is still to be discerned in the thought and feeling even of those men who most resolutely reject its stricter manifestations. It is one of the things that give nerve and fibre to the seventeenth century at its subtlest moments and a certain reality to its most fantastic impulses.

The conventional catastrophic view of history has been accustomed to see in the seventeenth century the dissolution of a civilization and the emerging of a civilization. Under the repeated blows of the Renaissance and the Reformation the world of the Middle Ages was disintegrating, and even those new provisional worlds created by the two great crises were passing away. And through all the holes and chinks, seeping through the rotten foundations of ancient worlds, the new world of rationalism and materialism, the modern world par excellence, was rising in a great tide, presently to carry away the wreckage of ancient civilizations on its triumphant flood. But that comparatively simple and tidy picture is no longer possible to us. No world quite passes away; no world is ever quite born. Only currents set in the broad stream of history, now swift, now slow, and sometimes the whole movement is one and dominating, but most often the waters are swirling, embroiled with torrents from many directions. If from the point of view of the passionate idealist, no hope is ever realized in the fullness of perfection of the imagination, so the cynic may in his turn remember that no vital influence is ever quite lost.

Especially is this true of the seventeenth century. The sudden, dramatic character that used to be attributed to the Renaissance has been challenged by studies that demonstrate long preparation of some of its most distinctive manifestations and provide ancient pedigrees for some of its most startling innovations. But when all allowances have been made, there does remain the fact of a great release, of a sudden quickening, of a renewed aggressiveness, of the human spirit in its relations with its environment. Not perhaps the most original of periods, certainly by no means unique in its creative energy, the Renaissance is yet a time of magnificent expansiveness and of joyous self-aggrandizement. The other-worldliness of the Middle Ages has been too often exaggerated and misunderstood for us to take too literally that view of the Renaissance which sees in it mainly a return to this world.[4] Nor is any age ever homogeneous, least of all, an age like the Renaissance. But the consciousness of the goodness of man's life here and now beat hotly in the veins of the sixteenth century, and the awareness of his own limitless and immediate powers fired many a bold spirit to fresh conquest in every field of a gloriously opulent world.

The consideration of the splendor of the earth and of the majestic possibilities of man has led the religious spirit more than once to a deeper appreciation of the source and sustaining life of that wonder. Something of this tendency is doubtless to be seen in the intensification of Platonic influence in the religious thought and feeling of the time. But for the less religious spirit, the temptation to an absorption in what is so basically satisfactory is obvious. For many men the step from the joy of life to a naive form of naturalism is not a great one. And such a development was made all the easier by the prevailing enthusiasm for classical literature, which gave confidence and rational conviction to instincts that hitherto had confronted the challenge of religion and morality with only the extenuations of too palpable human weakness to plead. There is no reason to believe that human nature in the sixteenth century was very different from human nature in the fourteenth, but there was an unquestioned difference in the way in which frail human nature regarded itself in the two periods. There were a great many reasons for that change, but Ovid was not the least of them, and one of his greatest claims to our recognition is the fact that he helped the poets of Elizabethan England to make poetry of it. The medieval body was not so pinched nor the medieval soul so proud as some commonplaces imply, but certainly the body came into its own with glory in the Renaissance, the full summer of Ovid distilled in the bright April and June of Shakespeare.

A fair case might be made out for the thesis that the basic difference between men is that between those who would take man as he is and those who would try to do something with him. Like most theses it would be too simple for truth, but it would deserve as much assent as do most propositions—that there is something to it. And that something is a fact that the world's idealists and the world's reformers forget at their peril. The naturalism of the Renaissance seems to a more sophisticated age a very mixed and embryonic one. Michel de Montaigne, however enamoured of himself and prepared to rest content with his pleasant deficiencies, was no child of nature. But his readiness to take himself as he found himself was something that neither Bernard, Abbott of twelfth-century Clairvaux, nor Master Calvin of sixteenth-century Geneva would have understood.

Much of what is most fresh and delightful in the age of the Renaissance goes back to that innocent complacency of the Sieur de Montaigne. But with spirits less gentle, less urbane, less disciplined, the story is a different one. For the cultivated indulgence of taste and whim in spirits less sceptical and accommodating becomes that rampage of appetite and passion that shadows the most brilliant pages of the Renaissance story. Again, private turbulence and public violence are no new appearance in the sixteenth century. The passion for self-aggrandizement and the greed for power know no distinction of time or creed, but the secularism that followed hard upon the naturalism of the Renaissance undoubtedly helped to give conscience and range to personal greed and ambition. As Signor Mario Praz has pointed out in his study of the Elizabethan reputation of Machiavelli, "The theocratic, collectivist ideals of the Middle Ages were being replaced by a conception of life based on the pre-Christian polity and the individuum." [5]

This general Renaissance tendency found particularly favorable conditions in the England of the time.[6] The breakdown of the ancient feudal nobility had been well under way before the Renaissance reached England. But its place during the reigns of Henry and Elizabeth was being rapidly taken by a new nobility, enriched by the spoils of the monasteries. For various reasons, one of the most important the extravagance of the court to which they were bound, this new nobility was scattering its possessions rather lavishly among other classes of society. With the spread of land speculation, there was a considerable opportunity for men of lower social position to enrich themselves quickly and with relative ease. The result is a rather fluid economic and social situation that offered highly speculative but on occasion richly remunerative inducements to men of energy and parts to advance their fortunes. Even though industrial and commercial life were as yet but imperfectly competitive, the great world centering in the court, say of Elizabeth or James, offers all the elements of a singularly ruthless and rapacious individualism.

There is, of course, another side to this growth of individualism. That brilliant development of personality that every student of the period has noted with delight is one of the richest and most stimulating gifts of the time to the poet and the artist. No small part of this is due, again, to a shifting of emphasis, of attention. One has only to compare the typical medieval saint's life with the studies in personality that are beginning to be written by poet and prose writer alike. For the medieval hagiographer the personality of his hero was of little direct account. The virtues of his subject were of value because of example and the delight that all aspiring amateurs take in a championship player. His shortcomings, his weaknesses were of interest only because they showed what divine grace might make of the poorest of human materials. But the center of medieval hagiography was the greatness and goodness of God, and the saint was cherished as a witness and an instrument and an occasion of that goodness. The whim, the idiosyncracy, the innocent weakness, that constitute the favorite material of the modern biographer, often survive this pious centralization and focus; but only casually and incidentally. That they are there at all is due to the realism of the medieval writer and not to his purpose. This difference between the medieval and modern approach is significant, and much of that difference we owe to the Renaissance cultivation of the individual.

Some of this may be due, also, to the fact that a good deal of the literature of antiquity came to the Renaissance with a very lively sense of its individual figures and without a corresponding grasp of its implied context. I have heard a European complain that the American individual is just an individual without the coloring and the deepening of race that play so large a part in European identity. It seemed never to have occurred to him that there might be invisible contexts and assumptions in the groundwork of American personality of which he was as yet but imperfectly aware.

The motives of self-aggrandizement that prompt so much of the individualism of the Renaissance assume probably their noblest because most impersonal form when the ambitious spirit of the time turns its aggression upon the world about it. Nowhere, certainly, was the fruit of the Renaissance richer or of more lasting good than where the creative energy of the time devoted itself to the conquest of nature. The story of that conquest properly belongs to the rationalist movement of the seventeenth century and the rise of the new science. But that impatience with ancient ignorance and the ambition to use the new science for "the glory of the Creator and the relief of man's estate," as the motives of the great scientific advance were defined by the most famous of the early defenders of the new movement in England, are Renaissance motives.[7] So, too, is that passionate exhilaration with which the champions of the new science will proclaim their emancipation from the timidity and the restrictions of the past. That combined sense of emancipation and rebellion, short-sighted and dogmatic as it was in so many ways, yet in its dynamic belongs essentially to the mood of release and renewal of the wonder of life characteristic of the time.

Like all revolutionaries, these of the Renaissance had a great impatience with the past and a generous confidence in the future. That tendency to throw away a badly-spoiled world, to stake all on the scheduled working-out of their hopes, represents a very large capacity for faith in the essential amenableness of the world to the dreamer's desire. That these men had. And it supplied to them a dynamic of incalculable potency.

But this positive, energetic expansion of the imagination is only one side of the intellectual life of the Renaissance. The other is that critical, speculative movement of rationalism, which, present almost at the beginning of the period, was only fully to come into its own when the first energy of the Renaissance was spent, and which was to produce consequences in many ways so opposite to its origin in spirit and direction.

Much has been said of the part which the rise of the middle classes played in the successive dramas of the sixteenth century, and of the part which the lay impatience of clerical dominance played in the various rebellions of the time. Less has been said of the revolt of the common man against the prescriptions and the suggestions of the uncommon. That simple natural realism which seems to be one of the salient features of the man in the street, whatever his social origins, is a force ultimately to be reckoned with. So, also, is his preference for simple explanations. In both he may be betrayed, and there is a good deal of reason to feel that in both he was betrayed by the Renaissance. For the gulf between the common man and the intelligentsia has probably widened rather than narrowed in the years since, and that in spite of all the efforts of the modern world at popularization.

But in the beginning, it was not so. Mr. Basil Willey has

suggested that the most important feature of the development of the rationalistic approach to the world is to be found in a change in attitude as to what constituted a satisfactory explanation of the natural world, "Instead of the kind of 'truth' which is consistent with authoritative teaching, men began to desire the kind which would enable them to measure, to weigh and to control the things around them." [8] The *why* dear to the heart of the child and the speculative was abandoned for that study of the *how* that was speedily to yield such astonishing power over the natural world. And the wide-ranging aggressiveness of the Renaissance, that at the beginning of the century took "all knowledge for its province" was to yield before its close to the new humility that beheld itself spending a lifetime picking up pebbles on the shore of a great sea. Yet even that humility was not proof against the exhilaration of the vast prospects of the new science and of the sense of command that in the beginning it gave man over the universe it was stripping of terror and mystery.

The shift of the scientist's interest from metaphysics to physics was more than a discovery of a new technique or a new method of attack upon the world. It was essentially a reorientation of the mind and the imagination. It is difficult for us who are accustomed to a world controlled through elaborate statistical processes to appreciate how pre-statistical, fundamentally unsystematic was the world at the beginning of the seventeenth century. Reliable figures even of population, for instance, were scarcely to be had.[9] The very fact of the existence of the great polymaths, with their ambition to sweep up all of knowledge and extract from it the secret of the world, is still a witness to the unsystematic state of knowledge with the lines between the specialist and the amateur or even dilettante as yet undrawn.[10] In such a world the possibility of an orderly, systematic, limited attack upon nature, point by point, problem by problem, was one to commend itself to the practical man's respect, and its results were such as he could appreciate and take into his intellectual possession.

As the seventeenth century advanced, the mathematical diagram more and more took the place of the full image with all its varieties and suggestions of context, and the world became a larger, a surer, a clearer, but also a less varied and less mysterious place.[11] This was a slow process, only beginning to be felt in the first half of the century, hardly defined before the middle; yet it is to be reckoned with in our study even of the first part. The common man's love of the wonderful, his distaste for the overturning of accepted premises, his restlessness in too rigid a framework, were all to have their revenges in various fashions from witchcraft [12] to Philistinism, but there was much to satisfy him in these early developments, and their triumphs were among the most impressive that the race has beheld, although for their full splendor we must look to a later date.

Again, the revolutionary drive of the spirit of the time must not be overlooked. The new approach was not suffered to take possession of the field without opposition. Every consideration of vested interest, of intellectual rigidity and inertia, of unwillingness to trust the truth to take care of itself, played its part in the resistance to the spread of the experimental method. And the valiant fighting spirit of the new science returned hatred with contempt; and the break with the immediate past, that unhistorical breach of the continuity of human experience, implicit in so much of the activity of the Renaissance, was deepened. Walls were thrown down, and fresh walls built against the tyranny of the past. The exhilaration of a new heaven and a new earth come to pass was warmed and heightened, and the turmoil and the contentiousness of the time further embroiled.

But what was involved in this struggle was more than the shift from library to laboratory, more than the triumph of that experimental approach and method to which we are indebted for so much not only of the material success of our day but also of the freedom from ancient superstition and the possession of larger understandings. Other currents of the Renaissance and the rise of rationalism flowed together. Mr. Robert Shafer has reminded us in his studies of *Christianity and Naturalism* that there is nothing new in the clash of naturalism and religion.[13] The roots of both lie deep in fundamental dispositions of feeling and imagination as well as intellect. It is exceedingly difficult for the religious human being to comprehend that that whole great world of experience that seems to him the richest, most revealing, most thoroughly satisfying of his deepest needs, the most completely expressive of his surest intuitions of value and purpose and reality, hardly exists for his brother. And it is quite as difficult for the naturalistically-minded to believe that what seems to him an illusion and a figment of weakness and blindness can be more than wilful self-deception for the religious.

Even the spacious and elastic and accommodating Church of the Middle Ages pressed hard upon not a few natures. For such men the revival of the naturalism and the materialism of antiquity must have brought congenial doctrine and the satisfaction of the rationalization of their own deepest repugnances and inclinations. The insistence of orthodox Christianity on the natural witness to truth planted deep in all human beings must have long given to the most conscientious of the naturalistically-minded a sense of estrangement; so it is not surprising if the triumphant revival of the materialism and naturalism of antiquity gave them a sense of sudden enfranchisement.[14] And this sense would be all the deeper because the religious admissions and assumptions often implicit in ancient materialism and naturalism would by their very unfamiliarity escape attention or at least put up no bar to the sense of escape from too well-known commitments. It would probably be a mistake to

21439

seek in this a cause of the Renaissance rebellion against authority, but there is no doubt that on specific issues such rebellion found support and justification in the example of antiquity.

To a world that had found the marks of truth in universality and in invariability, there was something profoundly disturbing and yet exciting in the recognition of variation of opinion on such important issues as the law of nature and the witness of God in the human consciousness.[15] It will be remembered that it was his discovery that the ancients had disagreed as to the point of reference for the spatial system that drove Copernicus to consider a different point of reference from that usually assumed by the astronomy of his day.[16] To a great many minds the presence of such a variety of theories as the Renaissance set in circulation on such a large variety of the basis issues of human life was but a fresh spur to the pursuit of truth. The medieval confidence in the capacity of the human mind to compass truth was as yet relatively unshaken. And the belief that there was knowledge to be obtained which would explain the riddles of life was widespread. For such minds the search for truth untrammeled by the cautions of authority opened up at this time with glorious possibilities.

But there were those for whom the thirst for truth was less compelling than the delight of the mind in its own motions. For such temperaments the allurements of novelty and of liveliness played a much larger part than the austerer compulsions of truth. Much of the brilliance and the intellectual warmth of the Renaissance is to be found in such a passion for ideas for their own sake, and there is abundant justification for the parallels that various authors have drawn between the humanists of the time and the sophists of antiquity.[17] Particularly is this to be remembered when the intellectual pilgrimage of certain Renaissance figures is studied in its youthful aspects. The capacity of a young Donne to try on various metaphysical caps should not be lost sight of when we are tempted to take too seriously certain youthful scintillations.

John Donne was not the man to rest content with even the most exhilarating swirl of conflicting ideas, or to be satisfied to let notion chase notion through the swinging doors of a lively fancy. The passion for truth even in his most "hydroptique" youthful days was too sharp and too inexorable. But for many of his contemporaries the very strength and multiplicity of the winds of doctrine of the time swept away any confidence they may have had as to the ability of the human mind to discover truth, and the scepticism which had at first been content to scrutinize faith was presently turned full upon the claims of reason. To the delighted amateur of the little world of mood and feeling and impulse in an age in which the conflict of ideas was almost daily sharpening to present savagery, there was much temptation to the Pyrrhonism of the ancients.[18] For the Pyrrhonist could meet the demands of the fanaticism of his day with a shrug of the shoulder, and at a moment when each and every party was claiming his adherence on the score of universal and self-evident reason, he could challenge the evidence of the senses and the competence of the reason.

The fact that the sceptic was so often, like Montaigne, a conservative, content to put up with the known shortcomings of the existent order, if it would be content to exact of him nothing more stringent than his conformity, may suggest something of self-protection in the supercilious indifference of the too enlightened. But it is hard to blame the type of temper better suited to the amenities than to the heroics of life for seeking some defence from a world growing daily more exigent in its demands for passionate and one-sided action. The absolutism of the seventeenth century may well explain if not justify some of the less heroic devices of the speculative. Indeed, in the various forms of fideism current in the seventeenth century faith itself begins to call scepticism to its assistance against the not always clearly comprehended assaults of reason, and rationalism begins to turn upon itself and devour its own children.[19]

This tremendous renewal of life and multiplication of reactions upon life is nowhere so richly and so terribly reflected as in the field of religion. In itself the sense of the coming of the hour of renewal and purification was nothing new; neither was the criticism of the existing order. Many of the charges of the Protestant Reformers had been advanced again and again by perfectly loyal and often saintly Catholics in ages past, and, indeed, the Council of Trent by the measures it took recognized the validity of a great many of those charges. But there was something more here, a deep consciousness of something past mending, a determination to go to the root of the problem, an insistence on a thorough-going and immediate putting right of things according to the scheme of the critics, at many points the substitution of totally new premises, in short a genuinely revolutionary frame of mind. The spirit of reconciliation, of the preservation of seeming incompatibles, of accommodation to times and men, was not unknown to the sixteenth century. It is nobly and richly born witness to in the various forms of Christian humanism which sought to appropriate the new riches of the Renaissance to the Christian life and faith, and in time all the confessions came to feel its influence. But in the beginning it could do little to stop the revolutionary spirit that drove forward the Reformation.

In the definition and direction of that tremendous force a great many things played their part and made their contribution. The intensification of national feeling, the growing consciousness and self-assertiveness of the middle classes, the intellectualism that if not caused by the invention of printing and the cheapening of books was so much intensified by these conveniences, the impact of more primitive religious patterns upon an unhistorical mind through the literal application of the

Bible, the revolt of the common man against the standards and the demands of priest and mystic, all of these elements unquestionably played their part. But the essential thing was the protest against the existing order and the determination in the mind of each of the Reformers to make it over to what he thought it should be.

Something of the terror of a world that in some of its aspects is disintegrating is to be found here. The doctrine of the seventeenth century that seems most comfortless to the twentieth century, that of predestination, was to many of its day sweetness and peace.[20] Hell was yawning beneath the feet of the sixteenth and early seventeenth centuries, and many of the most confident spirits could no longer put their trust in the traditional agencies of help afforded by the corporate life of the Church. Face to face with a God whom the Armageddon mood of the time saw not a little in its own likeness, it behooved the single soul to make itself certain of its standing. Something, too, of the individualism of the time came in. Each man reading his own Bible and finding his own salvation therein— here was an ideal to fire the imagination and express some of the deepest instincts of the age.

Too often the modern, surveying with deep pity and sympathy the heroic sufferings of those who by one side or the other were not permitted to hold in peace the tenets on which their whole spiritual life depended, is filled with indignation at men who would not allow to their neighbors the tolerance they defended as their own right. But that point of view on the whole is a modern one, certainly not an early seventeenth-century one. The belief that the common reason of man would lead all men to the same conclusion was deeply ingrained in the sixteenth and seventeenth-century consciousness. None of the great leaders of the Reformation was in the least doubt that he had hold of the heart of the matter, and that his defence and imposition of his own point of view was his duty to the truth and to right reason. The Scotch Presbyterians in 1637 quite properly cried out upon the attempt of Charles and Laud to impose upon them a Prayer Book modeled on that of the Church of England as an intolerable coercion of conscience and an unforgivable piece of ecclesiastical tyranny.[21] But when, only half a dozen years later, their turn came to make terms with Parliament, the imposition of the discipline of the Kirk upon the Church of England seemed to them a moderate and reasonable measure which all good men should submit to for the profit of their own souls.[22] It was an almost universal state of mind with all the strength that comes from such a deep conviction of absolute rightness.

That same passion for precise and manageable notions that plays so large a part in the acceptance of the new science was earlier manifest in the field of theology. Grace and Free Will had collided before the Reformation period, and the difficulties inherent in the recognition of the two at once had been canvassed pretty thoroughly, but yet Christianity had managed to hold on to both sides. But to the seventeenth-century mind, it was one or the other. So, too, in the field of ritual and liturgy. The Puritan who had determined that Transubstantiation was idolatrous felt that to sit at his ease at the table for the Supper and to bring the wine in a pewter tankard to that matter-of-fact board was the safest way of conserving the realities of the situation. Much of the fanaticism of the seventeenth century is due to that very passion for precision and consistency that in the field of science was to achieve such notable results.

But in the field of religion it led inevitably to segmentation and to the multiplication of sects. From some points of view that multiplication might have been taken as evidence of life, of the richness of the flowering of the spirit, but that was not the mood of the seventeenth century, for which uniformity and invariability were still canons of truth. And the bitterness of the collision of points of view bent on immediate domination, and in no wise disposed to wait until the harvest, shook Christendom. Before the seventeenth century opened, it was clear that religious controversy might wreck the work of the Reformation. The principle of private judgment had certainly promoted theological speculation among the masses and had made the individual Christian lay hold vigorously upon the problems of his religion, but the authority which the Protestant had rejected had not been replaced. Calvin strove vainly to replace the rejected authority of the Church, but the authority of the Bible privately interpreted rested ultimately upon the belief that each enlightened Christian had within him a guide to enable him to take the Bible in the sense which the Holy Spirit had intended it, in other words, the Inner Light. And before the seventeenth century was spent, the history of the Enthusiastic sects on the Continent and in England had demonstrated that the forms which the Inner Light might take were limitless, subject to no bounds of what the seventeenth century or, perhaps, any other time would call reason.

Harmless as many of the most fantastic of these sects may seem today, it must not be forgotten that in the seventeenth century no sect thought of itself as one contribution among many to the riches of the religious life, but each and every one was prepared to take possession of the entire Christian edifice at the first calling. Moreover, the social interrelations of religious theory and government were so close that very few religious issues were considered strictly or exclusively on their spiritual merits. The history of seventeenth-century religious controversy is an appalling one from any approach. A disregard of the circumstances of the times might easily make it seem completely irrational.

It is not surprising that those in Church and State who found themselves responsible for the guardianship of civilization regarded the multiplication of religious controversies as a menace to the peace of society. Even before the end of the sixteenth century the emphasis on doctrine with the resulting embroilment of the religious life in controversy was seen by discerning men on both the Protestant and Catholic sides to be a serious menace to the cultivation of other aspects of the spiritual life. Obviously, any religious group that found itself in control of its area would be tempted to invoke the peace argument against those who might jeopardize its privileges. And, equally obviously, a minority group pressing hard upon a more settled and indifferent majority with some prospect of imposing its more aggressive energy and intense will upon that majority, or any active competitor in a more evenly distributed imbroglio, would be more disposed to spend its energy on the winning of its ground. But even these very human considerations aside, a good many men by the beginning of the seventeenth century were weary of the fighting and fearful lest the life of the spirit be completely devastated by the unending strife over doctrine and discipline and rite. Conspicuous among this number were the men whose poetry forms the main subject of this study.

The climate of the seventeenth century is a very confused and yet a strongly marked one. The winds are strong winds, and they are blowing hard from all directions. And sensitive men are quite aware of them. The exhilaration of the Renaissance is not yet spent by the beginning of the seventeenth century, and something of the exhilaration of the new rationalism is to be felt already in the air. But there is also bitter disillusionment. This is not the first time in the world's history when the free and impassioned pursuit of the beauty of the flesh has ended in the contemplation of "a bracelet of bright haire about the bone." [23] Nor is it the first time that the magnificent exploitation of the world has brought a queen's favorite to the scaffold and left his friends to think long and bitter thoughts of the brevity of glory and the arrogance of power. Nor is it the first time that the hope of all knowledge in one brain has left the heart empty and made the over-labored spirit reel with the dry vanity of all wisdom and its seeking. But in the seventeenth century these moods are seen with a certain sharpness of contrast and a certain hard substance, as if the winds of the time hurling themselves against some bare mountain crag had left the impact of their blow and the swirl of their passing etched in the unyielding granite.

CHAPTER II

THE RELIGIOUS CLIMATE

THE religious poetry of seventeenth-century England was in no sense the monopoly of any one party or movement within the Christian Churches of the time or without. The Catholic Recusants both at home and over seas wrote hymns and memorial verses and meditations on the various privileges and hardships of their suppressed life, and some of these, notably the poems of Father Southwell from the end of the preceding century, enjoyed a good deal of esteem even in circles to which their principles were anathema and the fate of their author well-deserved. Likewise, the Puritans in the time of their struggle and in the time of their defeat expressed themselves with energy and grace, and though the number of their real poets is exceedingly few, the greatest poet of the century, with however many qualifications and distinctions, belongs as much to them as to anybody else. It says much for the universality of religious feeling and the currency of good poetry that here the boundaries of party and creed, however implicit, seem not to have restricted either the movement or the appreciation of the best religious poetry of the time.

But in the nature of things certain groups did not enjoy the same opportunities for poetic expression of religious feeling as did others, nor did all religious groups offer equal appeal to poetic talent. Some of the finest mystical and devotional writing of the time was produced on the English Mission and in the convents of the Recusants on the Continent, but for the most part it is confined to prose. This may be simply the accident

49

of genius; but it may also be true that in that suppressed and persecuted group the issues of bare survival were so urgent that religious energy sought more direct and active expression. Then, too, the exclusion from the main currents of life at home and the wrenching of all ties for those who took refuge beyond the seas may well have left the springs of poetry dry. For the poet is more dependent than most men on free access to the sources of life of his age. Whatever the reason or reasons, the Recusant output in poetry for the first half of the seventeenth century is, so far as we know, slender and fugitive.

Something of the same is true of the Puritans and the other minority groups of the Protestant confession. The Elizabethan Settlement of the English Church, dictated as it was to so large an extent by considerations of practical expediency, had stopped far short of what the adherents of Geneva thought a thorough-going and godly reformation. Hooker's great work of definition and defence had avowedly taken up a position conceived of as halfway between Rome and Geneva and therefore sure to satisfy neither. Indeed, the official alignment of the English Church on the Protestant side had served only to influence and exasperate Calvinist hopes. And the practical necessities of government in an age so rich in lessons of the consequences of religious embroilment had made the late sixteenth and early seventeenth-century state Church put up bars against the progress of the still more radical religious sects.

For all of these groups the time was one of restlessness and strenuous effort. In the most favorable of times they were bitterly disappointed and outraged by the official coddling of what seemed to them at best frivolity and "lewdness" and at worst downright immorality and idolatry. In harder times, when, for instance, Laud was striving to enforce the conformity that seemed to him, as to most seventeenth-century statesmen, essential to Christian peace, they suffered suppression and persecution. At all times they were continually on the stretch, striving with every means at their disposal to advance the principles to which they were devoted and to tear down all that stood in their way. Under such circumstances, it is not surprising that their best intellectual energy was devoted to religious controversy, or that their attention was on the whole focussed on action rather than contemplation.

Other factors entered into their cultural situation, to degrees not easy to determine. Social and economic conditions undoubtedly played their accustomed parts. The extreme "Enthusiastic" groups, like, for instance, the Family of Love, drew heavily on the lower classes. The Puritans depended for the most part on the middle classes, though their adherents were to be found in all layers of society. Means and opportunity for education, for leisure, for intellectual stimulus, for access to the arts and the amenities would, of course, vary from class to class, and though the want of these things would not be a bar to the greatest genius, it would seriously condition and limit the development of belles lettres in such groups. Then, too, the Puritan and the "Enthusiast" had in their view of the world certain elements discouraging to poetry. The picture of the Puritan as a sour middle-class fanatic hating the raw sports of his neighbors not for their brutality but for the grudged pleasure they gave the participants, has been overdone. The fathers of John Milton and Mrs. Hutchinson were not the only members of that group who loved learning and beauty. But, in general, the Puritan was one of the victims of the invention of printing. He tended to confine himself to the printed page among the arts, and among the possible motions of the mind his preference was for the more ratiocinative. His passion for truth, heroic as it was, bore heavily on imagination and sensibility, and his real fault is not so much the strenuousness for which he has been so unjustly blamed as the literalness and the self-sufficiency which his detractors have not always scrupled to emulate.

As for those issues of form and ceremony that bulk so large in the seventeenth-century religious world, one possible explanation has not received the attention it may deserve. And that is the part that class taste and instinct played in the differences that so gravely divided religious society. It must not be forgotten that the passion of the aristocracy for display reached a peak in the Renaissance both in Italy and in England. In a simpler society where the opportunities for luxury were relatively limited, display in dress and arms and personal adornment had been the mark of rank and importance. The elaboration of the etiquette and ceremony of daily life had been one of the ways in which the vanity of power defined itself and expressed its own and the world's sense of its significance. As rank and wealth tended to sequester themselves in courts and separate their state from the physical necessities of their function, something artificial came into what had in an earlier age been immediately significant. The middle classes, on the other hand, whether because of a past in which the acquisition of power and resource had been to no small extent dependent upon prudence and modesty or because of a habit of judging of value by more purely utilitarian considerations, had neither the taste nor the capacity for such self-expressiveness. At any rate, the taste of the Puritan for the plain and the literal and the undecorated was at least not encouraging to the flight of fancy.

It is possible, too, that like the sceptic and the satirist the poet tends to be conservative in the presence of a strict enthusiasm. Whatever the ultimate outcome, the immediate effect of the Puritan movement in the first half of the seventeenth century was not such as to promise the spaciousness or the freedom of life upon which the poet is so much dependent. It is tempting for him to break out of a too strict or confining conventionality of social or religious feeling. On such an issue the poet has often been found in the vanguard of revolution. But the immediate promise of the Puritan and Enthusiastic movements was hardly one of a richer or more supple milieu than the one in which he found himself. It is not surprising, therefore, that, with one great exception, the religious poets of eminence, particularly the mystical and devotional poets, come out of the more conservative, or, as they considered themselves, the more moderate and central tradition of the English Church. And even the great exception, epic and speculative rather than lyric or contemplative as the genius of Milton is, serves rather to support the generalization. Donne, Herbert, Crashaw, Vaughan, Traherne, all come out of what is essentially the same tradition. Only one of the five was a layman; the rest are all clerical, even the least orthodox of them, Traherne. And the layman, the physician Vaughan, shared their point of view, and the language in which he laments the religious vicissitudes of the Civil War is essentially theirs. One of them, only, departed from that communion, Crashaw, and he found his way to Rome. But he had his first nourishment among them, and practically all of his work was done when he was still of them, though almost from the start of his career he was responsive to other influences. But so in some degree were they all.

The keynote of the group to which these men belonged was "moderation," not in the sense of lack of fervor, but in the sense of respect for reason and measure. They liked to think of themselves as midway between Rome and Geneva, availing themselves of the strength and avoiding the extremes of both. Such an attitude, of course, at bottom begged the question, or, to be more exact, rested on assumptions by no means universally granted. Rome could hardly view half-way to Geneva as anything but half-way to error, and Geneva was not disposed to be any milder in its estimate of the half-way station in the other direction. The assumption of reasonableness, with its implications as to the state of mind of its opponents, which characterized the position of this group was, therefore, calculated to infuriate rather than conciliate those whom it labelled "extremists" in an age when even the most extreme viewed that denomination with horror.

Two considerations, however, this group might plead in justification of its position, and though they may not affect our estimate of the realities of the situation, they are essential to an understanding of the state of mind of these men. The first is that the Elizabethan Settlement was conceived of in an atmosphere of compromise. It was designed not as a revolution nor even as a reformation. It was quite literally a settlement, an attempt to establish order in such a fashion as to keep as large a part of the nation together as possible, while conciliating certain powerful minorities. Of course, it was neither scientific nor disinterested. Moreover, very different points of view were represented among those who made that settlement. Queen Elizabeth and Archbishop Parker certainly did not see eye to eye on a great many issues of discipline and ceremonial. And always behind were issues of political and economic interest no less important because not always recognized or understood.

The men who made of this Settlement a church, of whom the most important is admitted to be Hooker, were aware of and paid attention to the points of view of both the Protestants and the Catholics of their day. Hooker, in particular, while adhering to the major Protestant positions of the day showed himself sensitive to and appreciative of many of the values of Catholic practice and tradition. He claimed a mediate position for the Anglican Church, and he built up an elaborate structure of argument to justify that claim.

What Hooker began for the Anglican Church in theology Andrewes carried on in the field of devotional thought and writing, and Laud tried to carry on in ritual and government. This was not the only tradition in the English Church. But the group to which the poets in whom we are interested belonged believed it was the central group. The question of whether they were right or not is one that has been argued ever since, but it is not one that concerns us in our present study.

For the first half of the seventeenth century we have, fortunately, a very full and illuminating expression of this tradition or point of view in the preaching of one of these poets, John Donne. Donne, whose mighty shadow lies over so large a proportion of the literary developments of the first half of the century, had been born a Catholic of the blood of More and Rastell. The history of his conversion we shall have occasion to discuss later. The point is that as an English churchman Donne held this "moderate" view of the Church of England, and from his pulpit at Saint Paul's he expounded it with all the resources of a singularly rich and cultivated mind and with all the eloquence of one of the greatest of English preachers.

There is more than a touch of the drama characteristic of the time in the fact that one so fervent, in some things of so fanatical a temperament as John Donne, should have found himself a leader in even so qualified a moderation. There was nothing moderate in his love poems, certainly nothing moderate in some of the excursions of his imagination in the purlieus of death. There was even more certainly nothing moderate in his diatribes against the Jesuits and the Anabaptists, but in his fundamental outlook and in the point of view which he inculcated from the pulpit or the cross of Saint Paul's, Donne was a moderate in the sense defined above, and he threw his somewhat enigmatic influence to that cause. That in so doing he expressed something central to the religious opinion and feeling of his day is attested by the fact that he was generally recognized as the most distinguished London preacher of his day.[1]

To begin with, Donne defended the English Reformation against the assaults of both sides with spirit and confidence on the ground that by this reformation, as he once put it in a quotation from James I, *"Papistry was driven out, and Puritan-isme kept out,* and *wee delivered from the Superstition of the Papist,* and *the madnesse of the Anabaptists."* [2] In the same sermon, preached at Paul's Cross in September of 1622, Donne made it quite clear that though he was opposed to what he regarded as the indecent brawling of the sectaries within this moderate church, he was willing to have enough controversy to keep the Church of England in that middle position between the Catholics and the Anabaptists. As for the theory of inclusiveness, the favorite modus vivendi of later times, that was not yet dreamed of in the Church of England, for it was foreign to every instinct of the time.

The difficulties and the possibilities of this "moderate" position can be seen more clearly in the line which Donne took on some of the moot questions of his day. The issue of ceremonies is as good a one as any. Donne granted without any argument that there is nothing indispensable or efficacious in ceremonies as ceremonies, but he labored to justify them on grounds of expediency and comeliness, "Ceremonies are *nothing;* but where there are no Ceremonies, order, and uniformity, and obedience, and at last, (and quickely) Religion it selfe will vanish." [3] Viewed historically and abstractly, that is perhaps a moderate position, but there was little in it to commend itself to a man who believed that ceremonies were at best a superstitious superfluity and at worst anything from a stumbling block to sheer idolatry. And possibilities of trouble from this quarter became even clearer when in another of the same collection of sermons Donne is found arraigning with very little moderation the man who is so indifferent to beauty "that from a glorious Masse to a sordid *Conventicle,* all's one to him." [4] In that sentence the fundamental discrepancies of taste that underlay the whole struggle between the bishops and the Puritans on the issue of ceremony are laid bare. A man to whom a Mass could be a glorious thing would in that day find thing a little brittle in it, something that will not long stand the fierce onset of the extremist's certainty.

It is not surprising, therefore, that Donne like the rest of his group should be anxious to safeguard these positions from the type of attack they were not especially designed to meet. He and those with whom he held felt with a fair show of reason that they were the official interpreters of the English Church. They could certainly count on their side the statesmen who had achieved the Elizabethan Settlement, Hooker, who had done more than any other man to give that Settlement standing among the theologians and controversialists of Europe, and Andrewes, who enjoyed so high a reputation for his scholarship and his piety, and finally, but in no way least in immediate importance, the court and the high officials of the King. In many ways they were the party in possession, and, not unnaturally, they took a line different from that taken by the Puritans who were trying to convert their congregations to what they felt should be the position of the Church of England rather than what they felt was the position of the Church of England.

Still another element of a good deal of importance in the situation for Donne at least is the general composition of the audiences which flocked to Paul's Cross or crowded the enormous interior of old Saint Paul's to hear him preach. We can draw some very fair conclusions from the sermons themselves, for if in their swelling periods we find the portrait of the preacher himself drawn with dramatic and at times sensational brilliance, we also find there the no less vivid likeness of the men who listened to him. They are the prosperous and the high-placed of this world. Especially when he is calling them to account in the not infrequent sociological passages of his sermons, it is clear that they are the fortunate, the privileged, with all the temptations of the masters of wealth and power. The following adjuration is a fair example, "Till this defalcation, this scrutiny be made, that you know what's your owne,

what's other mens, as your Tombe shall be but a monument
of your rotten bones, how much gold or marble soever be be-
stowed upon it, so that Hospitall, that free-schoole, that Col-
ledge that you shall build, and endow, will bee but a monument
of your bribery, your extortion, your oppression; and God,
who will not be in debt, (though he owe you nothing that
built it) may be pleased to give the reward of all that, to
them, from whom that which was spent upon it, was unjustly
taken." [13]

It is not surprising, then, that on those issues of the relations
of piety to the world, of the part which the children of light
should play in secular affairs, of the relations of earthly ambition to heavenly aspiration, of those century-old strains and
conflicts between the life of the world and the life of the spirit,
Donne's is essentially the attitude of those who from their
position are disposed to make the best of both worlds. This
point of view is perhaps best summed up in the following
sentence from the *Essayes in Divinity*, "By which, as thou
didst so make Heaven, as thou didst not neglect Earth, and
madest them answerable and agreeable to one another, so let
my Soul's Creatures have that temper and Harmony, that they
be not by a misdevout consideration of the next life, stupidly
and trecherously negligent of the offices and duties which thou
enjoynest amongst us in this life; nor so anxious in these, that
the other (which is our better business, though this also must
be attended) be the less endeavored." [14] But though this passage occurs in the *Essayes in Divinity,* it only expresses what is
the prevailing theory and practice of the sermons. There is
much to suggest that no small part of Donne's success in the
pulpit as well as in the drawing room was due to this sensitiveness to the varying capacities of men, to his constant and
delicate remembrance of the law which he once phrased with
consummate perfection in one of his sermons, "Every man
must know how much water his own vessel draws, and not to

for their own sake, perhaps their richest satisfaction. But as he saw clearly, there was no necessary connection between these movements of the mind and the movements of the grace of true religion in the spirit of the average Christian. Indeed, the preoccupations of controversy might well make it very hard for grace to work at all. "That day of the Lord will be darknesse and not light, and that darknesse will be, that you shall not discerne the Lords body. You shall scatter all your thoughts upon wrangling and controversies, de modo, how the Lords body can be there, and you shall not discerne by the effects, nor in your own conscience, that the Lords body is there at all." [18] In other words, the fundamental need of the average human being is not to study controversy but "to study the Mystery of godlinesse, which is without all controversie." [19]

To that end he sought to discourage the excessive preoccupation with doctrine that plagued so much of seventeenth-century religious thinking. And especially did he attack it in its stronghold, the interpretation of the Scriptures, in which for the time it had wrought probably its most serious damage: "They therefore which stub up these severall roots, and mangle them into chips, in making the word of God not such . . . they, I say, do what they can this way, to make God, whose word, it is pretended to be, no God. They which build, must take the solid stone, not the rubbish." [20] In other words, "oftentimes, where fewest Expositors contribute their helpes, the Spirit of God alone enlightens us best; for many lights cast many shadows, and since controverted Divinity became an occupation, the Distortions and violencing of Scriptures, by Christians themselves, have wounded the Scriptures more, then the old Philosophy or Turcism." [21]

Here Donne's principles bore as heavily on his own predilections as on his opponents'. For his temptation was that with which he once admiringly charged Pico della Mirandola when he described him as "a man of an incontinent wit, and subject to the concupiscence of inaccessible knowledges and transcendencies." [22] Such a man did he know himself to be, and there lay one of his bosom temptations. It is peculiarly interesting, therefore, to find him taking such a critical attitude toward what he well knew to be next to his constant thirst for experience, his master passion. To some extent, of course, this suspicion is to be traced to his constant fear of the extremes of fantasy into which the excess of any good impulse might carry the fervent. But in this matter it was more than his usual good sense that prompted his suspicion of curiosity. It was rather his sense of the nature of the universe. Something of that, God meant to keep hid from the eyes of man: "And besides, when I remember that it was God which hid Moses's body, And the Divell which laboured to reveal it, I use it thus, that there are some things which the Author of light hides from us, and the prince of darkness strives to shew to us; but with no other light, then his firebrands of Contention, and curiosity." [23]

But strong as was Donne's concern for the danger of fantasy, even stronger was his anxiety that nothing should distract the attention of the Christian from the main business of his profession, the business of salvation. Conduct was the center of religious activity for Donne—"To search so farre into the nature, and unrevealed purposes of God, as to forget the nature, and duties of man, this is a shrewd surfet, though of hony, and a dangerous vomit." [24] And Donne believed, with that confidence of the seventeenth-century man that God would see the world from the same angle from which he saw it, that for God, too, the moral good of man was paramount. So with the revelation of His truth. Once in speaking of the vision of God which the saved might look forward to enjoying, Donne expressed this faith with singular completeness: "What shall we see, by seeing him so, *face to face?* not to inlarge our selves into *Gregories* wild speculation, *Qui videt videntem omnia,*

omnia videt, because we shall see him that sees all things, we shall see all things in him, (for then we should see the thoughts of men) rest we in the testimony of a safer witnesse, a Councell, *In speculo Divinitatis quicquid eorum intersit illucescet;* In that glasse we shall see, whatsoever we can be the better for seeing." [25]

But though Donne shared the passionate concern of his time for personal morality, his usual moderation is to be seen in what he has to say of the minutiae of the ethical life. The godly in the seventeenth century were wont to devote a good deal of thought to various devices of mortification in dress and in diet and in occupation. Donne's parishioners were no exception to this fashion of piety. The principle underlying the detailed advice which Donne gave on this point is very clearly set forth in one of the sermons: "For, neither spirit, nor flesh must be destroyed in us; a spiritual man is not all spirit, he is a man still. But then is flesh and spirit reconciled in Christ, when in all the faculties of the soule, and all the organs of the body we glorifie him in this world; for then, in the next world wee shall be glorified by him, and with him, in soule, and in body too." [26] In terms of equal reprobation Donne condemns both the absorption in the affairs of this world to the neglect of the interests of the next and, as we have seen, the neglect of the offices of this world because of a "misdevout consideration of the next life." [27] Indeed, he goes so far as to enjoin upon his hearers a grateful enjoying in this life of the good things which God has given unto his own: "Pay therefore this debt of surveying thine estate, and then pay thy selfe thine own too, by a chearfull enjoying and using that which is truly thine, and doe not deny nor defraud thy selfe of those things which are thine, and so become a wretched debtor, to thy back, or to thy belly, as though the world had not enough, or God knew not what were enough for thee." [28]

It is interesting, too, to notice in this connection how the

sociability that was so integral a part of Donne's nature re-
enforces the Protestant suspicion of the monastic life in the
vigor with which he urges his hearers "not to run away from
that Service of God, by hiding ourselves in a superstitious
Monastery, or in a secular Monastery, in our owne house, by
an unprofitable retirednesse, and absenting our selves from the
necessary businesses of this world." [29] Something of the same
sociable regard for the way of the world is to be found, also,
in what he has to say of dress, that favorite subject of endless
reflection for the pious lady of the seventeenth century and her
adviser, whether Catholic, or Puritan, or Anglican. It is pleasant to remember that the model whom he held up for the happy
mean he himself advocated in this regard was his own good and
gracious friend, Magdalen Herbert. Even of all the charming
things that have been said of that great lady, nothing more
charming survives than this from her funeral sermon in which
her friend, the Dean of Saint Paul's, tells how she solved the
problem of godliness and dress: "And for her *Attire*, (which
is another *personall* circumstance) it was never *sumptuous*,
never *sordid;* But alwayes agreeable to her *quality*, and agreeable to her *company;* Such as shee might, and such, as others,
such as shee was, did weare. For, in such things of *indifferency*
in themselves, many times, a *singularity* may be a little worse,
then a fellowship in that, which is not altogether so good. It
may be *worse,* nay, it may be a *worse pride,* to weare worse
things, then others doe. Her *rule* was *mediocrity*." [30]

And this same mediocrity—the word then had a happier
connotation than now—as an ideal led Donne to speak more
kindly of social and esthetic pleasure than many of the godly
of his time would have thought consistent with his profession
as a candidate for salvation. Here again Donne kept to his
rule that the abuse of a thing is no reason for destroying it—
"Every thing that hath, or may be abused, must not therefore
be abandoned; the turning of a thing out of the way, is not a

taking of that thing away, but good things deflected to ill uses, by some, may be by others reduced to their first goodnesse." [31] So long as the sources of pleasure are used with moderation they are good, and the godly may enjoy them with a clear conscience—"Feare not thou, that a chearefulnesse and alacrity in using Gods blessings, feare not that a moderate delight in musique, in conversation, in recreations, shall be imputed to thee for a fault, for, it is conceived by the Holy Ghost, and is the off-spring of a peacefull conscience." [32] In that sentence one breathes a larger and humaner air than is always associated with the piety of the seventeenth century, but the writings of John Donne are full of evidence that he and his friends breathed that air more frequently than we sometimes think. They deserve to be remembered gratefully as a powerful source of influence for the liberalizing and humanizing of the perilously earnest civilization of the England of the first half of the seventeenth century. [33]

CHAPTER III

METAPHYSICAL POETRY

IN metaphysical poetry the religious lyrists of the seventeenth century found ready to their hand an instrument of expression that was to prove peculiarly stimulating to their capacities and adaptable to their purpose. And, it should be added, like every other artistic instrument that fits the hand of the user, it was to prove compliant with their weakness as well as their strength. It was a singularly ductile instrument, becoming a very different thing in the hands of Crashaw from what it was in the hands of Herbert, and in Vaughan's something still different, as individual genius discovered and developed fresh possibilities and applied them to new ends. Indeed, so striking is this variety and individuality that English metaphysical poetry from Donne to Traherne is better viewed as a movement than as a type, and a movement in the English rather than in the Continental sense, with the emphasis on diversity and general and casual influence rather than on self-conscious co-operation to clearly envisaged ends. But, in spite of this diversity and individualism, it still remains true that all these major religious lyrists are metaphysicals, with certain clearly discernible likenesses in objective and operation.

Of recent years there has been a good deal of interest in metaphysical poetry, and not a little excellent work has been done in the definition and elucidation of the type. While for the most part discriminating, this study has been thoroughly sympathetic. For most of the recent critics have been keenly aware of the likenesses between the world in which these men lived and the world in which we live, and of the light to be shed on our problems by the contemplation of theirs. Even so objective and historically minded a study as the recent one of Mr. J. B. Leishman [1] owes no small part of its momentum to its author's appreciation of these values, an appreciation very seldom expressed but implicit in the selection of issues for discussion and the careful focussing of conclusions. So, too, for a man like Mr. T. S. Eliot who, both as critic and creative artist, is so widely involved in the ethical and esthetic discussion of the present time, the study of the metaphysicals affords a veritable arsenal of instructive parallels and possible correctives. The criticism of metaphysical poetry is, therefore, a very live issue of contemporary criticism, and a good deal more than disengaged curiosity or sympathetic antiquarianism enters into its discussion.

Whatever their theories as to the origin or value of metaphysical poetry, all critics from Dr. Johnson to Miss Joan Bennet are agreed that the distinctive characteristic of the type is its intellectual emphasis, an emphasis apparent both in the preoccupations of the poet and in his procedure. All critics agree, too, that the metaphysical poets sometimes overdid intellectual emphasis, but there is very wide disagreement to the extent of this excess, its seriousness, and its artistic human consequences. For Dr. Johnson, the fact that they emphasized the intellectual element is the definitive of their claims to literary immortality in poetry.[2] For Eliot the fact that they sometimes overdid it does not so much of a fault when you consider how the others, for instance, underdid it.[3] The devil you know may be less of a risk, but he is certainly more of a burden than the one you do not happen to have on your hands. At the same time, as Mr. T. S. Eliot well knows, it is easy to exaggerate the heinousness of the sins one is not tempted to fall into at the expense of those one is. Since our immediate problem is neither the direction of contemporary criticism nor the absolute value of metaphysical poetry, but an understanding of its possibilities and implications as an instrument for the religious lyrists of the time, it is well for us to begin at least with an inquiry as to what exactly it was that the metaphysical poets had to work with in this instrument of expression.

Probably the most satisfactory brief definition of the type is Professor Grierson's, "Metaphysical Poetry, in the full sense of the term, is a poetry which, like that of the *Divina Commedia,* the *De Natura Rerum,* perhaps Goethe's *Faust,* has been inspired by a philosophical conception of the universe and of the rôle assigned to the human spirit in the great drama of existence." [4] That definition is especially valuable, because it reminds us that metaphysical poetry is no isolated phenomenon peculiar to the seventeenth century, but a recurrent aspect universal poetry. It also sets up as a starting point the id of a full and complete development of what we find only part and to a degree in the seventeenth-century lyric. Grierson then proceeds to give us a working clue to the p and the embryonic, "The distinctive note of 'metaph poetry is the blend of passionate feeling and paradoxical nation." [5] That definition, however, takes us out general field and into the poetry of one individual, John

The question of how far the course of any move this may be attributed to the work of one individual large one, not likely ever to be definitely settled. F most thoroughgoing opponents of the heroic theo would grant that a movement may be illuminating the work of one man, if he can be fairly regarded and typical. All students of the English metaphysical would agree that Donne is the central figure in the group. C tainly not because Donne is typical, for it would be a very rash man indeed who would claim that Donne was typical of anybody but himself, but all students agree that he is the most metaphysical of the English metaphysicals in the sense of having perhaps more of the distinctively metaphysical qualities than any other poet of his time. Moreover, he was, it is generally agreed, the enkindling influence, the seminal force, for the entire group.

The beginnings of John Donne's poetry are distinctly secular, not to say profane, and they are highly personal, but they are significant for the whole development of English metaphysical poetry. For here in these early love poems meet two elements of crucial importance, a change in the movement of the spirit of the time, and a man who in temperament and experience was fitted to seize upon the emergent elements in the life about him.

When John Donne began to write his love poems, Elizabethan literature was in the heyday of its splendor. The first burst of pure song had, it is true, pretty much spent itself, but the emotional and imaginative brilliance of the Elizabethan genius was beginning to enjoy more than compensating self-expression in the drama. There was still the lavish and unconscious outpouring of energy characteristic of any great period of creative art. This does not mean that there were not shadows on that poetry as there were on the life of the time, but there was a reckless abandon, a confidence of energy that showered its forces upon the slightest undertaking without any fear that the life-giving waters would ever cease to flow. The result we all know, an almost unparallelled brilliance and passion and abundance of beauty and life. Every success in this imperfect world seems to bring its own defects in its train. Lack of coherence, lack of plan, lack of economy, all these are different names for what was to prove the great deficiency of Elizabethan literature, lack of control. The results are to be seen in the formlessness and the extravagance and the often grotesque incongruity of even the greatest of

Elizabethan geniuses. But in Donne's first poems these liabilities are still redeemed by the beauty and vitality of youth.

It is that last word that gives us the clue to the problem.
For the extravagance of youth so easily slips over into fantasy,
and with the passing of the years fantasy hardens into the
eccentricity of maturity. That in itself is a factor in the development of some of the less happy aspects of metaphysical
poetry that has not received so much attention as it deserves.
But Miss Kathleen Lea has suggested that just as the Elizabethan conceit is heavily indebted to the Italian conceit through
the habit of the Elizabethan of skimming over Italian poetry
and taking up the figures and ideas which attracted him without reference to the context, so the much-puzzled-over metaphysical comparison is really a development of Elizabethan
exuberance in the use of the simile.[6] Certainly, extravagance
and forcing of relations between images and ideas is not to be
considered a Jacobean invention.

On the other hand, there does seem to have been some flag-
ging of imaginative energy at the end of the sixteenth century.
What happened then may simply be just another example of
the way in which the human mind and imagination become
used to strong fare, so that that which at first offered all necessary stimulus has presently by familiarity become commonplace, and the overstimulated nerves are craving something
stronger than what has ceased to satiate their appetite.[7] The
large element of ingenuity in Elizabethan poetry may also have
contributed its share to the passion for novelty that is one of
the characteristics of an oversophisticated time. But there
is another factor that has not as yet received much consideration that may well account for not a little of this change in
temper. For when the general passion of the seventeenth
century for tightening man's grip on his world is considered,
it would be surprising if it did not affect the poetry of the time.
Certainly something self-conscious and deliberate comes into

the art of the new century, and something of the old spacious freedom and casualness of less rigorous times is lost. And as the swirl of conflicting forces latent in the movements of the age deepens, this effort to control the exuberance of the energies of the time, wise and inevitable at it may seem, in itself intensifies the intellectualism of Renaissance poetry.

Something should be said, too, of the development of Elizabethan literature in the direction of the ideal and the formal. So living, so fresh, is the first lyric outburst of the Elizabethan genius that it is tempting to forget how derivative and how ideal much of it was. The throbbing of English hearts through the symbols of ancient mythology and the breathing of the winds of English life and nature into the figures of ancient poesy are too much of a reality for it to be easy for us to remember how conventional much of Elizabethan love poetry was even in its heyday. But with the passing of time, some of those figures were bound to wear a little thin, and the voice of poetic enthusiasm to grow a little sharper, while artistic skill, maturing, would more and more translate the first happy borrowings of youthful emulation into the studied elegance of conscious imitation.

It is, it must never be forgotten, a little society in which these things are happening. It is a society which enjoys a central position in its day, enriched with the converging of all the streams of the life of the time upon its walls. But it is a section only of the society of its time, this of London, pretty much confined to the ranks of greatness and fashion. It has its own standards, its own pretensions, its own vanities, even. One of them is a taste for some of the elegances of learning without the labors. To the common human weakness for the striking and the dramatic it adds the taste of all small societies for the topical and the timely. So while it shows little ardor for pursuing the business of learning to any heights or depths, it makes a good deal of effort to "keep up." It has no monopoly on genius or even talent, but holding as it does the sources of wealth and power, it can very effectively pull toward itself whatever of aspiring talent there is outside its charmed circles. And it knows how, very effectively, because quite tacitly, to impose its own standards, its taste for display, its passion for self-aggrandizement and prestige, its faith in its own sphere of power and action rather than of contemplation, on the art it patronizes and sustains. Chapman, we know, wearied of the pretensions of this society and addressed himself to more strenuous and highly trained understandings, with an assumption of obscurity that is familiar to us, for much the same reasons, in a good deal of the high-brow literature of our own day.[8] What Donne really thought of the various noble ladies he courted for patronage we have little way of knowing, but there is an extraordinary difference in tone and value between what he implies in his various letters and dedications to his female patronesses and what he says of their sex in sermon and satire. It would look as if he compensated for the attendance he danced on their by no means unexacting and uncritical presences by a very low view of their sex in general (though, it should be added in fairness, pretty much the prevailing view of his day), particularly as regards judgment and intellect. Be that as it may, there is no question that the great bulk of Donne's verse was written with an eye to the smart world in which he aspired to play a conspicuous part.

The metaphysical poetry of Donne is, then, what might reasonably be expected at such a juncture from such a man. Donne flouts but does not entirely sweep aside the conventions of his day in the most conventional field of all, love poetry. Some of his lyrics are pure Petrarchanism, with all the burnings and humble aspirations to the "inexpressive she" that any lovesick young man about Elizabeth's London could desire. But a large number are of the other type that has made him famous. They are a revolt against a literary convention, one of the most brilliant rebellions known to English literature, a revolt against what was restrictive and artificial and hackneyed and stale in that convention, it is true, but also a revolt against what was ideal and graceful in it.

One can fancy the young Donne saying to himself, "Love is all that you have been saying about it all these years, but it is also this—hate, and contempt, and hunger, and revulsion, and curiosity, and vanity, and wild ecstasy, all in one." One can fancy him saying that his fellow poets had done justice to love and the heart and the fancy and the adoring eyes, but that love was also an affair of the nerves and the curious hands and the restless brain. One can fancy him saying, too, that enough had been said of love in gardens and on balconies; he was going to sing of love in the crowded and whispering houses and lanes of London, and the camps and the inns he knew.

Donne has an eye for the life about him. It is very easy to lose sight of that fact in the contemplation of his curious and often remote learning, just as so many readers of his sermons have been so much impressed by the magnificent passages on man's mortality and the fear of death that they have failed to note the countless flashes of the world of the time in which some contemporary attitude or mood is suggested in a line or two, or some aspect of the day-to-day scene is etched unforgettably in a moral example or a psychological illustration. Many of the types of the time, the middle-class merchant, the returned traveller with his tobacco and his fantastic costume, the Puritan, the young man about town, the soldier from foreign parts, the peddler with his chaffering, jostle their way through his pages. The various crafts of the day, the coinage, the sports, the games, the small inventions, some hardly above the level of gadgets, the petty formalities of the law, the mysteries of navigation, the physic of the time, the whipping of madmen, the ruined abbeys, the hangings in the queen's palace, all these yield their tribute of comparison and allusion. So do the day-to-day happenings of London, the Russian merchants, the plague bill, news from Virginia, the popular sympathy for Essex after his death, the various minor officials, pursuivants and informers, that battened on the misfortunes of the Recusants, to name only a few, come into the verses, grave and grimly gay, of the young John Donne. There is much to justify the words of Edmund Gosse, "Donne was . . . by far the most modern and contemporaneous of the writers of his time." [9] And with hardly an exception, this stream of contemporaneity is urban, almost exclusively of London.

Moreover, much of this daily material is handled with that candor, that absence of any impulse to idealism, that emphasis on the component physical detail, the literal and uncontexted sense reaction, that is in our day described as realism. And in Donne's case, as in ours, the detail so presented ranges anywhere from the dull and sluggish to the nauseous and the hideous, and the reaction anywhere from contempt to loathing. That effect which, in speaking of the sermons, Signor Praz has so eloquently described as "a livid subterranean stream of macabre realism," [10] is no less characteristic of the poems. This does not mean that grace and charm do not come within the purview of Donne's roving eye. They do, and they may easily be taken for granted or disregarded by the student who is interested in the more novel and sensational aspect of Donne's work. After all, the creator of Juliet and Imogen noticed that Marion's nose was red and raw. It is simply that the reader who has been living with the more chivalric and delicate sonneteers of Donne's generation cannot fail to be struck by this aspect of Donne's genius and may well be pardoned if, as so often happens, he takes this "realism" for the characteristic note of the poet.

But this realistic element, striking as it is, is only one element in the imaginative effect of Donne's verses. There is, also, that element of passionate awareness of implications

was to an extraordinary degree conversant with the movements
of his own time in religious controversy, in political thinking,
in science in all its branches, in the reports of discovery, and
in all those borderland branches of human curiosity where
fantasy jostles fact as in alchemy and Hermetism. To judge
from the use he made of this learning in the citation of authorities in his prose writings and his sermons, he must have
taken careful notes on his reading. And to judge from the
allusions in his verse, he must have read with a very lively
attention to everything picturesque and striking as well as to
the main arguments of his authors. But the most interesting
thing about this learning was that much of it was acquired
in the days of his youth and his early manhood when nothing
was farther from his thoughts than the career of learning
and piety to which he was destined. It was acquired, partly
from a desire to work out his own intellectual problems (he
read heavily in the controversy between Canterbury and Rome,
for instance), partly out of a fashion of learning, for learning
was in those days a grace of society and an embellishment of
the statecraft and courtiership to which Donne aspired, but
most, we may be sure, out of that wide-ranging curiosity that
is one of the dominating traits of his mind, that thirst for
knowledge that is one of the manifestations of his great and
basic thirst for life.

In that fascinating portrait of the young Donne which Professor Grierson has prefixed to his edition of Donne's verse,
there are two things that look out of the alert gravity of the
face, a deep sense of himself, a consciousness of the life surging
within his own identity, and a hunger and thirst, that might
almost be called a greed, for life. Much has been made in a
somewhat levelling modernity, of the dichotomy between learning and life, between books and living. Like all of the idols
of the marketplace, it has some justification in partial human
fact.[1] There are unquestionably a good many men, students

even, for whom the stream of life swerves aside around the walls of the library, and they will never believe that such an academic ox-bow is not a universal experience. But there are other men for whom the waters of life flow through all areas of their consciousness, for whom there are no walls between the various types of experience. Such a one was the young Donne, who plunged into the speculations of Plato or Paracelsus or Pico with the same zest with which he plunged into the varieties of amatory experience which sixteenth-century London offered to the young man about town. The discriminations of scholasticism served to define the shades of romantic experience in his youth, as in his maturity the memory of youthful sensuality and passion illuminated the oscillations of religious aspiration and defeat.[13] Everything alike was a part of that experience which he craved with a thirst even more immoderate and "hydroptique" than that which he attributed to Pico della Mirandola.

This enviable unity of consciousness was due in part, or perhaps rather, was possible, because Donne was still living in the era of universal knowledge. As Mr. Basil Willey has reminded us, "The major interests of life had not as yet been mechanically apportioned to specialists, so that one must dedicate oneself wholly to fact, or wholly to value."[14] The result was that a roving imagination could draw upon a wide variety of fields of learning and experience alike without being troubled by any difference in kind of its grasp upon them, and so make use of their common relevances and their total implications. But quite as important as this freedom of appropriation was the way in which it was carried out, not merely a matter of intellectual attitude but also of emotional reaction. The essence of the matter is to be found in the fact that to Donne what he read, what he thought, had the same kind of immediate potency of stimulus and energy that sense experience had. As Mr. T. S. Eliot has said: "A thought to Donne was an experience; it modified his sensibility. When a poet's mind is perfectly equipped for its work, it is constantly amalgamating disparate experience; the ordinary man's experience is chaotic, irregular, fragmentary. . . . The poets of the seventeenth century, the successors of the dramatists of the sixteenth, possessed a mechanism of sensibility which could devour any kind of experience." [15]

Obviously in minds such as these the reflective elements in experience play a larger part than they do in most minds, as Mr. Eliot very well suggests in the essay from which the passage above is taken.[16] There is warmth in the response of such men to ideas that leave the ordinary man puzzled or cold. The result is that surprising reality with which unexpected feeling invests abstractions that usually remain unassimilably outside the day-to-day range of experience. The familiarity with which Donne so often embraces eternity, that final extension of time, the least tangible of the familiar dimensions of experience, is one evidence. The result is that combination of the expansion of wonder with the tension of apprehension that Mr. Herbert Read has so well summed up in his phrase, "the emotional apprehension of thought." [17] But this emotional element in Donne's apprehension of thought does not, as emotion so often does, blur or deflect the operations of the mind. As Mr. Leishman has pointed out so comprehensively: "He [Donne] does not idealize his experiences or transform them by association into splendid visions; he grapples with them, carefully analyzes them, and often tries to interpret them by means of intellectual conceptions. But though a philosophic or metaphysical poet, he is still a poet, because he always tries to communicate the concrete experience itself, and not merely the results of his reflection upon it." [18]

It is that emotional blending of analysis and realistic illustration, in which satire jostles wonder and whimsy awe, that gives us the fascination of a passage like the following:

Eternall God, (for whom who ever dare
Seeke new expressions, doe the Circle square,
And thrust into strait corners of poore wit
Thee, who art cornerlesse and infinite)
I would but blesse thy Name, not name thee now.[19]

In such a passage not the least astonishing of its qualities is this emotional versatility. It is reminiscent of that mingling of emotions that is one of the distinguishing qualities of sophisticated and decadent art in any age. One thinks of the mingling of magnificence and pain in a brocade-bedizened cross-bearing Christ of the Spanish Golden Age, like that of Montanes at Seville,[20] or of the scream of torture breaking the rapture of youthful beauty and delight in the opera *Aphrodite*. But the emotional complexity of Donne's work is really a very different affair with more of the baroque than the Gongoristic or decadent in it. It is not just a mingling of emotion, one feeling suddenly shot through with another, for the elements of Donne's experience tend to preserve at once their identity and their interpenetrability. It is rather the swift setting of emotion against emotion with the same defiance of perspective that we have seen already in the handling of imagery. Ordinary human feeling moves much less quickly, clings more tenaciously to the purchase it has already won, retreats before a new emotional onslaught more slowly. It is sluggish in its rich diffusion, and when it is finally threatened by a shift in direction, it does not move with such clean completeness as does the emotion of Donne. Yet at the same time there is nothing trivial or mercurial in this mobility of feeling.

The explanation is, of course, that in Donne feeling like imagination is submissive to the operations of the logical faculty. It is the expression of thought that is the center of his purpose, with the stress on the relation of separate identities, and not the rich diversity of the creative fancy. It is one of the forward-looking and anticipatory elements in Donne's genius, this tight clutch of the mind on its own operations. It is not of that Elizabethan world to which the abundance of his imagination still belongs, but it looks forward rather to the age of prose and reason. So often one feels in a particularly rich passage of Elizabethan poetry that the author has simply plunged into a pool of imagination and feeling in which he is thrashing about, trusting that sooner or later he will touch shore. But the Jacobean will leave nothing to chance. He is not disposed to stay in calm waters; he has the same taste for the high seas that his Elizabethan brother has, but one feels in his case that an objective is in his eye and that however broken the rhythm of his progress, he is heading steadily toward it. True, as yet, rationalism is impeded by the richness of its materials, so that often the effect is ingenious and the operation of the mind tortuous, but the direction is discernible.

This does not mean that Donne is immune to the seductions of the casual and incidental comparison. No Elizabethan is more sensitive to the allurements of the particular detail, the chance-caught analogy, the fine-spun association than Donne, but always he pushes through to the complete adumbration of the thought on which he started. It is at this point that the metaphysical conceit is most liable to alienate at some time or other its hardiest admirer. For the very absorption in the un-ravelling of the intricate logical relations behind the metaphor distracts a little that complete surrender that most of us find necessary for the appreciation of emotion. Yet as Mr. T. S. Eliot has warned us again and again, we must not set our level of poetic enjoyment so low that the delight of thinking is in-terdicted. For ecstasy is the transcending and not the remission of thought. As Mr. Herbert Read puts it, "Metaphysical poetry is determined logically: its emotion is a joy that comes with the triumph of the reason, and is not a simple instinctive ecstasy." [21]

Joy and delight, however, are highly relative terms, and no-where more so than where the equilibrium between thought and feeling is in question. There are very few readers of poetry who would not at some time or other recognize the delight of seeing a complicated matter reduced to simplicity, a mass of discordant elements brought to unity. This purely intellectual satisfaction is to be had again and again in Donne as in all his followers. But there is another type of intellectual operation of which the delight is less certain, from the point of view, at least, of poetry. One of the main features of the development of seventeenth-century thought is the imposition of mathematical pattern upon the multiplicity of reality. More and more, experience is reduced to a diagram, a process, a development, the logical conclusion of which we have seen in our own day in some of the mechanistic conceptions of human nature in which all the mysteries of perception and will are subsumed under formulae of automatic stimulus and response. As Mr. Willey has suggested, such a process is attempted and carried through because it answers some need or predisposition of the human mind.[22] That reaching for a clear notion, an outline from which the accidents of the particular are sloughed off in the piling up of cases and illustrations, is to be seen at work in Donne more than has usually been realized. One striking example is the fascination which the map figure seems to have had for his imagination. The solemn and lovely "Hymne to God my God, in my sicknesse," with which, according to Walton, Donne comforted himself on his death bed, affords perhaps the most brilliant instance of his employment of that figure with which he had played ever since the youthful "The good-morrow," and which now at the gates of death could yet hold once more his roving thoughts:

> Whilst my Physitians by their love are growne
>   Cosmographers, and I their Mapp, who lie
> Flat on this bed, that by them may be showne
>   That this is my South-west discoverie
>   *Per fretum febris,* by these streights to die,

I joy, that in these straits, I see my West;
  For, though theire currants yeeld returne to none,
What shall my West hurt me? As West and East
  In all flatt Maps (and I am one) are one,
So death doth touch the Resurrection.[23]

Metaphysical poetry after Donne was used for all sorts of
purposes, from a trifle like John Cleveland's "Fuscara, or the
Bee Errant" to Edward Benlowes' "Theophila." It may be
said at once that its full possibilities for English poetry were
probably never fairly tested or exploited in the one genre that
would do full justice to them, a full-dress philosophic poem.
But many of them were developed to a very distinguished result in the more fragmentary lyric forms of Donne's successors
in the school of devotional poetry, Herbert, Crashaw, Vaughan,
and Traherne. It would be a mistake to attribute all or even
a majority of the characteristic effects of these poets to either
the example of Donne or the type of verse he so brilliantly
adumbrated. But there were unquestionably peculiar advantages in the metaphysical idiom for the expression of religious
experience.

In the first place, the very fact of the existence of a highly
intellectual and yet enkindling poetry was of great importance
to an age that more than most was basically intellectual in its
approach to religion. That absorption in controversy that so
many of the most thoughtful of the religious leaders of the time
deplored was in itself, in spite of its too frequent aridity, a
witness to the seriousness with which these men took the necessity of thinking through their religious convictions. The precise
definition of belief, the exegesis of the implications of belief,
the defence of one's own belief against the various assaults of
other points of view, all these intellectual aspects of the matter
held the center in the religious activity of the time. Consequently, however much the devotional poets might deplore the
doctrinal over-emphasis of the time and however much they

might seek in their own experience for something more inward and more varied, the intellectual aspects of religion were bound to play a very considerable part in their writing. The intellectual element is not, of course, of the same importance in the work of all of Donne's successors. Herbert and Vaughan, for instance, vary a good deal in philosophic interest and philosophic capacity. But for all, the problem of expressing religious ideas in verse is a real one. Consequently, an example so striking as Donne's and a technique so firm were bound to prove of great service in the solution of this problem. And, it should be added in view of the lush crop of weeds that was to spring up in this field, the faults of Donne were not minimized in the use his followers made of his example. That loss of context and blindness to the involvement of more than one party in poetic communication that are responsible for some of Donne's aridities and failures of taste were not to be redeemed, for instance, in Crashaw. For good and for ill, then, Donne's intellectualism was to affect his successors.

The same is true of his contribution to the solution of another of the major problems of seventeenth-century religious poetry, the problem of mediation between religious feeling and those instruments of sense and imagination that, under the conditions of human communication, are indispensable for the expression of thought and feeling in any field. The elaborate medieval apparatus that had so well served Dante and the other religious poets of the Middle Ages had been rejected by the Reformation. The familiar symbols of the world after death, the human intermediation of the saints, expressed in a thousand legends of this world and the next, the symbolism and pageantry of church rite and festival, with all the accumulated imaginative and emotional values that had gathered about them for fifteen hundred years, these things had for the most part been rejected. The figure of Mary the Virgin and Mother, though not entirely excluded from the thought of the time, was under suspicion. Iconoclasm with its fear of idolatry and its resolution against superstition was at the door of the Protestant consciousness, and much of what had given food to the Christian imagination for centuries was shut without. Even the human life of Christ had lost some of its direct imaginative appeal in the prevailing theological preoccupations. The Old Testament held its own fairly well in parallel and illustration, and those portions of the New dealing with the organization and customs of the early Church were in the center of contemporary controversy. Moreover, the large part played by the Psalms in the literary life of the time must never be forgotten. But, again, it is the revelatory and authoritarian aspects of the Bible rather than its imaginative richness and suggestiveness that dominate the general consciousness. It is tempting to wonder what would have happened if the invention of printing had become generally effective in the thirteenth century or been delayed until the eighteenth. Certainly, the history of the Reformation period would have been very different, but it is idle to speculate whether or not the emphasis of Protestant religious experience would have been more imaginative and less intellectual, and the instruments of its first expression less verbal and more symbolic. The fact remains that the general state of mind furnished a very considerable problem for the religious poet.

It was a problem to which there was more than one solution, of course. One, Milton was to find, and though his solution presupposed a more spacious attitude toward the questions of symbol and allegory than the average Puritan of his time would have been able to compass, it remains a very satisfactory one. But even so, it was probably better suited to epic than to lyric poetry. Another is suggested by the intellectual objective which (in the words of Mr. Willey) the Platonist, John Smith, set up as the goal of the enlightened believer, "to think of God without allowing the busy imagination to stain his white radiance with its phantasms." [24] That is a very lofty view of religious purpose, but one better suited to the capacities and the objectives of the mystic and the philosopher than of the poet. On the contrary, Donne's use of scholastic philosophy, of contemporary science, of the daily life of London, opened up rich possibilities for the sensuous coinage which religious values need for imaginatively effective communication. One of the great dangers of religious symbolism is that it may become remote, too well-worn, too specialized in its connotations for the wider stimulus needful for religious life. Of these evils there was little danger in the wide range of imaginative material that, as we have seen, Donne invoked.

Fortunately, no one of his successors tried to follow his example literally in the precise constituents of his imagery. In some ways Herbert comes closest, but there is a domestic tinge to the homeliness of Herbert's day-to-day imagery that Donne's lacks, and that makes it Herbert's own. Then, too, the pageantry of the ecclesiastical year, not as it is splendidly realized in cathedrals but as quietly observed in a parish church, comes to enrich his material of figure and allusion. Vaughan, likewise, extends the field of metaphysical imagery. For the urban Donne, nature, with the exception of a very few gorgeous descriptions of natural phenomena viewed pictorially, meant the "book of the creatures," ensconced and confined within the theological hierarchy. Vaughan opens up a whole new field of sense impression and of imaginative implication when he enriches that traditional conception with the discoveries of his own very individual sensitiveness to the beauty and wonder of the natural world. Traherne, in his turn, carries the awareness of nature as a treasure house of the revealing of God in some ways farther, while in other directions he adds new realms to the self-consciousness of Donne in his reminiscences of the childish self Donne seems to have forgotten. Crashaw returns to sources which Donne had rejected, and carries that blend of sense and divinity to which Donne had given credit to heights and in some ways to extremes beyond Donne's reach. But in varying degrees and in different directions all of these poets profited by the freshening and widening of the imagery of religious poetry which Donne had accomplished.

The same is true of what Donne achieved in the more purely musical aspects of his verse. Later Elizabethan secular poetry had been growing sweeter, smoother, more elegant, in its less happy moments, more facile. There is hardly any strength in art but which carries in its very realization the seeds of its own exaggeration, its own corruption. The early seventeenth century in England was an age when piety was taken for granted in large sections of society and yet, in some ways, insulated from large sections of the common life by a greater strenuousness of application. It is not surprising that under such conditions piety was relatively voluble and self-expressive, and yet religious feeling was to some degree stultified by over-definition and controversy. In such an age the religious poet needs to have a special care for freshness and variety of expression, for that accent and discrimination that constitute distinction of style. This is the more necessary because, as we have seen, religious poetry is a mixed genre, where two standards have jurisdiction and one may be accepted, mistakenly, as satisfaction for the other. So generous is the passion for edification in its acceptances that too often piety is allowed to cloak shallowness and banality of expression.

The very sharpness and precision of the working of Donne's mind and imagination are reflected in the felicity of his diction, a felicity in which precision is never sacrificed to grace and very seldom even to the sensational effect dear to Donne's heart. That precision goes to the length at times of a coinage or an adaptation, but, as a rule, Donne's command of the general vocabulary, enriched, of course, by the special terms of science and philosophy, is wide enough and pliant enough for his purposes. The same is true of his syntax. A transferred epithet, a compression of idiom, an inversion or a transposition for emphasis, these elements of surprise and of novelty are often to be found, but again, for the most part, Donne follows the movement of talk.[25] It is, to be sure, that glorified and pregnant talk that was the ideal of Matthew Arnold, but often there is no sign that the poet is emulous of anything but conversational directness and energy until the moment comes when suddenly he soars quite out of his plane. Yet even after these flashes of splendor he can be counted upon to return to that middle ground on which he habitually moves.

This is one reason for the freshness and trenchancy of his music. But it is not the only one. Like practically all Elizabethans, Donne experimented with variety of form in line and stanza pattern. Like almost all of these masters of singing he bent each pattern to his own ends. A notable example is to be found in the "Holy Sonnets." True, they have fourteen lines and a sonnet rhyme scheme. But within the line Donne certainly makes the most of that liberty of variation that is the one sure note of English prosody. The following is a somewhat extreme example but valuable for the evidence of how far Donne could go in a thoroughly serious, not to say solemn poem:

> And can that tongue adjudge thee unto hell,
> Which pray'd forgivenesse for his foes fierce spight?
> No, no; but as in my idolatrie
> I said to all my profane mistresses,
> Beauty, of pitty, foulnesse onely is
> A signe of rigour: so I say to thee,
> To wicked spirits are horrid shapes assign'd,
> This beauteous forme assures a pitious minde.[26]

Much more typical of the usual Donne effect is that of the opening lines of the tenth of these sonnets:

Death be not proud, though some have called thee
Mighty and dreadfull, for, thou art not soe,
For, those, whom thou think'st, thou dost overthrow,
Die not, poore death, nor yet canst thou kill mee.[27]

Indeed, here is the perfect musical counterpart of that emotional effect found so often in Donne where the imagination seems to fly out into infinity only to be caught swiftly and noiselessly back. Anyone who has ever been in Venice on St. Mark's feast day will remember how the lion of the Evangelist floats on silken standards before the great church. As the April winds from the sea swell and fling out their shining folds, that exquisite heraldry fills the whole radiant scene, and then as the breeze fails, they swing crumpling back to the literal banners, tethered to their unyielding standards. So it is with the music of John Donne.

For always there is to be felt the grip of an unseen and implicit principle of control, and that is the argument, the closely articulated, persistently held thread of the comparison, or the exposition, or the analysis, or the proof, that here, as in the realms of feeling and imagination, is, for Donne, ultimately supreme. The shortcomings of the resulting music are obvious. Not its dissonances, not its deliberate cacophanies, not even its broken chords, with their sudden jets and starts of melody, are its most teasing deficiency, but this truncation of splendor, this sudden thwarting of starbound beauty. But even the defects of Donne's music have their value for devotional poetry. The unimpeded pursuit of the infinite has its predestined repulses, and he who hopes to compress the ineffable into words had best take care of facility or the intoxication of his own rapture. For both the music of Donne is tonic.

The genius of Herbert was for the smoother, more limpid modes, and that of Crashaw for the higher and the more sustained flights of feeling. At his best finer and freer than Donne, Vaughan yet could not hold his music on the higher ranges which Donne deliberately rejected, and Traherne's gifts were nowhere less those of poetry than in this matter of singing. Yet all of them owe much of their best strength and distinction, even in their own peculiar achievements, to the astringent freshness, the vigorous reality, of Donne's music.

CHAPTER IV

THE CONVERSIONS OF JOHN DONNE

THE first and in some ways the most important thing to remember for Donne's life was that he had an unrivalled chance by birth and inheritance to be hanged, drawn, and quartered in the best Elizabethan manner, and that he rejected that chance. He was by his mother born into one of the great martyr families on the Catholic side. To judge from what we know of his education and from what we can infer from allusions in his works, he was brought up carefully in the ancestral faith. But through a series of changes which nobody can trace with any certainty and still less date, he ceased to be a Catholic, and eventually he became a priest of the Church of England. There is much to suggest that it was by very gradual changes that he moved from his first position to his second. And, as we have seen from his own writings, in a good many fundamentals of taste and feeling he always remained a Catholic rather than a Protestant. Indeed, there is one poem that suggests that even after he had, so to speak, become an officer on the Protestant side, he yet found himself at times uncertain and uneasy in that allegiance.[1]

If we were to accept that poem as evidence of a continuing state of mind, then there would be no question of a human tragedy of grim proportions. Here was a man who without caring very much for the differences between one church and another, quite willing in fact to make the shifts in allegiance necessary to give him a wider life, was yet held to the most thorough-going defence of just those aspects of the new allegiance that would seem to his temperament least important. One can hardly imagine a situation more galling to a man of any sensitiveness or honesty of spirit than to be thus forced to transform an opportunistic compromise into a life-work. Happily for that pity which the outworn miseries of the dead so often claim, there is too much evidence against this theory for it to stand. But it does point to some very important elements in Donne's intellectual and spiritual development.

One of the trials that every convert must face is the scrutiny of his motives. The world is not wont to search the most generous of the possible impulses to a dubious action. And nowhere is this truer than when the obvious material interests of the convert are so well served as they were in the conversion of Donne. That typically Elizabethan punishment referred to above was not unlikely to be his portion if he became a priest. If he stayed a layman, the best he could hope for was a constant restriction, an exposure to suspicion and to tyranny, insufferably galling to so proud a spirit. If the general difficulties of the Catholics increased, as they threatened to, then he faced a lifetime of forced concealment and obscurity, of complete stultification, even more intolerable to such arrogant energy.[1a]

Yet whatever the world's cynic practice, there can be no question that for the purposes of understanding any human problem, it is safer to risk the more generous interpretation. We shall be surer at least of seeing the man as he saw himself. From everything we know of the young John Donne we may be sure that nothing was farther from his thoughts than a religious vocation, and nothing could well be more foreign to everything we know of him than the kind of religious vocation that awaited the English Catholic of his day. There was, as we have seen, no dearth of opportunity for adventure for the Catholic priest in the England of his day; it was sometimes complained by the more conservative of the English Catholic leaders that too many rash young men enlisted on the English

Mission for the sake of the undoubted adventure in the enterprise. But it was a kind of adventure that required a self-surrender, a self-devotion, a self-abnegation, very difficult of compass for one so strongly individual and so completely aware of himself as an individual as Donne. Moreover, it involved an odium that so social a temperament as his could hardly be expected to covet, and a restriction of experience that might well appal one who had taken all experience for his province.

Whatever the elements involved, this issue was probably settled pretty early in Donne's life. One of his uncles, Jasper Heywood, was a leading Jesuit of the time.[2] From what we know of him, though talented, he was singularly lacking in that kind of discretion that enables a man to gauge fairly accurately the controlling elements in a situation before him. And he was very strong in loyalty and enthusiasm for his cause. The Jesuits of that day owed much of their success and no small part of their reputation to the skill with which they made use of the materials of this world. We may be sure, therefore, that the magnificent young human animal straining at the leash that may easily be seen in the fascinating portrait of the young Donne would not have discouraged his uncle. This is only guess-work. And we must not forget that Jasper Heywood was exiled from England when Donne was only about eleven. What we know is that the older Donne wrote of the Jesuits with a bitterness and a scurrility that makes the hypothesis of a personal grudge tempting, and that all his life he referred to them with a personal ferocity quite beyond what he brought to anything else he attacked.[3] And it is further suggestive that what he especially arraigned them for was the way in which they sought to enslave men's minds to their purposes. It would be hard to devise a theory that would account for these facts better than the theory that in his extreme youth he had suffered from the importunities of his Jesuit relative.

Clearly, then, Donne refused to be drawn anywhere in the

direction of Tyburn Tree. And what he said of those who did take that bloody road suggests in its constant brutality a very definite personal repudiation. So Donne did not cross the seas for a Recusant seminary, but went in 1584, when he was only eleven, to Hart Hall, Oxford. After three years there, he is said to have gone to Trinity College, Cambridge, and from there, after another three-year period back to London, to Lincoln's Inn to study law.[4] Then, as later, the Inns of Court afforded one of the best ways of seeing the world of London, probably the best way for a young man who, though financially well-off, had his way to make. That he did make his way in the gay and brilliant and dissolute younger world of London we know. "Popery" would not be much of a handicap in such circles, and Donne brought those gifts of audacity and boundless appetite and wit that would ensure his success in that careless society. But when he looked ahead toward that career at court which he seems early to have coveted, he must have seen a different picture. We may be sure that any misgivings which he already had as to his own prospects as a Catholic would be intensified in 1593 by what he must have felt at the death of his younger brother in the prison to which he had been committed for harboring a Jesuit.

Such an experience would have roused in many a young man a thirst for vengeance, in some a profound disgust for such a world, in a few a passion for rectification. But there is no trace in the younger or the older Donne of any thirst for setting the world right. Rather, he took it as he found it, eager to explore its resources, ambitious to command it.

Here, for all their difference in temperament, there is much in the nature of John Donne which brings to mind Francis Bacon. To understand both we must suspend the same modern premise, that there is something incompatible between the worldling and the artist, the philosopher, the scholar. That was a notion unknown to the Renaissance. We are not un-

familiar with the idea of the artist and scientist alike securing
the indispensable resources of their calling from the bounty of
the worldling. But the Renaissance aristocrat thought of a more
direct access to the sources of power. In other words, Donne
like Bacon looked to high office for himself as the most direct
way of realizing his dreams of achievement. So viewed, the
worldliness of the Renaissance is seen in its nobler aspects, and
the little compliances, the courtly servilities that strike the
bourgeois independence and self-respect of the average modern
critic so unpleasantly, are seen in their due perspective as the
means accepted and generally regarded as unavoidable to an
end by no means contemptible.

Moreover, as Signor Mario Praz has so well pointed out in
his brilliant study of Donne, the statesman was the ideal of the
Renaissance, the rôle above all others which the man like Donne
or Bacon, who came even on the fringes of the great world,
could be counted on to respect and to seek.[5] In the great world
of London, of court and tavern and noble's house, and in the
country houses of Twickenham and Polesworth and Mitcham,
Donne would find then not only his most congenial social contacts and exercise but also the most practical and direct way
of compassing his ends in a world where so much went by
favor and by influence. That explains a solicitude for social
contact that in our day is on the whole more readily condoned
in a woman than in a man, and a delight in being at the center
of affairs that would usually suggest the man of less original
and confident genius. All of these elements in the situation with
which the ambitious man must reckon in that day were in
Donne's case intensified by the fact that he had no powerful
relatives to push his fortunes at court, and that his wealth was
early, if not exhausted, at least depleted, so that by his late
twenties he seems to have had very much his own way to make.

As we shall see, Donne was not incapable of throwing the
world away for a devotion, but when he began to look hard

at his religious allegiance, he was at an age when religious passion runs at its lowest in most men. There is no question that if he had found himself in a world where his religious faith was the prevailing one, he would never have dreamed of changing it. He would probably have been just as anti-Jesuit; there was nothing in that incompatible with being a loyal and even a devout Catholic.

For in Donne's youth the Jesuits were quite as unpopular with many of their fellow Catholics as with the rest of their countrymen. The Elizabethan Settlement had been designed to keep as large a portion of the nation as possible in their old parish churches. The actual changes in church life from one reign to another had been so confusing that it was not always easy for the average man to gauge the magnitude or the permanence of these changes. And it should not be forgotten that the death of the Protestant queen and the succession of a Catholic might at any moment bring the whole English Church back to the Catholic fold. A good many Catholics, therefore, were inclined to bide their time without coming into any more conflict with the present order than need be. And it is not surprising that some of them were resentful of the Jesuits who made them face issues which they were in no hurry to face. It needs no stretch of the imagination, in view of the evidence suggested above, to see the young Donne among these.

But there was one issue in the very complicated religious situation of the time on which Donne seems early to have taken a more positive position. It seems fairly clear now that in all the confusion of motive and point of view of the English Reformation, the question of extra-national control was for the majority of the English people the issue on which they could be most easily roused to Protestant sympathies. It was on that more than on any other issue that Henry and later Elizabeth felt most strongly, and on that more than on any other that they carried their people with them. And on this

point Donne seems to have made up his mind to take his stand
with the majority of his countrymen. It is hardly a philosophic
question, but for that time and for a man in Donne's position it
was the central one. And it so remained. In all he ever wrote
on this subject there is every sign of conviction and assurance.
To question his sincerity on this point is to call in question his
fundamental honesty, for there is no evidence of even the
slightest doubt, or misgiving, or reserve. Even if he did sometimes wonder which was the true church, he certainly never
had any doubt, once he had made up his mind, who should
govern the English Church. Next to the Jesuits the claims of
the Pope called forth his most passionate reprobation.[6]

Yet, to one familiar with the classic seventeenth-century
Protestant attack on Rome, the most striking thing about the
"converted" Donne's diatribes on his old church is their conventionality. It is as if, having enlisted for the Protestant
cause, he had adopted the platform of his new side wholesale
without much critical scrutiny. This was the easier because,
as we have seen, the Protestantism which Donne embraced was
the moderate and partial Protestantism of that wing of the
Church of England that was farthest from Edinburgh and
Geneva. Whole-heartedly and enthusiastically he maintained
the position of his party, but he made no effort to advance it
in any direction. In the realm of controversy even, he is a
zealous party man, but neither an innovator nor a leader. This
aspect of the first conversion of John Donne has not always
been appreciated at its full value.

As for the date of this first conversion, it must always be remembered that such a change is more or less consummated when
a man first becomes aware of the possibility that he may alter
his opinions. Seldom does one find the line of advance of his
thought in any realm a straight or even one. On some points
it may be questioned if Donne ever thoroughly made up his
mind, but it seems safe to assume that he must have at least

settled the main question of allegiance before he undertook to help Dr. Morton in his controversies with Rome in 1605.[7] To doubt that would be to do less than justice to what we know of Donne's self-respect, to say nothing of his honesty.

But this is to leap ahead. We may be sure that in spite of what Donne later said about his careful study of all the Anglo-Roman controversy before he made up his mind to change his church allegiance, his first study was of the rich life of London. That he pursued that study with all the zest of a young man of extraordinary energy and the recklessness of a youth of uncommonly strong passions, we may be sure from what he tells us in his early poetry. Nothing is easier than to make the mistake of taking what a young poet says as literal fact. It is a standing temptation to read a man's biography into his verse, and in Donne's case there is more excuse for doing so than in the work of most poets, for his own verdict on his youthful license and what his contemporaries said of his life fully bear out the conclusions drawn from the poems themselves. Whatever the facts as to any particular event, the type of life which the young Donne drew upon for his poetry is unmistakable, and the kind of imagination and nature that made possible such experience is clear. For the life of the senses it was high tide, and full tide at that.

Some critics, notably Mr. Louis Bredvold, have discovered in these youthful poems evidence that at this time Donne fell under the influence of those sceptical and naturalistic ideas that we now know were more common in the Renaissance than men used to think. Mr. Bredvold has certainly made out an admirable case for the general influence of Libertine ideas on the young Donne.[8] But there is another element that should not be forgotten, and that is the time, both in history and in the young man's life. Young men of strong passions provided with plenty of opportunity to indulge those passions are apt in all ages to find abundant reason to think well of themselves and ill of those who would interfere with their course. There is much evidence in literature and history to suggest that the language of the passions is the same in all ages. Certainly the broadsides of the time offer tempting parallels to Donne's poems so far as point of view and ideas are concerned. That Donne meant what he said in these poems with all his heart when he said it is clear; to doubt that would be to miss a good deal of the wonder and the power of them, but the circumstances must be remembered before we take their general point of view too seriously as a considered philosophy of life. What we have here is a mind of singular fertility and range taking possession of itself and of its experiences with extraordinary zest and frankness.

What is of more immediate consequence than the question of naturalistic philosophy is the kind of temperament and imagination revealed in these poems. Donne was a man of strong passions, which he recognized for pretty much what they were. He was the kind of man that generations of naturalistic poets and novelists have dreamed of as their hero, as some one has wittily said, the kind of man Lord Byron wanted the world to think he was. And he was that kind of man not only in his senses but in his mind, in his imagination. Some of his later sermons bear out the evidence of the poetry here. But at the end of the career suggested in these verses, sophisticated and satiate, as some of the poems suggest he was, he was yet capable of a great love that could sweep him off his feet, that could lift him above all his ambitions and his plans for a brilliant career, and make him risk certain prospects for the perfection of that love. It is one of the most profoundly attractive things in all his career. Here for once one of the major tensions of his nature, the constant struggle between the moderation which his mind counselled and the excess dreamed of by imagination and feeling, was exultantly resolved in a major indiscretion and a sublime victory. And clearly as he came to realize what this romantic impulse cost him in the miserable and thwarted years that followed, there is not the slightest evidence that he ever grumbled at the price or wished it undone. Nor is there anything to suggest that having chosen the sober content of marriage he ever returned to the gay promiscuity of the days in which he had flouted the restraints of convention. That was his second conversion and a real one.

It is idle to inquire what Donne's career might have been but for his elopement with Ann More in 1601. What we know is that, having cast all away for love, Donne found that the world took the romantic hero at his word, with the result that he paid the price of his ecstasy in years of bitter privation and futility. Even the most successful of men finds the world a little less than his dreams, and the most occupied is conscious of some part of his nature's endowment that is doomed by fortune to rust unused and unknown. But in Donne's case a man of genius was doomed literally to beg for a chance to employ himself in order to secure the bare necessities of life, and to sue for the opportunity to expend unrivalled gifts for mediocre and obscure ends. It is one of the most pitiful cases in all the sad annals of courtiership. Even when he was forty, he found himself still seeking but the first rung on the ladder. He burned with the fire of his manhood's prime energy, but soon the night would come, and that fire would smoulder and die without its heat or its light ever having been enjoyed. And still he clung desperately to that hope of a great career. He had suffered all the vanities of the world's fortune, and he had not been cured of his lust for its prizes.

Even if we do not take at face value the theological studies which pious age imputed to a youth that we know to have been fully enough occupied otherwise, it is certain that Donne's theological studies began at a very early age and were pursued long and enthusiastically. It is very hard for the modern mind to appreciate the magnetism of theology when it held the center of the world's stage, and its intricacies challenged the minds of saint and worldling alike; but it must not be forgotten if we are to understand John Donne's early interest in theological studies. For the young Donne found in them a satisfaction for the hunger of his mind that would not be possible in any other field. Here he could penetrate into the deepest mysteries of the world about him, here his mind could take possession of the most ancient experience of his race, and here its hunger could go farthest on its own quest of ultimate reality. In all this there was nothing specifically religious, or perhaps to be more exact, nothing of religion as separate from and different from the other objects of his devotion. It was merely another segment of that rich world which his ravenous mind was taking into its possession.

Viewed from the angle of intellectual activity, it was a singularly congenial field, for it gave full scope to the opulence of his imagination and to the subtlety of his reason. He was one of those rare people for whom the abstractions of the mind have the same reality as the things of the senses.[9] And there is much to suggest that even his most vivid experiences owed no small part of their reality to the action of the mind through which they passed. He had to take possession of his experience with his mind before he could count it his. That is probably the mainspring of that extraordinary keenness of self-observation, that quite phenomenal fertility of self-aware-ness that is the secret of his most characteristic effects.

Another aspect of theology made an especial appeal to Donne, and that was the controversial. It must never be for-gotten that, with all his extraordinary persistence and refine-ment of introspection, there was very little of the introvert in Donne's temperament. There is something by nature solitary in the passions and the operations of most of the world's intel-lectuals, but there was nothing solitary in the nature of John Donne. His was a mind that sharpened its edge on the minds of

others. The bitterest thing about the circumscription of the
poverty-stricken years at Mitcham was that it shut him off from
the society upon which he was so dependent for stimulation.
Even at the peak of his religious career, when his mind was
plumbing depths of remorse and scaling heights of contemplation of the mercy and goodness of God that are usually reserved
for solitary venturing, even then in the *Devotions* with which he
solaced his famous illness of the year 1623 we find him com-
plaining that solitude is a torture to which even the damned in
hell are not subjected.[10] Theological controversy, in which
mind strikes spark from mind and all the passions for power
and for dominance that so often characterize the social nature
find their freest outlet and their most complete justification
in the consciousness of advancing God's truth, was therefore
ideally suited to the mind of John Donne, at once so sensitive
to the reactions of his milieu and so eager for the most unimpeded self-expression. Here his peculiar gifts would and did
find a rare degree of satisfaction.

In an age when the pulpit fulfilled the functions of the
modern newspaper, and when it furnished perhaps the most
satisfying source of entertainment and stimulus which the
serious-minded could with good conscience enjoy, it naturally
offered almost unrivalled opportunities for influence, and, dealing as it did with the most universally appreciated themes of
man's thought and experience, quite unrivalled opportunities
for dramatic self-expression and dramatic effect.[11] But at the
same time it must not be forgotten that the social prestige of
the preacher, though high among the middle classes, was from
the point of view of the court circle, mean. This condition is
witnessed to by an abundance of evidence in the records of this
century, Donne's reassuring apology for the sacred office in
his lines to Mr. Tilman on the occasion of his ordination, being as complete and explicit as any.[12] One might be sure therefore that Donne would not dream of entering the Church so

long as there was any chance of his realizing his earlier purpose.

But in the long suitorship for an opening into the kind of career he desired, Donne was destined to plumb the depths of disappointment and the agonies of hope deferred which are the traditional lot of the courtier. Under the strain he grew desperate. Yet it is significant that hope died hard, and there is not much to suggest that he became really disillusioned. It was that practical common sense of which there is so much evidence in the sermons that made him realize at last that he must soon have some firm ground under his feet if he were going to fulfil his duty to his wife and children and turn to any account the great gifts of which he could not but be conscious. When in 1614 James I with that canniness that so often shone out of his fantastic and warped mind made clear that there was advancement for Donne in the Church but nowhere else, Donne bowed to the inevitable.[13] It was not the first time that the Church had been suggested to him. As early as the days of his association with Morton, in 1607, the possibility had been offered to him, and he had rejected it, partly because, as he intimated to Morton, he felt himself unfit for that high calling and in all probability even more because he still hoped to realize his first ambition.[14] Later, in 1612, he had himself broached the subject to Rochester and been discouraged.[15] But now, when he was in his forty-second year, a certain career must have seemed a much wiser choice than a hope that with the years had proved more and more a mirage.

With his customary frankness he faced the undoubted liability of his youthful reputation, now redeemed in fact by a sober married life but quite obvious to all and not likely to be forgotten so long as his poems retained their vogue. Indeed, he might be sure that his present decision would insure their continued vogue. True, there have been other churchmen equipped with youthful pasts like Donne's, and such pasts have at least provided dramatic contrast to the piety of their age. Donne's own beloved Saint Augustine is a brilliant case in point. But the seventeenth-century taste in ministers of the gospel was different. It is true that Isaac Walton expresses a middle class rather than an aristocratic point of view, but his *Life* of Donne presents very graphically the kind of man English piety of the time liked to find in its parsons. Quite obviously Donne might ask himself if he could ever fill the rôle of such a man, let alone be such a man. His tried friend, Lucy, Countess of Bedford, apparently thought not, for, if we can judge from some obscure allusions in a letter which Donne wrote to Sir Henry Goodyer in March 1615, she let him know that in her opinion the life which he had led did not qualify him for such a calling.[16] It was characteristic of Donne that he faced the difficulties of his situation without apology or compromise.

But whatever the complication of motives and feelings that underlay the circumstances of his taking orders in 1615, there is no question of the earnestness and the sincerity with which he set out to realize the pattern of the perfect clergyman. This involved less of a change in his nature and his spiritual way of life than might appear at first sight. Donne himself once shrewdly observed that a conversion did not change what a man was so much as change the ends to which he was directed.

> Thou art the same materials, as before,
> Onely the stampe is changed; but no more,

he said to the modest Mr. Tilman on the occasion of his taking orders.[17] Of no one was this ever truer than of the author of those lines.

It is probable that the actual taking of orders involved very little of a conversion in itself, but rather a settling down manfully to the discharge of the obligations he had undertaken.

But certain things favorable to conversion had happened. For one thing he was speedily freed of the material anxiety which had long hounded his private life. For another, he had had closed to him a whole range of teasing possibilities. In a certain sense his life had narrowed, and for a man of Donne's temperament, that was a valuable aid to the concentration foreign to one half of his nature, inexorably required by the other. So much has been said of the conflict between the pagan and the Christian, the man of the world and the man of religion, in Donne that not enough attention has been paid to the even more fundamental conflict between the enthusiast and the man of balance, the man of versatile interest and power and the man of concentrated devotion, the amateur and the artist. It is the great conflict at the heart of the English Church in the first half of the seventeenth century, and it is the great conflict at the heart of Donne.

It was resolved in a characteristic fashion. While there is every evidence that Donne set about the discharge of his new professional duties with conscientiousness and zeal, it is clear that it was the preaching rather than the pastoral aspect of his calling that inspired his genius. It was par excellence the age of the preacher, particularly in educated and sophisticated circles like those of Lincoln's Inn and the court. For Donne the artist, quite as much as for Donne the religious genius, it proved a golden opportunity. For his preaching was to release again those creative energies that had found such brilliant expression in the poems of his youth. Only now there was a marked change in degree and in emphasis. It is not always easy for us who are interested in literature, for whom the Donne of the poems is the most important Donne, to remember that those early poems were not in the least professional, but the by-products of the brilliant career of an aristocratic young man about town for whom verse-writing was merely an elegant accomplishment, a casual incidental to a career of larger interests and of more serious concerns. Now the artist in Donne came to the fore. For however hard Dr. Donne labored in his library over the "parting" of his text and the assembling of the learned impedimenta which the seventeenth century deemed essential to the proper setting-up of a sermon, it is clear that for the first time in his life, the artist had the center of the stage. The faithfulness with which Donne labored in the perfection of his sermon, the care with which he prepared himself by rest and recreation for the delivery of it, show that he himself recognized the paramount importance of his appearance at court or at Lincoln's Inn or later at Saint Paul's.[18] His vast energies, so long left to rust and to devour themselves, now found not only their release but their most adequate channel. The hour sermon was the funnel into which he poured all the treasures of his life. In nothing that he had hitherto done had this man found such full scope for the dual aspect of his nature, his necessity for self-possession and for self-expression. The dramatic needs of his whole being were now at last fully satisfied. And the rapt eyes of the audiences that strained to hear every word of the most famous preacher of the day, who sometimes, according to what he himself says in an admonition to his hearers in one of his sermons, could not restrain themselves from applause,[19] wrought their alchemy on his social nature.

We have no way of knowing how many Donne's brilliant preaching converted, but of one convert we may be sure, and that was his first convert, himself. The almost mesmeric power of those mighty periods has long been recognized as one of the triumphs of English prose, but there is a large element of self-hypnotism as well. He was preaching to himself first. That is the secret of his success. And in that field there can be no question of his triumph. There is much to suggest that it was a conversion forever being carried on, never quite consummated, but never the least in question or in doubt.

The greatest preachers of the race have struck men as being

messengers. Thus notably Saint Paul, as Saint Augustine, no mean judge of such matters, so brilliantly appreciated when among the three supreme things he would choose to witness, should he be free to summon up the choicest experiences of all past time, he put the chance to hear Saint Paul preach. It was the hope of the direct word, the direct contact, that more than anything else drew the crowds around the great preachers of the Middle Ages, about Bernard or Peter the Hermit, that was later to draw the crowds about George Fox or John Wesley. In Donne's case the nature of his audience must not be forgotten. From everything one knows of the court of James I the modern reader may be pardoned the suspicion that that company was not craving anything so rashly disturbing as direct contact with God. Yet, however insulated by custom and by prevailing taste, the human heart still responds to certain fundamental stimuli.

Now with the (very few) exceptions to be discussed presently, one does not feel in the sermons of John Donne that blinding contact with the Reality of the world, with God, that one feels in the sermons of a preacher like Saint Paul. Here is not God speaking to man. Rather what one here enjoys is the spectacle of a man speaking to God. And here is where the secret of the great power and the great effect of Donne's preaching is to be found. The hearer in Saint Paul's Cathedral or in Saint Dunstan's in the West whom those sermons held spell-bound was so held not by any vision of the celestial city or assurance of the glory and the tenderness of God, but by the extraordinary power and vividness and intimacy of understanding with which the preacher spoke for him, for those shades of sentiment so delicately elusive that the average man is but aware of their inquietude and in no way capable of finding any relief or any mastery of them through word or even thought. There is, then, in Donne's preaching not only a large element of sheer mesmerism but an even larger element of sheer exorcism. The dumb miseries of the average man, the blind gropings, the faint regrets, the dim nostalgias of us all here find on this extraordinary tongue their universal voice.

That it was here that the great power of Donne's preaching lay, and that it is in this direction that his significance is to be sought, becomes clear when we examine these sermons in detail.

To begin with, in spite of the magnificent range of allusion and of figure in Donne's preaching, the range of theme is fairly limited. Every student of Donne's sermons has been struck by the large part which the theme of penitence plays in them and by the even more brilliant part which the theme of death plays. But the themes of penitence and of death played a very large part in all the religious thinking of the time; indeed, they were at the center. The problem of salvation is, of course, the key problem of all religion, but in the first half of the seventeenth century it was that, more nakedly and more strenuously than at probably any other time since those first centuries in which the Christian had taken refuge in the Church from the doomed pagan world. There is something almost legalistic in the insistence of the time on this core problem that gives a peculiar rigor and in a certain sense dryness to its handling of it, easy to distinguish from the rigor of later and of earlier ages. Nowhere is this legalism more apparent than in the seventeenth-century concentration on the redemptive aspects of Christ's mission. It was He who gave satisfaction for our sins. That is the center. Such concentration has its unfortunate aspects; the seventeenth-century picture of Christ lacks the beauty and the richness of the medieval and the homely appositeness of the modern Christ. But it is equally true that this limitation has like all concentrations its positive advantages; it results in a depth and intensity generally unknown to richer and broader conceptions, a power, even a reality, beside which more diffused notions seem a little sentimental. Of no preacher of the time is this more true than of Donne.

There is something of the same terrible strictness to be seen in Donne's wrestling with another of the fundamental religious conceptions of his day. As we have seen above, the sixteenth century found in the beginning both consolation and hope for its overwhelming sense of sin in what the English Prayer Book, for example, styled "a most wholesome Doctrine, and very full of comfort." Indeed, the Catholic neighbors insisted that justification by faith would prove a loophole for the lazy and the over-confident who would offer heaven faith as an excuse for bad behavior. Donne himself never lost this Catholic suspicion of the moral hazards of the central Protestant position. But as the seventeenth century opened, it was clear that for no inconsiderable number of the most serious and conscientious of the godly, those for whom the comforts of the dogma of justification by faith were especially designed, the danger actually involved was quite the opposite, that terrible despair that rose from the fear that one was not of the elect. By definition faith was essential to the efficacy of Christ's sacrifice for the individual; it therefore behooved the individual to make sure that he had the requisite faith.

Every age has its own peculiar pattern for the essentials of human life and feeling. The seventeenth-century pattern of faith was an exalted one. Those backslidings, those hesitations, those despairs, those moments of devastating aridity and chill, to which practically all the great warriors of faith have borne witness were not provided for in the ideal of that time. The result was that the pious strove for a steady, unbroken firmness of faith accessible by temperament to very few of even the most fervently aspiring, and read into the inevitable vicissitudes of human confidence the unhappiest of omens.

By temper the restless, conflict-torn John Donne was the man to know all there is to know of this struggle. The fervor of his aspirations, that habit of nature which made him throw himself whole-heartedly into everything he undertook, would make him thoroughly familiar with all the dark places of seventeenth-century melancholy and despair,[20] and the long years of frustration and of futility which he had known would inevitably make him self-critical beyond most. But striking as is Donne's sensitiveness and self-condemnation, no less striking is his common sense. Indeed, as suggested above, a very good case might be made out for the point of view that the basic conflict in the soul of Donne was that between fanaticism and common sense. Every instinct of self-confidence (and in many ways Donne was almost arrogantly self-confident) and of healthy, balanced sanity would and did make him fight that despair of his salvation which was the form the self-disillusionment of the time so often took in the souls of the religious. By that paradox that lies at the heart of the seventeenth century and at the heart of Donne, one of its most representative figures, what to the modern mind seems one of the grimmest things in Donne, this constant preoccupation with the fear of damnation, was actually one of the sanest.

With such an orientation of religious life, inevitably death played a central rôle in all religious feeling. Again, Donne exceeds rather than differs from his contemporaries in the stress which he places upon death. The vividness, one is tempted to say the sensuality, of his imagination, made inevitable a high coloring of what for another man might remain decently remote in theological abstraction. On this point one should remember not only the preachers of the first half of the seventeenth century but also the poets. Apparently nothing makes a man so sensitive to the physical horrors of decay as a full appreciation of the beauty and the glory of the world of the senses. Not only the seventeenth-century poets but their masters the Latin lyrists abundantly demonstrate that the hedonists are the sublime panegyrists of man's mortality.

There is then a perfection of nausea in some of Donne's reflections on death that would be possible only to the poet of the beauty of the world, and this poet, it must never be forgotten, was not extinguished but only purified and carried up to more exquisite fulfilment in the great preacher of Saint Paul's.

But there is another aspect of the sermons that has not received anything like its due appreciation at the hands of the lovers of the great apologist of man's remorse and his mortality, and that is represented especially by the sermons in which Donne dwells on the goodness and beauty of God and the glory of the prospect that opens before man's eyes when he lifts them from this theater of his weakness and his defeat to the sure heights of his triumph. Here Donne's magnificent powers of imagination and his passion for beauty served him no less memorably than in the terrible passages on death. In this Donne was, though of his time, yet above it. For on the whole the seventeenth-century preachers find their greatest exhilaration in their grimmer themes. In most of their works one searches in vain for anything like the warmth and tenderness and full glow of exultant beauty that give magnificence to a passage like the following:

The light of glory is such a light, as that our School-men dare not say confidently, That every beam of it, is not all of it. When some of them say, That some soules see some things in God, and others, others, because all have not the same measure of the light of glory, the rest cry down that opinion, and say, that as the Essence of God is indivisible, and he that sees any of it, sees all of it, so is the light of glory communicated intirely to every blessed soul. God made light first, and three dayes after, that light became a Sun, a more glorious Light: God gave me the light of Nature, when I quickned in my mothers wombe by receiving a reasonable soule; and God gave me the light of faith, when I quickned in my second mothers womb, the Church, by receiving my baptisme; but in my third day, when my mortality shall put on immortality, he shall give me the light of glory, by which I shall see himselfe. To this light of glory, the light of honour is but a glow-worm; and majesty it self but a twilight; The Cherubims and Seraphims are but Candles; and that Gospel it self, which the Apostle calls the glorious Gospel, but a Star of the least magnitude. And if I cannot tell, what to call this light, by which I shall see it, what shall I call that which I shall see by it, The Essence of God himself? and yet there is something else then this sight of God, intended in that which remaines, I shall not only *see God face to face*, but I shall *know* him, (which, as you have seen all the way, is above sight) and *know him, even as also I am knowne*.[21]

For anything to parallel this one must go to the great mystics, to Saint Augustine and to John of Ruysbroeck, and to some of the Hindu masters. And here arises one of the questions that will not down and yet for which it may be asked if there is any really satisfactory answer possible, and that is, Was John Donne a mystic? It is a question which we must try to answer, for it concerns the heart of our inquiry, the precise nature of the third conversion of Donne, and the final outcome of all three.

The first difficulty about this question is the one we have already noted, the great vagueness with which the term "mystic" is ordinarily used. To take perhaps the commonest use, most people would give the name of mystic to anybody who, strongly impressed by the existence of data of experience other than that of the everyday sense variety, devotes himself to this unseen world. Clearly in that sense, Donne was a mystic, but the classification includes a very large variety of people. Much more explicit and definitive is that suggested in the opening chapter of this discussion—a mystic is one who devotes himself to the effort to come into direct and immediate contact with reality, into direct experience of reality, and succeeds in that enterprise. Here again a good case may be made out for John Donne, though not so strong a one as on the other interpretation. For here the question of degree arises in an especially teasing fashion.

There is no dispute as to the fact that in the later years of his life religion was the center of Donne's world, the focus of all his scattered energies, the catalytic that made possible the final compounding of his discordant powers. There is no question but that Donne quite deliberately devoted all of his energy to setting himself into harmony with God. But at this point our certainty ends. It is worth while, though in no sense definitive, to ask whether John Donne would have considered himself a mystic. Although it is hard to demonstrate any answer to that question, yet there is much to suggest that he would not. And that, not for any modesty but for the very plain reason that he did not consider mysticism a prudent thing to meddle with. In the twenty-fourth of the *XXVI Sermons* he repudiates the claims of Catholic mysticism in terms that make clear his distrust of whatever departs from the appointed terms of this life:

There is a Pureness, a cleanness imagin'd (rather dream't of) in the *Romane Church,* by which (as their words are) the soul is abstracted, not onely *a Passionibus,* but *a Phantasmatibus,* not onely from passions, and perturbations, but from the ordinary way of coming to know any thing; the soul (say they) of men so purified, understands no longer, *per phantasmata rerum corporalium;* not by having any thing presented by the fantasie to the senses, and so to the understanding, but altogether by a familiar conversation with God, and an immediate revelation from God; whereas Christ himself contented himself with the ordinary way; He was hungry, and a fig-tree presented it self to him upon the way, and he went to it to eat.[22]

In other words Donne had a very definite sense of what was the proper business of this life, and what belonged to the next, and it is clear that he would have regarded any effort to anticipate the experience of the next life in this as presumptuous and ill-advised. "It is the posture reserved for heaven, to sit down, at the right hand of God; Here our consolation is, that God reaches out his hand to the receiving of those who come towards him."[23]

Avid as was his mind, in certain fields and at certain times

even brooding, it is clear that the center of his religious endeavor was action, not contemplation. The battle of the will
is the central business of this life, the vision of God the promise
of the next. As he put it in his deathbed hymn, he was in this
life but tuning the instrument of himself for the heavenly choir.
Any transgression of the limits of this world would in Donne's
judgment have savored of "Enthusiasm," and there can be no
doubt of what he thought of "Enthusiasm." It should be added
that the majority of his colleagues in the Church of England
at this time would have shared his point of view and approved
his reservations.

All this has to do with point of view. But here, as so often,
certain elements of temperament re-enforce his metaphysic if
they do not inspire it. The first to be noted is the audacity of
imagination with which we are already familiar in the youthful poems. The twenty-third of the *LXXX Sermons* shows how
Donne's mind not only probed the depths of hell as in the
famous *Devotions* but how it also at times slipped its pious
leash and with no less brilliance of energy dashed up the heights
of heaven. No one can be blamed for writing Donne a mystic
on the strength of a passage like that on the glory of God cited
above. But when one takes Donne's work as a whole, particularly the remarkably detailed and intimate revelations of
the *Devotions,* then it becomes clear that in certain of his
qualities Donne was very different from most mystics.

The first of these has been already touched upon in several
connections, for it is one of the mainsprings of Donne's extraordinary power as an artist. That is his exquisite and
thoroughgoing individuality, his gloriously full realization of
his own entity and of the thousands of unique moments of consciousness that have piled up the store of his experience. That
is a great gift, but it is the gift of the artist rather than of the
mystic. It has been called "egotism," but that is an un-
necessarily harsh word. Certain it is, however, that it is at the

opposite pole from the self-surrender of the mystic who has ever taken literally the Scriptural promise that he that loses his life shall find it.

Much the same thing is true of his versatility. It is one of his charms, one of his greatest charms, but it is the charm of the amateur rather than of the specialist, and versatile as so many of the world's great mystics have been, it still remains true that the mystic is at heart a specialist. He is essentially a man for whom one thing in the world is more important than anything else, a man who would cheerfully give the whole world for that one thing needful. Only half of Donne is such a specialist, and it is not the half of him that he would have himself most approved.

Finally, Donne was too sociable for a mystic. His theater was the world of men, and he had a gift for taking the center of the stage. His death is the final evidence of that undeniably dramatic impulse that may be discovered in so much of his life and writing. In that last solemn prospect of his dissolution, to use the word that his age loved, he saw his chance to express with final effect the fullness of his realization of man's life, to take possession with completeness of the last experience he should know on this earth. There was no wistful lingering of doubt or uncertainty in the impulse that prompted him to rise from his deathbed and, standing on an urn in his winding sheet, pose for the drawing that was to be translated into stone for his memorial in St. Paul's.[24] He was going to his reward, to the glory he had so often feared to lose, and of which he now felt certain. Nor was there any last clinging of the sensualist to the materials of which he was soon to be deprived. Rather, this was the last scene of his earthly existence, and he was going to play it adequately, drawing from it every fine shade of its meaning. Death was not a hospital affair to be slept through and huddled quickly out of sight. It was the culmination of the personal life, something not only to be prepared for but to be executed with as much competence as possible.[25] A man of rich expressiveness and versatility of talent like Donne would want to do it as well as possible with the maximum of effectiveness and style.

But there was more to such a scene than the self-expression of even a genius in self-expression. Death to the seventeenth century was an occasion of considerable social obligation. It was the time for the final witness of the devout, a witness of great importance not only for the edification it afforded the bystanders but for the reassurance it gave in a time of confusion and uncertainty. It is characteristic of the temperament of Donne that his last testimony should be dramatic, not a singing of psalms or a giving of words of comfort, but the taking of his own effigy with its fervent embrace of death and its legend of confidence. It is as if he knew with that exquisite self-awareness of his that he was still his best text and his own most moving illustration.

"And now," as Isaac Walton put it, "he was so happy as to have nothing to do but to dye; to do which, he stood in need of no longer time, for he had studied it long." [26] In other words his last conversion was complete.

CHAPTER V

THE DIVINE POETRY OF JOHN DONNE

THE religious verse of John Donne owes very little of its distinction to either its quantity or its variety. Measured by pages in Professor Grierson's edition, it constitutes about a seventh of the total of verses certainly ascribed to him by the most authoritative of modern students of his poetry. Even if augmented by the perhaps more speculative than religious commemorative and elegiac poems, it is still not much more than two-fifths of the total. Quantitatively, it cuts a still more modest figure when set beside the one hundred and fifty-odd sermons that we have from the same pen and the various controversial and devotional treatises in which Donne expresses his religious opinions and feelings. Moreover, like everything Donne touched, it challenges comparison with the finest of its genre; yet in the end it leaves the enthusiastic reader perplexed with a recurrent sense of aberration and self-thwarting. Finally, if any scales of comparison between the different fields of human endeavor were possible, it would certainly hold a much humbler position in the hierarchy of religious poetry than the love poems would in that of love.

But in certain respects this sacred poetry of Donne's has a very remarkable interest for the student of religious verse. Self-revelatory like everything Donne ever wrote, it has the initial human value of giving us an inward picture of one of the most notable religious personalities in English history. We have the sermons and the meditations written during his sickness to enable us to appreciate the significance of the poems (for the most part, they are quite sufficiently self-explanatory), and they confirm the impression of the poems themselves that in them we have the heart of the matter. If we knew only the religious poems, we might not appreciate the range of Donne's learning or his command of the problems of his day, but the heart of his spiritual experience is here. The themes, the approach, the general point of view, the habit of mind, the temper and the tone of these poems, are in general those of the sermons, in a more concentrated and, in many ways, more bare and austere form. The tendency to self-dramatization, apparently inescapable for such a type of pulpit artist, is here reduced to a minimum, and a certain elusiveness and reserve, so astonishing in one as candid and self-revealing as Donne, gives a very real dignity and even a certain air of objectivity to their pages. From the personal end, then, these poems are important and engaging.

But they have a larger interest than that. Individual and complicated as Donne is, he is yet a man of his time. His uniqueness lies in the way in which he goes behind and ahead of his day, in that versatility of mind and temperament that cuts across the lines of his age and embraces elements usually dissevered in the more partial general experience. In the operations of his intellect and imagination, Saint Thomas Aquinas jostles Montaigne and Galileo, and Cavalcanti and Marino bring on Dryden and Pope. But through it all he never ceases to be unmistakably a man of the seventeenth century, catching in the mirror of his mind more of the facets of that many-lighted age than almost any of his contemporaries, and expressing them with the genius of a poet, surpassed only by the greatest of his day. And this is especially true of his religious verse, in which the most characteristic movements of the thought and feeling of the time are expressed with the fullness and incisiveness of genius.

It is this combination of timeliness and personal originality

that made Donne's *Divine Poems* so stimulating to his contemporaries and so influential for his successors. Directly or
indirectly, every one of the great religious lyrists who followed
him is in his debt. The more central Herbert, the more mystical Crashaw, the more luminous Vaughan, the more original
Traherne, all owe to him the debt of high example and enkindling. It may be that he did not so much show them how to
write great religious lyrics as to make it seem significant and
worth while to do it. For the men of his tradition, the very
fact of his devotion to the genre gave it encouragement and
authority, all the stronger because both the prestige of his religious eminence and the drama of his unconverted past con-
ferred upon his work an authenticity for which neither the
poetry nor the piety alone would have quite sufficed.

For like everything he ever touched, the *Divine Poems* bear
the impress of the extraordinary personality of John Donne.
And, as always, most appropriately so. For the purely devotional lyric is properly the most personal type of religious
verse. Of that semi-dramatic devotional lyric which is one of
the great glories of medieval Latin poetry there is almost
nothing in Donne. The "La Corona" sonnets come closest to
the medieval pattern perhaps, but even in them, there is but
brief dwelling on the pictorial and dramatic possibilities of
the scenes and events invoked and nothing of that rich building-up of emotional suggestion that is the great charm of the
medieval prototype. For the scene itself, even when most
happily suggested, is but the springboard for the theological
and spiritual reflections that are the main purpose of the artist
as of the preacher. Not Jacopone da Todi but Ignatius of
Loyola is the proper patron of their technique, even where the
disciplined analysis of the *Spiritual Exercises* has yielded to
the swift suggestiveness of the metaphysical lyric.

They are lyric and reflective, almost exclusively, these
divine poems. The center of interest is the devotee, not the

Divinity. And it is the devotee in the singular person. The corporate "we" of the preacher and the hymn-writer plays little part in these poems even as a rhetorical device, and practically none as a psychological fact. It is not the priest who speaks here but the individual soul. Donne's sermons show a very rich and immediate sense of the social problems of his day. And though there is in them very little of that sense of bearing the burdens of his flock that so pervades, for instance, the *Devotions* of Bishop Andrewes, there is everywhere apparent a very constant and shrewd awareness of his audience. But in the *Divine Poems* Donne is thinking primarily of himself in his lay and human capacity and not in his official ministry. This does not in any way detract from the estimate of Donne which we have formed from his sermons, for even in his most solemn and oracular preaching Donne's greatest gift to his flock was himself, that sharing of his own experience, so searching and so complete that what he spoke out of the heart of one man went home to the bosoms of all. But here there is nothing social or official in the pouring-out of his soul. It is of himself alone that he is thinking as he argues with himself, strives to reassure himself, cries to his God for mercy, in happier moments gives thanks to his Saviour for his patience. This is the fundamental orientation of these poems, and in this is to be found their first claim upon our interest.

This personal quality is also one of the things that most clearly marks their relation to their time. For, as we have seen, one of the most characteristic efforts of the late sixteenth and early seventeenth centuries was to deepen the inner life of the believer. The great shift of attention from God to man which the Renaissance had wrought and the Reformation re-enforced had found its consequence in the endeavor of all parties to strike to new life the individual consciousness. That cleansing and that release of ancient springs of spiritual energy which led to the wonderful mystical revival of sixteenth-century Spain and early-seventeenth-century France, that passionate travail for the inward light that sweetens the amplest spirits among the German religious enthusiasts, finds its counterpart here in the Englishman's effort to make sure of the grounds of his salvation. Something of what had been lost by the rejection of contemplation and the suspicion of mysticism in the orthodox Protestant confessions was in a small measure restored by the necessity which the doctrine of justification put upon the individual consciousness for finding the warrant of its confidence within its own personal awareness. But, unfortunately, the first effect in a time of widespread social and intellectual crisis was to aggravate the basic spiritual insecurity of the sensitive conscience and to deepen the general anxiety about one's salvation and the craving for immediate and certain confidence until it became the central spring in seventeenth-century religion.

So the human soul was driven back upon itself, and alone, craving for reassurance, faced its God. In the case of a man like Donne who had had to re-examine his basic allegiances, who, whatever certainty he had been able to arrive at on purely intellectual grounds, would yet forever have given hostages of ancient faith and inalienable taste to an enemy camp, the sense of basic insecurity would be especially sharp and the pressure of the very organism itself for some confidence would be peculiarly heavy. And the burden would not be relieved by that self-consciousness that seems to be an inescapable by-product of such a highly sophisticated age.

Nothing in the seventeenth century is more baffling or more fascinating than its self-consciousness. To understand that would be to probe the heart of its mystery. Perhaps a complete study of the "melancholy" that plays so large a part in the literature of the time, that melancholy which Shakespeare mocked so blithely in Jaques and wrestled with so doubtfully in Hamlet, would solve the problem. Certain it is that the most penetrating spirits of the time were aware of the difficulty and appreciative of its gravity, and the boldest did battle with it. The cheerfulness which Donne commends is one answer of the time.[1] There is, also, in his admonitions a note of moral resolution that suggests the healthy concern of Augustine Baker for the maunderings of scrupulosity.[2] One is reminded of that old foe of medieval spirituality which two such scholastics as Baker and Donne might be counted on to remember, that acedia against which John of Ruysbroeck inveighed so energetically on behalf of all good mystics.[3] Only, in the seventeenth century, as Shakespeare so well saw in his Hamlet brooding over the dust of Alexander stopping a beer barrel, there is some additional tinge of too much thinking added to the brooding of the sick will. Even the old sins take on the hues of the speculative malady of the period.

It may be one of the many revenges which the overstretched mind took upon itself in this tortured time. But whatever the immediate origin, two general causes suggest themselves in the confused and shifting social picture of the age. One is the passionate and uncompromising idealism which informs the insurgent energies of a large section of the middle class, not the middle class of trade, but the middle class of the gown and the stole and the book and the altar. As we shall see in a moment, Donne for all his laughing man-of-the-world-liness was not immune to the noblest virus of the class to which he belonged. And the terror and the glory of the seventeenth century is in no small measure both directly and indirectly to be laid to the resultant fanaticism of this part of society and its influence upon the rest of the social order.

Still another cause may be sought in that great force which gives so much of the color and the violence of the sixteenth century but which has in no way spent its energy in the seventeenth. That is the passion for many-sided self-expression and self-aggrandizement of the new aristocracies of the Renaissance. The tremendous successes, the fierce competitions, the constant jeopardies, the sudden and overwhelming defeats, that were the day-to-day experience of the court of Elizabeth, and, with even more sordid implications, of the court of James, must have done much to breed self-consciousness and all its gnawing sicknesses, the bitterer for the idealisms that flourished even on that inhospitable soil. The ironmonger's son who became the darling of the brilliant younger set of Elizabeth's London and the most admired preacher of the court of James had every chance to know the goad of the first of these forces and the bitter sting of the second.

There is hardly a line that Donne ever wrote but bears on its face the impress of his extraordinary capacity for self-observation. The cynic finding him so often at the keyhole of his heart might be tempted to challenge the candor of that unremitting self-spying, but Donne's sincerity, in his lyrics at least, is beyond question, bearing on the face of it the surest of all authentications, its own. His finger may be ever on the pulse of his feelings, but the pulse beats not a whit the slower or the feebler for it. There is, indeed, in the very fact that his self-observation neither checks his fancies nor dries the springs of his passion a witness to the integrity of his feeling far more transparent than any simplicity or reserve.

> I am a little world made cunningly
> Of Elements,[4]

the beginning of the fifth of the "Holy Sonnets," puts the matter in a word. It might be taken as the text of all of Donne's verse, sacred and profane alike. And the parting of the text, so dear to the heart of the seventeenth-century preacher, may be found at length in the nineteenth of the same series, so amazing in its candor when it is recalled that the main burden of his self-censure falls not upon his unconverted past but upon his treacherous present:

Oh, to vex me, contraryes meet in one:
Inconstancy unnaturally hath begott
A constant habit; that when I would not
I change in vowes, and in devotione.
As humorous is my contritione
As my prophane Love, and as soone forgott:
As ridlingly distemper'd, cold and hott,
As praying, as mute; as infinite, as none.
I durst not view heaven yesterday; and to day
In prayers, and flattering speaches I court God:
To morrow I quake with true feare of his rod.
So my devout fitts come and go away
Like a fantastique Ague: save that here
Those are my best dayes, when I shake with feare.[5]

But the finest instance of this perfection of self-awareness to be found in the religious verse owes its beauty not to the amplitude of the preacher but to the swift and brief certainty of the poet, to what Browning would have called "a flash of the will that can."[6] It is the opening of one of the last things Donne wrote, the noble and final "Hymne to God the Father":

Wilt thou forgive that sinne where I begunne,
  Which was my sin, though it were done before?
Wilt thou forgive that sinne; through which I runne,
  And do run still: though still I do deplore?[7]

How much of the history of the human race is summed up in those four lines! In that universality of contrition the self-awareness of Donne rises above any narrow egotism and becomes the timeless voice of his kind, of those much-tried, never-victorious and never-defeated souls who in every age have held to some ideal higher than their practice and in all their vicissitudes have clung to the hope of some performance better than their capacity.

Mr. Logan Pearsall Smith has pointed out in his interesting

essay on Donne's sermons that Donne the preacher has but
three themes, sin, death, God.[8] Of Donne the religious poet,
the same may be said, and of these the first and the greatest
is sin.

Donne's view of sin is essentially that of his age. He confesses that sin is a rebellion against God, that in his impenitence
he has crucified his Saviour daily.[9] For him, as for all the
orthodox Christianity of his day, the warfare between the soul
and the body is a daily reality, but he sees more clearly than
do many of the moralists of his time that the issue is primarily
one of value. In other words, the root of his sin is idolatry.
As he puts it very plainly in "The Litanie":

> When senses, which thy souldiers are,
> Wee arme against thee, and they fight for sinne,
> When want, sent but to tame, doth warre
> And worke despaire a breach to enter in,
> When plenty, Gods image, and seale
> Makes us Idolatrous,
> And love it, not him, whom it should reveale,
> When wee are mov'd to seeme religious
> Only to vent wit, Lord deliver us.[10]

All students of the seventeenth century are familiar with
those lurid confessions of past iniquity in which the piety
of the age delighted, and all students of the time have smiled
at the very mild residue of fact which is often all that can be discerned beneath so much smoke and tears. The high spirits
of the young Bunyan that could not resist village games and
boyish pranks are a classic example. But Donne's past is a
very different matter. One has only to look at the moving and
eloquent picture of the young Donne which Professor Grierson
set as the frontispiece to his edition of the poems to appreciate
the first-hand knowledge which Donne had of the fierce appetites of the Renaissance. In that tensely live young face are

smouldering all of what the older poet was to describe as "youths fires, of pride and lust." [11] It is not necessary to accept the biographical reconstructions which Gosse attempted in his famous *The Life and Letters of John Donne* to admit that Donne knew what he was talking about when he charged himself with a sinful past. The kind of man the regenerate Donne said he had been in his youth is too clearly revealed in his early poems for anyone to doubt the essential justice of his later estimate.

As to the nature of that later estimate, we have abundant evidence in the references to his past to be found in his religious verses. That those references should be direct and candid without any hint of self-justification or minimizing is what any reader of the love poems would expect of their author, converted or unconverted. That is not, however, the remarkable thing about Donne's attitude toward his past, for after all, his past was, as we have seen, no secret. The remarkable thing is rather that he made so little of it. For once, his strong instinct for the dramatic failed, and he left his past there, simply as it was, the too well-known occasion of his repentance and his aspiration. Not on the ashes of those youthful fires but upon his fear of the death that was ever in his thoughts and of the God he had offended did he spend his genius and his tears.

It was not that he had ceased to follow the delicate pulses and the sinuous and devious ways of the lusts and the vanities of the human spirit. There are some terribly subtle and opulent studies of the psychology of weakness in the sermons. One of them, that long sentence in the seventh of the *XXVI Sermons* beginning, "There is a sin before these; a speechless sin, a whispering sin, which nobody hears, but our own conscience," [12] is a masterpiece of the stream-of-consciousness ethics. But the sins of the past, though never long out of his consciousness, were something which he had put from him.

What concerned his maturer spiritual judgment was the sinfulness of the present.

Here, again, the mind of Donne is the mind of his time, but with a difference. That idealism, so lofty in its aspiration, so exacting in its demands upon self and society, which is one of the most dramatic features of the seventeenth-century mind, is his. Even as he knew his time to be one of aridness and degeneracy, so did he know himself a traitor to his own best insight. But again there is more to his continual arraignment of himself than this universal consciousness of every sensitive and aspiring nature. Whatever its cause (and, as we have seen in our study of Donne's religious history, it is not easy to be sure of the part which various elements in his experience played), there are several definite channels which his sense of shortcoming invariably takes, and interestingly enough, these are the common channels of the sermons and the devotional prose works as well. The first of these is the consciousness of his own instability, his changeableness, his incapacity for that steady equilibrium which is one of the great ideals of the spiritual life of his age. Every age makes its own demands, wise or foolish, upon human nature. The seventeenth century was, as we have seen, very hard upon the unevenness of human energy. Its basic passion for the essential, for the literal enforcement of the law, was bound to bear very hard upon the temperamental, the emotionally unsteady. Its ideal of faith on the whole put more confidence in a steady certainty and serene assurance than in swallow flights of inspiration. Especially was this true of the English Church in the years of its most resolute battle against idiosyncrasy and fanaticism.

For a man of Donne's temperament, as we have seen, forever pulled between the poles of resolute and immovable common sense and warm and brittle intensity, this was bound to be especially hard. "This intermitting aguish Pietie" he called it once with bitter self-contempt.[13] Some of this restlessness is that which is incident to any ardent and impressionable nature, but more is due to that want of concentration, that constant liability to distraction, of which he was himself so sharply aware. Some of the most eloquent and picturesque passages of the sermons adumbrate this problem of the divided consciousness. It is also one of the recurring themes of that "Litanie" in which Donne reveals so much of his religious experience. But it finds its most dramatic expression in the close of "A Hymne to Christ, at the Authors last going into Germany":

> Seale then this bill of my Divorce to All,
> On whom those fainter beames of love did fall;
> Marry those loves, which in youth scattered bee
> On Fame, Wit, Hopes (false mistresses) to thee.
> Churches are best for Prayer, that have least light:
> To see God only, I goe out of sight:
>   And to scape stormy dayes, I chuse
>   An Everlasting night.[14]

As Mr. T. S. Eliot so well points out in his essay on Donne's colleague in prayer and pulpit, Lancelot Andrewes, the root of this distraction is probably Donne's incapacity to let go of himself, to surrender that acute and pervasive self-awareness that is the secret of his genius and his fascination.[15] It is richly shown in those passages from the sermons referred to above, to which Mr. Eliot, quoting Mr. Logan Pearsall Smith, does such admirable justice. But what is not shown even in those passages is the most remarkable and moving thing of all. Donne with his omniscient self-awareness knew this, too, at least once when in his illness he penned that most candid confession of all, the high-water mark, I am inclined to think, of even his self-revelation, "And I have sinned *before thy face*, in my *hypocricies* in Prayer, in my *ostentation*, and the mingling a respect of *my selfe* in preaching thy Word." [16]

Knowing these things of himself, it is small wonder that he should write:

> I dare not move my dimme eyes any way,
> Despaire behind, and death before doth cast
> Such terrour.[17]

Rather it is the triumph of some unfailing spring of life within him that he should still dream of renewal and pray for that

> fiery zeale
> Of thee and thy house, which doth in eating heale.[18]

With such an approach to the religious problem it is not surprising that Donne's conception of God should, on the whole, be an austere one. That deep sense of the "otherness" of God that runs through the Protestant Reformation fills Donne's heart with awe. The Creator and the Governor of the Universe, God is for Donne, as for most men of his time, defined in terms of power and will. He is the Judge who fills the sinner's heart with terror when he asks himself, "What if this present were the worlds last night?" [19] The wrath of God is for the sinner John Donne an ever-present terror, not to be forgotten in the many beautiful things he has said and sung of the mercy and the love of God.

Especially is the wrath of God important for an appreciation of the full measure of the wonder of the Incarnation and the Redemption. Here is a theme of which Donne never wearied, for here faith ministered to his deepest need. But though enthusiastic, his treatment of the Redemption is highly selective. For instance, he has very little to say of the human life and the human personality of Christ. The pity for the unhoused Child so splendidly expressed in the sonnet "Nativitie" is a rare tribute to the humanity of the God-Man. For, on the whole, Donne does not devote much time or thought to the details of that life. It was in general not the way of the Protestantism of his day, busied as it was with the terrors of law and the mystery of divine mercy. It seems as if the bare significance of the transaction itself held their thought to the exclusion of any regard for the human accidents. That concentration may be part of the absolutism of the time, of that passion for going to the core of the matter and clinging there, scornful of any distraction from or any amelioration of the stark grandeur of the bare fact. It may be, too, something of that legalism that in the early seventeenth century is to be found in so many aspects of English feeling. Nor should the passion of the time for a clear and relatively simple diagram of the mystery of the world be forgotten. Whatever it is due to, there is a tendency to keep to the official outlines of these great traditions in Donne's thought as in the thought of most of his contemporaries.

But it would be a mistake to conclude that some of those passages in which Donne seems to be reminding Deity of facts and theories which Omniscience might be trusted not to forget came as dryly and as coolly from his mind as they so often fall on our ears today. There is something far from official and conventional in the passion of praise and thanks that breathes through almost any one of the *Divine Poems*. Donne knew the bitter need of that for which he gave thanks, and whatever of confidence or assurance he mustered to face a world the mystery of which he never ceased to appreciate, he owed, and knew he owed, to the faith he set forth with such, at times, monotonous iteration. Even when the passion is all but smothered in the ingenuity of his exposition, there is yet apparent a warm tension of feeling. And once at least the full surge of his love and faith broke forth into glorious eloquence. It is in the sonnet on the "Ascension," of which the second movement is as follows:

> Behold the Highest, parting hence away,
> Lightens the darke clouds, which hee treads upon,
> Nor doth hee by ascending, show alone,
> But first hee, and hee first enters the way.[20]

This is in the temper of a hundred passages in the sermons and the *Divine Poems,* but in a moment the rather somber movement breaks into one of the most splendid invocations in English religious poetry:

> O strong Ramme, which hast batter'd heaven for mee,
> Mild Lambe, which with thy blood, hast mark'd the path;
> Bright Torch, which shin'st, that I the way may see,
> Oh, with thy owne blood quench thy owne just wrath,
> And if thy holy Spirit, my Muse did raise,
> *Deigne at my hands this crowne of prayer and praise.*

Of the more mystical conceptions of God, there is very little in Donne.[21] The "Beauty of ancient days, yet ever new" of Saint Augustine [22] does not come into Donne's scheme of thought, nor does the God who is revealed in a thousand casual places and homely incidents. God the Holy Ghost, "whose temple I am", finds His place in the list of salutations of "The Litanie," [23] but He plays little part in Donne's thought, much as one might have judged that the magnificently mysterious implications of His rôle in the life of the universe would have appealed to Donne's speculative imagination. Even the ultimate Unknown God beyond all the dim lights of human categories comes but little into the lucid discriminations of Donne's thought. But once, under the inspiration of the Sidneys, Donne's thought and feeling launched forth into the realm of the mystics in a beautiful invocation:

> Eternall God, (for whom who ever dare
> Seeke new expressions, doe the Circle square,
> And thrust into strait corners of poore wit
> Thee, who art cornerlesse and infinite)
> I would but blesse thy Name, not name thee now.[24]

Here, as so often in Donne's religious thinking, the range and variety of concept is limited, but the idea is in his verse invested with a warmth and intensity of feeling that make of it something rich and glowing in its narrow self. Whether it

be the sinner's fear or the creature's wonder at the divine condescension that stooped to share his lot, or the seeker's prayer
for light as to the true church, always when Donne speaks of
or to his God, there is a note of sure and intense feeling. Within
the sphere (to borrow a figure he loved) of his mind and
heart all is quick and living in his faith and his affection. But
there is little of tenderness in it, and very little of intimacy,
such as a Herbert on one level or a Crashaw on another would
know. Thirst and passion and intensity, these are here, and
the swift glancing of awe and beauty, but of the divine suddenly coming near in a breath or the eternal opening out in
spacious serenity from the taut moment, there is only now and
then a breathless hint, withdrawn almost as soon as given.

But in no way does this mean that Donne thought of man
and God in separate compartments of being, with little commerce across the epistemological gulf between, as some of his
successors have done. On the human side, Donne held two
views that would have made such a gulf impossible, however
large a part fear might play in his religious psychology. The
first of these two mediating tenets was the old belief that man
was a microcosm:

> If men be worlds, there is in every one
> Some thing to answere in some proportion
> All the worlds riches.[25]

And the second was the confidence that however fallen or sin-
bemired, this man is after all the temple of God.[26] Indeed, the
very cry of the sinner for help is the voice of God speaking
within him and his surest guarantee of being heard:

> Heare us, for till thou heare us, Lord
> We know not what to say;
> Thine eare to'our sighes, teares, thoughts gives voice and word.
> O Thou who Satan heard'st in Jobs sicke day,
> Heare thy selfe now, for thou in us dost pray.[27]

For if man seeks God, no less does God seek man, like adamant drawing his iron heart, in one of those scientific figures in which Donne so much delighted,[28] or, more tenderly, wooing him, as in the sonnet written after the death of his wife.[29] And in the last and ultimate passage of death the love of God in the Incarnate Christ brings to the fearful soul its final peace and assurance:

> I have a sinne of feare, that when I have spunne
> My last thred, I shall perish on the shore;
> But sweare by thy selfe, that at my death thy sonne
> Shall shine as he shines now, and heretofore;
> And, having done that, Thou haste done,
> I feare no more.[30]

So death, to which Donne as both preacher and poet had paid so long and such macabrely rich tribute, is finally exorcised not only of its terror but its fascination. Curiously enough, death enjoys much less of a pre-eminence in these last poems than in either the sermons or the earlier verses of the unconverted Donne. This was due to no failure of appreciation of the dramatic possibilities of that ultimate scene in man's earthly life. If there were any doubt of that, it would be put to rest by the care with which, as we have seen, Donne prepared for his own death. It is, rather, that there is some loss of the old brooding wonder that in the earlier poems intrudes every so often upon the most unlikely contexts. It may be that for the convert the contemplation of man's mortality had no such horrid power as for the sensualist. For death was a challenge and a reminder to the converted sinner, ultimately a hope of rest and a passage to a greater peace. Therefore, its contrast to the pomp and circumstance of the flesh could exercise no such power over an emancipated imagination as over that of the youth still enthralled with the prides and lusts of his age. Perhaps, too, something of its mystery had evaporated, and something of its strange beauty tarnished in the long contemplation he had devoted to it, and, naturalized as it were in the many theological speculations and the more restricted certainties of these last years, it had lost something at once of its terror and its magnificence.

A somewhat analogous development seems to have taken place in Donne's attitude toward the thirst for knowledge and the delight in speculation that are so characteristic of his earlier verse. Miss Ramsay in her admirable survey of Donne's scientific attainments has suggested that there must have been some conflict between science and religion for one so alert to the modern developments in both.[31] In the judgment of the present writer to take that view is gravely to misunderstand Donne's position and the position of most of the scientists of his day. Donne did keep up with the advances of science to an extraordinary degree. Both in extent and in up-to-dateness the range of his scientific allusions is remarkable. But it should not be forgotten that he is quite as well-informed and as actively interested in the theories of pseudo-science and quasi-science. The figures of the unnatural history which the Elizabethan Age had inherited from the Middle Ages and used with such avidity for all sorts of purposes are no less striking than those drawn from the new science. The same is true of these comparisons drawn from alchemy and the various schools of Hermetic thought. In other words, Donne is no Bacon trying to win his generation to a new attitude, doing battle with ancient super- stitions and prejudices, in every way advancing the cause of a new learning.

Donne is primarily a speculative. For him there is no distinction of time or age. True, he appreciated the importance of the new science as did perhaps few of his contemporaries. In *Ignatius his Conclave* of 1611 he makes Copernicus describe himself as one who had "turned the whole frame of the world, and am thereby almost a new creator."[32] But to him the new science was much like the new discoveries of the explorers, matter for wonder and for exhilaration. As he wrote to the Countess of Bedford in one of those eloquent and revealing verse letters which shed so much light on not only his intellectual processes but his intellectual feelings:

> We' have added to the world Virginia,' and sent
> Two new starres lately to the firmament.[33]

The motive of his studies was curiosity, and the result an exhilaration in the addition of more strange and wonderful information to his already considerable store, a personal exhilaration that was deepened by a quite spontaneous and unaffected rejoicing in the expansion of human knowledge and the widening of the possibilities of human experience.

Donne's intellectual digestion is of the best and his appetite for strange knowledges unfailing. The frequency and the gusto of his allusions to the physic and the physics, the astronomy, the anatomy, of the time show at once a very high degree of impressionableness and an unusual capacity for the assimilation of all sorts of intellectual material. As Miss Ramsay has pointed out, his attitude toward science was at once largely metaphysical and scholastic,[34] not, it should be added, in the sense of that timid and academic scholasticism that declined to look through Galileo's glasses, or of that caricature of official conservatism and scepticism that in every age has afforded the apocalyptic and millenarian wing of educational reform its indispensable devil. Rather it was the more robust scholasticism of an earlier time, with a larger catholicism of intellectual appetite and a freer range of curiosity. The problem of being was still at the center for Donne. He was singularly unaware of the issues of methodology implicit in the scientific developments he so uncritically welcomed, and in spite of a good many passages on the relations of faith and reason, he was not much interested in epistemology. Not the least fascinating quality of the mind of Donne is his ability to leave a good many issues hanging in suspense at the same time that every fact or idea is at once moving and active.

There was, then, no clash between science and religion for Donne. But there are certain signs of a stress between faith and reason that suggest the great conflict of the coming years. There is, for instance, in "The Progresse of the Soule," a characteristically ambiguous flash of positivism:

> As lightning, which one scarce dares say, he saw,
> 'Tis so soone gone, (and better proofe the law
> Of sense, then faith requires) swiftly she flew
> To a dark and foggie Plot.[85]

There is, also, in the generally more coherent and sober "Holy Sonnets" a passage in the fourteenth sonnet that suggests a similar tension between faith and reason. Here what in the passage above was but a moment's mockery is expressed in a profoundly serious prayer to the three-personed God:

> I, like an usurpt towne, to'another due,
> Labour to'admit you, but Oh, to no end,
> Reason your viceroy in mee, mee should defend,
> But is captiv'd, and proves weake or untrue.[86]

Then there is that apostrophe in "The Litanie":

> O Blessed glorious Trinity,
> Bones to Philosophy, but milke to faith.[37]

And the prayer at the end of the passage of the same poem on the Patriarchs:

> Let not my minde be blinder by more light
> Nor Faith, by Reason added, lose her sight.[38]

All of these passages, and they are by no means the only ones, suggest unmistakably a strain between faith and reason, a strain in at least one case seen as arising from "more light."

The obvious conclusion to be drawn from passages such as the above is that Donne was finding it difficult to reconcile faith and learning. But here, as always, the past of Donne should not be forgotten. His first way into religion was through speculation, or to be more exact, it was the intellectual side of religion that first engaged the interest of the unregenerate Donne. When he was still far from any thought of orders and dreaming of a career of power and influence and brilliant display at court, Donne had found the study of theology of absorbing interest. Part of this was due, no doubt, to his position as a Catholic unwilling to cut himself off from the life of his country and time. But, unquestionably, much was due to the fascination of such studies in and for themselves. The sermons and other prose writings abound in evidence of the pursuit of theological speculation for its own sole delight. And the secular poetry, even the most indecorous, affords ground for that one of the petitions in "The Litanie" that to the contemporary reader must seem the most extraordinary:

> When wee are mov'd to seeme religious
> Only to vent wit, Lord deliver us.[39]

It is in "The Litanie," too, that, invoking the prophets and the heavenly poets, he asks them to pray:

> That I by them excuse not my excesse
> In seeking secrets, or Poëtiquenesse.[40]

And in this connection it should not be forgotten that the fruit of the apple which the serpent gave the woman to eat is in "The Progresse of the Soule" described as the excess of speculation to which Donne attributes the fantasies of the heretics.[41]

The feeling so frequently expressed in the sermons that faith is jeopardized by the license of speculation entered, then, very deeply and actively into Donne's later thinking. It is not science that he is ultimately afraid of but the fecundity of his lively fancy and roving intellect. It is easy to see in this the dislike of the Dean of Saint Paul's for any activity that might stir the waters of accepted faith and doctrine, but the personal concern of the passages above is unmistakable. It is of something in his own nature that he is afraid. It is not any censorship of his institution, it is not the opinion of the sober and godly among his fellow churchmen, that rises like a shadow before that restless mind of his. It is the fear that his mind may carry him away from God.

Much has been made of the un-English elements in Donne's temperament and culture. Such speculations are always hazardous, resting as they do on precarious generalizations as to national character and temper, and assuming trains of causation that can from the nature of things hardly be demonstrated. But they are nonetheless tempting. For there are elements in Donne's nature as revealed in his writings that are strikingly different from what one finds in general among his countrymen. Again it is not the elements in themselves that are curious so much as their combination.

To begin with, in the early work it is the combination of intellectual passion and intellectual wantonness that is so striking. Ideas matter tremendously to the young Donne, but they matter in themselves and not just for their reference to truth. It is a state of mind common in the Italian Renaissance and not common in the last decades of sixteenth and early seventeenth-century England, a state of mind sure to be misunderstood in the England of the time. There seems to have been something of this delight in ideas for their own sake in Sir Thomas More's *Utopia*, which has led to that work's being taken with a literal seriousness that would have astonished its lively-minded author. Sir Walter Raleigh had something of the same delight in speculation, and the rumors which drifted out of the small circles and gatherings in which he vented his speculations led to those accusations of atheism which are so hard to understand on the basis of anything he ever wrote. So Donne in his youthful days and, indeed, into his maturity played with ideas with extraordinary light-heartedness and freedom. He was not indifferent to that quest for truth which absorbed the energies of his more stable-minded contemporaries, but speculation for its own sake was a standing temptation to him. And to judge from the tone of his later poems, it remained to the end an ever-present temptation.

But on the other hand, Donne saw this speculative delight for what it was. And as more and more he came to feel that the appropriation of truth, the living and the doing and the feeling of religious faith, were the essentials of religious experience, and not the thinking about it, least of all the arguing about it, he became more and more suspicious of this part of his own nature. Seen from the outside, this subordination of speculation to faith might seem a failure of confidence, a disinclination for certain inevitable risks. But viewed against Donne's whole experience, it is rather, I think, the consequence of his final focussing of his interests upon the quest for the essential insight and his complete devotion to it. It is not timidity but his own critical scepticism of himself that prompts him to this late caution. It is perhaps the final evidence of that curious dualism that runs through his nature and makes its least expression so interesting.

There is one final question which any serious study of Donne's religious poetry must try to answer, and that is the question, "Is this mystical poetry?" Like the question of whether or not Donne himself was a mystic, that is not an easy question to answer, because it involves considerations of both kind and degree.

To begin with the more general conception of mysticism suggested in an earlier chapter, there are certain elements in the religious poetry of Donne that are definitely mystical. In the first place, Donne is operating in what we may in a somewhat general sense call the region of the mystical. He is concerned primarily with God and his relation to God. Of that there is no question. But however essential to mysticism, that interest is not distinctively mystical, for it is the central interest of all religion. The question is whether or not he is concerned with God and his relationship to God in the way the mystics are.

That is a question that cannot be answered in terms of particular passages or on the strength even of piling up passages. It is a matter of tone, of direction, of scope, and of intention. Practically all students of Donne who have gone through the sermons and the various devotional works as well as the poems have agreed as to the impression they make of deep earnestness and even intensity of longing and of application. It is impossible to read the wonderful twenty-third of the *LXXX Sermons,* for instance, without feeling the passion and magnificence of his aspiration to God. Nothing less than the full possession of the presence of God will satisfy the hunger and thirst there so beautifully expressed, or fill the great stretch of that imagination so glowingly revealed. The same passion burns in the *Devotions,* "I have not the *righteousnesse of Job, but I have the desire of Job, I would speak to the Almightie and I would reason with God.*" [42]

The audacity and the immediacy of a sentence like that certainly come from the world of the mystics, but the speaking with God and the reasoning with God are a different matter. What the difference is becomes clear, I think, in a passage from the wonderful twenty-third sermon already several times referred to. Donne is explaining to his doubtless rapt auditory the four ways of knowing of "the Schoole," that is, of the scholastic philosophers, "They make their second way Contemplation, that is, An Union of God in this life; which is truly the same thing that we meane by Faith; for we do not call an assent to the Gospell, faith, but faith is the application of the Gospell to our selves; not an assent that Christ dyed, but an assurance that Christ dyed for all." [43]

It is clear to even the most elementary acquaintance with the contemplative teachings of the scholastics that such an explanation involves a grave misunderstanding. Donne is quite right that the scholastic philosophers meant by contemplation "An Union of God in this life," but he is quite as mistaken when he says that that is the same as what an Anglican of his day meant by "faith." It is as if up to a certain point Donne had gone along with the plain sense of the thing he was expounding, and then suddenly switched into what for a man who had gone so far is an amazing misunderstanding. It is no defect of learning that is responsible for that misunderstanding, for Donne is familiar with, and in one place or another in his works quotes from, most of the classic masters of the contemplative life. Plato, Plotinus, Philo Judaeus, Porphyry, Clement, Saint Augustine, the pseudo-Dionysius, Hugh of Saint Victor, Bernard of Clairvaux, Pico della Mirandola, to name only a few of the most important, all figure in his quotations. Yet curiously enough, Donne cites the great contemplatives for almost anything but contemplation. And when he does cite them for contemplation or refer to their mystical experience or reputation, it is almost always to misunderstand them as he does here. It is as if the older Donne were using a notebook that the younger Donne had filled in the days of his theological researches.

But whatever the immediate occasion of such misunderstanding, the final explanation is undoubtedly to be sought in the basic constitution of Donne's mind. It is, as we have seen, a mind of extraordinary sensitiveness and reactive power, but it is not primarily contemplative. Even of beauty, to the pursuit of which the young Donne must have given considerable thought, he has relatively little to say that suggests the impersonal, nonpossessive delight of contemplation. For him beauty is excitement, direct and immediate. In "Farewell to love" he says:

> I'll no more dote and runne
> To pursue things which had indammag'd me.
> And when I come where moving beauties be,
> As men doe when the summers Sunne
> Growes great,
> Though I admire their greatnesse, shun their heat.[44]

This is probably the explanation of the fact that has struck some students of Donne's love poetry, how little beauty counts in the reckoning, how rare are any suggestions of descriptive detail even in the most sensuously abundant of his love poems. After all, the appreciation of beauty demands a surrender of the self not constitutionally easy for so unremitting a self-awareness as Donne's.

Even deeper than this incapacity for self-surrender in Donne's mind is a curious ambivalence that runs through all his thinking and imagination. It is especially obvious in passages like those above where he seems to come to the doors of mystic understanding and then quite of his own accord to draw back. The reason is, I think, a conflict in the way his imagination worked. Even the most casual reader of Donne can hardly fail to be impressed by the magnificent sweep and range of his imagination. The way in which he strides over the world gathering up the homeliest detail and the sublimest implication in one swift and sharp gust of poetry is one of the most striking marks of his genius, and dull would he be of soul indeed who could keep his critical feet on the ground in such a mighty wind. What has not been equally appreciated is the passion for particularity, for definiteness, even precision, that informs both his imagery and the movement of his thought. Nowhere is the transitional, the ambisecular aspect of his genius more clearly manifest than here, where in the audacity of his assault upon a theme and the richness of the associations he brings to its unfolding, he looks back to the Elizabethans, and in the precision with which he seeks to gather all the strands of his thought into his hand, he looks forward to the Augustans. Only the tautness with which he pulls them together betrays the seventeenth-century tension in the classic lucidity. There are two passages on death that dramatically illustrate this difference between the Elizabethan and the Augustan tendencies in Donne. The first is from that famous tenth among the "Holy Sonnets," with the rich opening out of implication in the adjectives:

> Death be not proud, though some have called thee
> Mighty and dreadfull, for, thou art not soe.[45]

The second is less well-known, the opening of an elegy called simply "Death," but it is easy to catch in it the coming footfalls of a new age:

> Language thou art too narrow, and too weake
>   To ease us now; great sorrow cannot speake;
> If we could sigh out accents, and weepe words,
>   Griefe weares, and lessens, that tears breath affords.[46]

Of all the contraries that met in the personality of Donne, this is, I think, the ultimate intellectual and imaginative one. It bears the same relation to the history of mind and imagination that the tension between his aspiration for self-transcendence and his self-consciousness bears to his emotional and spiritual history, that the struggle between intensity and versatility bears to his moral history. There was something in Donne's imagination that drove it out in those magnificent figures that sweep up earth and sky, but whatever emotion such passages arouse in us, Donne was not the man to lose himself with Sir Thomas Browne in an "O Altitudo." In another world beyond the orient release of death, he hoped to see his God face to face, age without end. But he was not disposed to anticipate the privileges of that world in this, nor even in general to try to do so. Consequently, he was sceptical about the claims of those who were said to have succeeded, always, of course, with the exception of the Scripturally-vouched-for rapture of Saint Paul.[47] The result is that in most of the mystical passages in both his poetry and his prose, the marvellous thrust into the ineffable is followed by a quick pull-back into the world of here and now with its lucid sense-detail and its ineluctable common sense. It is much like a child's ball on an elastic string. It swings out as if in its free arc it would cut the outermost rim of the horizon, and in a moment it has snapped back.

That is the ultimate reason why Donne cannot be considered a mystic. But though doomed to self-thwarting, the outward swing is there, and it never loses its power or its beauty. That is, I think, the great secret of the undoubted power which Donne was to exercise upon the hearts and imaginations of all the religious poets who followed him. It is the secret of the unique stimulus he gave to them. For it must not be forgotten that what Donne was to be directly to Herbert, and less directly to Crashaw and Vaughan, was something more than model or example. He was to be the spark that set fire to their genius, that lighted out their way for them, even where that way was to carry them farther than ever he could himself explicitly go. It is something beyond the analysis which Donne loved, something to be known in the nerves and the heart as well as in the picture-making brain. It is that something that owes no small part of its potency to the magic of words and yet is something more. It is the triumphant challenge of the seventh of the "Holy Sonnets":

> At the round earths imagin'd corners, blow
> Your trumpets, Angells, and arise, arise
> From death, you numberlesse infinities

Of soules, and to your scattred bodies goe,
All whom the flood did, and fire shall o'erthrow,
All whom warre, dearth, age, agues, tyrannies,
Despaire, law, chance, hath slaine, and you whose eyes,
Shall behold God, and never tast deaths woe.[48]

It is the trumpet call to the mystical poets of his tradition.

CHAPTER VI

GEORGE HERBERT AND THE ROAD TO BEMERTON

THERE is no more impressive witness to the currency of genius than the way in which one age appropriates the heroes of another in spite of the fact that it would indignantly repudiate every value implicit in the grounds on which they were first acclaimed. What is true of the hero is no less true of the artist and of the saint. The "holy Mr. Herbert" of Izaak Walton [1] would certainly not seem at first sight the man for the author of *Point Counter Point;* yet Mr. Aldous Huxley has paid striking tribute to the power of "The Collar" as a poem, "among the most moving, to my mind, in all our literature." [2] True, the reason which Mr. Huxley gives for his judgment would shock Walton and, I think, surprise Herbert: "If Herbert replied, *My Lord,* and obediently turned his eyes away from the flowers and cordial fruits, it was not so much through fear of hell as from an intimate conviction that Cockayne was no place for him and that the Being which had summoned him was a projection of his most real, his essential self. That is why the poem still has such power to move us." [3] Such a reason would ring very hollow to the seventeenth-century ear, but the witness to the infectiousness of genius is all the more impressive.

Either estimate, Walton's or Huxley's, would, I think, have troubled Herbert. Walton was less naive than he has sometimes been assumed to be. The seventeenth-century like the nineteenth-century lovers of piety cherished the ideal of a pure and stainless holiness, but they were less disposed to insist upon innocence as one of its prerequisites. And readier, too, to grant that for the most part, saints are not born but made. Walton is so obsessed by the "holy Mr. Herbert" of the Bemerton days that he does unquestionably let his picture slip out of focus and present us the whole life in the contemplative luminousness of the latter end. But he does not suppress all trace of the shadows as Victorian hagiography so often does. The worldliness that neglected the cloistered seclusion of Cambridge unless the King was in the neighborhood, the aristocratic reserve, the elegance in dress, and the willingness to defer the long-resolved-upon ordination, all are to be found in Walton's pages. But it was the outcome that interested Walton, and the desire to share his edification at that end that prompted him to write. Herbert would have been distressed at the result, for however joyfully he would recognize that the Lord had brought him to his goal, he would be the last man to want to conceal the vicissitudes of that pilgrimage. For though he was too humble to deem that his experience would swell the mighty witness of the glory of God, he was, as his sending of the manuscript of *The Temple* to Ferrar on his deathbed shows, charitably sensible of the encouragement his struggles might afford some other bemired wayfarer.

For the modern reader, Walton's piety has had more disastrous consequences. As the author of one of the tercentenary articles on Herbert pointed out, "George Herbert suffers as a poet from having been too easily and too simply beatified." [4] To an age all too disposed to equate simplicity of heart with simplicity of mind and both with dullness, the picture which Walton draws of the gentle saint of Bemerton may be a real bar to the appreciation of the fiber of his spiritual life and the energy of his mind.

Not for nothing, as the most recent students of Herbert have insisted, was he born of the proud and warlike lords of the Welsh marches. He had, as his brother Edward tells us (and

Edward was quite aware and even proud of his brother's reputation for sanctity) his share of the family "passion and choler."[5] Allied to some of the most powerful nobles of his day (he was a cousin of William, Earl of Pembroke), with a mother, the famous Magdalen Newport, whose wit and grace of mind and manner had won her the friendship and loyal admiration of some of the most notable men of her time, George Herbert was by birth and rearing free of the great world. On the other hand, the fact that he was an orphan, not too well-supplied with wealth, a younger son in a junior branch of the family, should not be forgotten.[6] It is always easier to make little of claims freely acknowledged than of claims to race and position not substantiated by immediate wealth and power. As the history of two at least of his brothers suggests, Herbert's position was one to stimulate and encourage ambition, not one to make it superfluous.

All the evidence points to the richness of Herbert's native endowment. Handsome, graceful in person, elegant in manner, witty and gracious, he was, for once, the sort of man whose external appearance did justice to his very real powers of mind and spirit. Good sense, taste, a sense of beauty, a clear, vigorous mind, creative power, all these were his. If his mind seems more orderly, less wide-ranging than that of his mother's great friend, John Donne, it should be added that it yields nothing to that extraordinary mind in alertness and perhaps surpasses it in precision. Bishop Andrewes is said to have admired his handling of some problems of theological scholarship,[7] and Lord Bacon to have valued his judgment in philosophy, or at least the writing of philosophy.[8] We have sufficient evidence of the relations between Herbert and Bacon in the former's Latin verse [9] and the latter's dedication of his own translation of the Psalms.[10] The references to the developments of contemporary science are less varied and striking in Herbert's work than in Donne's, and they have received less justice, but there are several references in Herbert's verse, both English and Latin, that suggest that he was even more aware than Donne of the significance of the revolution that was then taking place under their eyes in the world of thought, and at least one passage that suggests that his enthusiasm for the new age was qualified by an almost prophetic insight into its possible shortcomings.[11]

Herbert was, then, the kind of man likely to do well in the great world of his day, and recognized as such. Indeed, in the end he was censured, as Barnabas Oley, the friend of Ferrar and biographer of Herbert, tells us, for not making more of his powers,[12] and, as we shall see presently, when we come to examine his poems, he was himself conscious of the obligations of ability and fretted not a little over unrealized potentialities. The Renaissance passion for personal power and achievement had been a good deal tarnished but by no means spent in the England of Herbert's youth, especially in the circles in which he moved.

George Herbert began well with the best that his country could afford in education. That he made the most of his opportunities is suggested not only by the appointment as King's scholar which he won at Westminster School and the legends of his masters' approval,[13] but also by the fact that his boyish Latin verses against Melville were allowed to survive. The golden hopes he had raised in his school days certainly would seem to have been realized in the impression he made at Cambridge.

There was only one flaw in his equipment for a brilliant career, and that was his health. Soldiering was the family profession, but his health seems to have been early recognized as too delicate for that. Ill-health plays a large part in the annals of religious genius, and from age to age and from religious tradition to religious tradition, men have varied a good deal in the way they have dealt with the problem. By and large, ill-

health, though common, seems to have been viewed more as a
calamity than as an opportunity for sanctity in seventeenth-
century England. Herbert himself would seem from various
allusions and from his translation of Cornaro's *A Treatise of
Temperance and Sobriety* to have taken a good deal of interest
in diet and its problems. Certainly, he did not easily acquiesce
in or accept its handicaps and its opportunities, but it was
later to play a very important part in the working-out of his
fortunes. Probably in the beginning, the fact that he was
judged too frail for "the way that takes the town," [14] only
whetted his ambition and strengthened his resolution to distinguish himself in those fields where he could, learning and
verse and courtiership.

It seems likely, though we have no way of telling, that the
initiative in his choice of vocation was taken by his mother.
It was not at that time the normal choice for a man in his
position in society, and, when, finally, he consummated his
choice by ordination, his friends felt that they had been edified
by an uncommon display of humility. We know what John
Donne wrote to Mr. Tilman, and it is certain that the leading
figures in the Church of England of his day, men like Laud
and Williams and Andrewes, were of a birth much inferior
to his. [15] Magdalen Herbert was, as we can tell from, among
other evidences, the testimony of Donne, a deeply religious
woman, [16] who would certainly have a very high notion of the
sacred calling. On the other hand, we have no reason to think
that she made any effort to thwart her son's efforts for preferment at Cambridge. The one possible indication that she may
have wished to hasten her son's action is that he did carry out
his long-deferred purpose so soon after her death in 1627,
but, as we shall see, so many other factors conspired to the
same end about that time that it seems rash to hazard so particular an inference. One possibility should be considered here
that Herbert's biographers have tended to overlook, and that

is that even a deeply religious aristocrat like Magdalen Herbert may have regarded court favor and success in the great world as more of a resource for the service of an Established Church than his generally middle-class and often Puritan biographers would realize. The statesman-ecclesiastic certainly makes less appeal to the taste of our day than the pattern of primitive holiness, but the type has, with some shocking warnings, some triumphs to its credit, and they would appeal to the still considerable Renaissance elements in the consciousness of a woman like Magdalen Herbert.

Although it is always hazardous to draw any biographical conclusions from a man's poems, it is significant in this connection that Herbert's conscience, a very sensitive one, was troubled apparently quite as much by the futility of the way in which he had spent his life as by the distraction of it. And if one can judge from the general effect of his verse, Herbert would seem to have been seriously pursuing his internal way even while he was seeking worldly preferment at Cambridge. It is not surprising that the boy of seventeen who knew the early "holy hymns and sonnets" of Dr. John Donne [17] and their famous author intimately at his mother's house and who was, there is reason to believe, already admitted to the friendship of the saintly Andrewes,[18] should write scornfully of the rich secular poetry of his day and resolve to devote himself to the service of the divine muse.[19] What is more significant is that when he began to write seriously, it was, so far as we can tell from what has survived of his work, religious poetry almost exclusively that he wrote. Poetry was not only something that Herbert took seriously, but perhaps the most profound expression of his personal energy and identity. It is particularly revealing, then, that with few exceptions it is his religious experience that moves him to such expression. Whatever else he does in the course of his life, it would seem to be this religious experience that cuts deepest into his consciousness.[19a]

But for the next few years there can be no question that it was his worldly fortunes that he was pushing most assiduously. In 1612 he took his B.A. degree, in 1614 he became a fellow of Trinity College. In 1616 he took his M.A. degree, and in 1618 he was appointed praelector or reader in rhetoric, to note only the major steps of his academic advancement. He was poor. Whatever the thirty pounds a year that the eldest son of the family at his mother's solicitation settled on his younger brothers might do for the living of a scholar at Cambridge in 1617, it was clearly inadequate for the promotion of a Herbert.[20] True, there was the cost of books, the most ancient of the pretexts of a student's begging letters. Significantly enough, there was, too, the cost of ill-health. And never is there any suggestion of doubt about his ultimate destination being holy orders.

That assumption of his future vocation still holds two years later when he is canvassing his friends for the post of University Orator. One of his patrons, Sir Francis Nethersole, has apparently expressed to his stepfather his fear that the much-coveted oratorship will mean the postponing of his taking of orders. He hastens to reassure his stepfather on this point,[21] even though we know from a letter of some months before that he is quite aware of those considerations of prestige and honor that, he admitted, then appealed to his youthful ambition to make a figure in the world.[22] The author of the letter is obviously making a case for himself, perhaps shutting his eyes to certain implications, but he is honest, and he is not playing the prig, at any rate. He succeeded in obtaining the oratorship, and he proceeded unquestionably to use this post as he had used his readership in rhetoric to push his fortunes with the King and court. The letters he wrote for the university and the orations he delivered on certain occasions of high ceremony have come in for some harsh criticism of adulation, and his general conduct of his office has exposed him to the charge of gross servility and self-seeking. It is no defence to say that

Donne was guilty of much worse, but neither should we forget, first, that the custom of the time in formal greeting and in dedication and in other species of compliment was normally florid and extravagant, and, second, that King James and other "noble" recipients of these compliments bulked very much larger in the eyes of their contemporaries than they do in ours. It is true that, except for a certain dexterity in the art, a certain elegance in the sentiments, there is nothing much to Herbert's credit in these productions, but it is safer to draw conclusions as to the kind of audience for which they were produced than as to the kind of man who wrote them.

For most of the eight years during which he held the oratorship of Cambridge University, Herbert's suit for wealth and place seems to have progressed happily. It is a tribute to his personality and his general culture that he kept the respect of his colleagues, even though most of his time seems to have been passed in more exalted circles. If we may believe Walton, Herbert had, as early as 1620, attracted the notice of King James by the letter which he wrote in the name of the University to acknowledge the King's gift of the *Basilicon Doron*.[23] And if we may again believe the same source (it should be added that corroboration for Walton's story has been sought in vain), some three years later King James followed up this initial expression of interest by the substantial evidence of the lay rectorship of Whitford, a sinecure that assured Herbert of an income of £120 a year, a very substantial sum for those days.[24] This does not in any way seem to have increased Herbert's sense of responsibility to the Church (the lay sinecureship was a recognized form of royal encouragement to aspiring courtiers) but rather to have whetted his ambition for secular preferment. The success of his family (his brother Edward had been since 1619 English ambassador to the French court, and his brother Henry became in 1623 Master of the Revels at the court of King James) may also have encouraged him to aspire to the position of a Secretary of State, a position which, all his biographers agree, was the object of his hopes for the next several years. During all this time George Herbert must have been pushing forward his general reading, a general reading which, as we have seen, put him in possession of the movements of his day, in certain fields at least, to a degree beyond that of most of his contemporaries. One likes to think of him visiting his mother now and then in the beautiful Italian gardens which her young husband, Sir John Danvers, had laid out at their home in Chelsea, and there perhaps deepening that friendship with John Donne which was to prove one of the most important influences of his life. And while it is impossible to date more than a few of his poems, he must have been producing at least enough verse to consolidate the kind of reputation as a poet that a man in his position in society would have—the reputation for verses passed from hand to hand and admiringly copied into commonplace books.

Precisely what ended this promising career it is not easy to say. A series of deaths among Herbert's actual or prospective patrons—the Duke of Richmond in 1623, the Duke of Lennox in 1624, the King and the Marquis of Hamilton in 1625, Bacon and Bishop Andrewes in 1626—is the reason most commonly given.[25] Such a series of deaths might well discourage the hardiest of suitors in a world where everything went by favor, and where competition was so ruthless and public opinion so pitiless that the least check to a rising man's fortunes might prove ruinous. But for a man of Herbert's connections and gifts, the blow would not at first sight seem necessarily fatal, if his suitorship had held any great conviction. But if we assume, what there is no reason to doubt, that Herbert had always intended to take orders (the letter to his stepfather of March 18, 1617, is incontrovertible evidence of his original intention), then his suitorship must have been that of a man with a divided conscience. And the deferring of success, to take the most cheerful view of what happened between 1625 and 1626, would gradually confirm, if it did not suggest, the suspicion that he was on the wrong track. Then, too, the ebbing of hope would seem more final for a man who, as we know from the letter of one of his friends, had been seriously ill in or about 1622 and was to be stricken with a prolonged illness six years later.[26]

As we shall see presently, we have reason to believe that Herbert was coming to worry about the passing of time, very much as Donne had worried under not entirely dissimilar circumstances. But we must be careful not to stress unduly the crisis character of what happened in these years. Precipitate as Herbert could be on occasion, he certainly did nothing hurried now. When he was ordained deacon is uncertain, but he was officially described *diaconus* in a document of July, 1626.[27] On the fifth of that month he was instituted by proxy as Prebend of Leighton Bromswold in the diocese of Lincoln. There does not seem to be any reason why if he were still of the same mind as three years before, he should not treat this simply as a sinecure, a further reënforcement of prospering fortunes. Instead, he seems almost immediately to have embarked upon the project of restoring the ruined church, which remained one of his main interests until his death. But he still kept his University oratorship, though there is reason to think that he spent much of the year of 1626–27 with his mother in Chelsea.[28] The fact that he had taken the diaconate before he renounced his Cambridge connections suggests that he continued for some time to think a career of courtly success not incompatible with orders. It is interesting that the one reaction we have of his mother to his course of life in these years is a fear that he was exceeding his means in undertaking to renew the church of Leighton Bromswold.[29]

What is suggestive in this guesswork is that immediately

after his mother's death in 1627 Herbert did give up his Cambridge career. There has been considerable speculation as to Herbert's relations to the remarkable woman who was his mother. The extant letters are formal, startlingly so. But letters were usually formal in those days, and those of a student of divinity probably more edifying than most. There is, however, the unmistakable evidence of Herbert's deathbed as to the place his mother had held in her son's consciousness.[30] And whatever one may think of the terms in which they are expressed in the *Parentalia,* there can be no question of the reality of the feelings of grief which her son there expressed in those extraordinary classical circumlocutions.[31] His mother's death, the desolation with which he faced the mortality of man's energies, the sad thought which any parting involves of the things not done and now forever withheld, the peculiar sense of life passing out of one's hands that such a loss entails, all of these things very probably led Herbert to a more searching self-scrutiny than any he had yet essayed. The first result that we can put our hands on is the resignation of the Cambridge oratorship, soon followed by the surrender of his fellowship at Trinity College.

We do not know much of Herbert's movements in the months following. Most of 1628 he would seem to have spent, ill, at the house of his brother Henry at Woodford in Essex.[32] Then on March 5, 1629, he married. Walton tells a dramatic story of a three days' wooing. Herbert himself in *The Country Parson* advises his parson to choose his wife by ear rather than eye.[33] Herbert may well have known Jane Danvers by report, and Walton assures us that she had long known of Herbert.[34] She was beautiful, comfortably provided for, and so far as one can tell from what is reported of her in the biographies of her husband, gracious and compliant with his wishes. There is nothing romantic about the ideas which some very good Englishmen of the seventeenth century held about marriage,

and not much in their ideas about women to commend them
to a woman of the twentieth. But we must not forget that here,
as so often, actual human relations may sweeten unpromising
formulae. There are some rather appalling expressions in
Donne's sermons of what one may call the remedial view of
marriage; yet he was, as we know, capable not only of heroic
passion but of—what under the circumstances was still more
heroic—enduring tenderness and love. It is significant, however, that Jane Danvers, though she won the commendations
of her husband's biographers, never, so far as one can tell,
entered that deeper consciousness of her husband that finds
expression in his verse. As for the motives for the step, one
is free to guess. There is no evidence, unless one wishes to take
the advice which Herbert gives his country parson as to the
general advantages of marriage as a preliminary to orders.[35]

But if that was his intention, in contrast to the three days'
courtship which Walton claims, Herbert lingered yet another
year. There is no reason to doubt Walton's story that it was
only the extraordinary persuasions of Laud that overcame
Herbert's reluctance to accept the living of Fuggleston and
Bemerton which the King offered him in April of 1630.[36]
Although we have no evidence whatever to suppose that Herbert
had any such past as Donne's to make him feel unworthy of
the honor of orders, yet there seems no reason to doubt the
reality of the scruples which he advanced. And if one can
judge from the treatise on the life which a country parson
should lead that Herbert wrote and the life which he himself
led, his conception of the obligations of such a step might
well make a modest man hesitate. Moreover, as we shall see
shortly, there is reason to believe that Herbert's interior life
had been taking a direction that would make his conception
of the demands of such a religious function still more exacting,
in a certain measure perhaps beyond his scope and power. The
interpretation of a man's interior life from what he writes is

always risky, but, as we shall see, it is very difficult to read Herbert's poetry and escape the conclusion that his standard of the fullness of relation between the soul of a Christian and his Maker was something much higher and steadier than he could well believe himself capable of achieving, let alone helping others achieve. That, however, is a matter of conjecture, the evidence for which properly belongs to the study of Herbert's poetry, where it will presently be considered.

Herbert was finally ordained on the nineteenth of September, 1630.[37] What his thoughts were as he lay before the altar he was to spend the rest of his life in serving we can only guess. He told his friend, Arthur Woodnoth, according to Walton, that then he took measures for the further management of his life.[38] In default of other evidence the main tenor of these resolutions may be conjectured from what he wrote somewhere about this time in *The Country Parson*. As for the degree to which he succeeded in realizing his ideal, we can judge from the reputation which his priesthood at Bemerton has enjoyed from that day to this. The classic description is Walton's, concentrated in that single picture of the ploughmen in the fields dropping their labor at the sound of the bell from Bemerton Church to join their prayers with the morning or evening prayers of their beloved pastor.[39] The tact and the courtesy which Herbert had enjoined upon his country parson must have been his to a singular degree, so warmly did he succeed in commending his ministry to those simple country folk in the less than three years he was to exercise it.[40]

Herbert was seriously ill of an ague, to use the diagnosis of the time, not much more than a year before he went to Bemerton. The second year of his ministry was hardly finished when his health began to fail again, and now the frailty and the many illnesses of his life took their final course into what the medicine of the time described, apparently quite accurately, as a consumption. It was a bitter cup, this, to have health and power fail when at last one was ready to use both to their final and supreme end and so redeem the years of uncertainty and waste, and some of the poems of *The Temple* suggest that Herbert drank of it to the full. But the deathbed on which he sang his own "The Sundaies of man's life" was, if we may believe Walton, a serene and confident one. He was buried in the little church he had made famous, on the third of March, 1633.[41]

What was it that made that brief ministry of less than three years so memorable in the history of his church? Its practical accomplishments were considerable: the restoration of the church, the renovation of the vicarage, the establishment of the full liturgy of the country church, the daily work of the ministry with its coming to know the around three hundred souls committed to his care. Then there were those things about which most of his parishioners probably knew nothing but which are so important for us—the completion of the manuscript of *The Temple* and probably the completion of *The Country Parson*, the writing of the comments on Valdesso, and in all likelihood other writings now lost to us. All these were very substantial achievements for a man who for a good part of these months was ill and at best not strong, living in the midst of a very considerable household, and, if we can judge from the letters that have come down to us from this period in his life, fully alive and responsive to family obligations.[42]

But impressive as they are, they are not in the last analysis the explanation of the peculiar fascination which this portion of Herbert's life has exercised on the imaginations of men of very different theological sympathies from his, or the profound way in which this life has come to seem to his fellow churchmen the embodiment of so many of their finest ideals, the pattern of one of their great types of devotion. There is something very dramatic, as all Herbert's biographers from Walton down have felt, in the aspiring and ambitious man of position and gift turning from the court and the university and the city to bury himself in an obscure village in the country, but there is nothing sensational in it. There is, for instance, nothing of the peculiar fascination of asceticism about it. The house which Herbert put in order for himself and his successors was simple and unpretentious, but it had a garden to the laying-out of which its master apparently gave considerable thought, and it was served, as his will bears evidence, by two men servants and four maid servants,[43] for those days not a pretentious establishment but certainly one far removed from anchoritic standards. One is glad to know, too, that Herbert refreshed himself with music, going to the cathedral in Salisbury for musical service twice in the week, and making one of certain private musical parties.

It was, rather, the spirit with which he exercised a modest and unpretentious ministry that impressed all who came in contact with him. Those were years of stress in things ecclesiastical, of bitter controversy over church government and church practice, years in which sensitive men must often have felt that the spirit of religious life was being made all but impossible by the strife, not over unessentials, as men have sometimes since rather carelessly charged, but over every premise of faith and discipline. Persecution has its own peculiar gifts for the religious spirit, but controversy such as that which was already casting its premonitory shadows over the tall spire of Salisbury Cathedral in the disputes between city and chapter, is more apt to blight and desolate. Especially is this true for that ideal of settled, quiet, orderly, modulated religious life which was the ideal of Herbert's tradition. What he did, therefore, in the way of realizing that ideal was to be remembered in the harassed and distracted days that were coming upon his group with the peculiar awe and tenderness with which men look back upon the realization of a dream which it seems can never again be realized on this earth.

But if that were all there were to Herbert, critics and

scholars for whom that ideal has lost not only possibility but
even appeal, would not today be reading Herbert with respect.
There is something more to those years and to that suddenly
not wasted or futile life than that. There is the accomplishment of a purpose, the achievement of a quest, the rounding-
out of an experience, to shift the metaphor somewhat frivo-
lously from century to century. Here was a man who with much
to engage him in what he was and what he found open to him
in the world about him, yet looked beyond the instinctive
interests and appetites of the moment to a profounder scrutiny
of the meaning of his life and its relation to meaning beyond.
And having found that meaning, that answer to the imperfec-
tion and the hunger of his own experience in God, he was not
content to rest in a mere thought of that God, a remote meditation about His nature and working, but must strive to draw
near, to yield himself to that God, to live in the most intimate
relation possible with Him. It is that, essentially mystical,
aspiration, I think, that gives Herbert's ministry its distinctive
character and accounts for the peculiar effect it has exercised
upon all who have come in contact with it, whether by actual
experience or by report.

To understand that we must turn to the consideration of
Herbert's inner life. Here we are unusually fortunate in the
possession of a relatively large number of lyrics on the per-
sonally revelatory character of which all students of Herbert
have been agreed. But it is evidence which must be used
with care. For Herbert is no naive and innocent dévot singing
with unpremeditated spontaneity, but a highly conscious and
deliberate artist, as is coming to be more and more appreciated
among Herbert scholars. With all the hungers and ideals and
ambitions of the young poet, he deliberately decided that of
the two loves which have filled the heart of the poet from time
immemorial he would choose the divine one of which to sing
his praise, and to that end he would bring all the resources of

his experience and his art. The nature of a poet's experience is notoriously composite and tortuous, comprising many elements of vivid and intense awareness besides the literal fact of his own day-to-day life, and what it becomes in his imagination is still more incalculable. However, one may from such intensely and fully self-revelatory verse as Herbert's glean much as to the constant preoccupations and aspirations of their author. In a general way, one may conclude that certain thoughts and feelings engaged his imagination and penetrated to the depths of his consciousness. If they recur in varying contexts with different implications, one may take it that in this realm there were certain developments in the poet's appreciation of these experiences and in his reaction to them. One can answer the qustion, "What?" but the questions "When?" and "How?" that so much occupy the authors of the modern psycho-history cannot be answered with such confidence, for the creative imagination is notoriously careless of contexts and contemptuous of dates.

In Herbert's case the problem is peculiarly teasing. For *The Temple* in the form in which it is usually printed, a form, it should be added, that we have every reason to believe is substantially the form in which Herbert left his verse, presents us at the outset a very interesting problem in the determination of its basic plan. It begins in a very business-like fashion, "Dedication," "The Church Porch, Perirrhanterium" (the utensil for sprinkling holy water),[44] "Superliminare" (the lintel or upper door-post),[45] and then advances into the church proper. Here we come directly to what was the essential thing for a man in Herbert's ecclesiastical party, "The Altar." There is a marked shift in technique and in point of view in the next poem, "The Sacrifice," but the connection is obvious. So is that of the next poem, "The Thanksgiving," and that of the next, "The Reprisall," but in each case, the connection is with the last poem, rather than with the series. In other words, there has been a shift in categories, and whatever the main line of march envisaged at the start, it has been dropped for the immediate openings of each particular poem. One is reminded of some of those associational classifications which Wordsworth made of his poems. There is an organization, but it is metaphysical in the sense in which Dr. Johnson objected to metaphysical and not in the dominance of logic that is characteristic of Donne's and of Herbert's own metaphysical organization within the individual poem. Sometimes, in fact, Herbert seems rather to become bogged in a mass of reflections about roughly the same problem as in "The Reprisall," "The Agonie," "The Sinner." "Good-Friday," "Redemption," "Sepulchre," "Eafter," with its pendant, "The Song," and "Easter Wings," seem again to be marching on a straight line. But the line rather swerves in the first "Holy Baptisme," stands still in the second "Holy Baptisme," and, to shift the figure rather outrageously from Herbert's time, jumps the track in "Nature." "Sinne" is what one would expect the author of "Nature" to be thinking about in general philosophical terms, but "Affliction" is quite clearly the personal history of the man who wrote "Nature," told in temptingly personal detail. One is relieved that the assurance of "Repentance" and "Faith" comes to his aid. But the immediate connection of "Prayer" with what goes before is not apparent. More reasonable, but in no way inevitable, seems the succession of "The Holy Communion." And less inevitable still, though from another point of view quite appropriate, is the following of "Antiphon." The magnificent outburst of "Immortal Love, author of this great frame," in "Love, I" may well be taken as its own occasion for being, and the first poem called "The Temper" is worthy to follow, while the second may be taken to represent a quite familiar reaction from the ecstasy of the first. It is very hard to see what "Jordan" has to do with any of what has immediately gone before, and "Employment" carries on the thoughts raised by "Jordan" rather than returning to what went before. So it goes.

In justice to Herbert it must be remembered that when he chose "The Temple" as the vehicle of his poetic and religious expression, he chose a symbol capable of more than one reference. It might be used for the actual church building, for its ordering, its furnishing, its implications, it might be used for that Mystical Body of the Lord, the Church, with its foundation Scripture, its indwelling Spirit, its rites and ordinances, its feasts and fasts, its intercessions, its mighty commemorations, and it might be used for that recognized temple of the Holy Ghost, the spirit of the individual Christian in its struggles and its illuminations, its repentances and its confidences. What Herbert seems to have done is to take up now one plane, now another, sometimes with an obvious reason for the shifting of his point of view, very often, so far as we can tell, without any. Finally, we must not forget that in view of the fact that the manuscript to which we owe the existing form of the series was a deathbed legacy, we cannot be sure that the order in which the poems were left has any final meaning, that it in any way represents a perfected order in its author's intention.

Yet, as the above very partial analysis suggests, the poems are not left in chaos. They tend, rather, to gravitate into little centers and to form, as it were, beads of verse, sometimes loosely strung along the thread of a central procedure, more often not. Is this partial order due perhaps to their date of composition? The evidence is against that. There is not, it is true, much external, objective evidence available, and even that is by no means clear in its implications. It consists mainly of a manuscript known as the Williams Manuscript (from Dr. Williams' Library in London, in which it is now kept) [46] in what is generally agreed to be a Little Gidding hand, with corrections in the handwriting of Herbert. This manuscript contains considerably over a third of the one hundred and sixty-odd poems published in the 1633 edition of *The Temple,* and six poems of the same type but not included in the 1633 edition. Some of these poems, common to both manuscript and first edition, occur in very different forms in the two collections. There are, also, a considerable number of minor differences that must represent still further reworking of the poems between the Williams Manuscript and the manuscript Herbert sent to Ferrar on his deathbed. Containing as it does some extensive revisions in Herbert's own hand, the manuscript is of incalculable value for the light it throws on his religious and poetic development. Especially does it have value for that matter on which we have so little evidence, the chronological development of his work.

Clearly, this partial collection represents an earlier stage of the poems which are reprinted in the 1633 edition, an edition which, practically all Herbert scholars agree, was printed with, perhaps, one manuscript between and, almost certainly, some minor revisions, from the famous little book which Herbert on his deathbed sent to his friend, Nicholas Ferrar. And in the case of a number of the poems, the Williams Manuscript represents at least two earlier stages, that of the apparently very good copy, Herbert's own or somebody else's, which Herbert then either worked on directly or brought up to date with a more recent revision. There must have been at least one more revision still by Herbert, for even the revised versions of these poems differ in some cases from the 1633 version to an extent and a consequence that only the author could have essayed. There is no question, then, that the Williams Manuscript represents an earlier version than the printed, but the question is, how much earlier? The late George Herbert Palmer thought that the fact that none of these poems refers specifically to the priesthood while some of the poems not in the manuscript do is evidence enough to warrant our attributing the Williams poems to some date before Herbert's taking orders in 1630.[47] That to the present writer seems quite reasonable. It is true that the number of poems that refer specifically to the fact that Herbert is a priest even in the final form of *The Temple* is rather smaller than one would expect. But the absence of any reference in this group seems significant.

Another interesting item is the fact, which Mr. Palmer noted, too, that while the order of the Williams poems differs from that of the first edition and the traditional order, the Williams poems are, with the exception of the six poems not printed in the 1633 edition, and seven poems which are placed at the end of *The Temple*, all printed in what is roughly the first half of the final form of *The Temple*.[48] There are under a score of non-Williams poems printed in the first half of *The Temple*, and between "Obedience" on page 104 of the Oxford edition and "The Elixer" on page 191, there are no Williams poems. But in that list of seventy-three poems do occur a number of poems referring, a very few quite explicitly, to the priesthood, and more to a state of mind that would better consort with what we know of his Bemerton days than with what we know of him before. In most of these cases, however, it is not wise to be too dogmatic, for while the revelations of state of mind are quite clear, those of circumstance are at best indirect; and he would be a very confident man who would undertake to determine whether a certain poem of discouragement belonged to Bemerton days or earlier. On the other hand, one could find a good deal of evidence for the thesis that the discouragement poems of Bemerton tend to conclude with a note of reassurance where those of the earlier period more often end simply with longing or resolve. "The Collar," for instance, becomes more poignant in its rebellion and despair if we can assume that it was written at Bemerton, and "The Pearl" opens up new vistas as to the pre-Bemerton state of mind, if we can be sure that it was written before. But I do not see how we can be sure. All we can say is that most of the Williams poems sound as if they were written before Bemerton. There is no one of them for which one must presuppose Bemerton to make sense of it. But that is equally true of a good many of the poems that are not in the Williams Manuscript. And it is a curious thing that if it was Herbert who arranged *The Temple* in its present order, he put at the end of this long series of verses not found in the Williams Manuscript, seven poems (five in the same order in which they came in the earlier collection) which were included in the Williams Manuscript, and which were, therefore, in all probability written earlier than a large number of the verses that precede them.

The explanation of these circumstances that seems most reasonable to the present writer is that most of these verses were written when Herbert came to Bemerton, and that, perhaps feeling his health failing, he tried to get them into some order. He would not seem to have attempted any chronological order, either of writing or of experience, for he thrusts a poem like "Affliction," which must come after his leaving Cambridge in 1627, between two poems from the Williams Manuscript, which may well belong to an earlier time. It is even possible that he was stopped by failing health in the middle of the process, so that what we have now is but a partially organized whole. Whatever the facts, there is certainly plenty of material for speculation in the arrangement of *The Temple*, but nothing for conclusion. Nor should it ever be forgotten that while the presence of a poem in the Williams Manuscript is proof that it was existent at some unspecified time before the completion of the present form of *The Temple*, probably even before Herbert went to Bemerton, we cannot argue from its absence from the Williams Manuscript that it was not in existence at the time of its making or even earlier.

It is for this reason that I regard the late George Herbert Palmer's division of the poems into the Cambridge period (to 1627), the Crisis period (from then to 1630), and the Bemerton period (from 1630 to his death) as more suggestive than conclusive.[49] The distinction between the Williams and non-Williams poems that underlies such an arrangement seems to me too precarious. Moreover, marked changes in one's way of living are not usually conducive to that high degree of concentration of the involuntary faculties of the mind that seems to be necessary for poetry, and very recent experience does not always come through to expression with the same immediacy of emotional effect as more removed feeling and imagining. I should, myself, incline to put as few poems as possible into the Bemerton period and as many as possible into the first period. For as Mr. Palmer well points out, Herbert must have had some considerable body of work in circulation by 1625 to call forth the witness to his poetical eminence that Bacon's dedication of his translation of the Psalms implies.[50] But again it must never be forgotten that all this is conjecture. And at the bottom of some of my unwillingness to accept Mr. Palmer's findings is doubtless the purely subjective fact that I am not so impressed as George Herbert Palmer was by the specifically priestly character of the non-Williams poems. Very few of them seem to me to betray priestly as against purely Christian and churchmanly preoccupations. There is nothing surprising in this. After all, a priest has all the spiritual concerns of a private soul, on the one hand, and, on the other, he has in a liturgy like that to which Herbert was devoted, plenty of opportunity to express his pastoral concern. It is a negative argument this but not to be disregarded in the study of such an attempt as George Herbert Palmer's.

Palmer's grouping of the poems within the main divisions, according to topics treated, seems to me open to even more serious objection. The classification in itself is a singularly discriminating and illuminating one, and in that sense very valuable. For what it attempts to do, it could hardly be bettered. Its eleven divisions only need to be named for their suggestiveness and aptness to be appreciated—I. The Church-Porch; II. The Resolve; III. The Church; IV. Meditation; V. The Inner Life; VI. The Crisis; VII. The Happy Priest; VIII. Bemerton Study; IX. Restlessness; X. Suffering; XI. Death; XII. Additional and Doubtful Poems. Palmer has boldly faced the fact that the Bemerton experience was not entirely one of peace after storm. Yet one cannot help regretting that his closing with death would make *The Temple* end with "A Dialogue-Antheme" between the Christian and Death instead of the exquisite "Love bade me welcome; yet my soul drew back," with which *The Temple* traditionally (and in the Williams Manuscript) ends. It is not only that this latter poem seems better to correspond with Walton's account of that happy death at Bemerton, but that there seems to be more of the peculiar and distinctive contribution which Herbert made to the religious life of the time in the loving confidence and tenderness of its reassurance.

And, on less subjective grounds, this grouping of Palmer's is open to question in that it reduces to order and topical coherence what Herbert, by intention or necessity, left less closely organized and less specifically directed. Valuable as Palmer's grouping is for our understanding of the range and direction of Herbert's experience, it is from another point of view misleading both as to the incidence of the different elements in Herbert's experience and as to their total effect. We have only one clue as to the poet's view of his work, and that is to be found in what he told Mr. Duncon when he gave him the little book for his brother Ferrar, containing, as he put it according to Walton, *"a picture of the many spiritual Conflicts that have passed betwixt God and my Soul, before I could subject mine to the will of Jesus my Master: in whose service I have now found perfect freedom."* [51] The accompanying directions are significant for what he thought of the main effect of the poems, *"if he can think it may turn to the advantage of any dejected poor Soul, let it be made publick; if not, let him burn it."* [52] It was for the encouragement of the troubled in spirit, then, that Herbert thus tentatively offered it to the world, and it may have been with that intention to give comfort and reassurance, that he put those seven earlier poems at the end of the very mixed lot of more recent verse. But the two things that emerge from Herbert's own words (as reported) are that for him the conflicts, the inner struggles, were the heart of *The Temple,* and that looking back upon them all now on the edge of eternity, he found their issue triumphant and believed that their recounting would encourage other victims of a troubled conscience and struggling heart. Apparently, Ferrar agreed with him.

This seems to me the best clue to *The Temple.* It is the story of a man's struggles. It is not the triumphant account of a pilgrimage proceeding by dramatic and well-defined stages; it is not even a lyric version of the mystic way. The fact of the struggle, the elements that went to it, and the poet's own confidence in the outcome and the significance of it, these are the important things for Herbert, and they are the elements that impress themselves upon the attention of anyone who reads through the poems as they are printed in the traditional order. This does not mean that very definite elements of growth and development cannot be discerned. As we shall see presently, we have in a study of the revisions of some of the poems from the Williams Manuscript some very striking evidence of such change. But these developmental elements are, I believe, incidental to the unfolding and the expression of the conflict and of the certainty that that conflict had vindicated.

In such a progress the gentle Mr. Herbert of Bemerton, the pattern of a primitive peace and innocence and holiness to which Barnabas Oley looked back out of the midst of the devastation of the Civil War, yields to a much more complicated personality, a combination of poet and, in seeking at least, mystic. One's respect for Herbert's shrewdness and vigor of mind rises. So, too, does one's sense of his capacity for self-scrutiny, for discrimination, for holding to the essential, for profound spiritual insight of a very unpretentious sort. So, finally, does one's appreciation of the victory he ultimately won and of the worth of his example.

CHAPTER VII

GEORGE HERBERT AND *THE TEMPLE*

HOWEVER intense and prolonged the inner struggle of George Herbert, there was one fundamental issue on which, unlike John Donne, for instance, he enjoyed from the beginning peace. There is no sign anywhere in his life or writings of any question as to which was the right church, and where the path of salvation was to be found. He had never known any church but one, and he never was, so far as we know, abroad. Moreover, from a very early age he had a settled conviction as to what that church was and what it should be. In other words, he began at a point which Donne reached only after many painful years. Religious controversy as such held no fascination for him as it had for the troubled mind of John Donne. The handling of the theological issues in, for instance, "The Holy Communion," found in the Williams Manuscript, not by the way one of his best poems, is crude, and the poet's conviction that what happens in that rite is more important than the "how" is unmistakable. That this is due rather to lack of interest than capacity is to be seen in the comments on Valdesso. Here in the question of the possible dangers to faith in the writings of the Spanish reformer was an issue that seemed of crucial importance to Herbert, the problem of the competence of private judgment in theological matters, the opposition of the Inner Light to institutional religion. And here Herbert was quicker than Ferrar, I think, in his concern about the final effect of Valdesso's stress on the Spirit in the handling of Scripture, and whatever the reader may think of the issues involved, his judgment was, I think, sounder than Ferrar's in his apprehension of danger to the position of the Church of England, in which they both believed.[1] Other instances might be cited to show that Herbert's lack of doctrinal preoccupation did not arise from indifference to the importance of theology or lack of capacity for the necessary discriminations, but simply from the fact that his main concern was with another aspect of church life.

For Herbert is basically a churchman in the sense that for him the regulations, the forms, the accumulations and customs of the Church, are a source of inspiration, of spiritual extension and revival. For him these things did not stifle or usurp the place of personal spiritual life, but they recharged it and nourished it. Here we have, it cannot be too much insisted, one of the basic differences in human orientation that lie at the bottom of the troubles in the English Church of the seventeenth century. Readers of Baxter's autobiography will remember the passionate contempt with which that great Presbyterian leader speaks of the "Readers" who in his youth held the charge of the neighboring churches.[2] Herbert was no more blind than Baxter or, for that matter, Laud, to the dangers of formalism, to the perennial temptations of human slackness and laziness. He has some very sharp words in "The Church Porch" on "England, full of sinne, but most of sloth!"[3] But the remedy to him was not to abolish the church offices and prayers but to infuse fresh energy into the use of them and realize their possibilities. It is, though Herbert's generation would hardly have agreed, one of the basic issues of all reformations.

The important thing is that Herbert had a chance for that easy and spacious apprehension, for that growth of association and meaning, for that enrichment of affection, that periods of quiet development give men. That is why he so constantly defends the uses of his beloved church with the word, "reasonable." It is easy to point out that the force of such a claim depends entirely on the criteria of reasonableness upon which it is based. But there is really no doubt as to what the word meant when used by Herbert and the men of his group. It meant that the institution and the man had grown into each other, that he felt no strain or impediment in his relations to his church. Particularly is this apparent in those issues of faith and works and justification that so worried Donne, and that hold in such a tight vise so much of the devotional writing of the period. The closest Herbert comes to what is the great devotional commonplace of the pious Puritan of the time, and to what holds so large a place even in Donne's thought, is the poem "Judgment" in which he envisages the great Judge asking for "ev'ry man's peculiar book." It is hard to imagine even the audacity of Donne compassing so logical a simplicity as Herbert's conclusion:

> But I resolve, when Thou shalt call for mine,
>   That to decline,
> And thrust a Testament into Thy hand:
>   Let that be scann'd.
> There Thou shalt find my faults are Thine.[4]

That failure of faith that so much tried some of the best of his contemporaries is not what troubles Herbert. And, conversely, there is less stress on the legalistic aspects of the redemption in his verse than in the devotional utterances of his contemporaries, not excluding even Donne.

In general, Herbert feels no strain in his faith. He knows where he is. He rejoices in the ordinances and the authority of the Church which his Puritan contemporaries found so onerous, and he finds freedom in what seem to him the clear acceptances of faith. In general, he does not seem to be conscious, as his friend Ferrar was, of the attractions of Rome. But there is one very interesting exception, "To All Angels and Saints." Here he explains to these "glorious spirits:"

Not out of envie or maliciousnesse
Do I forbear to crave your speciall aid:
    I would addresse
My vows to thee most gladly, blessèd Maid,
And Mother of my God, in my distresse:

   ·   ·   ·   ·   ·   ·   ·

Chiefly to thee would I my soul unfold.

But now, alas, I dare not; for our King,
Whom we do all joyntly adore and praise,
    Bids no such thing;
And where His pleasure no injunction layes—
'Tis your own case—ye never move a wing.[5]

This is, in essence, it might be added, the same argument which the Puritans advanced against the ordinances of Herbert's own church. As a whole, the poem is interesting because it shows Herbert's feeling and imagination for once pressing against the bounds of his belief.

In general, however, there is very little of this strictness of interpretation in Herbert, this careful watching for warrant and justification, that is the core of the intellectual discipline of so many of his contemporaries. Strictness there is in Herbert, as we shall see in a moment, but it is in general of a very different kind. Nowhere is the essential range of his view, with due regard, of course, to his time, better seen than in his conceptions of God. The wrath of God, the justice of God, the will of God, the order of God, the power of God, these mainsprings of sevententh-century religion are to be found in Herbert as in all his contemporaries. But, also, playing an active part in the inspiration of thought, awakening imagination and kindling feeling, are to be found the wonder of God, the closeness of God, the pity of God, the tenderness of God, all those gentler manifestations of divinity that implement the love of God. It is not always easy for the modern reader to do

justice to the logical force and, in a sense, inevitability of the
grimmer aspects of the sevententh-century conception of God.
The aberrations of the pagan Renaissance, the fanaticisms
of the Christian reaction, the cataclysmic confusion of a period
of religious revolution, all of these forces had bred a rigor of
mood that could hardly fail to see its God in its own grim
temper. Practically all English religious thought of the opening
years of the sevententh century begins in a devastating sense
of sin. That is a good beginning for a strenuous religious life,
but that initial tension must relax a little before an ampler spirit
can begin to apprehend the larger aspects of the race's experience of God.

This is what Herbert did, or perhaps, to be vaguer and yet
more accurate, what happened to Herbert. By and large, as
every lover of Donne becomes aware, the strength of his genius
lies in his exquisite awareness of the soul's feeling for God.
What he says of God is much less interesting because much
less warmly and richly experienced. But Herbert thinks a
good deal of God, of God in Himself, and not just of what he
asks or wants of God. He thinks of God in all the world. In
general, as we have seen, seventeenth-century religious thought
in its preoccupation with the law and the word of God makes
very little of the immanence of God. But Herbert sees the
essence of God's providence in His indwelling in the world he
has made:

> Thou art in small things great, not small in any;
> Thy even praise can neither rise nor fall;
> Thou art in all things one, in each thing many;
> For Thou art infinite in one and all.[6]

And with the immanence of God comes that sense of the
mystery of God which the seventeenth century in its desperate
eagerness to have everything clear so commonly forgets or
shies away from:

> But Thou art Light and darkness both togeather:
> If that bee dark we cannot see,
> The sunn is darker then a tree,
> And Thou more dark then either.[7]

The most distinctive thing about Herbert's God, however, is his yearning for man. Even in its severest clinging to the eternal decrees, and its most arduous self-searchings as to the possession of saving faith, the seventeenth century did not forget that God had so loved the world that He had given his only begotten Son to save it from itself. But, as a rule, that century was too much preoccupied with its own unloveableness to conceive of a daily and immediate love seeking out with particular yearning the least of its creatures. That is the beautiful conclusion of the well-known "The Pulley," the implication of the first stanza of the exquisite Easter song:

> I got me flowers to straw Thy way,
> I got me boughs off many a tree;
> But Thou wast up by break of day,
> And brought'st Thy sweets along with Thee.[8]

It is Herbert's apprehension of God's yearning for man that enables him to do what so few seventeenth-century English writers can do, put into God's mouth words that are what He might conceivably use. The type of speech which the seventeenth century usually gives to God is painfully pedagogical and official, in fact a theological instruction or at best homily, nothing that one could imagine God saying in his private, humanly speaking, personal capacity. Of the long patience of God, of that sparingness of words that might be expected of One who through the ages must have had quite enough of words, there is in these conventional speeches of God no suspicion. Herbert tried his hand at that sort of thing once in "The Sacrifice." [9] In spite of a pungent summary like "Man stole the fruit, but I must climbe the tree," it is probably unfortunate that that long and in many ways vivid summary of the Passion is put into the lips of its chief figure, for it is hard for piety to remember the decencies of drama. Even the broken cry of the Cross,

> But, O My God, My God, why leav'st Thou Me,
> The Sonne in Whom Thou dost delight to be?
> My God, My God—

is pulled back into the almost too-oft repeated refrain of the poem, "Was ever grief like Mine?" with only the slight variation of "Never was grief like Mine."

But such lengthiness and overexplicitness as disfigure this poem are rare with Herbert. Consequently, it is only fair to set against that failure the poem that is the triumph of his forbearance and reserve in this most difficult of all the fields of religious expression. It is that poem to which Mr. Aldous Huxley has done such noble though incomplete justice,[10] "The Collar." We do not know when "The Collar" was written. It is not in the Williams Manuscript, and the modern taste for shadows on light will make us like to think it was written at Bemerton. We may be sure that the anguish that so cried out in it was not the last word in the history of Bemerton or the poem would not have ended as it did:

> I struck the board, and cry'd, "No more;
> I will abroad."
> What, shall I ever sigh and pine?
> My lines and life are free; free as the road,
> Loose as the winde, as large as store.
> Shall I be still in suit?
> Have I no harvest but a thorn
> To let me bloud, and not restore
> What I have lost with cordiall fruit?
> Sure there was wine

Before my sighs did drie it; there was corn
Before my tears did drown it;
Is the year onely lost to me?
Have I no bayes to crown it,
No flowers, no garlands gay? all blasted,
All wasted?
Not so, my heart; but there is fruit,
And thou hast hands.
Recover all thy sigh-blown age
On double pleasures; leave thy cold dispute
Of what is fit and not; forsake thy cage,
Thy rope of sands
Which pettie thoughts have made; and made to thee
Good cable, to enforce and draw,
And be thy law,
While thou didst wink and wouldst not see.
Away! take heed;
I will abroad.
Call in thy death's-head there, tie up thy fears;
He that forbears
To suit and serve his need
Deserves his load.
But as I rav'd and grew more fierce and wilde
At every word,
Methought I heard one calling, "Childe";
And I reply'd, "My Lord." [11]

Seldom have the arguments against a life of strict religious renunciation and devotion been presented with more directness and energy. Seldom have the elements of possible illusion and possible sterility, the two great charges of the world against Herbert's course, been presented with more vigor. It is interesting, too, to note how as the frenzy deepens, the line of argument falls from the humanist to the materialist and opportunist level. Then comes the single word, the whistling of the thrown lifeline when the dikes of reason have been swept down by passion. The one thing, the only thing that can be set against that terrible unanswerableness of outraged nature, the cry that in a single word appeals to a more ultimate nature, calls to a real fulfillment, comes through the roar of self-tormenting, and the soul knows its illusion and its destiny. Nowhere in English poetry has the profound cogency and expressiveness of the one word been more dramatically or more simply vindicated. It is a great moment when the artist lays away his art with all its strength and beauty and yields himself to the bare "thing in itself." This is such a moment.

For the great thing in the religious experience of Herbert was that he wished to know his God for His own sake alone:

> Ah, my deare God, though I am clean forgot,
> Let me not love Thee, if I love Thee not.[12]

And he wished not only to know Him but to know Him at once here and now in that world of intimacy in which the bounds between here and there, and then and now, disappear. In that sense one may say that Herbert has the purpose and the longing of all the mystics.

It is not without significance that one of the most moving expressions of that longing should be one in which the sense of doubt and estrangement is hurled as it were into the face of his God. That hurling is perhaps one of the soundest things in Herbert, because there he faces the raggedness of human experience with something of the honesty and confidence of the mystics themselves. "Even as I am known"—one of the great difficulties of the strenuous mood of the seventeenth century, one of the prices of its heroism, is a certain straitening of its imagination, a certain pulling taut of its emotions. Human feeling probably never runs along one level, high or low, certainly not that irritable sensitiveness of feeling which is so often the portion of the poet. Yet, we have seen, the passion of the seventeenth century was for steadiness of emotion. The vicissitudes of ardor frightened it and discouraged it, just as did the distractions of the imagination, which so troubled Donne. There was good reason for this concern, as there was for almost everything else that looks like fanaticism in that rather relentless time. But the hand which moral strenuousness laid on religious passion was often pretty heavy. There is, therefore, something profoundly honest and courageous in Herbert's expression of his rebellion as the occasion of his illumination.

In the realm of the imagination, too, the strenuousness of the time bore rather hard on Herbert. The poetic imagination, enamored as it so often is of harmony and peace, zealous as it so often has proved in every field in the pursuit of the one thing needful, yet craves a certain variety, a certain multiplicity of stimuli. However it may lift its head towards the One, its roots are in the Many. It is an interesting thing that, while Herbert has given but relatively scant expression to his delight in the Many (the delicacy of his incidental allusions bears witness to a keen and loving eye for nature, for the casual and incidental details of daily life), yet the consciousness of distraction, of the ungirt loin and the unlit lamp, is one of the mainsprings of his poetry. More than once there is the suggestion so clearly given above in "The Collar," of a feeling that some part of his nature is being denied, that one of the gifts God gave is being wasted. The seventeenth century was strenuous in its demands for concentration. The region of the neutral, the innocent, the transmutable, was perilously narrow between the two embattled camps of God and the world. That is why so much of its religious poetry seems to a contemporary reader arid. That is why there is so little of that large peace in which the loves of man by finding their relative positions in a reintegrated world of order come home to their destinies in the One Love.

With a man like Donne, it does not so much matter. The

pain is there past *that* lifting. But for a man who like Herbert could see that

> All may of Thee partake:
> Nothing can be so mean
> Which with his tincture, "for Thy sake,"
> Will not grow bright and clean,[18]

it is a pity that the rigor of the time was not more hospitable to the sacramental principle.

But to say even this much is to wish the seventeenth century were not itself and to surrender some of the characteristic interest and life of Herbert's verse. For it is to the realization of his own lack of concentration, as well as to the painful sense of the instability of his own feelings, that we owe the dramatic interest of Herbert's religious and poetic history. The first has on the whole received more attention from Herbert students than the second. It is one of the classic dramas of the seventeenth century, none the less poignant and real even if Herbert had probably not been any great sinner in the external sense. After all, he had been guilty of what for a man of his feeling and insight would be the supreme sin, the running-away from even a muffled call, the trying to hide even a dim light, the shuffling-away from what must have been a pretty clear conviction relatively early in life. It is the second, the realization of the instability of his feelings, the unevenness of his inmost temper, the uncertainty of even his deepest love, that has received little attention. Nor is that surprising. It is probably the consequence of the first, and not a primary mainspring at all. It takes a good deal of discipline on the lower levels of thought and will to insure any degree of steadiness on the higher levels of feeling. And probably even then only a very humble degree of stability is possible to the children of men. At any rate, we have here in Herbert's despondency over his own weakness what might be called the chief malady of the mystics. And, I think, a further evidence that what Herbert was essentially seeking was the steady, unbroken consciousness of the presence of God, and that what troubled him was the brittleness, the uneven texture, of his experience of that consciousness.

As Mr. Osmond some years ago pointed out, "A Parodie" may be taken as the key to *The Temple*,[14] though I think in a more specific sense than Mr. Osmond perhaps intended:

> Soul's joy, when Thou art gone,
> And I alone,
> Which cannot be,
> Because Thou dost abide with me,
> And I depend on Thee;
>
> Yet when Thou dost suppresse
> The cheerfulnesse
> Of Thy abode,
> And in my powers not stirre abroad,
> But leave me to my load,—
>
> O what a damp and shade
> Doth me invade!
> No stormie night
> Can so afflict, or so affright,
> As Thy eclipsèd light.[15]

It is not failure to achieve what he seeks that here moves Herbert to cry out. It is rather failure to keep a firm hold on what he has actually known and experienced. One is reminded at once of that Dark Night of the Soul that plays so considerable a part in the mystical experience of Saint John of the Cross. But to push that general resemblance to the point of identity is to misunderstand Herbert. The terrible anguish of the mystic is not to be found here. It is rather the weight of unrelieved human nature, the depression of light withdrawn. There is no mistaking its sincerity, its reality, but between it and the experience of the great mystics there is a vast difference in intensity. Yet the essential mark of the mystic region is there. It is the privation of light that is the burden of his grief, not any possible consequence. In other words, Herbert's eye is on the mark, but he cannot always reach it.

What is this joy the privation of which so heavily weighs upon his spirit? Not ecstasy, I think. Not that ecstasy is unknown to Herbert. In one of the Holy Communion poems, he cries:

> Give me my captive soul, or take
> My bodie also thither.[16]

And in "Church Musick" he thus addresses the music:

> Now I in you without a bodie move,
> Rising and falling with your wings.[17]

But it is interesting to note that in the first poem the verse never quite takes off into the free air of ecstasy. It remains cramped, and Herbert's verse is not usually cramped. And in the second the echoes of Shakespeare suggest rather the effort to give expression to a feeling than the transport of ecstasy. The truth is, I think, that ecstasy is not Herbert's region. In general his religious tradition did not much approve of such heights of feeling. It cared too much for decorum, for clarity, for control. Its basic problem, we must never forget, was the problem of order. Harmony, integrity, peace—these are great ideals, and there is nothing negative or passive in either their nature or their acquisition, particularly for people who started as Elizabethans, but their achievement has, like all human achievements, its price.

It was with as much difficulty as any of his contemporaries that Herbert achieved what he did. The difficulty of concentration, the indirection, the hesitation, the distraction of those years in which he knew that eventually he was going to take orders, had their consequences in the sense of instability, of fruitlessness, of incapacity to hold close what he knew and loved, that is the constantly recurring theme of *The Temple*. That was the secret of whatever of grief dogged those swift Bemerton years, and of the shadows that lie on the surface of his verse. But it should never be forgotten that even the most disheartened of his poems ends with the steady reassurance of the presence of his God. He may not be able to see the light behind the darkness of the immediate moment, but he never long falters in his confidence that it is really there. That confidence is no parsonic unwillingness to yield even the moment to the enemy, but it is the most persistent and central thing in Herbert's religious consciousness and the source of the peculiar power of his verse.

How this confidence grew and deepened is to be found in a study of one of those seven poems that, separated from the other poems of the Williams Manuscript, were printed at the end of *The Temple* in the edition of 1633. Here we are peculiarly fortunate in having available three quite different versions of the same poem, and that one of the most beautiful and meaningful of all Herbert's poems. Indeed, most people asked to pick out a typical Herbert poem would probably choose this one. Certainly it could not be left out of any list of the half dozen universal favorites. The first version we have (there may have been other versions before) is the version which was copied into the Williams Manuscript presumably from some copy of Herbert's own. To judge from the nature of Herbert's corrections, it was a good copy, for the changes he makes are for the most part changes in the substance of the verse and not mere corrections of text. Then Herbert took up this manuscript and went over it, in some cases making slight changes, in others quite reworking the original. This is the most extensive of his revisions, carried out, it should be remembered, in his own handwriting. There must have been at least one more revision (possibly more than one) before the final form was printed after Herbert's death, for that is strikingly different even from the version which Herbert left in the Williams Manuscript. We have, then, three distinct and different versions of this poem, representing at least three distinct stages in its development. It seems, therefore, worth while for purpose of comparison to print the three versions as three separate poems.

PERFECTION

Lord teach mee to referr
All things I doe to thee
That I not onely may not erre
But allso pleasing bee.

A man that looks on glass
On it may stay his eye:
Or if he pleaseth, through it pass
And then the Heav'en espy.

He that does ought for thee,
Marketh that deed for thine:
And when the Divel shakes the tree,
Thou saist, this fruit is mine.

All may of thee pertake:
Nothing can be so low
Which with his tincture (for thy sake)
Will not to Heaven grow.

A servant with this clause,
Makes drudgery divine.
Who sweeps a chamber for thy Lawes,
Makes that, and th' action fine.

But these are high perfections:
Happy are they that dare
Lett in the light to all their actions
And show them as they are.[18]

The Elixir

Lord teach mee to referr
All things I doe to thee
That I not onely may not erre
But allso pleasing bee.

A man that looks on glass
On it may stay his eye:
Or if he pleaseth, through it pass
And then the Heav'en espy.

All may of thee pertake:
Nothing can be so meane
Which with his tincture (for thy sake)
Will not grow bright & cleane.

A servant with this clause,
Makes drudgery divine.
Who sweeps a roome as for thy Lawes,
Makes that, and th' action fine.

This is the famous stone
That turneth all to gold;
For that which God doth touch & owne
Can not for less be told.[19]

The Elixer

Teach me, my God and King,
In all things Thee to see,
And what I do in any thing
To do it as for Thee.

Not rudely, as a beast,
To runne into an action
But still to make Thee prepossest,
And give it his perfection.

> A man that looks on glasse,
>   On it may stay his eye;
> Or if he pleaseth, through it passe,
>   And then the heav'n espie.
>
> All may of Thee partake:
>   Nothing can be so mean
> Which with his tincture, "for Thy sake,"
>   Will not grow bright and clean.
>
> A servant with this clause
>   Makes drudgerie divine;
> Who sweeps a room as for Thy laws
>   Makes that and th' action fine.
>
> This is the famous stone
>   That turneth all to gold;
> For that which God doth touch and own
>   Cannot for lesse be told.[20]

What has happened to this poem in the course of these successive revisions? The most striking thing is the fact that whole stanzas are eliminated, thrown away (in spite of the universal tenderness of the artist for the children of his brain), and that new stanzas appear. The omissions are striking. The third stanza is the first to disappear, crossed out in strong strokes of the same ink as Herbert used for the other corrections, unmistakably his own. It is an effective stanza with a certain gnomic vigor. And it is more dramatic than the rather dry stanza, with the astonishing opening-up under the surface, that precedes it. It is easy to find the Herbert who humorously and lovingly treasured up popular proverbs and sayings in this third stanza. Yet it went. There is not much of the devil in Herbert's work, particularly in those poems that from evidence of form and style would seem to have been written well on in his life. It is Sin that plays the rôle of the sceptic and the accuser in "A

Parodie," for instance. There may have been too much of the rigid theological transaction about the stanza to suit the unfolding tastes of Herbert. At any rate it went.

So did the last stanza. But here the reason is, I think, more apparent. There is in that stanza something agnostic, something reconciled to the imperfectibility of the world, or at least too easily acquiescent in its recognition of the fewness of the Chosen. There is certainly nothing to be discarded in its form or language. But Herbert's view of his theme had ripened and strengthened since it was written, for there is something positive and aggressive in that last stanza which he now adds beneath the rejected one, a stanza that in the somewhat rigid alchemical figure brilliantly sums up the whole poem, with the completeness and firmness of arc that is one of the characteristic movements of Herbert's mind. There has, also, been some growth in that quiet confidence that is, in later years, to be the final note of so much even of his most troubled poetry.

There is one other striking change in the second version of the poem. The old fourth stanza, now the third, is revised in the direction of greater precision and humility. It is a change that holds in reserve the force of the conclusion, not so much a change in feeling or point of view as in rhetoric. Yet even in passing we should notice, I think, that the emotional tone is made firmer by this focussing of feeling as well as attention on the point of the conclusion. The passion for the essential is tightening its grip on Herbert.

Something of the same passion we may see in what is, after the substitution of the new close, the most considerable of Herbert's revisions from the poetic as well as the philosophic point of view. The opening of what we may for convenience call the first and second versions is precise enough in its declaration of Herbert's passing from the fear of sin to the desire to please his Lord. But there is still a remoteness, a thinking about the issues and the discriminations involved, that becomes apparent at once when set beside the direct plunge of the last version. After that plunge, "In all things Thee to see," there is no need of discrimination between the fear of sin and the desire of pleasing God. "As for Thee" says all there is any need of saying. The essential thing is there. One is almost sorry not to rest with that. But the additional new stanza provides the logical connecting link between this beginning and the old second stanza. Under its apparent simplicity, under what may even seem a certain naiveté of emotional insistence, there is a precision and an economy of statement that does justice to but also hides the fine elaboration of the thought. Here as so often, the forthrightness of Herbert's expression of value almost conceals the exquisiteness of his mental operations. But the sum-total of the revisions is, I think, quite apparent. "The Elixer" is now a much more positive, much homelier, much more intimate and direct thing than it was in the beginning. And this intimacy and directness is not to be found, as in Donne, in the expression of the poet's feeling, but in his apprehension of and surrender to his subject.

That is the secret of the intimacy of feeling that has struck every student of Herbert's verse from his day to ours. Other poets in Herbert's own age, as before and since, have done richer and more magnificent justice to the majesty and the power of God. But of God found and known here and now in the little passages of daily life and the small circumstances of our common environment, Herbert has the most to say of any seventeenth-century poet I know. To find anything just like "Ah, my deare angrie Lord," [21] "How sweetly doth 'My Master' sound! 'My Master!' " [22] "Sweetest Saviour, if my soul Were but worth the having," [23] one has to wait for the generation of Francis Thompson and Alice Meynell and some of the Irish poets of only yesterday. It is interesting how the same motive may lead a poet out of the forms of his day to anticipate the

forms of a later day. When one remembers the Scripture para-
phrase, the catechising (sometimes one is tempted to say that
the devotee was trying to make sure that God was properly in-
structed and fenced against straying from theological bounds
that were now and then perhaps suspected to be not so rigorously enforced in another world as in this!), the prayer for
the averting of wrath, the rehearsing of a semi-legal transaction,
that constituted so much of the stock of religious poetry of his
time, it is refreshing to turn to the more imaginative types
that this very intimacy of Herbert's religious consciousness
revived if not created. The incident, the divine anecdote, as it
were, in a poem like "Artillerie," the dialogue as in "Love-
unknown," the voice heard as in "The Holdfast," the vision in
"Humilitie" ("I saw the Vertues sitting hand in hand"), the
use of the ejaculation in "A True Hymne," the overhearing of
his own heart in "The Familie," the charming legend of the
present day as in "Christmas," the allegory again and again as
in "The World," and "Life"—these are but a few of the most
striking types and forms in which Herbert again releases that
myth-making faculty of the imagination of which the religious
literalism of the time, grandfather to the scientific literalism
of a later time, had been making such havoc.

Some of the standing preoccupations of the time come to a
fresh and magic life under the spell of that quick sense of the
nearness of God. There is a stanza in "Decay" in which the
poet brings back for a moment the wonder of those Old Testament days when God himself walked in the world he had
made:

> One might have sought and found Thee presently
> At some fair oak, or bush, or cave, or well:
> "Is my God this way?" "No," they would reply;
> "He is to Sinai gone, as we heard tell;
> List, ye may heare great Aaron's bell." [24]

But more constantly than in the forms of his verse, this intimacy of consciousness is revealed in the peculiar homeliness of the terms in which Herbert tries to communicate his sense of the divine. There is splendor in Herbert, and some of that startling magnificence that is to be found in practically all writers of this period, in which the afterglow of the Elizabethan day still reddens and empurples the western sky. There is that happy, effortless felicity that, gathering up much meaning in a phrase, yet has leisure for charm, the essence of the classic spirit. But the distinctive contribution of Herbert to the poetic style of the period is to be found in none of these, but rather in a peculiar combination of homeliness and grace. John Donne knew how to use homeliness with telling effect for surprise or startling realism or vivacity. Some of his most sensational effects are due to this same command of the gifts of the everyday, but what Herbert does with this material is very different from what his predecessor made of it. Where Donne may even use the homely to carry his startled reader off the earth of the everyday into far regions, Herbert employs it to domesticate wonder, to bring the remote home to hearth and bosom, to give to the general, the sharp incidence of the particular, the breath-taking freshness of the just-happened.

Herbert can write that often and quite justly admired last stanza of "Vertue," which seems a calmer Donne, but still in the sphere of Donne:

> Only a sweet and vertuous soul,
> Like season'd timber, never gives;
> But though the whole world turn to coal,
> Then chiefly lives.[25]

There the devastating truth of the platitude finds for once something like the adequate figure.

But that stately splendor is not the habitual idiom of Herbert, not the habitual expression of the peculiar grasp which he has on the reality of spiritual feeling. Much more characteristic, though still within the bounds of the commonplaces of the seventeenth-century devotional life, is the lively beginning of "Doom's-day":

> Come away,
>   Make no delay;
> Summon all the dust to rise,
> Till it stirre and rubbe the eyes;
>   While this member jogs the other,
>   Each one whispring, "Live you, brother?" [26]

Or to take one of the loveliest things Herbert ever wrote, where the perfection of the music gives its own sweetness to the fresh vividness of the imagery:

> How fresh, O Lord, how sweet and clean
> Are Thy returns! ev'n as the flowers in Spring,
>   To which, besides their own demean,
> The late-past frosts tributes of pleasure bring;
>   Grief melts away,
>   Like snow in May,
>   As if there were no such cold thing.
>
> Who would have thought my shrivel'd heart
> Could have recover'd greennesse? It was gone
>   Quite under ground; as flowers depart
> To see their mother-root, when they have blown,
>   Where they together
>   All the hard weather,
>   Dead to the world, keep house unknown.[27]

Much has been made of Herbert's use of nature. There is no question of his sensitiveness to and his delight in the beauty of nature, particularly of nature in its commoner manifestations of flower and bird and the coming and the passing of the day's light. But he is hardly to be called a nature poet. His use of the roots and the flowers is not different in kind from his use of astronomy in "Divinitie," [28] of the life of the Court in the second of the two poems called "The Temper." In other words he is a metaphysical poet of the school of Donne with the same undivided consciousness of his tribe. But there is a homeliness of spirit in Herbert, arising out of the peculiar intimacy of his apprehension of the divine, that naturalizes all his mind touches to the purpose of his love. There is less of surprise in him than in most of the metaphysicals, more of inevitability. It is that, conjoined with the intimacy, that has led so many critics to apply the adjective "naive" to his verse.

One of the tests of this quality is to be found in an aspect of his work that has, perhaps happily, not received the attention it deserves. It has been said that Herbert gets certain effects in his poetry because he transfers the point of view and the emotional habits of the sonneteers to divine poetry. That is a reasonable hypothesis in view of the poem in which the young Herbert threw down to the poets the gauntlet of the other love in his early resolution to rescue poetry from its profane preoccupations. But it does not do entire justice to another movement of the time, perhaps more apparent in the Latin countries, the movement for a warmer, more intimate, perhaps more sensuous, handling of religious emotion. The emphasis on the affective aspects of the spiritual life which is to be seen in the flowering of the great mysticism of late sixteenth-century Spain and seventeenth-century France is, also, to be taken into account. The homogeneity of medieval Europe had been rudely shattered but by no means destroyed, and stones thrown into the spiritual pools of Spain or Italy often moved the island waters of England.

Some of the same forces that penned the ardors of certain seventeenth-century French devotional books, that informed some of the sculptures of the Roman churches, and the paintings of the Spanish masters, are to be found at work in Herbert as in Crashaw. Unfortunately, past history has to be approached across the excesses of its degenerations. What any movement was like in its beginning or even in its prime is hard to come at, because it is not easy to remember the circumstances which called forth its eccentricities. But we need only to recall the emphasis of early seventeenth-century religious feeling on the wrath of God, the justice of God, the terror of God, to appreciate how those who had come to joy in the beauty and the graciousness of God might run to excess in the expression of their delight. There are certain adjectives like "sweet" and "dear" that are unquestionably abused by Herbert. With that delight in the mixing of the genres that is an aspect of the metaphysical mind that has not received as much attention as it deserves, Herbert even distills an excess of his own, "sowre-sweet." Certain elements in human experience, like tears, that at various times have tempted men beyond the limits of discretion, are also overdone. The peculiarly seventeenth-century and generally Puritan affection for "groans" is another instance of how a good thing may be run into the ground. Herbert even gives evidence of Crashaw's nest obsession. But the suggestion which Miss Kathleen Lea has made on Crashaw's behalf applies quite as much to Herbert, that some of these words that seem to us to be used to the point where they cease to have any meaning, actually had for the men of that time an almost ritualistic potency of connotation, so that what they brought into any line they entered was a thing at once sharper and richer than we can now imagine.[29] Such a theory might well commend itself to any student of literary history, familiar with the way in which each period employs its favorite critical terms of blame and approval.

A good example of the rich and intense feeling of aspiration which might in that age invest what seems to the mind of today a very artificial figure is to be seen in the following stanza:

> Listen, sweet Dove, unto my song,
> And spread thy golden wings in me;
> Hatching my tender heart so long,
> Till it get wing, and flie away with Thee.[30]

If we scan the revisions of the Williams Manuscript and still more the differences between the Williams Manuscript and the edition of 1633, it is impossible to avoid the conclusion that Herbert was more or less consciously aware of his temptations in this direction, and that he tried to restrain them. Sometimes a little thing is more telling than a great. "King of all grief," "King of all wounds," he wrote first in the opening lines of "The Thanksgiving," and sometime between that form and the final he changed those apostrophes to the present "Oh King of grief," and "Oh King of wounds." [31]

The same tendency is to be seen in the close of "Prayer," where the poet warms to a riot of luscious expressions of delight:

> Softnesse, and peace, and joy, and love, and blisse,
> Exalted manna, gladnesse of the best,
> Heaven in ordinarie, man well drest,
> The milkie way, the bird of Paradise,
>
> Church-bels beyond the stars heard, the soul's bloud,
> The land of spices——

And then in tremendous finality he closes with the barest expression possible of the essence of the matter, "something understood." [32]

But in general what preserves the essential freshness and modesty of Herbert's verse is the dominating reality of what he is talking about. It is the presence of his Lord here and now in the homeliest of contexts, apprehended with quick intimacy and expressed with the simplicity of one who has found his center beyond himself.

Once in "The Forerunners" he saw the "sweet phrases, lovely metaphors," dear to his poet's heart, fleeing before the winds of coming winter. He tried to tell himself:

> True Beautie dwells on high; ours is a flame
> But borrow'd thence to light us thither.[33]

But it was a flame he spent the best of his art to keep alive, even when that art lay in nothing more than the gracious marshalling of the simple logic of his love. It was the poem "Love," not changed from the days of the Williams Manuscript that he chose to end *The Temple*. We can hardly do better than to imitate his example. It is not the greatest of his poems perhaps, but none is more characteristic nor more distinctive:

> Love bade me welcome; yet my soul drew back,
>   Guiltie of dust and sinne.
> But quick-ey'd Love, observing me grow slack
>   From my first entrance in,
> Drew nearer to me, sweetly questioning
>   If I lack'd any thing.
>
> "A guest," I answer'd, "worthy to be here":
>   Love said, "You shall be he."
> "I, the unkind, ungrateful? Ah, my dear,
>   I cannot look on Thee."
> Love took my hand, and smiling did reply,
>   "Who made the eyes but I?"
>
> "Truth, Lord; but I have marr'd them; let my shame
>   Go where it doth deserve."
> "And know you not," says Love, "Who bore the blame?"
>   "My dear, then I will serve."
> "You must sit down," says Love, "and taste My meat."
>   So I did sit and eat.[34]

Chapter VIII

RICHARD CRASHAW: LITTLE GIDDING TO ROME

At first sight, the story of Richard Crashaw seems the most dramatic of all the stories of this group. The son of a famous Anglican preacher and writer of marked Puritan sympathies, who had distinguished himself pre-eminently in the controversy with Rome, Crashaw died a canon in the Church of Loreto. Such an end to such a beginning might well suggest an evolution more dramatic than Donne's, a conversion more drastic still. Actually, it was neither. Of all these men, with the possible exception of Traherne, Crashaw changed least. Taking into account the conditions of the times, and the forces that influenced his development, that end in the angel-garlanded House of Loreto was the logical conclusion of a process of growth that must almost certainly have begun in his father's library in Whitechapel.

There is still extant a letter from William Crashaw of February 26, 1611, to his friend and patron, the Earl of Salisbury, the Lord High Treasurer of England, asking for the gift of certain "popishe bookes," which, he has just learned, have been seized and are in his lordship's hands.[1] That similar requests, if not that one, must have been granted, we learn from his own voluminous productions in the controversy with Rome. Much of this reading was quite clearly done with the righteous indignation and the intellectual malice of the born controversialist. But there is abundant evidence to be found in the devotions which he published and the translations he made of ancient hymns and prayers that this often rabidly anti-Roman preacher

loved good letters and tender feeling far too profoundly to be
held from either by difference of time or creed. Mr. Hutchinson is doing only justice to a staunch and sincere spirit when he
claims for him some part in the progeny of his son's gentler and
tenderer genius.[2]

Evidence of this more genial side of William Crashaw's nature cannot have been entirely lacking in his ordinary address. For the clever and beautiful and accomplished lady who
married him as his second wife in his forty-second year was herself, though much younger than he (she was twenty-six), still
quite old enough, and if we can judge from her funeral oration,
quite enough a woman of the world, not to be entirely beguiled
by an enthusiasm for piety if her suitor had been as dry and
fierce as some of his works suggest.[3]

Of Crashaw's mother, we know nothing beyond her name.
She is said to have been Helen, the daughter of John Routh.[4]
We do not even know the date of her death. But her husband
married her successor in 1619. Her son was born, we know, in
1612 or 1613. So even if he knew her, he cannot have been
more than five or at most six when she died. The second Mrs.
Crashaw distinguished herself by the kindness with which she
treated her stepson, but she died in childbed in 1620. To these
successive losses with brief intervals of maternal tenderness
Signor Praz attributes something of that susceptibility to fem-
inine influence in maternal guise that is to be found in the letter
concerning some woman friend, whom he calls, "My dearest
mother," generally considered to be Mary Collet, and in his
praises of Teresa of Avila and the Virgin.[5] It is a tempting
hypothesis, with much to sustain it in Crashaw's works but
naturally nothing in the way of direct evidence. All that we
can be sure of is that even if his mother died in infancy (not
a likely hypothesis when the remarrying habits of seventeenth-
century widowers are remembered), there was for the sensitive
and ardent boy the memory of at least one gracious and beauti-

ful woman, all the more precious and suggestive for its early transference to the ideal and the remembered.

Of the next years of Crashaw's life we know nothing. The foundations of an excellent education were doubtless being laid in the beginnings of that familiarity with the classic poets to which the Latin and Greek verse of his youth bears witness. Probably that familiarity with contemporary Latin poetry, notably that of the Jesuits, to which Signor Praz has paid such authoritative tribute, would come later. But whatever the peculiar emphasis or advantages of his father's home, they were to end with his father's early death. William Crashaw's will was proved in 1626, when his son was about fourteen years old. A mention of Crashaw in a list of people for whom mourning cloaks were provided for a funeral in 1627, with its possible suggestions of youthful social connections,[6] and Lloyd's testimony that Crashaw was left for guardianship in the hands of two distinguished lawyers of the time, undoubtedly friends of his father's Temple days,[7] give us all we know of the next few years. The first certain landmark after his father's death is his acceptance for admission to the Charterhouse in 1629, with a note that seems to indicate that he was older than the usual age for such admission.[8]

It has been suggested that the origins of the type of his early Latin epigrams are to be sought in the Sunday exercises of the Charterhouse which required the senior scholars to make verses in Latin and Greek on the Gospel and Epistle of the day.[9] Certainly, Crashaw distinguished himself in these brief years at the Charterhouse, as we can see from the terms in which he paid tribute to his master, Robert Brook, in an autograph address prefixed to a copy of the *Epigrammata Sacra* of 1634, terms in which a boy of brilliant promise would pay tribute to a sympathetic and encouraging master.[10] More substantial evidence we have in the exhibition to Pembroke College, Cambridge, which closed his school career, and in his election to the Greek Scholarship at that college on October 6, 1631.[11] This was followed by his matriculation in the next year as a pensioner at Pembroke.[12]

It has been suggested very reasonably that Crashaw must have brought with him to the University a considerable reputation as a youthful poet, for the many contributions he made to the collections of elegies in his first year, collections to which contributions were usually invited, would indicate a considerable school reputation for one still so young.[13] This impression of precocious recognition is borne out by the confidence with which the young poet in the address to the reader which he prefixed to the *Epigrammata Sacra* in 1634 declared his resolution to devote himself to sacred poetry, setting against the profane love which the poets have celebrated so lavishly and so wantonly the sacred love of the Christian.[14]

Probably the greatest single influence of these first Cambridge years was the influence of Little Gidding, that remarkable effort to acclimatize monasticism and the religious life in Protestant England which has so fascinated all students of the period. The founder and the head of the Little Gidding Community, Nicholas Ferrar, who had been the devoted friend of Herbert, may have been also the friend of Crashaw's father. Certainly, the elder Crashaw must have had some contact with Ferrar in the days when they were both interested in the Virginia Plantation, an enterprise that, however disastrous in its practical outcome, proved so singularly efficacious in bringing good men together in a common enthusiasm. It will be recalled that John Donne had been interested in this enterprise, and so had Sir Henry Wotton. Nicholas Ferrar devoted himself to its affairs with such high hopes that when all was brought to nought through Court intrigue, he seems to have felt that he was dispensed from further attendance upon the world of power and ambition.[15] It would be in the spirit of the Ferrars to befriend the son of their old friend, and Crashaw's acquaintance with the community, half patriarchal and half monastic, which dated from old Mrs. Ferrar's purchase of the manor of Little Gidding in 1625 and Nicholas Ferrar's ordination to the diaconate in 1626, may well have antedated his Cambridge days.[16] But we are on surer ground when we come to his University residence, for in one of the earliest accounts of the Ferrars, Crashaw is mentioned expressly as one of the Cambridge men who used to ride over to Little Gidding to share in the pious exercises of that devoted family, notably the night watches, which were so dramatic an innovation of their life.[17]

As to the details of Crashaw's relation to the Little Gidding Community we are still in the dark, but the reports that have come down to us with regard to the intimacy of his relation to the community are strikingly confirmed by the letter which he wrote from Leiden in the days of his exile to a friend who may be either John Ferrar or Mr. Collet.[18] On the strength of this letter, Miss E. Cruwys Sharland was ready to conclude that Crashaw was actually a member of the Little Academy, that intimate family group in which so many of the humanistic observances of the community centered.[19] While that opinion takes a good deal for granted, especially in view of the fact that, so far as we can tell, membership in it was confined to the family itself, there is no questioning the intimate terms on which Crashaw stood in regard to the group of people with whom the letter deals, and we know of no other group but that of Little Gidding to which the letter could refer. The whole tone and temper of the production, as well as the incidental allusions, make the Little Gidding reference as certain as anything can be in an affair in which the giving of names seems to be so carefully dodged. This letter, then, confirms the importance that tradition has assigned to Crashaw's connection with Little Gidding in such a fashion as to suggest that one of the major influences, not only of the early Cambridge years but of Crashaw's entire English life, is to be found in that group.

It is, therefore, very important to understand just what was the character of the Little Gidding Community and of the contribution which it made to the religious life of the time. From our point of view it is difficult to exaggerate its importance.[20] Ferrar had known Donne in their common interest in the Virginia Plantation Company,[21] and he was, as we have seen, a great admirer of George Herbert. With the latter he enjoyed, indeed, a friendship that if it was not nourished by personal association, of which there is some doubt, was yet grounded in a mutual admiration and understanding that gave to a relation sustained mainly by letters the character of a very deep personal intimacy.[22] It was to Herbert that Ferrar gave credit for counsel and support in the venturesome days of the start of their community,[23] and it was to Ferrar that Herbert on his deathbed entrusted the fate of *The Temple*. So impressive is that relation that it is easy to overlook the fact that in spite of all their sympathy there were some very fundamental differences between Herbert and Ferrar. In the same way, great as was the debt of Crashaw, and many as are the ways in which Little Gidding ministered to his spiritual nourishment and fulfillment, Crashaw's whole religious orientation was, long before the crisis of 1644–45, quite different from Ferrar's.

All three men belong to the same movement in the English Church of the seventeenth century, share many of the same basic sympathies, react to the same problems, cherish in many respects the same values. Either friends or enemies might well view them, indeed, have viewed them, as representing different stages in the same development. There is much to justify this view of the matter, if care is taken not to make that line of development a straight line. To take for a beginning the test of Rome, it is very doubtful if even the rabidly suspicious Puritans who made life so heavy for Nicholas Ferrar would have called Herbert papist. His whole temper and pattern of life are obviously Anglican. On the other hand, it is incompatible with everything one knows of the life of Little Gidding that Mary Collet, if it was she who was with Crashaw in Leiden, should go with him to Rome. But most students are agreed today, whatever their personal judgment of the wisdom or the rightness of his final course, that in becoming a Catholic Crashaw was carrying to their logical conclusion tendencies present in his work almost from the beginning. Rome was his spiritual destiny. But for Herbert Rome had no immediate appeal. He was fully occupied and profoundly satisfied where he was. For Ferrar, on the other hand, Rome had a very real appeal. But the conviction that made him as a young man, when he was deeply and, as it was to prove, lastingly, impressed by Catholic life in Italy, resist all efforts at conversion, stayed with him to the end. In later years, he was to reassure one of his worried visitors at Little Gidding, Edward Lenton, that he held as seriously as any part of his creed the general Protestant conviction that the Pope was Antichrist.[24]

For Herbert the Via Media was an accomplished fact. Its temper was his peace, its limitations his assurance. With reason the modern High Churchman cites his regard for the comeliness of the church and its service, his finding the center of the House of God in the altar, his confidence in the authority of the Church, as a vindication of the seventeenth-century succession from Hooker to Andrewes to Laud. But it is not without significance that, as the late Professor Palmer pointed out some years ago, Herbert has found many of his most enthusiastic devotees in nonconformity.[25] The Bemerton parsonage is securely within the Protestant tradition, whatever may be said of some of the verses that were written in its library. Herbert was never disturbed by any of the uncertainties of the convert Donne as to where the true church was, nor was he ever tempted to look beyond her calm fields for nourishment for his spirit or for inspiration to his ways. Valdesso, who so aroused Ferrar's enthusiasm that he translated his *Divine Considerations,* made Herbert uneasy, and, we are inclined to think, from his point of view rightly so.[26] There is nothing of the eclectic about Herbert. It is not without result that, so far as we know, he never left his native shores. There is the peace of the engirdling seas in his placid unawareness of the charms and the perils of the religious life of the Continent. This does not mean, as we have seen, that he is immune to the prevailing preoccupations of Protestantism or to those subtler influences of the revivals of the inner life that were stirring France and Italy and Spain. But there is no division in his conscience, no sense of any force pulling him beyond himself. The Church of England is his life with an institutional completeness that for all his devotion to chapel and liturgy it never was for Crashaw.

While Herbert was under no temptation to pay homage to the Pope, one cannot imagine him saying, as Ferrar said, that the Pope was Antichrist. There is a certain deep-rooted, stubbornly entrenched Protestantism in Ferrar that is quite foreign to the temper of Herbert. As suggested above, it is probably not unconnected with his youthful resistance to efforts at conversion, and it was probably intensified by the somewhat ambiguous position the Little Gidding experiment was forced into by the curiosity of Catholics and the hostility of Puritans. But firmly rooted as Ferrar was in the center of his convictions, he was strongly and irresistibly pulled from that center. It is always tempting to guess at influences when there is so little direct evidence and so much indirect as in Ferrar's case. It is risky to say of any one purpose or practice of Little Gidding, "This is due to such and such in Ferrar's Italian experience," but there are so many things in the practices of Little Gidding that suggest what we know to have been features of that rich life of devotion and charity that Ferrar came into touch with in those months of his youthful sojourn at Milan and Padua and Venice that the conclusion of inspiration and suggestion seems inescapable.[27] The catechisings of Saint Charles Borromeo at Milan, the meetings for devotional and humanistic intercourse of the oratory at Padua and the confraternities of devotion at Florence, to name but a few of the most dramatic of the features of Italian religious life at the time of his sojourn in Italy, may well have inspired the famous Sunday Psalm children, the Little Academy, and other features of the religious practice of Little Gidding. The collections of books of devotion and of prints and pictures which Nicholas Ferrar brought back from his youthful travels, are a physical symbol of one of the salient facts in the religious life of Ferrar, the enrichment of his island Protestantism with the artistic and devotional spoils of Continental humanism.[28]

In that sense Ferrar and his community belong to the movement in contemporary European life, which the Abbé Brémond has so eloquently described as "devout humanism." But the debt of the Ferrars is deeper than that. The Puritan charge of popery which found its classic expression in the collection of distortions known as *The Arminian Nunnery* could discover abundant justification even in the superficial appearances. One can find the roster of their iniquities in one of the opening sentences, in which the suspicious visitor reports a conversation with Nicholas Ferrar at Little Gidding: "I first told him what I had heard of the *Nunns* at *Gidding;* of *two watching and praying all night;* of their *Canonicall houres;* of their *Crosses* on the outside and inside of the *Chappell;* of an Altar richly decked with *Tapestry, Plate,* and *Tapers;* of their *Adorations, genuflections,* and *geniculations,* which I told them plainly might strongly savour of Superstition and Popery." [29]

In that inclusive sentence are comprehended the main charges of the Puritan party against Little Gidding: monasticism, extra-Scriptural religious observances, idolatrous decorations, superstitious practices. But though these stock charges are all delivered with fervor and conventional reprobation, it is clear that two features of the Community of Little Gidding beyond all others roused the indignation of the anonymous author. The

first is to be seen in the title, the abhorred name of "nun."
Ferrar expressed horror of the name of nun and of anything like
vows, but he encouraged his two nieces to continue in their
resolutions of a single life, and he never married himself.[30] But
though the unknown author of *The Arminian Nunnery* in his
choice of title and in the title-page picture of a nun holding a
chaplet of beads was clearly making the strongest appeal he
could to Protestant prejudice, there was another facet of the
matter that even more profoundly awakened his personal indignation. "Oh the stupid and blind devotion of these people,
for Men and Women in health of able and active bodies and
parts to have no particular *Callings,* or to quit their *Callings,*
and betake themselves to I wot not what new forme of *Fasting*
and *Prayer,* and a contemplative idle life, a lip-labour devotion,
and a will-worship, *Eccl. 4 & 17.* which by the word of God is
no better than a specious kind of idlenesse, as *St. Augustine*
termes them to be but *splendida peccata:* as if diligence in our
particular lawfull callings were no part of our service to God.[31]

There the unknown author, for all his distortion and inac-
curacy, puts his finger with a good deal of precision on the central issue. The very fact of this group retirement from the
business of the world, this living in community for the purposes
of religious exercise, this making of religious service the main
order of the day, and of the night, as this author noted with
fresh indignation ("They have promiscuous private Prayers all
the night long by nightly turnes, just as the English *Nunnes* at
Saint *Omers* and other Popish places"),[32] meant that Nicholas
Ferrar had moved out of the life of Protestantism into that of
Catholicism. This would alone be enough to account for
Puritan hostility to Little Gidding, for in this revival of monasticism, in however limited a form, Nicholas Ferrar was out-
raging Protestant sentiment at a point where in England, at
least, it had been richly cultivated. But in his approaches to
the contemplative life as well, he was running counter to the

whole practice and temper of the English Renaissance and of nascent Puritanism, in which, as perhaps never before, the social and practical characteristics of the English genius were most richly vindicated. Certainly, the contemplative emphasis of the Little Gidding Community belongs to the Counter-Reformation rather than to the Reformation.

But here again, even in his most sensational deviations from Protestant tradition to Catholic, Nicholas Ferrar keeps to the spirit and orientation of Protestantism much more profoundly than appears on the surface. For if he encouraged the resolution of his nieces to a single life, it was in an essentially patriarchal framework. The Community of Little Gidding, for all it numbered in its prime some forty souls, was essentially a household. The Ferrar family was that household under the rule of the mother of John and Nicholas Ferrar, and those members of the household who were not Ferrars by birth or marriage were attached to it either as schoolmasters or as servants.[33] John Ferrar left on record that thousands came to visit the community,[34] and from more than one source we know that various members of the neighboring Cambridge colleges were accustomed to ride over to share in its devotions, but there is nothing to indicate that one not a Ferrar or attached to the immediate service of the family ever became a member of the community.

Moreover, the younger members of the family were educated to go forth from Little Gidding and take their place in the world in homes of their own, and, almost without exception, those who lived to be old enough to marry did so.[35] The Virgin Sisters remained, though, after the founder, the main objects of dramatic interest in the community, the exception rather than the rule. And though the center of their life was religious observance of a more extensive and specialized type than was usual in that age of devout women, still the main lines of their activity are to be found in the teaching of country children, in the care of their household, in the preparation and the dispensing of medicines, and the care of the sick, in music and needlework, in other words, in the traditional activities of women of piety and intelligence of their class.[36] In general, the difference is in the quality of their charitable activity rather than in the type.

Two of their activities do, however, take them out of the class of women like Lettice, Viscountess Falkland, and these two are the bookmaking for which Little Gidding was famous [37] and the activities of the Little Academy.[38] The beautiful concordances, illustrated with prints from Flanders, France and Italy, represent in their exquisite taste and skill something of the medieval bookmaker's combination of craft and art. As for the meetings of the Little Academy, they suggest the influence of those assemblies of devout laymen which Philip Neri gathered in the Oratory at Rome.[39] And in the materials of those discussions as they have come down to us, there is much to suggest the Continental interest in stories of saint and martyr. Not only the Protestant witnesses to the faith who inspired the widespread devotion of the time to Foxe's *Book of Martyrs*, but the martyrs of the early Church who enjoyed so wide and enthusiastic a revival in the martyr cult of the time in Catholic countries are represented in the stories.[40] So are various noble men and women whose words and examples, quite within the scope of secular life, instruct and edify. There is much in these stories to suggest the devout humanism of the time in France, that combination of a desire to edify with a tenderness for the human love of entertainment to which some of the French leaders like Camus ministered so shrewdly and elegantly.[41] And one of the central theses of the martyr cult, that one which is so reminiscent of the debates of the ancient Stoics as to the possibilities of the good man's maintaining his peace of soul in the most trying circumstances, namely, that the martyr is sustained in the midst of torture by the sweetness of divine grace, finds clear and even drastic expression in one of the comments which the "Mother" contributes to that collection of martyr stories with which the group beguiled Christmastide of 1632, "He that lies broyling on a Gridiron in others eies, lies in his owne Conceit upon a Bed of Pleasure." [42] In general, however, the emphasis of these stories is moralistic, with their stress upon the stoutness of heart of the witness rather than upon the detailed experience of martyrdom with its ecstasies and its agonies.

There is the same mingling of diverse elements in what has been recorded of their devotions. The reading at meals, the visits in procession to the chapel, the services twice daily, the nightly watchings, the decoration of the chapel with needlework and flowers and candles, and the formal obeisances with which Nicholas Ferrar himself advanced to the reading desk, all of these suggest to us, as they did to contemporary visitors, the pattern of Catholic monastic observance. [43] But if one examines more closely into the material of these devotions, it becomes clear that here again Ferrar has been availing himself of the resources of Catholic life without basically departing from his central Protestant position. For where he goes beyond the patterns for service available in the Prayer Book, to which like Herbert he was so warmly attached, he is apt to keep pretty close to the Psalter and the hymns which had long been consecrated by Protestant custom. The object of those frequent meetings in chapel and "Upper Room," even of the night watchings, which are the most dramatic of his liturgical innovations, seems to have been divine service in the usual Anglican sense rather than anything of contemplation or mysticism. [44]

This does not mean that there was not a certain vein of mysticism in Ferrar's own nature. The asceticism which during his mother's lifetime expressed itself in a preference for sparingness of diet and sleep, on his mother's death seems to have intensified into something of the Catholic passion for mortification,[45] a passion not unknown among Puritans but more characteristic of mystics of the Counter-Reformation. His basic passion for retirement and solitude both belong to the world of the mystics, without in themselves being exclusively or necessarily mystical. But in general, Ferrar is the loyal and convinced Protestant whose tastes and capacities have led him to look beyond the circle of his own beliefs and habits, and whose passion for realizing the fullest possibilities of his faith has led him to lay hold upon any instrument or stimulus to life that he has come upon. In so doing he often departed from the lines and restrictions of his fellow churchmen, but whatever he took he made his own, and the temper of that transmutation is essentially that of the English Church of his time. In all he did or said there is something of the clean, airy, plain atmosphere of that house in the fields and gardens at Little Gidding. Even his most exotic undertakings are informed by the same paramount love of decency and sobriety. However many of the currents of the Counter-Reformation find their way through those quiet parlors and gardens, the result is essentially English, and for tone and temper Protestant in what seemed to him the reasonable, moderate fashion of the church in which he lived and died.

It has seemed worth while to dwell thus at length on the character and direction of the life at Little Gidding, for there is no question of the influence which this community exerted on the sensitive and earnest young son of the in many ways Puritan William Crashaw. But the extent of that influence is to be found in the encouragement it gave to Crashaw in his love of religious observance, in his affection for the beauty of the House of the Lord. It might open the imagination to possibilities beyond anything Crashaw had ever known in the church of his father and cultivate tastes and interests not appreciated even at Bemerton, but of itself it will not alone account for the direction which his genius took.

Other influences must be reckoned with. The first is to be sought in his contacts at Cambridge. The new chapel at Peterhouse, which in the richness and the character of its ornament was to stimulate such vigorous iconoclasm on the part of the Parliamentary forces, was begun in 1632 and consecrated in March of 1634.[46] We know that Crashaw later was to appeal for help toward its decoration and that he was himself to contribute to its furnishing.[47] Probably from the beginning he followed its advance with that keen anxiety for its comeliness and delight in its embellishment that one would expect from an habitué of Little Gidding. Cosin, to whom Crashaw is said to have owed his eventual appointment to a fellowship at that college in 1635,[48] became the head of Peterhouse in 1634. Like Lany, the head of Pembroke, to whom Crashaw dedicated his first publication of verse, Cosin was one of the leaders of the High Church party of the period, and he used his influence to intensify the already existent anti-Puritanism and High Anglicanism of the College. Therefore, when, probably toward the end of 1635, Crashaw came into residence at Peterhouse, he came into immediate contact with one of the centers of Catholic influence in the Church of his time.[49] That it would prove a congenial atmosphere we can be sure from the prevailing tone of the Latin epigrams which Crashaw had already published in 1634, the year in which he received his first degree. And his enthusiasm for the embellishment of the chapel is but one evidence of the zest with which he entered into the life of the place.

The fellowship itself is sufficient witness to the success of his university career. But it would seem likely that the reputation as a wit, as one of the famous wits of the English nation, antedates his reputation as a saint.[50] The precocity of his verse, the independence and resolution of spirit apparent in his early announcement of his allegiance to the sacred muse, have already been noticed. The perfection of his extensive linguistic attainments (he seems to have been in varying degrees master of five languages, Greek, Latin, Hebrew, French, Spanish, Italian) [51] must in part belong to these university years. And at some time during these years he must have been ordained, although there seems to be no record of the ceremony now in existence. But the fact seems beyond question.[52] Queen Henrietta Maria, in the famous letter in which she recommends the converted Crashaw to the attention of the Pope, says expressly that he had been "ministre" in England, and there is every reason to think that on such a point in such circumstances she would have been correctly informed.[53] Both Walker and Lord Chalmers without giving their evidence say categorically that Crashaw was curate and catechist at Little Saint Mary's, and this conclusion is supported by the traditional references to Crashaw's connection with Little Saint Mary's, and by Mr. Warren's discovery of Crashaw's election by the Fellows of Peterhouse as "Catechista & Curatus Ecclesiasticus" on April 15, 1642, and of various records of his catechising activities in village churches at that time having some sort of connection with Peterhouse.[54] Mr. Warren's discovery undoubtedly explains why only three pupils were assigned to Crashaw when Ferrar Collet came to Peterhouse.[55] And it gives still further plausibility to what Lloyd has to say of the popularity of Crashaw's preaching in his *Memoires* of 1668. "Philosophy," says Lloyd, "came as plausible from him as his Speeches or Sermons; those thronged Sermons on each Sunday and Holiday, that ravished more like Poems." [56] It is possible, of course, that Lloyd had confused the two Crashaws, especially in view of the thoroughly attested reputation of the elder as a forceful and admired preacher. But it is more likely from the terms in which he speaks that he had not. In that case, it is quite possible that if we could see some of Crashaw's sermons, we should have very seriously to revise the impression as to Crashaw's mental quality and intellectual interests that has been frequent among critics who have been more impressed by the rhapsodic character of his poetry than the intellectual. But all this is matter of conjecture.

We have more light on the progress of his religious opinions and the influences which shaped them. The dedication of the *Epigrammata Sacra* to Benjamin Lany, the Master of Pembroke, is quite explicit as to the intimacy that had subsisted between teacher and student.[57] Lany is said to have begun life with opinions not unlike those of the senior Crashaw, who was a friend of his, but he had in the course of the years moved to a position of opposition to the Puritans and support of the High Church group, of which he was now, indeed, one of the leaders at Cambridge.[58] The tribute to Andrewes of 1631, though in no sense expressing any doctrinal commitments, like the later tribute to Herbert's verse, is significant for the light it throws on the loyalties of the young theological student.[59] The plea for help for the adornment of the chapel of Peterhouse bears witness to the taste for church ornamentation and liturgy [60] that one would expect from the Little Gidding association. The most explicit of all of Crashaw's allusions to the troubles of the times, "An Epitaph upon Mr. Ashton, a conformable Citizen," cannot, in default of any positive identification of the subject, be certainly assigned to a date much earlier than that of its publication, 1646, but the reprobation of emphasis upon maintenance of doctrine of the Puritans, the satire of the tenderness of conscience that was the main plea of what Crashaw's group regarded as recalcitrancy to law and order, and the praise of the "conformable citizen" of whom the poet says:

> To th'Church hee did allow her Dresse,
> True *Beauty*, to true *Holinesse*,[61]

are all in the spirit of the group. And this impression is borne out by the character of the Latin epigrams themselves. Of the preoccupation with sin, the reassurances that Christ with his blood has ransomed sinners, the anxiety about the possession of faith, the placations of wrath, that are to be found in the verses of even a Herbert, there is almost nothing. Practically all the *Epigrammata,* as Lord Chalmers has pointed out, are based on the Gospels or Acts,[62] and while they are full of that semi-moralizing reflection that was considered the proper conclusion of Scripture reading at that time, their most striking characteristic is the effort to bring closer to the contemporary imagination the human aspects of Our Lord's life, and to realize the pictorial and dramatic possibilities of the Scriptural narrative.

The characteristic spirit of most of Crashaw's later work is to be discerned even in the earliest of his poems, notably in the epigram on Luke 18. 41, "Quid vis tibi faciam?' with its striking beginning:

> *Quid volo (Christe) rogas? quippe ah volo, Christe, videre:*
> *Quippe ah te (dulcis Christe) videre volo,*[63]

translated by Grosart:

> Askest, O Christ, my wish? My Christ, I wish to see:
> To see Thee, O my sweet Christ, to see Thee.[64]

Much the same thing is true of Crashaw's imaginative approach to his theme. For the highly characteristic treatment of the crucified Christ in his lines "Upon the Bleeding Crucifix" of 1646[65] is to be seen as early as 1634 in his Latin verses, "Vulnera Dei pendentis,"[66] with their equally characteristic indebtedness to Marino.[67]

At the same time it is quite apparent in the first work of Crashaw that he is still a long way from Rome. It is not certain that the rather heavy verses on the Gunpowder Treason, usually ascribed to him, are his (the first two sets seem to the present writer quite unlike Crashaw, and the third set very much like him),[68] but there is no mistaking the satiric ending to the epigram on Acts 5. 15,

O Petri umbra potens! quae non miracula praestat?
Nunc quoque, Papa, tuum sustinet illa decus,[69]

translated by Grosart:

> From Peter's shadow what may we not hope,
> Now all thy glory it sustains, O Pope! [70]

And still clearer are the implications of the ending of the address to Lany which dedicated to him the *Epigrammata Sacra*. Not the least dramatic is the protest against the slavishness with which England, despising her own voice, "only prizes those things to which having crossed the Alps and lived over the sea has given a value!" [71] a curious state of mind for one who was so preëminently to draw his spiritual nutriment from over the sea. Striking, too, are the terms in which he describes his resistance to some recent efforts at Jesuit propaganda, a resistance delivered apparently in very vigorous Anglican terms.[72]

But more insidious propaganda even than that of the Jesuits was to lay siege to Crashaw, and that within the apparently secure circle of his friends. The evidence of this is to be found in the poem "On a Treatise of Charity," which was first published in 1635 with Robert Shelford's *Five Pious and Learned Discourses*.[73] This work is something of a landmark in the theological developments of the period by reason of its fifth treatise, in which Shelford maintains that Antichrist has not yet come, in that claim undermining one of the strongholds of the Protestant attack on Rome. For Protestant polemics had been wont to find all the Scriptural marks of Antichrist in the Pope, and, therefore, in the Biblical passages on that picturesque theme a seemingly inexhaustible arsenal of vituperation. It is no wonder that James Ussher writes to a friend from Ireland, "The Jesuits of England sent over the book hither to confirm our papists in their obstinacy, and to assure them that we are now coming home to them as fast as we can." [74] But although

Crashaw in some mildly satiric passages on the Puritans takes cognizance of Shelford's pleas for decorum in church, it is clear both from the title of Crashaw's verses and from the points he takes for departure in his handling of the theme that the thing that most impressed him in the whole book was the second discourse, "A Sermon preferring holy Charity before Faith, Hope, and Knowledge." The main thesis of Shelford expressed in his quotation of "Knowledge puffeth up, but Charitie edifieth" [75] was one to commend itself even to the Crashaw of the epigrams. For he had learned early the truth of what Shelford went on to explain, "Faith converts the minde to God: but it is love and charitie that converts the heart and will to God, which is the greatest and last conversion, because we never seek anything untill we desire it." [76] The consequences which Shelford draws from this principle are to be seen in what he says by way of defence of the Sacraments of Baptism and Communion: "These Sacraments do that for us that all the preachers of the land cannot do . . . these preachers the Sacraments, besides the light which they give to our understanding, infuse, through Christs power and effectuall ordinance, grace into our souls, and make us acceptable before God." [77] The most interesting thing about Shelford's treatise from the spiritual point of view is the stress which it puts upon the affective aspects of religious life, which the age had in general either neglected or taken too much for granted. The realization of the importance of these emotional elements is of the first consequence for Crashaw's religious development. It would, I think, be a mistake to assume that he caught this from Shelford, but the presence of spiritual influences like that of the treatise of Shelford in his own milieu (Shelford was an M.A. of Peterhouse) is significant for Crashaw's development, especially at this period of his life.

Another important element in Crashaw's spiritual environment at this time, or only a little later, is to be found in the possibility of a congenial group of spirits at Cambridge who shared his taste for devotional literature of a warmer and more colorful type than that usually available in the Church of England of the time. The clue is to be found in a Latin oration of Crashaw's friend and intimate, Joseph Beaumont, the poet, delivered at Cambridge in 1638. In this oration, discoursing glowingly on the range of humane studies, the young Beaumont singles out St. Teresa for "special and rapturous encomium," "Sancta est TERESA, nomen vobis inauditum, credo, et Angelis magis familiare quam hominibus nostris." Mr. Warren, who discovered this oration in a manuscript volume, "A collection of my R. Father's Latin Speeches," which Joseph's son Charles presented to Peterhouse, believes that the phrase quoted above suggests that "Beaumont or Beaumont and his little circle of 'Arminian' and mystically-minded friends had just discovered the Saint." And he concludes very justly that if Beaumont knew of the saint at this period, Crashaw did too.[78] The present writer would certainly agree with Mr. Warren's conclusion, but would also suggest that the possibility of Crashaw's having already known of Teresa should not be overlooked. The canonization of Saint Teresa in 1622 had aroused wide interest in her life and work. And with reading habits formed in his father's library and encouraged by the collections of Continental books of devotion at Little Gidding, it would not be surprising if Crashaw had early come to know of the great Carmelite. But even if he had been familiar with the life and writings of Teresa before this, Beaumont's reference is of great value for its indication that at this time Crashaw would not be alone in his tastes at Cambridge.

The external evidences as to Crashaw's career for the next few years are, as for most of his life, meager. There is evidence in his poems of the interest with which he followed public affairs, especially the fortunes of the King. Crashaw may, indeed, have known the King. Certainly, he had a personal interest in

him, quite apart from the loyalty habitual with his party, for
as early as 1633 Charles had been at Little Gidding and had
since given substantial evidences of his interest in and regard
for that enterprise.[79]

Anthony à Wood records that an anonymous informant told
him that in 1641 Crashaw was incorporated a member of Oxford University. The fact, if it could be established, would be
important, suggesting as it does a growing reputation. But the
only confirmation is the Queen's use of the plural in speaking
of his university education in the letter to the Pope already referred to. And the honor may have been paid to Crashaw on
the occasion of a later visit.[80] But this is not of much importance
in view of the deepening crisis brought about by the rise of
the Puritan party to power. The bitterly Puritan satire of *The
Arminian Nunnery* would have grieved Crashaw in 1641. In
1642 he was, we know, one of the small group of Peterhouse
fellows who guaranteed a loan to the King.[81]

Early in 1643 he must have left Cambridge, for Mr. Warren
in his study of the buttery book has found that the last special
charge to Crashaw for diet is dated the week of January 20,
1643.[82] This conclusion is confirmed by the fact that in March
of that year Ferrar Collet signed for the receipt of a sum of
money which the college owed Crashaw.[83] He thus anticipated
by nearly a year the visit of the Parliamentary Commissioners
to Peterhouse, and he was spared the pain of witnessing the
spoliation of his beloved chapel by the Parliamentary Commissioners on December 20 and 23 of 1643.[84]

The court had been in residence at the town of Oxford from
July of 1643, and it is not unlikely that Crashaw like many
other Royalist sympathizers joined it. It has been suggested
that it was at this time that Crashaw was made a member of
the rival university, but again there is no evidence. Indeed, the
first certain date for this period is that of February, 1644, when
from the famous letter which he wrote from Leiden to a friend

in England we know that he was in that city, but recently parted from "my mother." [85] That letter is of peculiar interest for several reasons, chief among them the light it sheds on his circumstances and state of mind at this time. But suggestive as it is, there is something peculiarly elusive about it whenever matters of fact are alluded to. The absence of proper names is, of course, not surprising in a letter from one intimate friend to another. But it is hard to account for the almost studied vagueness of its statements. The writer is obviously eager to be understood by the person to whom he is writing, and yet he never seems quite to come to the point. Now that is not the usual habit of Crashaw's mind even in the least simple of his poems. It is almost as if Crashaw were afraid that his letter might fall into hands where specific information would make trouble (it may simply be that he does not want to seem to resign his fellowship unless it will do his candidate some good).

Certain facts emerge pretty clearly from Mr. Martin's admirable analysis of the letter.[86] Crashaw has been in Holland for some little time, at first, apparently, in close touch with if not actually resident with "his mother," who can hardly be anybody but Mary Collet, the niece of Nicholas Ferrar and the "mother" of the Little Academy at Little Gidding, but for two months now he has been forbidden to see her, apparently at the instance of her relatives rather than from any unwillingness of hers. He does not want to give up his fellowship (he must still be at least uncertain as to whether he will go to Rome, if the issue has even arisen), he is still hoping for the restoration of the King which he is confident "wilbe likewise a Restitution of all things," [87] but he realizes that this restoration may be some time in coming.[88] While one must always make allowances for the exaggerations of contemporary courtesy in the letters of the time, especially letters to anyone in a superior position (as the recipient of this letter is obviously, at least to the extent that he is an older man), still there seems no question that Crashaw has been badly distressed by this denial of his "mother's" company. At the same time he is in considerable uncertainty as to plans. Leiden is plainly too materialistic, too much given over to Mammon, to suit him. There is some possible suggestion of a monastic life in the phrase "severer courses," but we cannot be sure. His clinging to his fellowship would seem to preclude any formed decision in that direction. And, for all we can tell, the letter may concern simply his uncertainty as to where he is to turn to now that he is exiled from his "little contenfull kingdom." [89] But in view of what happened so soon after, it is tempting to think that he was hesitating between the two churches in these months when as he tells us, "I am so wretched that I am sometimes even carefull for some meanes whereby to maintaine my travells so as to keep me up from a necessity of engagement whethersoever I goe." [90]

The next sure date in Crashaw's life reveals him as now for some time a Catholic. That is the Queen's letter, dated September 7, 1646.[91] More than two and a half years have elapsed. What has happened during that time? If we can take the statements of the Queen's letter seriously, he has been living near her for about a year. That would mean that he had arrived in Paris toward the end of 1645. But the Queen says expressly that, having been converted by his reading and study, he had come to Paris from England to enjoy the freer exercise of his faith. That suggests that he had been in England again after the Leiden letter, say late in 1644 or early in 1645, when he may well have been at Oxford where the court was. Sometime then between early in 1644 and late in 1645 he became a Catholic. There is at least a year and a half for which no account of any sort can be given, and at any time during that period he may have taken the final step.

The reasons for that decision are to be sought, I think, not in further guessing about matters on which we have no evidence, but in looking at what was happening in the world he had left. We have no reason to believe that before the crisis of 1643 Crashaw had ever suffered any uncertainty as to which was the right church. There is nothing to suggest that the doubts that tortured Donne ever disturbed him. From the beginning his interest was, so far as we can judge, not in theological speculation or in questions of order and government, not in institutional problems at all. He had, it is true, very definite convictions as against the Puritans, whose tenets bore heavily on his delight in liturgy and music and comely behavior in church service, all of which he valued as the instruments of worship. But there is not much evidence in his work as a whole of that attachment to the ordered life of the Church that is so marked in Herbert. It is significant that even after his own conversion, when he is urging his patroness and friend the Countess of Denbigh to join his newly found church, when if ever, in a convert's enthusiasm, he might be expected to have something to say on the much-mooted differences between the two communions, he has nothing to say of doctrinal tenets, of issues or principles of allegiance.[92] He simply urges his friend to end delaying about what she is going to do any way and admit her Lord into her heart. He reminds her that it is perilous to hesitate in so vital a matter. But in his tactics, in the considerations which he advances for such a step, there is nothing different in kind from the arguments he used in his Anglican days when trying to persuade a young lady to whom he had sent a prayer book to embrace a life of piety as against a life of worldly vanity.[93]

The reason is probably that he had himself known very little change in point of view. The question of homage to the Virgin will do as well as anything else for a test in the matter of Catholic feeling in the seventeenth century. Herbert once expressed the High Anglican point of view of his time rather well when he explained to the Virgin that he would like to pay tribute to her, but that the fact that the Word of God did not

enjoin such devotion deterred him.[94] If we can trust Car's report in the complimentary verses which he prefixed to the
edition of 1652, Crashaw even in his Protestant days was so distinguished for his devotion to the Mother of Christ that he was
styled "the chaplaine of the virgine myld." [95]

He would be a rash man, indeed, who would undertake to tell
which of Crashaw's poems were written while he was still among
the Protestants and which after his change of allegiance. Perhaps the most significant difference to be noted is that the
Protestant Crashaw chose to translate Marino while the
Catholic turned to Saint Thomas, but it must be acknowledged
that even in the translations from Saint Thomas and the great
medieval hymn-writers, as Miss Wallerstein has pointed out,
the stylistic influence of Marino is still powerful.[96] Probably,
the explanation of this marked continuity is to be found in that
apology for the hymn to Saint Teresa which the edition of 1648
tells us was written when the author was still among the
Protestants. It is significant that it is not the "popery" of his
theme for which the poet apologizes but the "Spanishness"
of it.[97] Crashaw, whom T. S. Eliot once described as "primarily
a European," [98] is the last man to suspect of undue nationalism,
but it is more than possible that in those early years it was the
reflection that his was the Church of England that satisfied any
passing doubt which his Jesuit friends might have been able to
insinuate into that otherwise preoccupied mind and imagination. For him the Church was the aid, the means to the richer
worship of and communion with his Lord. That means he had
found in the chapel and oratory of Little Gidding and in the
chapel of Peterhouse and the church of Little Saint Mary's.
When he saw those cherished instruments of his devotion in
jeopardy, Crashaw apparently did not wait to be excluded
from his fellowship. And when they were swept away, it was
only logical that the new institutional life which denied his
deepest intuitions and condemned his profoundest insights

should no longer seem to him the church in which he could find his Lord and Master. Nor is it surprising that he should turn to the church in the writings of whose saints and poets he had long ago found help and congenial company in his endeavor to draw closer to his God.

This does not mean that the ejection from Peterhouse was not important. But it could hardly have been unexpected. The fears which the growing strife between King and Parliament raised in all peace-loving breasts must have been sadly reenforced by the discussions which preceded the loan to the King in 1642, and they must have seemed to be finally fulfilled in the desecration of Peterhouse Chapel by the Parliamentary Commissioners in December of 1643. Yet terrible as was his distress of mind when he wrote the letter from Leiden in February of 1644, he could still hope that the restoration of the King would put all right. It may well have been the news of the beheading of Archbishop Laud in January of 1645 that put an end to that hope.

The story of Crashaw's life as a Catholic is soon told. The Queen's letter seems to have brought no immediate notice, at least of any substantial character, from the Pope, and for a year Crashaw would seem to have been destitute.[99] Then in 1647 he is found by an English visitor, in the service of Cardinal Palotto, apparently a worthy master for such a follower. Difficulty with the Cardinal's entourage (Crashaw is said to have been so shocked by the behavior of some of his fellow servants that he complained to their master) led to the appreciative Cardinal's finding Crashaw a minor post in the House of Loreto in 1649. But a fever that he caught on the way ended his life only a few months after his arrival, on August twenty-first of that year.[100] There is, however, no reason to think that if he had lived longer, his life at Loreto would have been essentially different in its main objectives and methods from his life at Peterhouse and Little Saint Mary's.

It would have been interesting to see what the full and immediate realization of the possibilities that had already been adumbrated in spiritual reading and intercourse with chosen spirits in his English life would have proved in a world completely penetrated and dominated by Catholic tradition. As suggested above, the present writer is inclined to believe that his turning to the great Latin hymns of Thomas Aquinas and Thomas of Celano and Jacopone da Todi is not without its significance as to the development of his mind and feeling. But more than this we shall probably never know. In any case we may be sure that what Mr. Eliot says of his poetry has its bearings on his religious experience. Crashaw's was, as Mr. Eliot points out, a singularly homogeneous and mature genius. What we have lost by his premature death is probably no new manifestation of that genius, at least in kind.[101] What he would have written further would probably have been of the same type as that in which he had already achieved mastery. But the quality of the additions to the great Saint Teresa poems to be found in the edition of 1652 shows that Crashaw could still surpass himself even in his own field of ecstasy.

Chapter IX

RICHARD CRASHAW: "POET AND SAINT"

As for the degree and the extent to which Crashaw's powers did develop during the modest span of working years that were his, it is not easy to form a judgment because of the obvious difficulty of dating his work. The lapse of time between the publication of his first volume, the *Epigrammata Sacra* of 1634 and the *Steps to the Temple* of 1646, is considerable. With the exception of a few poems like his translation of the first book of the *Sospetto d'Herode,* which can be dated 1637, the majority of these poems are scattered over what is relatively too long a time for us to say anything very precise about the particular stage of development which any one represents. When the number and extent of the revisions between the edition of 1646 (the changes of 1648 are comparatively few) and that of 1652 is considered, two possibilities are open to us: either the editor of the 1646 edition did not have access to much of the latest of Crashaw's work or Crashaw did, comparatively speaking, a good deal of writing between 1646 and 1649. Probably both suppositions are true, but the large part played in this new work by translations of Latin hymns and liturgy rather confirms the latter.

Lord Chalmers has pointed out a development of Crashaw's work that is perhaps more properly to be described as a change in direction and concentration of interest rather than in point of view or capacity. The first volume of Crashaw's work, the *Epigrammata Sacra,* published in 1634, is, he reminds us,

wholly Latin and wholly sacred.[1] This concentration is probably due to the relation which Mr. Warren has seen between
these early poems and the poet's school and university exercises,[2] but whatever its cause, it is striking. The second
volume, *Steps to the Temple,* published in 1646, and again,
with additions, in 1648, is mingled humane and sacred, with
only one-seventh of its contents in Latin. *The Delights of the
Muses* of 1646, republished with additions in 1648, is likewise
sacred and profane, and roughly two-thirds English and one-
third Latin. The *Carmen Deo Nostro* of 1652 is exclusively
sacred and English. In other words, secular poetry and Latin
poetry are discarded. This, thinks Lord Chalmers, was a
deliberate and self-conscious process.[3] If Crashaw's European
connections are kept in mind, it is possible to discern in this
development a miniature of what had taken place in France
over a much more extended period. The first volume might
be taken to represent schoolboy piety, the second devout
humanism, shading already in the Teresa poems into mysticism,
the third, mysticism.[4] And the abandonment of the learned
language for the vernacular might represent the mature artist's
recognition of the fact that his gift was for English not Latin
poetry, and the mystic's effort to present as directly as possible
the experience of the heart. The fact of this change, however,
is the important thing.

But whatever evidences of change or growth the eye of the
critic may discern in the successive volumes of Crashaw's work,
the fact remains that from the young man's first defence of the
propriety of poetry for the theological student and of sacred
poetry against the world, Crashaw's work is homogeneous to an
extraordinary degree. It is essentially the same man singing on
the same themes to the same ends. It is for that reason that
considerations of date play so small a part in the study of
Crashaw's work that for practical purposes they can be disregarded.

Pretty much the same thing is true with regard to the development of his basic religious ideas. Whatever his specific church allegiance, his controlling religious attitudes are the same. His idea of God, to go at once to the center, is, from the start and throughout, the idea of a God very different from Donne's, and even from Herbert's. The God of wrath about whom Donne so movingly sought to reassure himself plays even less part in the thought of Crashaw than of Herbert. The most extended presentation of this familiar seventeenth-century deity is to be found in a poem that significantly enough is put into the lips of "Our Lord in his Circumcision to his Father." The audacity with which these lines treat the wrath of God would be blasphemous if represented as uttered by any but divine lips. For the traditional conception that the blood shed at the circumcision of Christ is but the first drops of the mighty shedding of the Passion is here taken up by the Son who hurls it like a challenge at the Father:

> Thy wrath that wades heere now, e're long shall swim
> The flood-gate shall be set wide ope for him.
> Then let him drinke, and drinke, and doe his worst,
> To drowne the wantonnesse of his wild thirst.[5]

Except for a passage like this, the God of wrath and justice has vanished from Crashaw's mind. It is the God who could not bear to abandon his creature to the misery of his own willfulness that fills the thoughts of Crashaw. Nothing could be in sharper contrast to the fear of Donne than the wonder with which "Charitas Nimia, or the Dear Bargain" begins:

> Lord, what is man? why should he coste thee
> So dear? what had his ruin lost thee?
> Lord what is man? that thou hast overbought
> So much a thing of nought?[6]

It occurred to Herbert once to wonder how the Passion of Christ seemed to the Sufferer himself, and the result he expressed in the somewhat stiff but moving lines of "The Sacrifice" with the piercing refrain, "Was ever grief like Mine?" But Crashaw goes farther back than that, back, indeed, of the prevailing theology of the time, which in the main held Herbert, to wonder about the primal pity that prompted that gracious and terrible undertaking. Another passage from "Charitas Nimia" begins familiarly enough with that splendor of dust so characteristic of the poets of the time, but as it proceeds, it passes quite beyond the limits of the time into that world of primitive speculation which the age for the most part avoided:

> Let froward Dust then doe it's kind;
> And give it self for sport to the proud wind.
> Why should a peice of peevish clay plead shares
> In the Æternity of thy old cares?
> Why shouldst thou bow thy awfull Brest to see
> What mine own madnesses have done with me?
>
> Should not the king still keepe his throne
> Because some desperate Fool's undone?
> Or will the world's Illustrious eyes
> Weep for every worm that dyes.[7]

This same wonder everywhere penetrates Crashaw's thought of the Incarnation. For him that was the central fact in the world's history. Not that Christ had died for man to satisfy God's justice and redeem his elect, but that God should have come into the world, stooping his glory to the meanness of earth, adding to his ancient cares the littleness of human life. Crashaw may have owed a good deal of his profound realization of this element in his religious faith to Marino,[8] but there

is no question of the personal ardor that invests his expression
of it even in a translation like that of the following passage
from the first book of the *Sospetto d'Herode* of Marino in
1637:

> How a pure Spirit should incarnate bee,
> And life it selfe weare Deaths fraile Livery.
>
> That the Great Angell-blinding light should shrinke
> His blaze, to shine in a poore Shepheards eye.
> That the unmeasur'd God so low should sinke,
> As Pris'ner in a few poore Rags to lye.
> That from his Mothers Brest hee milke should drinke,
> Who feeds with Nectar Heav'ns faire family.
>   That a vile Manger his low bed should prove,
>   Who in a Throne of stars Thunders above.
>
> That hee whom the Sun serves, should faintly peepe
> Through clouds of Infant flesh: that hee the old
> Eternall Word should bee a Child, and weepe.
> That hee who made the fire, should feare the cold;
> That Heav'ns high Majesty his Court should keepe
> In a clay-cottage, by each blast control'd.
>   That Glories selfe should serve our Griefs, & feares:
>   And free Eternity, submit to yeares.[9]

At first, thinking over this wonder, Crashaw seems to have
been most impressed by the condescension of Glory to the
misery of his creatures. But as this central theme of his
religious experience grew in loving contemplation, something
of the deep warmth of his own nature came to invest that
wonder. It has been said that we all tend to make God in our
own image. Perhaps, rather, as Saint John of the Cross once
put it, God is a well from which we may each draw according
to the measure of our capacity and in the kind of our sympathy.[10] At any rate when Crashaw wrote his famous letter

to the Countess of Denbigh, the passion of God for the soul of
his creature had assumed for him something of the startling
urgency which Francis Thompson was later to seize upon so
dramatically in the basic figure of *The Hound of Heaven:*

> When love of Us call'd Him to see
> If wee'd vouchsafe his company,
> He left his Father's Court, and came
> Lightly as a Lambent Flame,
> Leaping upon the Hills, to be
> The Humble King of You and Me.
> Nor can the cares of his whole Crown
> (When one poor Sigh sends for him down)
> Detain him, but he leaves behind
> The late wings of the lazy Wind,
> Spurns the tame Laws of Time and Place,
> And breaks through all ten Heav'ns to our embrace.[11]

Indeed, as Bernard of Clairvaux had already put it on behalf
of all the mystics, "he is loved who already loves." [12]

The human love which tries to rise to this divine love is, as
we shall see in a moment, a correspondingly lofty and radiant
love, but it is grounded in a very simple and direct intimacy
of feeling. The beginning of one of the songs is significant of
this approach:

> Lord, when the sense of thy sweet grace
> Sends up my soul to seek thy face.[13]

The same note enters into even the terrors of the contemplation
of the Judgment Day in the translation of the "Dies Irae":

> Dear, remember in that Day
> Who was the cause thou cams't this way.
> Thy sheep was stray'd; And thou wouldst be
> Even lost thy self in seeking me.[14]

It was this appreciation of the wonder of divine love conde-
scending and of human love yearning for intimacy that led
Crashaw to dwell so tenderly on the least aspects of the human life of Christ. On the whole, seventeenth-century religious feeling had been a little shy of the human aspects
of Christ's life. Much of this was due undoubtedly to the
dominating preoccupation with the themes of divine justice,
of condemnation and redemption, of justification and election.
But much was, I suspect, due to the instincts of the icono-
clasts. Down that road lay those intensely human hymns
and religious ballads of the Middle Ages, in which the life
of Galilee is treated much like life in the next village, and
Christ and his mother talk to each other very much as did
the villagers themselves. Still more dangerously, lay those
paintings and statues which, though burned and broken, yet
haunted the memories of that age, so terrified of superstition
and idolatry.

Crashaw seems to have been troubled by no such fears. For
from the earliest of his Latin epigrams he dwelt lovingly on the
human passages of the life of his Lord. Here no scruple of
reverence or awe kept his busy imagination from the homeliest
details. The sole guide is relevance to the central theme of
Christ's love and lovableness. It is significant that where his
early Latin poems range over a relatively wide field of speech
and incident from the New Testament, the mature English
poems concentrate on what were for Crashaw the main expressions of the love which brought Christ to earth, expressions in
which that love is offered in complete helplessness to man, in
the full surrender and patience of infancy, or the Circumcision,
or the Passion. And here it is not the things which Christ said,
the challenge, the argument, the teaching, the exposition which,
as so often in the work of contemporaries, are the important
thing, but the bare deed without any word. It is for that reason,
basically, that Crashaw devotes so much and such meticulous

detail, say to the child sleeping on his mother's breast, or the terrible figure of the "Bleeding Crucifix":

> Jesu, no more! It is full tide.
> From thy head & from thy feet,
> From thy hands & from thy side
> All the purple Rivers meet.[15]

But the main motive of all this emphasis on the human life of Christ is not that of bringing religion to earth, of naturalizing eternity in the everyday. The love of God is beyond all telling, and the man who would know that love to the full must aspire far above this poor earth. There is a very considerable vein of asceticism in Crashaw's verse as there was in his life. His friend, Thomas Car, when he tried to describe the poet's way of life in the introductory verses to the *Carmen Deo Nostro* of 1652, stressed the detachment of the mystic as well as the indifference of the poet, where material interests were concerned.[16] The seventeenth century is rich in exquisite statements of the transiency of beauty and the brevity of man's pride. Crashaw has the gift of his time, and can strike the authentic note of magnificence and despair. In some Latin verses usually ascribed to him:

> Eheu ver breve, & invidum!
> Eheu floriduli dies! [17]

In English:

> Come then, YOUTH, BEAUTY, & BLOOD!
>   All ye soft powres,
> Whose sylken flatteryes swell a few fond howres
> Into a false æternity. Come man;
> Hyberolized NOTHING! know thy span;
> Take thine own measure here; down, down, & bow
> Before thy self in thine idæa; thou
> Huge emptynes! contract thy self; & shrinke
> All thy Wild circle to a Point.[18]

In other words, Crashaw is quite aware of all that is to be said on that theme of "darke, dusty Man":[19]

> All-daring dust & ashes! only you
> Of all interpreters read Nature True.[20]

But the conscious asceticism of Crashaw comes fundamentally out of no low opinion of the world, out of no distaste for ordinary living, but out of a very deep passion for the love he has glimpsed, and a belief that it is only by passing beyond the limits of ordinary experience that he may hope to come to that love. It is, perhaps, best expressed in the beautiful ending of "An Apologie, for the Fore-going Hymne" (that "To the Name and Honor of the Admirable Sainte Teresa"). It is after his ingenious justification of his going to Spain for the wine of divine love where others go for the profane inebriation of sack that he soars out of dialectic into another region:

> Drink we till we prove more, not lesse, then men,
> And turn not beasts, but Angels. Let the king
> Me ever into these his cellars bring
> Where flowes such wine as we can have of none
> But HIM who trod the wine-presse all alone
> Wine of youth, life, & the sweet Deaths of love;
> Wine of immortall mixture; which can prove
> It's Tincture from the rosy nectar; wine
> That can exalt weak EARTH; & so refine
> Our dust, that at one draught, mortality
> May drink it self up, and forget to dy.[21]

Clearly in such a passage as this we are in the presence of a feeling very different from anything we have yet found in Donne or Herbert, or are indeed to find in Vaughan. Here is none of that care of a reasonable religion that is one of the main preoccupations of the group out of which Crashaw came. Rather we are in the presence of a passionate ardor that makes one think of that "Enthusiasm" which filled this group with so much horror. But it is "Enthusiasm" with a difference. For it is no private or personal revelation that is celebrated here. It is not any new discovery of truth that makes Crashaw praise Saint Teresa. It is not as the hierophant of a new revelation of belief or government that he extols this mother who moves him to ecstasy. There is one of the marked differences between Crashaw and the "Enthusiasts" of the day. For the center of interest in his work is not theological but devotional. It is no new insight which Crashaw prays for in the great final apostrophe to Saint Teresa which has so delighted practically every student of his work. It is rather for that exaltation of will, that firing of emotion, that may carry him out of himself into the ecstasy of love—of love for Him whom he already loves but as yet without that love that realizes the fullness of Teresa's. Only it is like Crashaw to devote his power not to telling what he lacks but what it is that he asks of Teresa, something more than inspiration, rather the lifting up of him into her own wingless flight:

> O thou undaunted daughter of desires!
> By all thy dowr of Lights & Fires;
> By all the eagle in thee, all the dove;
> By all thy lives & deaths of love;
> By thy larg draughts of intellectuall day,
> And by thy thirsts of love more large then they;
> By all thy brim-fill'd Bowles of feirce desire
> By thy last Morning's draught of liquid fire;
> By the full kingdome of that finall kisse
> That seiz'd thy parting Soul, & seal'd thee his;
> By all the heav'ns thou hast in him
> (Fair sister of the SERAPHIM!
> By all of HIM we have in THEE;
> Leave nothing of my SELF in me.
> Let me so read thy life, that I
> Unto all life of mine may dy.[22]

Is this mystical? That is not an easy question to answer. For there are several elements present in it, conspicuous among them the desire to express his wonder and delight in a fellow creature and the effort to analyze in some degree the sources of power that he has felt in the words of that creature. But there is, I think, no mistaking the central aspiration of a passage like this, the great yearning, the basic passion, that gives volume and meaning to the ecstasy of the verse. That is the desire for the immediate, the ineffable experience of the presence of God. Teresa is one of the greatest mystics of the century preceding Crashaw's, one of the most glowing, and most attractive Christian mystics of all time. Crashaw feels her power and feels it for the central, the mystical reason. This woman has found her way to Divine Love. It is that fire that has kindled her great heart and lightened her pages. Her fire kindles Crashaw, and looking at her, Crashaw feels himself closer to her goal. In that sense the beautiful passage above is mystical.

But it is not mystical in the sense that in itself it involves or expresses the poet's achievement of the purpose he shares with Teresa. Indeed, far from being absorbed in his own contemplation of God, the poet is quite aware of something in his own consciousness, apart from the object of that consciousness, and that he is expressing with singular passion and beauty. From this point of view, the passage is even less mystical than, say, the verses "Upon the Bleeding Crucifix," [23] or the beautiful song, "Lord, when the sense of thy sweet grace," [24] indeed than much of Crashaw's verse. But in its direction, in its aspiration, in its understanding and sympathy, it is mystical.

Was Crashaw, then, a mystic? It is very hard to answer that question categorically for a man who says so little of his own experience in any personal way and so little explicitly on the whole question, a man who, in other words, is a poet and not a theologian or writer of devotional treatises. Certainly, the admiration for Saint Teresa would not be definitive, for the ecstatic is the seventeenth-century type of saint, not in any sense peculiar to that century but especially revered by the Catholics of the time.[25] No other type save that of the martyr challenged anything like the interest which the ecstatic did, and even in the case of the martyr, one of the great sources of the appeal of his type, a type which the contemporary persecutions of Catholics in Protestant countries brought into fresh devotion, was its vindication of what one may call the ecstasy of suffering. What was for Catholicism an age of challenge and dispute, filled even in Catholic countries with the reports of almost unsupportable challenges met by their fellow believers in other lands, made the topic of martyrdom an urgent one for any sensitive or thoughtful Catholic.[26]

To all of this Crashaw had been exposed in his reading of the poets and prose-writers of Italy and France and Spain. And as the Puritan shadow deepened around Little Gidding and Peterhouse, the experience of the alien saints and writers must have come home to him the more keenly for the very esoteric character of his experience of them. But when all allowances have been made for the exotic nature of much of Crashaw's religious reading, it still remains fundamentally true that it came home to his business and bosom and answered something very deep in his experience. His approach to religion, his sense of religious values, was essentially that of the great ecstatics of the time in France and Italy and Spain, however different the form in which that orientation might express itself.

The actual word "mystic" is used by Crashaw more than by any other of these poets, but used as an adjective rather than as a noun. It is not easy to say just how much that means, for the adjective "mystic" was used in England in that day almost as loosely as it is in ours. Crashaw is no exception to the habit of his age. Sometimes he uses the adjective in the sense of "occult" or "hidden" with some connotation of unsuspected potency in that concealment. For instance, in "A Letter from

Mr. Crashaw to the Countess of Denbigh," Crashaw uses the word in a very general sense:

> What Magick-Bolts, what mystick Barrs
> Maintain the Will in these strange Warrs.[27]

There is more than that, some suggestion of the ineffable as well, in a passage like the following:

> A hundred thousand goods, glories, & graces,
>   And many a mystick thing
>   Which the divine embraces
> Of the deare spouse of spirits with them will bring
>   For which it is no shame
> That dull mortality must not know a name.[28]

But on the whole there is not much to be drawn from Crashaw's use of this much-abused word.

Very much more illuminating is what he has to say of the mystical process. As we have seen, Crashaw's poetry is not the place where one usually looks for explanations or anything savoring, even indirectly, of exegesis. But there are a couple of passages that tell us a good deal more than one would expect and much more directly and explicitly than usual. The first is the close to the famous "Description of a Religious House and Condition of Life (Out of Barclay)." The main line of thought of the poem is Barclay's, but as a comparison with Barclay's original will make clear, the clothing of the thought, the full realization of it, is, as usual, Crashaw's. It is the conclusion that gives so eloquent and so subtle an account of the aims and the processes of contemplation:

> But reverent discipline, & religious fear,
> And soft obedience, find sweet biding here;
> Silence, & sacred rest; peace & pure joyes;
> Kind loves keep house, ly close, and make no noise,
> And room enough for Monarchs, while none swells

Beyond the kingdomes of contentfull Cells.
The self-remembring SOUL sweetly recovers
Her kindred with the starrs; not basely hovers
Below: But meditates her immortall way
Home to the originall sourse of LIGHT & intellectuall Day.[29]

That is simple, fairly explicit, and about what one would expect from the subject, set forth with a good deal of imagination and winged with that quickening of feeling that one has learned to take for granted with Crashaw. The second important passage is much less well-known and even when noticed, not much appreciated. One very sympathetic critic has, indeed, expressed disappointment that in the Epiphany hymn Crashaw has contrived "to make the highly romantic figures of the three kings curiously dull."[30] Mr. Falls is quite right. The Epiphany hymn is dull beside the Christmas hymn, for it gives us something that Crashaw so seldom gives us that one is not quite prepared for it. To no small extent it is philosophical, to say nothing of exegetical. And philosophy usually makes but a poor figure beside rhapsody. Nor should we forget that however dear the trappings of the Three Kings may have proved to generations of painters, after all, it was not to them but to the shepherds that the angels sang that first "Gloria" on the midnight hills.

A moment ago, I said that this hymn is philosophic, not to say exegetical. That does not mean that the succeeding verses, sung first by one of the Three Kings and then by another, with a chorus sung by all three, lose in the end their character of song. Even in the passage below, what is in essence a piece of fairly straight-ahead explanation, such as is the staple of most of the religious poetry of the time, is suddenly swept up into pure rhapsody. There are several such passages as this in the poem, all with the authentic light and fire of Crashaw, and it is surprising that they have not been better appreciated. But they are so integrally related to a train of thought not always immediately apparent or on the surface lucid that it is not perhaps entirely surprising that they have been neglected.

One of the striking themes of the hymn is the anticipation of that darkening of the sun that is traditionally assigned to the day of the Crucifixion. Especially is this meaningful for those nations that formerly worshipped the sun, as had the Magi. It is from that event that the first of the Kings proceeded in the best emblem fashion of the time to draw out the significance of that eclipse. The second King now takes up the theme, to be followed presently by the third:

[2.] By the oblique ambush of this close night
Couch't in that conscious shade
The right-ey'd Areopagite
Shall with a vigorous guesse invade
And catche thy quick reflex; and sharply see
On this dark Ground
To descant THEE.
[3.] O prize of the rich SPIRIT! with what feirce chase
Of his strong soul, shall he
Leap at thy lofty FACE,
And seize the swift FLASH, in rebound
From this obsequious cloud;
Once call'd a sun;
Till dearly thus undone,
[Cho.] Till thus triumphantly tam'd (o ye two
Twinne SUNNES!) & taught now to negotiate you.
[1.] Thus shall that reverend child of light,
[2.] By being scholler first of that new night,
Come forth Great master of the mystick day;
[3.] And teach obscure MANKIND a more close way
By the frugall negative light
Of a most wise & well-abused Night
To read more legible thine originall Ray,
[Cho.] And make our Darknes serve THY day;

Maintaining t'wixt thy world & ours
A commerce of contrary powres,
    A mutuall trade
    'Twixt sun & SHADE,
By confederat BLACK & WHITE
Borrowing day & lending night.
[1.] Thus we, who when with all the noble powres
That (at thy cost) are call'd, not vainly, ours
    We vow to make brave way
Upwards, & presse on for the pure intelligentiall Prey;
[2.] At lest to play
    The amorous Spyes
And peep & proffer at thy sparkling Throne;
[3.] In stead of bringing in the blissfull PRIZE
    And fastening on thine eyes,
    Forfeit our own
    And nothing gain
But more Ambitious losse, at lest of brain;
[Cho.] Now by abased liddes shall learn to be
Eagles; and shutt our eyes that we may see.[31]

Seldom has the "negative way" been presented more vividly or directly than in this passage. And unlike many emulations of *The Mystical Theology* of Dionysius the Areopagite, this has something analogous to the conviction, the positive thrust of the reality beyond the categories, of the original. The glow of feeling, the fire of Crashaw, is to be caught even in the subtlest of these lines. Here Crashaw has succeeded in giving the equivalent of the intellectual ecstasy of Dionysius in his own more directly emotional medium.

But such direct expression of ideas is rare in Crashaw. Poetry for him is not an instrument of explication. He does not use it to tell a story or to explain a dogma, nor to enforce a moral, nor to exhort to right feeling. Those long addresses to the Deity, in which one suspects the poet of rehearsing God in dogma and prescription, that weigh down so much seventeenth-century poetry are not to be found in Crashaw. Still less does one find that highly subjective expression of personal feeling that is the great triumph of Donne and Herbert. One can elicit from the devotional verse of Herbert a very fair picture of those "many spiritual conflicts that have past betwixt God and my Soul," [32] as he himself described them. But the verse of Crashaw is devotional in a much more specialized and rigorous sense. It is devotional in the sense of Mr. T. S. Eliot, "Devotional poetry is religious poetry which falls within an exact faith and has precise objects for contemplation." [33] Crashaw's poetry is that in a sense that Herbert's verse seldom was and Donne's almost never. It is fundamentally contemplative and affective.

In one respect this concentration of Crashaw's has been misunderstood. It is not surprising that a reader fresh from the dazzling speculations of Donne, or from the ordered meditations of Herbert, should feel that Crashaw is so completely absorbed in feeling and image that he seldom or never thinks. Some critics who would not go as far as that would still insist that the intellectual side of Crashaw is unimportant or deficient. As a matter of fact, nothing could be farther from the truth. Crashaw was a learned man, trained in the theological disciplines of his tradition and ripely cultivated in the classical literature that was the stock of the humanism of his day. Moreover, as Signor Praz and Mr. Martin have shown, he had a wide acquaintance with the poetry of his own time not only at home but abroad. Indeed, in his own humbler degree Crashaw shares that grace of learned allusion that is one of the charms of Milton's poetry.

But Crashaw is intellectual in another sense to which justice has hardly been done. The piling up of rhapsodic images in "The Weeper" has blinded readers and even critics to the fact that the great bulk of Crashaw's work is very far from being what Praz so brilliantly described that poem as being, "a rosary of epigrams or madrigals loosely linked together." [34] As a matter of fact, the line of development of the usual Crashaw poem is as firm, basically, as the line of a baroque statue or building, and the logical mass as substantial. The distraction comes from the embellishment, but in general that embellishment is lateral, as it were. It may screen from view the logical advance of the poem; indeed, it often does distract from it, but the forward thrust is always there. Even when the reader feels that he has been swept off his feet by the wind of the poetry, he is being carried steadily to a usually definitive and resonant conclusion. The Nativity hymn and the Teresa poems are superb examples of this.

It is not for nothing that among all the wide range of mystical writers, the mature Crashaw chose for imitation and for praise and for translation two of the most intellectually vigorous, the two who almost more than any other mystics preserve the architectonic power of thought even in the transports of rapture, Teresa of Avila and Thomas Aquinas. For in his own much humbler degree he shows something of the capacity of both for keeping mental control of feeling. Only as with both of these much greater thinkers, there is nothing of the external or the restrictive about this control. It is organic and informative.[35] The thought is the ribbing of the leaf, the spring of the arch that flowers into grace and light.

Indeed, where Crashaw fails from the poetic standpoint, the lapse is usually due to his preoccupation with the thought of the poem at the expense of the image, and so of the feeling. The cherub whose song tasted all day of his breakfast on the Magdalen's tears is an extreme example.[36] The famous "walking baths" of the eyes of the Magdalen that have so effectively distracted generations of critics is another from the same poem.[37] Had Crashaw been a little vaguer in detail or a little less absorbed in the celebration of his theme, neither of these two classic "horrible examples" would have been perpetrated, nor a number of lesser ones. But the important thing to remember is that it is no failure of logical power, of activity or firmness of thinking, that is responsible for the lapses in Crashaw's style.

The substance of the matter is that Crashaw is a man with his eye on the object. His poems are not treatises or descriptions or analyses or idyls or self-revelations. They are rather emblems, contemplations, hymns, sometimes one of these at a time, more often all together. In so being, they are very much of his time, and can only be understood in terms of the time.

At the base of all of Crashaw's poems is the emblem, one of the most popular and one of the most characteristic artistic forms of his day.[38] Geffrey Whitney in his *A Choice of Emblemes, and other Devises* of 1586 gives a most complete description of type, a description which is revealing for Crashaw's secular as well as religious verse. Emblems he defines as:

suche figures, or workes, as are wroughte in plate, or in stones in the pavementes, or on the waules, or suche like, for the adorning of the place: havinge some wittie devise expressed with cunning woorkemanship, somethinge obscure to be perceived at the first, whereby, when with further consideration it is understood, it maie the greater delighte the beholder. And althoughe the worde dothe comprehende manie thinges, and divers matters maie be therein contained; yet all Emblemes for the most parte, maie be reduced into these three kindes, which is *Historicall, Naturall,* & *Morall. Historicall,* as representing the actes of some noble persons, being matter of historie. *Naturall,* as in expressing the natures of creatures, for example, the love of the yonge Storkes, to the oulde, or of suche like. *Morall,* pertaining to vertue and instruction of life, which is the chiefe of the three, and the other two maye bee in some sorte drawen into this head. For, all doe tende unto discipline, and morall preceptes of living.[39]

Now there is a very large element of the ornamental in the above definition. We are accustomed today to view ornament with some suspicion. That is partly the reaction to the deluge of cheap and vicious ornament with which the Industrial

Revolution has deluged us, partly to a somewhat Philistine utilitarianism which defends its efficiency from the distractions of beauty. Ornament had another meaning for Crashaw and his age. In the address to his tutor Lany with which he prefaced the *Epigrammata Sacra* in 1634, he thus defends the writing of sacred verse from the possible strictures of one who might think that such activity was unworthy of a serious student of theology, "Nor assuredly than this kind of writing, provided it have sufficiently discharged its proper functions, could anything be more suitable to theological leisure; for in it without doubt the very substance of theology being overlaid with poetic grace, sets off its grandeur by loveliness." [40] The ornament is, then, not something superimposed or affixed, but something immediately relevant that brings out the meaning of the thing ornamented and awakens the mind to an appreciation of it.

And for the large element of wit in the proceeding, for that element of the conceit that makes the emblem in so many ways one of the major sources of metaphysical poetry, we have the word of another student of the time, Tesauro, the seventeenth-century rhetorician and critic, "A witticism from the pulpit is nothing but a witty symbolical idea lightly hinted at by God: then gracefully unveiled by the talent of man: sharing the applause with God for having come across it." [41] There is, then, in the religious conceit a species of that virtuosity dear to the self-conscious artist in all ages, especially in this most self-conscious of times. But this virtuosity is seen to be of very minor importance when it is set beside its main objective, the worship of God by the discovery and the offering to Him of the beauties and wonders of His works, that is one of the main-springs of all ritual.

But there was, I think, another source of inspiration for these poems in which Crashaw takes some event in sacred history and tries to come as close as he can in a picture or a phrase to the apprehension of it, and that is the Ignatian meditation. *The Spiritual Exercises* of Saint Ignatius went all over Europe, and, gathering up as they did in a more systematic method many of the experiments of the time, they were enormously influential in all sorts of unexpected places. From our point of view, the first element to be noticed in the Ignatian technique is the "composition" for a visual meditation, that is, an imaginative reconstruction in which the aspirant to contemplation tries to bring before his eyes some episode or scene in sacred history, or the appropriate physical setting for an illustration of some theme in dogmatic theology.[42] Usually such a reconstruction is brief, precise, definite. The motive is not artistry, nor is it criticism. It is to bring the theme of the meditation so vividly before the mind that the thoughts will be elevated and concentrated, the feelings stirred, and the whole spirit absorbed in the contemplation of that theme.

The way in which the Nativity is conjured up before us in the opening lines of the Nativity hymn, the picture of the child Teresa starting out for the Moors and martyrdom, in the great Teresa poems, the use of the opening scene of the "Stabat Mater" in the "Sancta Maria Dolorum," are conspicuous examples of the moving use of this technique. But impressive as are these opening pictures, it must never be forgotten that they are but the starting-point. From them the poet springs into those sudden flights of rhapsody that are the never-failing wonder and delight of the lover of Crashaw.

In such passages the impulse of praise and love which gives rise to the hymn surpasses itself. There is nothing of introspection, nothing of the personal in the result.[43] For it is not of himself that the poet is thinking, save when perhaps in a moment of self-recollection he finds himself cumbered and begs for grace to pass beyond himself. It is of the saint, the Virgin, the Lord himself, that he is thinking, and always, whatever the specific theme, of the wonder and the love and the lovableness of God. That is what he is trying to express, no, what he is trying to rise into, to lose himself in. The ending of the hymn one always feels is the silence of the prayer of pure affection in which the fictions of the imagination, and the reflections of the reason, and the yearnings of the heart are at last stilled in the pure and unmediated contemplation and adoration of Divine Love.

That is why it is so difficult to do justice to Crashaw's imagery. It is striking, rich, full-bodied, even luscious, but it is not in general naturalistic. It does not exist for its own end. Indeed, its range is astonishingly narrow for its brilliance; yet there is no sign of economy or reserve. Over and over, Crashaw repeats his images with slight variation or adaptation. The same properties appear on the stage of his imagination again and again—roses and snow, the Pelican, the Phoenix out of its ashes, time after time, beyond even the limits of that legendary resurrection, the dove, sacred and profane, nests of various kinds, breasts of all sorts, blood, tears by seas, darkness and light, fire and flood, the womb, the tomb, wounds of every sort, deaths without end. It is impossible to avoid Miss Lea's conclusion that many of these images are used ritualistically, without any necessary intrusion of the everyday realism of the thing itself.[44] Even images that do not seem very malleable, by reason of their homeliness, not to say at times, brutality, seem to be so employed.

And certain words are used in much the same fashion until one begins to wonder if perhaps they had not for Crashaw some richer access of meaning, now perhaps lost to us, that kept their ceaseless repetition fresh and moving. "Fair and sweet," "sweet" and "sweetness" in all sorts of contexts, "soft," "dear," "delicious" in very unexpected places, like "delicious wounds" [45] —these adjectives are repeated so often that one begins to conceive a very mean opinion of the range of Crashaw's vocabulary. But it is not a matter of lack of words. Crashaw is capable on occasion of an extraordinarily delicate and precise use of words, and he takes the pleasure which all the metaphysical poets took in the use of words for the sheer delight of them. No, what we have here rather is the ritualistic use of images, in which the connotations that never can be exhausted freshen and enliven ceaseless repetition, where the emotional whole is served rather than hindered by repetition.[46] So the altar is decked for all the great feasts of the year with a few simple properties of candles and flowers and rigorously limited and fixed implements of linen and metal, and yet each time the heart is lifted afresh to the miracle of divine condescension and the wonder of communion.

Especially is this apparent in the many references to music and to odor, the least tangible and the most hauntingly suggestive of sense experiences. And above all is it true of the body of Crashaw's imagery that has aroused the most controversy always and of late an especial heightening of interest. It was inevitable that the handling of the two loves, the sacred and the profane, should shock the Puritan tradition of the nineteenth century and should exhilarate the Freudian of the twentieth. The Puritan is too much aware of the dangers of certain confusions, of the perils of certain parallels. The Freudian can never entirely remember that sex was known before Freud, and that its implications for the life of the whole man did not await twentieth-century discovery. And the last thing that either will appreciate is the matter-of-factness with which certain allusions were handled by a generation as yet unaware of the self-consciousness of both.

Some of the most interesting and significant pages in Signor Praz' brilliant study of Crashaw as the great expression in poetry of the spirit of the *seicento*, concern the effort of the time for the "spiritualizzamento del sense."[47] That is an admirable phrase to describe the work of winning a luxuriously sensual age to a concern about spiritual matters, which various groups in the Counter-Reformation undertook, notably those great popularizers of the time, the Jesuits. And Signor Praz' brilliant description of the consequences of that effort for the poetry of the time in the Latin countries may be accepted as authoritative from the point of view of the modern critic, since it is doubtful if there is any one with a knowledge comparable to his to contradict him. But it is clear that, as Signor Praz himself sees, such an approach to the matter may have very different consequences, according to the character of the artist involved. For one man such imagery may be little more than a literary fashion, to be exploited for all the varying motives of literary fashion. For another it may be the ardent expression of the purest religious enthusiasm. In the case of Crashaw there is no question of the sincerity of the religious feeling to the service of which all this imagery of the two loves is devoted.

But the question of the extent to which the connotations of the two loves were preserved in the poet's consciousness is an interesting one. Certainly, Crashaw was under no such compulsion as that which influenced some of the Catholic reformers and artists who were striving to raise a corrupt age to the contemplation of higher things by throwing an imaginative and emotional bridge between that better world and its usual habits of mind and heart. His interest was in no sense reforming or even hortatory. What is more likely to be true is that he was influenced by the imagery itself, finding that attraction in it that one always finds in the accidental form of an influence that has seized upon one outside of his daily and immediate milieu. Nowhere in the England of his day was he to hear divine love sung of with the warmth and quickening of emotion, the loftiness and richness, with which he heard it praised in some of the great poets of the Counter-Reformation. That imagery would have a power for him that any strong influence experienced from abroad or in a small group has on a sensitive and responsive person. On the other hand, it would be free of the attenuations, the distortions, the adulterations of imagery freely bandied about in daily intercourse. This is not to say that such imagery would be used by Crashaw without an awareness of its sensual and profane implications. But it does mean that it might be used with greater freedom and with less impediment for the ritualistic purposes suggested above.

After all, it is the experience of divine love which Crashaw is celebrating, and not that of human. Here as elsewhere it is the central impulse of his religious feeling that determines the direction which his poetry is to take. And so far as the form of his imagery at this point is concerned, whatever one's individual reaction to that type of imagery, it must not be forgotten that a good many mystics have found in such symbolism the best figure to express the love of the spirit.[48] And since Crashaw is a metaphysical poet as well as a mystical, it is well to remember that in these figures the points of contrast may be quite as illuminating as the points of resemblance. It is of the essence of the metaphysical as of the baroque tradition to use the exuberance of the flesh for the transcendence of the spirit.[49]

As he made clear in the passage cited above from the Epiphany hymn, Crashaw was preoccupied with the world beyond the ordinary categories of human experience. It is a rash preoccupation. Yet with his exuberance and his precision he did not fall into the sea of vagueness that waits for many such adventurers. That was not the metaphysical way. Rather, he ran his hazards in paradox and in the tension of contrasts, sometimes almost savagely unresolved, beneath the gracious surface. The numerous passages that mingle beauty and pain afford striking examples, some of which, like the richly embroidered verses "On the wounds of our crucified Lord," hardly pass beyond the stage of emotional confusion. But in most of these passages, whatever conflict there is arises from the nature of the feeling itself. Ecstasy is beyond the analytical, categorical resources of language. It defies the ordinary name-givings of "pleasant" and "unpleasant," for it stretches the capacities of the soul beyond the securities of its expectations. That is the meaning and the justification of a passage like the following, as one would expect, from the final version of "A Hymne to the Name and Honor of the Admirable Sainte Teresa":

> O how oft shalt thou complain
> Of a sweet & subtle PAIN.
> Of intolerable JOYES;
> Of a DEATH, in which who dyes
> Loves his death, and dyes again.
> And would for ever so be slain.
> And lives, & dyes; and knowes not why
> To live, But that he thus may never leave to DY.[50]

The foregoing is one of the most successful of these paradoxical expressions in precision and in competence. Yet I am not at all sure that it compares even in sheer communicability with a passage in which no such effort is made to bring together the discordant yet concurrent elements of feeling that in its character is essentially beyond categories. It is one of the stanzas from "The Weeper" that practically everybody agrees is successful even though it deals with that delicate matter of the physical appearance of the Magdalen's weeping:

> Not in the evening's eyes
> When they Red with weeping are
> For the Sun that dyes,
> Sitts sorrow with a face so fair,
> No where but here did ever meet
> Sweetnesse so sad, sadnesse so sweet.[51]

Here the naked constituents of the paradox are put side by side, and the work of integration is accomplished by the exquisite cadences of the music. What Miss Wallerstein says of some other poems of Crashaw applies to this passage: "The sensuous emotional ecstasy by which Crashaw approaches the central theme of the poem, failing somewhat in its images, finds another and complete form of expression in the verse music. And in the full tide of feeling along which we are swept by the intoxication of that music, all the elements are absorbed and subdued to one. It is literally through musical ecstasy that Crashaw lifts us into his theme, as it is through the music that he lifts himself into his experience." [52]

It is futile to try to separate the component elements of any genius though for the business of study one must make the endeavor. For all creation is a making of an image in another medium. It is impossible to keep from mixing figures when one attempts to speak of that mingling of fire and light and music that goes to the making of Crashaw's description of the effect upon his spirit of the ecstasy of the great Spanish mystic. Only the very experience of that supreme union with Divine Love would accomplish the purpose of the poet. And even in the last fullness of mystical communion, when the totality of all things comes into the waiting soul, even then in that supreme integrity, there must yet be some shadow of the unique, of the unrepeatable. For always there is the never-quite-yielded individuality of the human soul that, once having made, not even its Creator can obliterate. In the final analysis then, all expression is but an analogy, a parallel creation, in the deepest sense a metaphor.[53]

For that task, Crashaw had two great gifts. The first is the sheer power of music that, as in the passage from "The Weeper," through and beyond and above all imagery and suggestion of thought and feeling can rear its own airy towers and by its own proper magic scale the heights of ecstasy.[54] For sheer felicity of expression, in which sound and rhetoric and the movement of the music combine to create the physical vesture of the feeling, probably no English poet has ever quite surpassed Crashaw at his best, and he is at his best in a passage like the foregoing. There is nothing mystical in such an achievement. Rather it springs from what is a special gift in itself, from what may be used for any of a great variety of purposes and effects. Crashaw used it for a superb piece of virtuosity in "Musicks Duell," pretty generally recognized as one of the most dazzlingly successful efforts in the English tongue to translate the distinctive effects of one art into another. Once at least he used it for a charming love song, from the Italian, "To thy Lover." Again he used it for the wistfulness of love-dreaming in "Wishes to his (supposed) Mistresse." It was a gift available for the most secular of purposes, and Crashaw, who had a vein of humor that has not in general received its due, and a daintiness that suggests his profane brethren rather than the sacred poets of the time, might have added richly to the delights of the seventeenth-century profane muse. But though unlike Herbert, he did write secular masterpieces, like Herbert he found in the field of sacred poetry the opening of his particular treasure.

Here, too, he found the adequate theme for his other great poetic gift, that fire and intensity of feeling that gives reality to all his imagery, however foreign to our idiom it may seem, that gives warmth and immediacy to even his most precisely teasing and implicated phrasing. There is nothing diffuse, nothing vague, in that feeling. The allusiveness of the poet, the concentration of the mystic, are at one in the passion with which he turns his face God-ward, that passion that in the end is to carry him out of himself and beyond himself. The lights and fires of the first lines of that final apostrophe to Saint Teresa are so dazzling that it is easy to forget the end of it. But that is perhaps the most wonderful thing about that great poem. For in that simple, explicit statement of his ultimate aspiration all the splendor of music and feeling fall away from the bare thrust of the incandescent will:

> By all the heav'ns thou hast in him
> (Fair sister of the SERAPHIM!
> By all of HIM we have in THEE;
> Leave nothing of my SELF in me.
> Let me so read thy life, that I
> Unto all life of mine may dy.[55]

That is truly mystical, and from the religious point of view the most remarkable thing about Crashaw's verse, for his age or for ours.

CHAPTER X

HENRY VAUGHAN: THE COUNTRY DOCTOR

In a certain sense Henry Vaughan belongs to another age from that of the men whom we have been considering. And in some ways it is unfair to consider him at all with them, because the influences they shared were already spent when they reached him, and what was for them the dominant fashion of the moment becomes too often in his hands a reactionary turning from the life of his time to models more congenial to his own spirit. Moreover, he is weak precisely where these men are strong, so that in some ways they are the worst approach to him. The precision of Herbert sets in unpleasant relief the vagueness of Vaughan, and the sustained ecstasy of Crashaw leads us to unreasonable expectations of his successor's much smaller-arced inspiration. But not to consider him as a man of his time is to be still more unfair, is to view him, as so many nineteenth-century critics did, as a less great Wordsworth or as a vague nature-lover who forfeited his animistic birthright for a mess of seventeenth-century orthodoxy. Not to remember the source of all his religious ideas and tastes in the tradition which we have been studying is to miss the intellectual backbone of his work and to ask more of the emotional and imaginative elements than we have any right to ask. It is to reduce his less exciting verse to flatness and some of his finest flights of feeling and fancy to meaninglessness. Vaughan gains, therefore, by being set beside the men to whom he would have recognized his own kinship, for it is out of their world that for

259

good or ill his own springs, and more than most men of his time he appreciated the continuity of that succession.

Of the actual life of Vaughan we know very little, although much of what we do know is surprisingly authenticated by his own pen. His letters to the antiquarian Aubrey, who was a cousin of his, confirm the few facts current on his life and give a very definite, although, of course, lamentably brief and casual, glimpse of his personality. The facts themselves are few. He was born in 1622, the elder of twins, at Newton St. Bridget, Brecknockshire. His father came of an ancient Welsh family that as long ago as Agincourt had distinguished itself in battle, and in the person of Sir Thomas Vaughan had fallen a victim to Richard III and been commemorated by Shakespeare.[1] Of his mother nothing is known. There is reason to think that, as in the case of so many ancient families at this time, the Vaughans had fallen on leaner days, but some of his ancestral property Henry was to keep all his life. If we can believe Aubrey, on his own showing not an unbiassed witness, the elder Vaughan was not a very reliable or admirable character.[2] His son may refer indirectly to this somewhat dubious repute of his father in the praise he gives his schoolmaster, but the passage probably means little.[3] At any rate, Vaughan was fortunate in his teacher, to whom he and his brother were sent for instruction at eleven years of age, the Reverend Matthew Herbert of Llangattock, for both he and his brother wrote verses expressing rather more than conventional warmth of feeling for the master with whom they continued for the next half-dozen years.

Of this early life of Henry Vaughan's we can form no clear picture. We know that the country in which he spent these first years was a singularly beautiful one, but we must not forget that the seventeenth-century ideal of natural beauty was not the same as ours. For instance, the hills of his beloved Breconshire seem to have made very much less of an impression upon Vaughan than did the river Usk. However, when all due allowances have been made for difference of taste, it does remain true that the young Vaughan had a continued opportunity to enjoy picturesque and beautiful scenery that none of the other poets whom we have studied knew.[4] More important still, he had a chance to experience from the beginning of his life and first-hand that country life to which Herbert came only in his maturity and the urban Donne and the scholastic Crashaw not at all. Again, we must be wary of drawing conclusions. In his earliest verses there is quite as much to suggest that the young Vaughan was impressed by the town as that he was aware of the advantages of country life. Indeed, the coming to see the country for what it was may well be one of the important factors in that conversion that has so much exercised the curiosity of his critics. But in the place of his birth and childhood Vaughan had opened to him areas and possibilities of experience denied to the poets we have so far studied.

While there is no record of Henry's university matriculation, the letter which he wrote to Aubrey in 1673 confirms by implication the tradition that he accompanied his brother Thomas when he went to Oxford and entered Jesus College in 1638. But whereas Thomas remained in Oxford until he had received his B.A. and indeed, as Henry tells us, became a fellow of his college, Henry did not stay to take a degree but went up to London to study law, probably about 1640.[5]

What followed we cannot tell. The young Vaughan may actually have had some experience of the type of life he described with so much gusto in certain poems that he published in his first volume, that of 1646. He may have actually drunk with the wits and swaggered down the street with some of the gay young cavaliers of the time. But when one considers that these verses make little distinction between the mighty dead whom he could not have known and the living great whom he might have known, it is not certain that they are not right who have suggested that the literary intercourse like the loves described in these early poems may owe more to the poetic fashion of the time and the wistfulness of youthful literary ambition than to actual experience.[6] What is certain is that, as Vaughan himself wrote to Aubrey, "the sudden irruption of our late civil warres" cut short whatever hopes he may have had of a legal career.[7] For his Royalist and Anglican sympathies would seem to have been early defined, in all probability hereditary.

How long Vaughan remained in London is unknown, as is unknown when and how he procured his medical education. It is not known, either, when he married his first wife, Catherine Wise, the daughter of Charles Wise of Ritsonhall, Staffordshire, nor when the first or indeed any of his six children were born.[8] All we can be sure of is that by December 17, 1647, Vaughan is dating the preface of *Olor Iscanus* from Newton on Usk and that his publisher is no longer describing him on the title-page as "Henry Vaughan, Gent." but as "Mr. Henry Vaughan Silurist." It is generally assumed that some time before that, in all probability as early as 1645, he had returned to his home to practice medicine.

As to whether he had meanwhile taken part in the Civil War, there is some difference of opinion, but recent criticism seems to incline to the view that he had. The one fact usually put forward as evidence against the theory is that in one of his earliest poems he claims that his hands are clean of innocent blood.[9] Only a modern reader proceeding on modern hypotheses would conclude from that that he abstained from the conflict. No seventeenth-century cavalier would be misled any more than any seventeenth-century Puritan would be. For positive evidence, there are the humorous verses "Upon a Cloke lent him by Mr. J. Ridsley,"[10] which are quite clear in their implications of presence on the field of battle, and "An

Elegie on the death of Mr. R. Hall, slain at Pontefract, 1648," [11] with its reiterated contempt for those who "quitted action, to their shame." The late Louise Imogen Guiney, who in 1894 had thought that Vaughan was bedridden at the time of the call to arms in Wales,[12] by 1912 had found documentary evidence that Henry Vaughan was one of the Welsh bodyguard of cavalry-troopers that gathered about the King on the field of Rowton Heath on which his friend R. W. fell.[13] That evidence would seem never to have been published, being held for that volume on Henry Vaughan which Miss Guiney and her friend Miss Gwenllian E. F. Morgan had projected. Mr. E. K. Chambers suggests that Vaughan was one of the garrison of Beeston Castle, and that that imprisonment which he is supposed to have shared with his close friend Dr. Powell, to which he refers in one of his poems, may have been connected with the campaign of which the siege formed an important episode.[14] Were the documents in question published, they would, of course, settle the matter, but even on the evidence available in the poetry, Vaughan's participation in the Civil War in some degree seems probable.

What is certain is that by 1647 Henry Vaughan had bidden the great world adieu (if he had ever seriously courted it), and settled down in that active and useful retirement at Brecon into which the letters to Aubrey give us a glimpse. In that same year of 1647, his brother Thomas was deprived of his living on the classic charges of "drunkenness, swearing, incontinency, and carrying arms for the King," [15] and retired presently to Oxford. Henry would not seem to have kept in very close touch with Thomas, if we can judge from the uncertainty of some of the references to the latter years of his brother's life in the letters to Aubrey, for in view of the warm affection and admiration for his brother there displayed, his uncertainty as to the details of his brother's Oxford career hardly seems compatible with close contact.

The years from 1647 to 1650 are critical years in the history of Henry Vaughan. Practically all students of his life are agreed that something of critical importance for his spiritual development happened in those years, and some recent critics have gone so far as to suggest that what happened amounted to a conversion. Certainly, nothing could be more appropriate for a seventeenth-century poet who has been called mystic by more than half of his admirers. And there is no question that some of the things Vaughan said about his early verse,[16] and the fact that he seems to have withdrawn from the publication of *Olor Iscanus* after it was well under way, sound very much like a classic seventeenth-century conversion.[17] The difficulty which Vaughan critics have chiefly encountered with this conversion is the question of what Vaughan was converted from. Here again the difficulty is mainly due to the habit of all of us of reading any loved author in terms of our own time. Today if a man talks of conversion, we assume that he has been converted from something. But there is another sense in which a great many profoundly religious men both in the seventeenth century and today have felt themselves to be converts and that is in the sense of being roused out of lethargy and indifference into zeal and activity. Anyone who even for a moment has experienced (and who has not) the difference of moral and mental and emotional tone that exists between those times when he is alive and functioning with something like all his powers and those times when he is not, will understand how a person who has been able to consolidate his forces on the higher level will regard his former state with an abhorrence that may well suggest the terms in which, say a John Bunyan, describes his youthful self.

It may be something like such a change of heart that is back of what Vaughan has to say of his early verse and of what he now thinks of it after coming under the influence of George Herbert. Readers familiar with the possibilities of the verse of the time have been somewhat amused at the earnestness with which Vaughan beseeches his reader to forget his early work. Certainly, there is nothing in the first volume to bring the blush to the cheek of even the famous Victorian maiden. One wonders if there are other verses of those days that did not find their way into that first publication. It is just possible that there may be, for in that curious book of Vaughan's middle years, the *Thalia Rediviva* of 1678, in which verses written over a period of at least fifteen years are gathered together, there do occur in some of the Etesia effusions lines of a greater amatory freedom and warmth than almost anything found in the first volume.[18] Either Vaughan became less strict later on, or his editors were able to lay hands on some earlier verses which had not been used for the first editions. But the fact remains that for some reason Vaughan wanted to withdraw the poems of *Olor Iscanus* when the publication was too far advanced for the publisher to give it over without a struggle. That reason is certainly not to be found in anything intrinsically reprehensible in the verses actually published. What is more probable is that those verses had come to seem to their author feeble and meaningless.

For something did happen in those years between 1647 and 1650. The outward evidence of it is to be found in the *Silex Scintillans* of 1650. For where the earlier volumes give evidence of pleasant instincts and pleasant performance, here suddenly is real poetry, and, what is still more important, poetry that gives evidence of that profound personal experience that is indispensable to religious poetry. Whatever the faults of the verses, the spasmodic character of their inspiration and the lack of sustained power in their execution, for instance, it is clear that here a man has found himself. And in so doing he has opened up a vein of experience distinctive for both poetry and religion. For, as we shall see in a moment, the vein of religious experience opened here is different from anything to be found in Donne or Crashaw or Herbert. Indeed, the only other poet of the time who has anything like the key to what Vaughan is doing is the relatively unknown Traherne. The man who wrote "I saw Eternity the other night," [19] is a seventeenth-century poet, could, indeed, so far as English poetry is concerned belong only to the seventeenth century, but there is nothing like that poem to be found in the work of his predecessors, even of those whom he most devoutly imitated, Donne and Herbert. Here suddenly, a great poet looks out from the pages of what had promised to be merely another of the countless excellent minor poets in which that age is so singularly rich. True, he has not yet taken possession of himself. Indeed, he never will do so fully, but he has found himself.

It is possible that Vaughan was right when he said that the important thing was that he had read George Herbert. Much has been made of the secondary character of Vaughan's early talent. His love poems, his mildly bacchanalian wits poems, his poems of penitence, have all been brought under the suspicion of pure imitation. "A poet in search of a subject" is the verdict of several of his critics. [20] It is not an uncommon phenomenon in an age of literary sensitiveness and expressiveness like that of his youth. If that is all there is to it, Herbert would seem to have put his feet into the right way. And moved by boundless admiration, Vaughan would seem to have proceeded to emulate him as closely as he could. Certainly, he took the same subjects Herbert had treated, he took the same themes; consciously or unconsciously he took the same titles, he tried to express the same feelings, and in doing so he borrowed figures, ideas, images, even phrases. At first the lover of Herbert is irritated by these echoes, tantalizing in their repetitions and in their tendency, even at moments of acutest resemblance, to trail off into a vagueness foreign to Herbert. Some of these emulations of Herbert, particularly in the field of rhetoric, persisted throughout Vaughan's poetic career.

The trick of beginning a poem with an interrogation, a dramatic affirmation, an exclamation, an invocation of the Deity—this indebtedness to Herbert is to be seen in the two editions of *Silex Scintillans* and in *Thalia Rediviva*.

But impressive as this debt is, it may be doubted if it is as important in substance as in phrase. Vaughan, for better or for worse, changed, adapted, his borrowings. Where he agrees with Herbert, it may well be asked if Vaughan's general position would not already have disposed him to agreement with Herbert. And where he departs from Herbert, he does so much worse or so much better than his master that the question of indebtedness seems unimportant. When he strikes his own gait, when he soars into the brilliant passages of meditation on nature or night or eternity or death or the presence of God that are the distinctive triumph of his muse, he completely departs from the world of Herbert. It is as inspiration, as helping Vaughan to find himself that the influence of Herbert counts.[21] In that, of course, Herbert has done for Vaughan the greatest thing that teacher or master can do for an artist.

But it may be seriously doubted if Herbert is the whole story. Vaughan was twenty-five in 1647, when he seems to have come so strongly under the influence of Herbert. He had had some kind of war experience, probably including both service on the field of battle and imprisonment. He had had some kind of medical education after the disappointment in the legal career. Three years later, in 1650, he will have written a good deal more than half of all the poetry by which his name is known. But his writing will go on for a good many years still. Indeed, from the date of the publication of *Silex Scintillans* in 1650 to the issue of an enlarged edition of that work in 1655, he does an enormous amount of literary work, in spite of the references to ill health to be found in these volumes, in spite of the badness of the times, in spite of what one would think would be the labors of becoming established in a new profession. Indeed, one may say more—if the dates of dedicatory addresses can be taken seriously, and if one can assume that a man does not think of a dedicatory address until a book is nearing completion, this work was done before the end of 1653. It included the translation of two very substantial essays by Plutarch, of an even more substantial essay by Guevara, of an essay by Anselm, of a very much more extended essay by the Jesuit Nierembergius, and an essay by the Bishop, Eucherius, and a more or less original book of devotions of his own. That is a good deal of work to finish up at least, within the space of four years. We have, of course, no way of knowing how long before 1650 these things were under way, but it is doubtful, partly by reason of age and partly by reason of known activity, that much had been done on them before 1647. Taken all together, there is certainly something very suggestive in this rapid succession of publications.

Nor did this flood of production cease abruptly in 1653. In 1654 Vaughan published beside the translations from Nierembergius and Eucherius named above, an original life of Paulinus, Bishop of Nola, and in the next year besides the enlarged *Silex Scintillans*, a translation of the *Hermetical Physick* of Nollius. And then, so far as we know, he published nothing more until in 1678 a friend published for him, possibly without his consent, the "Thalia Rediviva" and other poems. From a letter to Aubrey of June 15, 1673, we have reason to believe that this volume was ready for the press five years earlier.[22] The title-piece of the volume was certainly written many years earlier, and the latest poem we can date with any certainty, the memorial of his brother Thomas, was probably written not long after his death in 1666. In other words, by 1655 Vaughan had done pretty nearly all the writing he was ever going to do. The rest of his story is the story of a successful country doctor, who would seem to have devoted his time to the exercise of his profession and to the acquisition of a considerable store of knowledge in the not surprising field of natural history.[23]

Clearly, then, there is plenty of reason for the oft-repeated question as to what happened in the years between 1647 and 1650. One answer we have from Vaughan, the reading of Herbert. Another we have from those who have been impressed by the allusions to ill-health found in Vaughan's own work. They point to the peculiar kind of sensitivity to certain natural phenomena, night and dawn, and the peculiar kind of looking back to childhood found in some of the poems of *Silex Scintillans.* These readers see in the years 1647 to 1650 a long and weakening illness with a protracted convalescence in which certain sensitivities were heightened and certain processes of recollection were awakened in a fashion not without parallel in the history alike of the artistic and the religious consciousness.[24]

Still another suggestion often advanced to account for the development of these years is the influence of Hermetic ideas, an influence which Henry Vaughan is assumed to have received through his brother Thomas.[25] There is no question but that there is in Henry's poetry, especially in his theories as to the relations between God and nature and man, a good deal to support that theory, as Miss Elizabeth Holmes has so abundantly demonstrated in her admirable study of *Henry Vaughan and the Hermetic Philosophy.* Nor is there any question of the competence of Thomas to account for such an influence. For he was one of the two notable adepts in Hermetic wisdom that Mr. A. E. Waite has been able to find in seventeenth-century England.[26] But there are certain difficulties in the way of dating the association between the two brothers. That they were educated together until Henry left Oxford, we know, but at that time they were only sixteen to eighteen at most. Then they may have been together a good deal after Thomas received his living in the neighborhood of their old home. But we must not forget Henry's statement that his brother remained at Oxford ten or twelve years.[27] That, of course, may mean that his brother was an absentee, or it may refer to his return to Oxford after the deprivation of his living. It is clear from Thomas' diary that at some time before 1658, his brother's wife and his wife were engaged in making eyewash together at the Pinner in Wakefield, and presumably his brother would be with them.[28] But against these slender evidences of association is to be set that uncertainty which Henry showed in his letters to Aubrey as to his brother's precise degree and his burial place, an uncertainty that, in view of the terms in which he refers to his brother and his works, suggests prolonged separation.[29] One other point should be suggested here, and that is that Henry Vaughan himself had in his middle life a very considerable reputation for learning. There are at least two passages in his poetry that suggest a consciousness that he had been looking for truth in the wrong place, in the paths of magic,[30] of which the more explicit is the following:

> And my false *Magic*, which I did believe,
> And mystic Lyes to *Saturn* I do give.[31]

It should be remembered, also, that two of the authors whose works he chose to translate, Nierembergius and Nollius, had a very considerable interest in and knowledge of Hermetic theory. It seems quite probable, therefore, that Henry Vaughan, without being in any sense an adept like his brother, did a good deal of Hermetical reading for himself.

Two other possibilities have been suggested, both by Miss Morgan of Brecon. In a letter to the Times of November 3, 1932, she says she has proof that Vaughan's conversion was due "primarily, to his careful study of the Bible, followed by the unexpected death" of his brother William on July 14, 1648.[32] We still wait for the publication of that proof. Until then we can only weigh this suggestion on its intrinsic merits. That

Vaughan felt his brother's death with especial keenness is beyond question. We have proof of the fact in several of his poems, especially as Mr. Paul Elmer More has pointed out,[33] in four of the most moving of the *Silex Scintillans* pieces, "Thou that know'st for whom I mourne," "Come, come, what doe I here?" "Silence, and stealth of dayes," "I walkt the other day."[34] And it should be added that this blow may well have come with the more force in that he had already lost one at least very good friend in the death in action of R. W. at Rowton Heath in 1645,[35] and was to lose another in the death of R. Hall killed likewise in action at Pontefract in 1648.[36] And these old wounds must have been opened afresh by the death of his friend Charles Walbeoffe in 1653 and possibly not much later, of his first wife, who died, we know, some time before 1658.[37] There is no question, then, that "They are all gone into the world of Light!" had abundant justification when it first appeared in the second part of *Silex Scintillans* in 1655, and we may well seek its origins in the series of losses chronicled above. But that is only one aspect of the new Vaughan. However powerful grief over personal loss may be in detaching a man from his old habits of thought and action, it does not seem an entirely competent explanation of the release of a whole new dynamic of thought and feeling. For that more would seem to be needed.

As for the theory that Vaughan's conversion was due to the reading of the Bible, that is again suggestive, but on the face of it scarcely adequate to account for so throughgoing a change. That Vaughan read the Bible to excellent result is abundantly witnessed by his verses, but it would be difficult to chart any path, say, from the passages he selected to write verses on. Again, being a man of his time, he had probably read his Bible all his life, and the suggestion that whatever new insights are to be seen in *Silex Scintillans* are to be sought in the Bible is not on the face of it as convincing as that they are to be sought in certain Hermetic influences. Miss Morgan's explanation of Vaughan's conversion is not impossible, but until the evidence is presented, it does not, on the face of it, seem entirely adequate to account for what happened.

For between 1647 and 1650 Vaughan took a new path, experienced something that resulted in an awakening of powers hitherto not apparent, and the release of a store of energy that in a few years found an expression quite unparalleled in all the many remaining years of his life. Some additional light on this problem is to be found, I think, in a scrutiny of the writings which Vaughan translated in these years. The first thing to notice about them is that they represent somewhat old-fashioned interests and influences. The moral writings of Plutarch, from which Vaughan made his first prose translations in *Of the Benefit We may get by our Enemies* and *Of the Diseases of the Mind and Body,* in 1651, had been influential in England for more than a hundred years.[38] They present the reasonableness of the Stoic point of view with a good deal of warmth and shrewdness, very much the sort of treatment of practical moral problems to commend itself to the mind of the English Renaissance. Guevara, whose *The Praise and Happinesse of the Countrie-Life* Vaughan translated at the same time, likewise, had been fashionable in the young manhood of John Donne. The particular treatise which Vaughan chose to translate savors much of the devout humanism of an earlier generation, in which the values that might be commended solely on grounds of piety are also developed in terms of reason and graciousness. A later, more sophisticated, more ardent stage of the same devout humanism is to be found in the *Flores Solitudinis* of Nierembergius. There is something striking, certainly not accidental, in this concentration on the theme of solitude and retirement. Anselm's *Man in Glory,* of which Vaughan published his translation in 1652, is sterner

fare, but not uncongenial in its handling of the temptations of
the world, and the same is to be said of *The World Contemned*
of Eucherius. There is, also, a good deal of the same point of
view, of the same scheme of values, in the compilation which
Vaughan made in *Primitive Holiness*. As for the collection
of devotions which Vaughan himself composed, they are a
species of taking order for a quiet Christian life in the main
tradition of the English Church of the time, with perhaps more
of the influence of Herbert than, say, of Andrewes.

But it is quite clear what Vaughan's mind has been busied
with—thoughts of self-mastery, independence of fortune, retirement, solitude, a certain degree of meditation and contemplation, the taking measures for the ordering of a Christian
life in the midst of a troubled time. It is not, I think, unreasonable to suppose that the decision to retire from a violent
and unjust world and to be content with an obscure life in the
country may have been hastened by a combination of experiences, of soldiering, of illness, of personal loss not least,
of the defeat of the side with which he sympathized. It is hard
in a matter of this sort to say which is cause and which effect,
but the main movement seems fairly clear. And the precipi-
tating circumstances may well have been, first, the failure of
Vaughan's London hopes, and then the defeat of the Royalist
cause in Wales. As for the elements of retreat from the life of
the time involved in such a decision, it must not be forgotten
that with the repeated victories of the Parliamentary forces,
the issue for a man with Vaughan's point of view and sympathies was already settled by circumstances.

Vaughan was, unlike the other poets we have studied, a layman. That is a fact which should never be lost sight of in any
discussion of his religious ideas, or of the philosophic ordon-
nance of his work. Laymen in Vaughan's day were often very
well versed in theological learning, as we have seen in the case
of the unordained Donne, which, though an extreme case, is

extreme only in degree. And as Vaughan was to complain, many of these laymen were not in the least averse to discussing theological ideas. But he himself belonged to that group in the Church of England which believed in authority and tradition. Consequently, he could be counted on not to dispose summarily of what he did not know about, and to spend more time on advocating the support of the Church and the clergy than in doing the work of either. Indeed, it is probable that the theological issues of the time did not in the abstract much engage him, that he was interested in the matters of taste and loyalty and practical observance at issue rather than in dogma or principles of church government. The Church was the Church for him, and he took pride in its traditions, its decency and its order, and its reverence. Needless to say, he strongly disliked the Puritans, who in his eyes were overthrowing all these things.

Mr. T. S. Eliot in a striking passage has declared that Vaughan's Anglicanism is in his judgment somewhat suspect. He does not feel in Vaughan the cheerful, more spacious, more democratic spirit of Laud, or for that matter, though Mr. Eliot does not add this, of his successors in the modern High Church party.[39] There is something to what Mr. Eliot says here. Vaughan had no sympathy with the democratic movements of his time, and he would hardly have had with those of our time. Even in the very real primitivism of the life of Paulinus of Nola and in the various passages of his work, both poetry and prose, that praise a country life, we note something aristocratic and highly selective. Welshman as he was, with a pedigree centuries old, Vaughan could and did laugh at pride of genealogy, just as he laughed at the splendor and fashion dear to the heart of the vanishing feudal order.[40] But he wrote of the populace in the spirit of one of Shakespeare's Romans on the mob.[41] At the same time, there was nothing of the spirit that prompted the issue of the *Book of Sports* in his religious tastes. He objected to the Puritans' banishing the festivals of Christmas and Easter, because it seemed to him that they were trying "to extinguish the *memory* of his [Christ's] *Incarnation* and *Passion*." [42] But he had no more love than the Puritans for the traditional popular, semi-pagan Christmas of the holly and the mummings and the wassail bowl. [43]

Although his intellectual range is wider than Herbert's, and though he is constantly alive to influences quite alien to Herbert, there is more in common between the moral complexion of the two men than is always recognized. There is a note of austerity in their love of order and graciousness of rite, a moral austerity than many lovers of the simple life and the open air have shared. Vaughan did very well to keep in Breconshire. He would not have liked the Cavalier refugees any more than he did the Puritans. One can see Crashaw moving in the group around the Queen in Paris, touching his environment in its love of color and elegance and ardor, but for the most part carrying his own atmosphere with him, probably quite unaware of the more worldly aspects of the life about him. But Vaughan would not have liked the Cavalier world any more than he liked the world of the Restoration. For after those early bohemian poems of his, he had turned distinctly sober. There is a tone of moral strenuousness in all the essays which he translated, even in the *Hermetical Physick* of Nollius, and this tone of moral strenuousness is to be found in his own work, both prose and verse. After all, he objected to the Puritans for making schism, for violence, and spiritual pride, and pretensions to sanctity, and not for austerity and religious fervor. [44]

As regards politics, Vaughan was a staunch royalist, writing eloquently and on occasion movingly of the sufferings of the King and his family, [45] but like so many supporters of authority then and since, he had his own criticisms of the social order. Indeed, one may note more of the passion of social criticism in Vaughan's verse than in that of any of the men we have been studying. Some items of his arraignment of the arrogance and folly of wealth are classical, of course, expressed in the Juvenal of his first translation, and the staple of thoughtful men's reflections before and since.[46] What he says of usurers, monopolists, holders of patents, and the whole tribe of the world's oppressors, is to be paralleled in the sermons of John Donne as in the reflections of all sorts of men in the verses and books of devotion of the time.[47] But he says it nevertheless with conviction and with energy, and while we have no reason to believe that he ever had any prospect of growing rich or wielding power, we may see in such passages one of the reasons why he settled down with content in a narrow and obscure world. Above all, he shows himself preoccupied very much as Herbert seems to have been, with the social morality of his time.

He was to a preëminent degree the good citizen, a supporter of authority and settled order in Church and State. We may be quite sure that the case of the Puritans against that authority and order never received anything like a fair hearing from him. The ability to see the justice of both sides was not a virtue in much esteem in the seventeenth century any more than it usually is in times of passionate conviction and rising energy. Vaughan wrote some very sharp things of the disturbers of his time. Indeed, he found it quite impossible to allude to the Puritans without contempt or indignation, and there is no question that the sharpness of his hatred adds a tang to a good many of his lines.[48] A primitive and ingenuous sweetness is not to be found in Henry Vaughan's political utterances, whatever theories one may have as to the influence of a love of nature on the human spirit. But one may claim for him, as one may claim for all his troubled and distracted contemporaries, whatever allowance is to be made for sharp provocation and the recalcitrances of the time. Certainly, in any scale that did justice to the masterpieces of spleen and obloquy that his century produced, he would fall so low as to be for all practical purposes out of sight. So much for the controversial side of his churchmanship.

As for the devotional side, it is less easy to speak with assurance, because as compared, say with Herbert, or, in a very different sense, with Crashaw, it plays so small a part in his religious life. Following Herbert's example, Vaughan does salute some of the great days of the Christian calendar with verse, and with verse that is not always to be dismissed as purely imitative. Those lines on the Nativity that were not printed until the *Thalia* volume, although dated 1656, are packed and vivid, with a flash or two of quick passion that is suggestive of the spirit of the great hymns of Crashaw.[49] Some lines in this poem are merely topical, but the prayer for peace which is the core of them is obviously sincere and distinctive. In this connection, it should not be forgotten that Vaughan wrote on the Communion, for instance, with a good deal of conviction and deep feeling. And he wrote not simply to affirm his conviction of the propriety of kneeling to receive the Communion as in "Dressing"[50] but also to express something much warmer and more personal as in "The Holy Communion." Here, indeed, the opening figure of the feast, a figure which Vaughan shares with Herbert as one of the commonplaces of Christian tradition, presently yields to the beautiful and characteristic figure of the going to God through darkness:

> Darkness, and day-light, life, and death
> Are but meer leaves turn'd by thy breath.[51]

Vaughan's churchmanship is in no sense nominal, but sacramental in the sense of Donne's or Herbert's.

This impression of the verse is borne out by the brief manual of devotions which Vaughan drew up in *The Mount of Olives*.[52] It is a book for solitary devotion as the subtitle, *Solitary De-*

votions, explains, and in that it belongs to a very large and rich body of pious literature to which almost every shade of opinion in the Church of Vaughan's day and the generation preceding his had contributed, but especially those who, like him, belonged to the tradition of Hooker and Donne and Andrewes and Herbert. In spite of the emphasis of the title, it is peculiarly a churchman's book. It opens with the usual admonitions to prayer, and then goes on to furnish forms for awaking, for arising, for the commending of one's self for the day. Then come prayers for preparation for a journey, for leaving home, and for travelling. Next are admonitions as to behavior in church, with prayers to be said going to church, and if alone, coming home, or, if not alone, on arrival. Admonitions for evening prayer with forms for sunset and evening, for going to bed, and for awaking in the night finish the Christian's day. More striking, because more characteristic of French piety than English, is the provision of a series of ejaculations, "When the Clock strikes," "Upon some suddaine fear," "Upon any disorderly thoughts," "Upon any Diffidence," "When thou hearest that any is dead," to name a few of them.[53] But more important than any of these are the Communion prayers, to which between a third and a half of the treatise is devoted. This section opens with "Admonitions, with Meditations and Prayers to be used before we come to the Lords Supper," stressing purity of conscience, purity of intention, fervent and effectual devotion. There is then provided a substantial "Prayer for the grace of repentance, together with a Confession of sins," which is followed by "A Meditation before the receiving of the holy Communion," "A Prayer when thou art upon going to the Lords Table," and one to be said immediately before the receiving of Communion. Then come "Admonitions after receiving the holy Communion," with an appropriate prayer. "A Prayer in time of persecution and Heresie" and "A Prayer in adversity, and troubles occasioned by our Enemies" hardly need explanation in view of the times and the writer's attitude toward them. But the striking thing about this collection of Communion prayers is the pains which the writer takes to bring home to the reader the nature of the sacrament, of which he takes a view similar to Herbert's and Donne's, and to make sure that the religious significance of the occasion is appreciated and reverenced, and the spiritual possibilities realized to the full. Of personal and intimate feeling such as one finds in the ardent pages of Crashaw there is very little. But there is no question of the reality, the sincerity, and the depth of the writer's feeling for the great rite of his church. And the direct and practical spirit in which he handles his theme is strongly suggestive of Herbert.

As for the general appropriation of the Christian tradition, Vaughan is in many ways as austere as Herbert but not so rigorous. There is more of the ranging of Christian humanism to be seen in his work, not only in his choice of materials for translation but also in the responsiveness he shows to the various influences of the age. This is due, of course, in part to the difference of time and to the perhaps more exposed position of the lay physician and student of nature. But more is due to temperament. Certain aspects of the Christian tradition which interested but seemed dangerous to Herbert aroused no such scruples in Vaughan. The hospitality to the idea of miracles implied in the poem "Religion":

> Or is't so, as some green heads say
> That now all miracles must cease?
> Though thou hast promis'd they should stay
> The tokens of the Church, and peace,[54]

is very different from the rather suspicious attitude of Donne and Herbert. In the same way, there is nothing in the praise given to the Virgin in "The Knot" that might offend the strictist Anglican theology as to her rôle in the process of redemption, but there is no mistaking the difference of feeling in the terms in which that praise is expressed, say, as compared with that of Herbert. It will be remembered how Herbert told the Virgin that he would very much like to give her honor, but hesitated to do so because he did not find it enjoined in Scripture.[55] There is no such hesitation in the warm opening of Vaughan's poem:

> Bright Queen of Heaven! Gods Virgin Spouse
> The glad worlds blessed maid!
> Whose beauty tyed life to thy house,
> And brought us saving ayd.[56]

It would be misleading to overemphasize the expression of appreciation of the aid of the saints given in an intimately personal commemoration like that of "Joy of my life!" but again there is a difference of atmosphere between what Vaughan says of the saints and their rôle in the life of the Christian and Herbert's explanation that he does not give honor because he cannot find warrant for doing so. It is a beautiful thing this, in various lines of which later commentators have seen sources for poets so widely different as Coleridge, Newman, and Masefield:

> Stars are of mighty use: The night
>   Is dark, and long;
> The Rode foul, and where one goes right,
>   Six may go wrong.
>   One twinkling ray
>   Shot o'r some cloud,
>   May clear much way
>   And guide a croud.
>
> Gods Saints are shining lights: who stays
>   Here long must passe
> O're dark hills, swift streames, and steep ways
>   As smooth as glasse;

> But these all night
> Like Candles, shed
> Their beams, and light
> Us into Bed.
>
> They are (indeed,) our Pillar-fires
>   Seen as we go,
> They are that Cities shining spires
>   We travell too;
> A swordlike gleame
> Kept man for sin
> First *Out;* This beame
> Will guide him *In.*[57]

In the same spirit, angels begin again to spring in the groves and shades of the banks of the Usk. It is not a point to be labored, but that stark Protestantism that in its terror of super-stition repudiated all friendly mediations and whitewashed the warm colors of the medieval imagination until the Scriptural landscape was left black and white like the interior of a Dutch cathedral, has been mitigated in Vaughan. The influence of the devout humanism of the Counter-Reformation, apparent in Vaughan's translations as in so much of the devotional literature of the time, may have had a good deal to do with it. It may be, too, that the danger of Rome did not seem so pressing in that hour of the triumph of Geneva. But whatever the causes, there is no mistaking the difference in atmosphere between Vaughan and his master Herbert or even the hospitable and far-ranging Ferrar.

This sensitiveness to influences other than those of his own immediate tradition is to be discerned, too, in the element in his view of the relations between the Creator and his world that wherever he obtained it, suggests the influence not only of Hermetical philosophy but also of that pre-Quaker ferment of religious ideas in which the immanence of God receives an emphasis that in general it had not enjoyed in England since the Reformation. But that influence is one to be studied in connection with Vaughan's nature ideas rather than here. Suffice it to say that real and convinced and organic as was Vaughan's churchmanship, the windows of his church were open to the many winds of doctrine that stirred the air of that exciting time.

CHAPTER XI

THE POETRY OF HENRY VAUGHAN

VAUGHAN begins, however, with the prevailing ideas of his tradition. That is, he begins where Donne and Herbert began, with the penitent, in a confession of sin and a prayer for forgiveness. It was the proper beginning for the Christian of his time, as indeed of any time. Vaughan uses the first person in his handling of the basic theological ideas of his tradition. Here he is unlike Crashaw, who, as we have seen, was much more preoccupied with his Redeemer than with himself, and here he is like Donne and Herbert. In a way, that is unfortunate for Vaughan, because Donne and Herbert are very hard to equal in the field of the sense of sin, and in the areas of their peculiar triumphs, impossible to surpass. There is nothing in Vaughan to match the truly awful terror of damnation of some of Donne's sermons, a terror that sheds its somber light over so many lines of his verse. Nor is there anything to match the blended passion of fear and remorse and challenge to heavenly justice that breathes through the finest of Herbert's highly personal penitential verses. Here Vaughan has been so unfortunate as to challenge comparison with masters of their grim genre in a field where he is adequate but in no sense first-rate.

Yet it is not quite fair to dismiss this aspect of Vaughan's work simply as a characteristic example of his imitation of Herbert. For it is older models that he is imitating here. When Vaughan began to cultivate the field of expression which Herbert had opened to him, he began with what was for him as for Herbert the basis of the entire personal religious life. He probably had no idea of what this new vein was to open for him; indeed, it is not impossible that he never knew how distinctive his contribution was ultimately to prove. Where he began was at the beginning, and the fact that he had nothing new to contribute at this point indicates not insincerity or unreality but simply that here his peculiar gifts as a religious genius and as a poet did not come together in such a fashion as to generate great poetry.

I am not sure that the real disservice that his devotion to his master did him was not in a very different field altogether. For the penitential poems of Herbert are among not only the most profoundly personal but the most profoundly deliberate and systematic of his creations. The strength of Vaughan is definitely not in the direct attack upon his subject. He has not the kind of mind that takes possession of his theme firmly and precisely. Rather his sensitivity outreaches his power of analysis, and his best intuitions would seem to come in a flash and all too often to vanish again when he tries to hold them or to fit their vague implications to a preconceived scheme. Here the very strength of Herbert would mislead him, and, I am inclined to think, did mislead him. Vaughan's humility was undoubtedly justified by the facts but not by its fruits. For Herbert was strong precisely where he was weak. If Vaughan could have added Herbert's gifts to his own, he would have been steadily the great poet he is now only in flashes. But he did not possess them, and the effect of their example, humbly appreciated and devoutly emulated, was unfortunate and misleading for the gifts which Vaughan did possess. Yet it must never be forgotten that had not Vaughan tried to do what Herbert had done and he could not do, he might never have found what he could do, as could no other poet of his time in his own limited but radiant genre. Here blame and regret are alike ungrateful and futile.

For an earlier generation this problem of sin had taken the form of a great concern for one thing, the making certain that one was among the elect, redeemed by the blood of the Saviour and so made acceptable to the great Judge. Predestination was at the beginning of the century the official theory of the English Church, but in practice, as we have seen, men like Donne had seriously modified it in the direction of free will. The state of mind, however, for which it was of the first importance to make sure that one had within himself the immediate and certain confidence of his own salvation, lingered long after intellectual accommodations were pretty widely accepted, and undoubtedly this was reënforced by the conversion and regeneration theories that came to play so large a part in the thought of the more "Enthusiastic" groups of the time.

Basically, there are two aspects to this problem of conversion or regeneration, whether it is faced in orthodox or heterodox groups, then or now. The first concerns illumination or the finding of God, the discovering of Him, the coming face to face with Him. The second concerns the relation which the worshipper seeks to establish with God on the basis of what he knows about Him. Both aspects may be envisaged in very different terms, depending on the religious tradition in which a man is working or his individual gifts and habits. For a man like Donne the nature of God, the ways of His dealings with men, the place where He is to be sought, the methods by which He is to be sought are not questions of discovery so much as of appropriation and realization. In the eyes of such a man, the Scriptures and the Church afford the Christian all he needs to know. That does not mean that Donne would close the field of speculation so much as that he would locate it and chart it. Herbert and Crashaw held pretty much the same view. But large groups of earnest and thoughtful men among their contemporaries were quite sure that not only the English

Church but all of the existing churches had as yet failed to make the right locations and still less the right interpretations. In that sense they were seekers for light and illumination, and many of them so called themselves.

On the other hand, there were then, as always, men who were not especially concerned with the intellectual problem. Some of them, especially among the more "Enthusiastic" groups, were not at all philosophical and intellectual. They were plain men. Probably the revolt of the plain man was a much more important factor in the troubles of the seventeenth century than has been commonly realized. For these men the speculations of the philosophers and the definitions of the theologians were alike remote and abstract. They wanted to come face to face with God, with the immediacy, the almost tactual directness and substantiality, that the plain man insists on. But there were still others, like the poet Crashaw, who paid little attention to philosophy because that was behind them, and they were pressing forward to the reality which the philosophy described. Crashaw knew the philosophic and theological formulations of his group and time and accepted them, but his interest was not in these formulations but in the reality for which they stood. For a man like him there was no conflict between the theology and the seeking, for one served the other, and the second fulfilled the first. Such a man is not really a seeker but rather a devotee, or a mystic, depending on the direction and the degree of integration of his effort.

Vaughan is related to both of these latter groups. There is little evidence of any passion of seeking, of any sharp hunger for fresh insight in his verses. He seems quite content with Scripture and Church. But there is evidence in his work, and this is, probably, the most startling thing about his verse, of precisely the sort of insight which many of the Seekers were looking for. It is as if what he were not looking for had come to him. His sense of the presence of God in nature is exactly the sort of thing which the Seekers, both the half-philosophic and the half-scientific like the Hermetists, and the more exclusively religious like some of the early Quakers, were interested in and looking for. Indeed, the resemblances between some of the ideas expressed in his verses and the ideas expressed in the Hermetical writings of his brother are so striking that it is difficult to avoid the conclusion, as we have seen, that there is some direct connection between the two. And the use which Vaughan made of Herbert's work suggests that it is not impossible that here again he has merely seized upon the poetic possibilities of a body of ideas. But it is interesting that while that precise charge of exploitation for poetic purposes has been made of his Herbert poems, no such theory seems ever to have been advanced of the Hermetic poems. For here there is something that in its surprise, in its freshness, bears upon its face the unmistakable evidence of its authenticity.

For Vaughan's appreciation of nature is not a matter of ideas or of perceptions but of sensitivity. It is not simply that he believes that God may be found in his creatures. It is rather that he has felt God there in his own immediate experience. Indeed, it is almost as if he had felt God there without at first being aware of what it was he had felt there, as if only after he had experienced in its fullness this overwhelming impression, had he been able to identify it. It is the feeling, the awareness, that comes first. It is the sensitivity that precedes the accounting for the experience, the explaining it, if you will. This is the opposite of literary exploitation, and all of Vaughan's readers seem to have recognized that fact at once. Indeed, they have rather tended to recognize that fact to the exclusion of other considerations just as important for an understanding of Vaughan's feeling for nature.

In the first place, the non-intellectual, primarily emotional character of Vaughan's experience has led a good many critics to regard it as an ideal type of primitive religious experience as contrasted with the more developed experiences of dogmatic religion. Now it is true that there is a good deal of evidence to suggest that a rather vague, undefined, only half self-conscious awareness of something other and beyond nature is not at all rare. A sense of the numinous, the German philosopher Rudolph Otto has defined this experience in his *The Idea of the Holy*.[1] This sense of the numinous may not rise above the level of a very vague and general feeling. It may also be defined in the direction of a sense of power or intention, and so become a sort of animism. It may be explained in terms of beauty or unity, and so become the foundation of a type of pantheism. It may take on moral connotations that make the latent sense of awe explicit as happens in some of Wordsworth's autobiographical verses, say that passage in the *Prelude* in which he recounts the episode of the stolen boat.[2] It may coexist with quite different forms of religious consciousness and color them, or be drawn into their orbit. This is suggested in a story of Saint Francis of Assisi of a locality which on his first acquaintance with it had made a deep impression on him. He said to a friend, "This is a holy place!" In all probability, the same basic emotional experience is involved in all these cases, but the point of reference, the context, varies from individual to individual, depending on the swiftness with which sensibility is re-enforced by reflection, and the kind and range of ideas which the individual brings to the interpretation of the original awareness.

In Vaughan's case, we may be pretty sure, the experience preceded any attempt at identification, any possibility of analysis. This probability is heightened by the fact that in at least two other fields, Vaughan seems to have possessed the same type and intensity of sensitivity—in his perception of the relations between life and death, one of those themes on which all men are sooner or later brought to some degree of reflection, and in the reminiscences of his childhood which involve not only the mystery of sin and sorrow but the still more fundamental mystery of the identity of the soul. Here Vaughan seems to have shown the same type of sensitivity as he showed in his grasp of the presence of God in nature, and to have experienced an awareness as piercing and as rich and as haunting as any of his experiences of nature. Indeed if one recognizes the beginning of his poem on "The World" as perhaps his most breath-taking flight, then perhaps even more so. But here his expression is not as complete or as sustained or as explicit as his expression of his intuition of nature. It is just possible that the difference is to be accounted for on the very ground that in the Hermetic theory of the relations of God and nature he had ready to hand an account, an explanation, that could do justice to his own personal experience of nature, and, it may be added, an explanation that could be fitted into the context of his very real and very sincere Christian belief.

But this does not mean that there was anything mechanical or conventional in that reference. Indeed, we shall see that quite the contrary is true if we recall the religious emphases of his time. For the very intensity with which the seventeenth century had laid hold upon certain aspects of the Christian tradition and the rigor with which it had devoted itself to the exploration and the apprehension of those truths had led to the neglect of certain other aspects of the Christian tradition. The spirit of the time, even when not specifically Puritan, was to a greater extent than is always remembered today, the product of a period of rigorous scrutiny and testing, of sharpened definition, of deliberate winnowing and selection, and, on the reverse side, of resolute rejection and elimination. The makers of the seventeenth-century Church of England believed that Christianity in the Middle Ages had become corrupt and adulterate. They tended, therefore, among other things, to focus and to concentrate their religious attention. For them the power and the justice of God the Creator and the Judge, and the love and sacrifice of God the Son and Redeemer held the center of the religious stage, and the relations of fallen and predestined man to these central facts rigorously defined and even confined theological speculation. The result was that God the Holy Spirit with all the magnificent and at times, it must be confessed, mysterious implications of the rôle of the Third Person in the Trinity, tended to be confined to the witnessing to, and the insistence upon, the foregoing dogmas. Even the so-called "Enthusiastic groups" who were not satisfied with the official definitions of the fundamental Christian positions tended to confine their invocation of the Holy Spirit to the discovery and ratification of other definitions and conclusions on the same issues. That God was everywhere was a position to which all Christians would have agreed, as they would have agreed that the whole universe and its creatures was the work of His hands. But in their preoccupations with the central issues of justice and mercy, of power and satisfaction, of sin and justification, they were on the whole not disposed to emphasize, still less to do justice to, the implications of the Christian doctrine of the immanence of God in the world of his creation.

It is not surprising, therefore, that in the welter of "Enthusiasm" and "Brownism" in which some of the omissions of the orthodoxy of the time were vindicated, this of the immanence of God should find its place. Some of this "Enthusiasm" was due probably to a very understandable revolt against the restrictions of the religion of order and authority which Hooker and Andrewes had sought to erect as a barricade against the fantasies of the private spirit. Some was due to a more or less self-conscious reaction against the definitions of moderation and decency which the official religion had set up. But to no small extent, especially in those tendencies that anticipated the Quaker movement of later in the century, there was a thoroughly organic effort to recover the full power of an element in the Christian tradition that had been of recent years neglected. And this tendency in the groups to the Geneva side was re-enforced in the other direction by those further developments of the Counter-Reformation that led in Catholic countries to what the late Abbé Brémond so vividly described as "The Mystic Invasion." [3] It would be rash to try to orient Vaughan by means of Crashaw and George Fox, but it is true that tendencies seemingly moving in opposite directions were co-operating to restore to the religious consciousness of the seventeenth century one of the most perilous but also one of the most stimulating and enriching conceptions of the Christian tradition.

Vaughan does noble justice to the possibilities of this conception even in those passages of direct and explicit statement that are usually not his happiest form of poetic expression.

> O thou! whose spirit did at first inflame
>   And warm the dead.
> And by a sacred Incubation fed
>   With life this frame
> Which once had neither being, forme, nor name,
>   Grant I may so
>   Thy steps track here below,
>
> That in these Masques and shadows I may see
>   Thy sacred way,
> And by those hid ascents climb to that day
>   Which breaks from thee
> Who art in all things, though invisibly: [4]

so he prays in one of those nameless poems of *Silex Scintillans* that contain some of his most exquisitely complete and winged utterances. It is his prevailing point of view, expressed over and over again in his praise of God as the preserving spirit of his Creation and as the source of all the life of the world. It is expressed less directly but no less explicitly when he declares that the whole of Creation is implicit in the part, or praises his God as discovered in his creatures. [5]

In all this there is nothing contrary in doctrine to the Christian theory of Vaughan's day, nothing incompatible in implication. Donne again and again in his sermons speaks of the "Book of the Creatures" as the second book of revelation. But Donne's emphasis is on God as the Creator and on the creatures as his handiwork, and still more on the intention and as it were the lesson of the Creation. Not so Vaughan's. His interest is in God the Inspirer and the Life that enters into the Creation, and it is for the witness of their being and their action that he values the "Book of the Creatures." Yet though Vaughan goes beyond the sources of his official position, he still remains in the tradition of his time. Sensitive as he is to the charm of nature, it is not the wonder and the beauty and the mysterious radiance of the Creation that primarily engages his attention. Rather it is the lesson which the creatures afford to man, that creature so grievously in need of lessoning for Vaughan as for all seventeenth-century religious thinkers.

For that reason his view of nature cannot be understood without a glance at his view of man. That view of man no doubt is colored by his experience of himself. Most views are. But it is a view of man grounded, as can easily be seen from his prefaces as well as from his poetry, in a sustained and deeply concerned scrutiny of his own time. It is the rebelliousness, the readiness to follow after strange gods, the instability and the distraction of human nature, that pained him in his melancholy and often indignant contemplation of the human scene actually before him. It is these qualities that seem to him the prevailing and persistent characteristics of fallen man. Against this distraction, this instability, this deep-rooted rebellion, he finds in the processes of nature, particularly in the instinctive life of animals, and the sustained routine of the motions of the heavenly bodies, and the undistracted patience of the inanimate things of earth, a majestic contrast of obedience, order, stability, and peace.[6] And there is something not only sublime in this spectacle but also something pathetic in that the faithless and turbulent rebel to divine order and peace is that creature which the Creator set above all the rest of the Creation, as the voice of the whole inarticulate universe. In rebelling and so falling from his destined grace and glory, man has betrayed not only himself but these helpless creatures, too.[7] And yet they still keep their ancient ways, and in majestic obedience and faithfulness they raise the quire of universal praise which the sinfulness of man has not scrupled to omit. Nothing, therefore, can afford so majestic a contrast to man's behavior or so shameful a rebuke or so challenging an example to him as this steadfastness of the faithful and innocent creatures.

In this emphasis Vaughan yields to the moral preoccupation of his time. In so doing he makes some sacrifice in cosmic range and perhaps in esthetic subtlety, but he gains immensely in relevance, integrity, and emotional direction. There is a certain drive of moral purpose that transforms what might so easily have been sentimental and merely idyllic into something central to the life and feeling of his age. That is something which the view of Vaughan that sees in him primarily the animist clipped and confined by Christian dogmatism, misses.

So far there is nothing in Vaughan's expression of his awareness of nature alien or extraneous to the main traditions of Christianity. But when it comes to the development of these ideas, there are certain elements which are definitely not Christian in their origins. These elements have engaged the attention of a number of scholars, culminating in Miss Elizabeth Holmes' study of the Hermetic elements in his work.[8] There are a number of these elements which might be discussed. In a brief study like this, however, two will do for the whole group. The first is the idea of a definite and involved relation between the different parts of the creation, between the different orders of the creatures. The second is the idea that there is a definite commerce between heaven and earth, a commerce of which man may take advantage by studying and contemplating the creatures.

The notion of the relation between the microcosm and the macrocosm, the microcosm the little nature of man, the macrocosm the great and extended nature of the universe, is of course older than Christianity and is to be found present in some form in all periods of Christian thought. Donne was fascinated by it, for instance, but we cannot be sure that the fact that this notion was widespread among the Christian thinkers of the time in any way suggests a specifically Christian appropriation of the idea, for Donne like many of his contemporaries was familiar with Hermetic ideas and probably with Hermetic literature. The extension of this conception to include the "creatures" was, however, foreign to Donne as to his time. But it is the central conception of the Hermetic tradition. "The greater and lesser worlds corresponded both in outline and in detail . . . This correspondence, with the 'sympathy' it involves, is the secret of the Hermetic medicine," says Miss Holmes.[9] And the power that holds together these corresponding elements is that "tye of bodies" which binds the herbs and the stars together in verse after verse of Vaughan.[10] It is very hard to determine the provenience of ideas in an age so eclectic as that of the seventeenth-century doctor, an age in which ideas of very diverse origin gravitate to central points of view and are made to confirm or to extend cherished beliefs. The peculiar fascination which the phenomena of magnetism exerted on the mind of Vaughan is not peculiarly or necessarily Hermetic.[11] But it is not unlikely that the scientific illustration it seemed to afford of the practical working of the sympathy of the universe was what made it so deeply appeal to him. And it should be added that any contemplation of this type of the mysteriously ordered and, as it seemed, purposive working of natural processes would re-enforce the penitent Christian's awe before the spectacle of the obedience of unfallen nature.

But the contemplation of nature for its own sake was not the province of the English religious poet of the seventeenth century, nor is it that of Vaughan. However much of a naturalist he may have been, as one of the letters to Aubrey suggests, that was not his main interest.[12] His main interest was the illumination of man, his possible salvation. "When I take up a stone or clod of earth and look upon it; then I see that which is above, and that which is below, yea, the whole world therein," said Boehme.[13] But for Vaughan it was not merely a matter of seeing. It was also a matter of hearing what these creatures spoke to him. There was nothing passive anywhere in the universe. The least of the creatures contained the eloquent presence of God, and each of them, sentient, radiant with that Presence, gave its message to the wistful and homesick soul of man. For the creatures had preserved that intercourse between heaven and earth that man in his wilfulness had broken. That is the message of "Cock-crowing," one of the most revealing of all Vaughan's poems with its subtle and by no means entirely extricable blend of Hermetism, of Christian tradition, and probably also of that potent blend of the two in German mysticism of which the most influential example for England at this time was to be found in the works of Jacob Boehme.

The Hermetists in spite of all the fantasies of their language and the perversions to which some of their alchemistic inquiries were exposed seem on the whole to have had a taste for religious conformity, for as a rule both in the Middle Ages and at the time of the Reformation they made profession of Christian orthodoxy according to the prevailing beliefs of the milieu in which they found themselves.[14] And there is no reason to suspect the sincerity of those professions unless one is inclined, as are some students of the out-of-the-way in religious psychology, to suspect the sincerity of all orthodox profession on the part of the eclectically interested. For it should not be forgotten that orthodoxy in certain sections at least of seventeenth-century religious feeling in England was curious in its inquiries and hospitable in its speculations. There was no zone of quarantine around its passionately-held preserves. That is one of the most characteristic and most interesting of its qualities. Of this there is probably no better example in the poetry of the time than Vaughan's "Cock-crowing":

> Father of lights! what Sunnie seed,
> What glance of day hast thou confin'd
> Into this bird? To all the breed
> This busie Ray thou hast assign'd;
> > Their magnetisme works all night,
> > And dreams of Paradise and light.

> Their eyes watch for the morning hue,
> Their little grain expelling night
> So shines and sings, as if it knew
> The path unto the house of light.
> > It seems their candle, howe'r done,
> > Was tinn'd and lighted at the sunne.

> If such a tincture, such a touch,
> So firm a longing can impowre
> Shall thy own image think it much
> To watch for thy appearing hour?
> > If a meer blast so fill the sail,
> > Shall not the breath of God prevail?

> O thou immortall light and heat!
> Whose hand so shines through all this frame,
> That by the beauty of the seat,
> We plainly see, who made the same.
> > Seeing thy seed abides in me,
> > Dwell thou in it, and I in thee.

> To sleep without thee, is to die;
> Yea, 'tis a death partakes of hell:
> For where thou dost not close the eye

It never opens, I can tell.
In such a dark, Ægyptian border,
The shades of death dwell and disorder.

If joyes, and hopes, and earnest throws,
And hearts, whose Pulse beats still for light
Are given to birds; who, but thee, knows
A love-sick souls exalted flight?
Can souls be track'd by any eye
But his, who gave them wings to flie?

Onely this Veyle which thou hast broke,
And must be broken yet in me,
This veyle, I say, is all the cloke
And cloud which shadows thee from me.
This veyle thy full-ey'd love denies,
And onely gleams and fractions spies.

O take it off! make no delay,
But brush me with thy light, that I
May shine unto a perfect day,
And warme me at thy glorious Eye!
O take it off! or till it flee,
Though with no Lilie, stay with me! [15]

But this poem, so rich in its implications, so sustained in its
flight, is important, too, for the light it throws on still other elements in Vaughan's "nature mysticism." The first of these is
the sense of a veil between the soul of man and the world which
he looks out upon. In common with the German mystics
Vaughan found the saddest consequence of the fall in the
blindness and the deadness of the spirit of man. Here in certain
natural phenomena, notably those of the ending of night and
the breaking of dawn, Vaughan found that the veil wore thin,
and something of the light behind the darkness of this world
shone through. There were other occasions when Vaughan
found the same thing happening—when he thought of the dead

and the relations between life and death, when he thought of the past, and it rose clear behind the mists of the present in the innocence of childhood or the sweet freshness of the primitive world, and finally when he thought of any of the diverse manifestations of the conflict between light and darkness in nature or in the soul of man.[16]

It is significant that Vaughan did not share the point of view of the Christian Platonists who saw the world in an ascending series from the humilities of the little life of earth to the footsteps of the throne of God. Rather like the Hermetists he saw the earth in a descending series, with the mighty influences of the heavens descending upon the earth, and the earth joyously acknowledging their power. Hence that prayer to God that all the world may become "thy cloudless glass." [17] Hence that specific and even dramatically alive commerce between heaven and earth, remembered from the insights of childhood, yearned for in the exile and estrangement of fallen maturity.[18] Hence, too, that yearning to re-establish that bright intercourse, to restore that broken communion.

It is a pity that the use which a later and greater poet made of some of Vaughan's speculations as to the relations between man and God in nature and in the innocence of childhood has focussed attention rather upon those points in which Vaughan is like Wordsworth than upon those points in which he is like nobody else. It is true that he recalls with wistfulness a nearness of heaven to innocent and responsive childhood to which the adult man has long been a stranger. It is true that he gives some striking glimpses of the human spirit come from aboriginal light into the darkness of common day and the distraction of the common lot. And men have debated whether or not he believed in the pre-existence of the soul. But even more striking than Vaughan's picture of the light of childhood and its fresh joy in the natural world is his vision of the beginning of the world, of the radiant earth before the fall, and the sweetness of the as yet not wholly estranged childhood of the race. Like the ancient Greeks for whom in a time of confusion the dim memory of a more settled and less ambitious world bred the great dream of the golden age, so Vaughan in the confusion and seeming destruction of his time turned to a world in which communications were not yet broken and simpler men lived in closer relation to God in obedience and worship, conserving, even though fallen, the ancient sanctities:

> I walk the fields of *Bethani* which shine
> All now as fresh as *Eden,* and as fine.
> Such was the bright world, on the first seventh day,
> Before man brought forth sin, and sin decay;
> When like a Virgin clad in *Flowers* and *green*
> The pure earth sat, and the fair woods had seen
> No frost, but flourish'd in that youthful vest,
> With which their great Creator had them drest:
> When Heav'n above them shin'd like molten glass,
> While all the Planets did unclouded pass;
> And Springs, like dissolv'd Pearls their Streams did pour
> Ne'r marr'd with floods, nor anger'd with a showre.[19]

In this looking back to Eden there is of course nothing peculiar to Vaughan. It was one of the favorite speculations of the more "Enthusiastic" groups of the time. It is almost as if the Reformation retreat from the Middle Ages to the primitive Church, with all the disputes as to that institution that had arisen out of the controversies of the sixteenth century, had brought the seventeenth-century heirs of those primitivists to go still farther back into the days before a church was needed, to find the unbroken communion of Eden. Among these seekers of Eden there is something which the reader with Wordsworthian preoccupations is apt to overlook in Vaughan. There is, it is true, sometimes a wistfulness and a nostalgia in this remembering of Eden, but more often there is a very distinct aggressiveness in this seeking of the first innocence, a faith that it can be recaptured, and a determination to re-win it. This Vaughan shares, and it is, I think, the secret of the peculiar rapture with which he develops the theme of the primal innocence. Here is something that quite literally sweeps him off his feet. It is something entirely different from the note of exile and longing in "They are all gone into the world of light!" the sense of wonder and bafflement as to where the fled soul of bird or loved one has gone from the abandoned shell of the body. It is a passion of seeking, a hope of finding, that gives an entirely different dynamic to his verse and wings with poetry its most unexpected expressions.

> I soar and rise
> Up to the skies,
>   Leaving the world their day,
> And in my flight,
> For the true light
>   Go seeking all the way;

he sings in "Ascension-day," and in the "Ascension-Hymn" that follows these verses he speaks with even more sureness of accent:

> Dust and clay
> Mans antient wear!
> Here you must stay,
> But I elsewhere;
> Souls sojourn here, but may not rest;
> Who will ascend must be undrest.

> And yet some
> That know to die
> Before death come,
> Walk to the skie
> Even in this life.[20]

Vaughan has the authentic thirst of the mystic for the reaching of God here and now in the individual soul. It is Crashaw's desire but with a difference. For Vaughan's God is fundamentally different from Crashaw's. He is not the human Incarnation of Divine Love to be traced in every least line or episode of the Gospel story, to be sought after with all the passion of human need and affection, to be apprehended in the simple, human passages and contexts of man's life and love. His God is Divine Providence, to whose will man should submit, with which man should identify himself, and He is, as we have seen, the life and light of the universe. This does not mean that one may not find even a number of passages in which Christ or God is invoked in terms of quick feeling ranging anywhere from the intimacy of tenderness to ecstasy. There is for instance, that poem on "Jesus Weeping" with the direct address of the opening, "My dear, Almighty Lord! why dost thou weep?" But though the verses gradually intensify until they reach a climax of feeling, it is interesting to see how the somewhat Crashaw-like treatment of the emotion for its own sake slips into the habitual theme of the inspiration and the redemption of the world:

> O holy groans! Groans of the Dove!
> O healing tears! the tears of love!
> Dew of the dead! which makes dust move
> And spring, how is't that you so sadly grieve,
> Who can relieve? [21]

Basically, it is not the contemplation of God or the adoration of God that moves the journeying heart of Vaughan. It is rather the light and the quickening of God, that true life which he set against the phantom and deceitful life of the world's clinging. Beautifully he drew that distinction in one of the strangest and most moving of his verses, "Quickness":

Thou art a toylsom Mole, or less
    A moving mist
But life is, what none can express,
A quickness, which my God hath kist.[22]

It is this God, seen not in the creatures of his hand so much as against the darkness and illusion of the world of man's perception and consciousness, that Vaughan seeks in some of the least contemporary of his lines. It is God beheld out of the confusion and the mystery of life by means of that "Ray," that spark of light which He has sent into the soul of man, which makes him see in darkness, and if one may for a moment confuse the senses, hear in silence. That is the theme of one of the most Dionysian of his poems, "The Night," especially in the following passage of direct apostrophe:

Dear night! this worlds defeat;
The stop to busie fools; cares check and curb;
The day of Spirits; my souls calm retreat
        Which none disturb!
Christs progress, and his prayer time;
The hours to which high Heaven doth chime

    Gods silent, searching flight:
When my Lords head is fill'd with dew, and all
His locks are wet with the clear drops of night;
        His still, soft call;
    His knocking time; The souls dumb watch,
    When Spirits their fair kinred catch.

                .   .   .   .   .

    There is in God (some say)
A deep, but dazling darkness; As men here
Say it is late and dusky, because they
        See not all clear;
    O for that night! where I in him
    Might live invisible and dim.[23]

It is this thought of light out of darkness, that prompts Vaughan's many and beautiful passages in praise of death, and that gives distinction to his handling of that favorite theme of all seventeenth-century poetry and piety. True, Vaughan has his share of the characteristic seventeenth-century mortuary splendor. He can invoke the ultimate dust with all that lucidity of horror and that mockery of pride in which the age revelled, and he has his share of the solemn pomp and pageantry with which that imaginative time half shrouded, half exploited, its one whole-hearted tribute to the basic mysteries of life. But it is not death as the leveller of all pride and the dissolution of beauty that he celebrates, but death as the dark gate to the radiance of eternity. Vaughan's was a peculiarly tenacious tenderness of affection, and he seems unable to resign the lost to the usual sanctities of seventeenth-century piety. The result is that some of the loveliest of his poems are those nameless verses in which he rises from the lament of various loved ones who have taken their ways to other climes to a vision of that world which now holds them from his sight. And the loving memory of them he employs not to harrow grief or to enhance penitence, as do so many of his contemporaries, but to pierce the veil that hides their world from his earth-darkened eyes.[24]

Of these the finest is the famous "They are all gone into the world of light!" so fine that it seems a pity to quote only a part of it. But beautiful as is the beginning, the distinctive tribute to death is to be found a little farther on, in the following rapt apostrophe and the stanzas that develop its theme:

Dear, beauteous death! the Jewel of the Just,
    Shining no where, but in the dark;
What mysteries do lie beyond thy dust;
    Could man outlook that mark!

He that hath found some fledg'd birds nest, may know
    At first sight, if the bird be flown;

But what fair Well, or Grove he sings in now,
　That is to him unknown.

And yet, as Angels in some brighter dreams
　Call to the soul, when man doth sleep:
So some strange thoughts transcend our wonted theams,
　And into glory peep.

If a star were confin'd into a Tomb
　Her captive flames must needs burn there;
But when the hand that lockt her up, gives room,
　She'l shine through all the sphaere.

O Father of eternal life, and all
　Created glories under thee!
Resume thy spirit from this world of thrall
　Into true liberty.[25]

Seldom has the view of death as the release of the spirit from the bondage of material existence been more glowingly expressed. It is, of course, one of the classic themes of Christian poetry and of the poetry of the time, but Vaughan gives to his handling of it his own peculiar accent. The sense of the mystery of what was here but a moment ago as actual as the consciousness that contemplated it, and now is gone, he knows not where, is part of the magic of the preceding passage. So is the luminous sense of the impingement of eternity upon time, not as something strange, but as the innermost desire of the human spirit, its true home. Even more directly is the same idea expressed in the conclusion of "The Water-fall":

　　　O my invisible estate,
　　　My glorious liberty, still late!
　　　Thou art the Channel my soul seeks,
　　　Not this with Cataracts and Creeks.[26]

Whatever his theme, this is the ultimate objective of Vaughan. And this is the source of the sincerity rising at times

even to passion that breathes through his work, and that wings
his most brilliant and characteristic passages. It is, in a certain
sense, the defining mark of his mysticism, and upon our estimate of the intensity and direction of this force depends our
answer to that question on which Vaughan's critics have so
strikingly divided. For some Vaughan is pretty nearly the
most mystical of all these poets,[27] for others, notably Mr. T. S.
Eliot, he is not a mystic in any sense worth mentioning.[28] It
is ultimately a question of what one means by mysticism, depending on whether one is primarily impressed by the range
of a man's awareness of and sensitiveness to mystical elements,
or whether one insists, rather, on the central core of real, developed mystical experience. That Vaughan has the mystic's
desire for immediate contact with reality behind all the shows
of things, there can be, I think, no question. But when one
compares his seeking for reality with, say, Crashaw's, one is
immediately struck by an essential difference. There is an in-
tensiveness, a direction, a precision even of feeling, in Crashaw
that one seeks for on the whole in vain in Vaughan.

The difference goes back ultimately to the nature of their
experience of the reality which they seek. Probably all mystical experience begins in rather vague intuitions. The story of
the awakening of the Buddha as told in one of the famous birth
stories which Warren has included in his interesting volume
of Buddhist translations shows how vague uneasiness is presently transformed under the stress of the three "showings" into
a very sharp and definite conviction of the worthlessness of human life.[29] That vague sense of the incompleteness of the immediately present Vaughan had without question.

He had more. Definite as were his doctrinal commitments,
he had also a sense of the environing mystery of the universe,
of those things that are beyond the reach of the senses and of
the formulations of the mind. He was frankly sceptical of the
competence of the human reason to perceive all the relevant

aspects of the world.[30] In an age of passionate inquiry and speculation, in which, as we have seen, he shared fully, he was not at all sure that some even of the passive and seemingly inanimate creatures did not possess a surer grasp on the essentials of the universe than the restless mind of man.[31] And he was quite unlike most of his contemporaries even among the religious poets in appreciating the perceptive value of wonder. There is, it is true, a good deal of evidence of appreciation of the preëminently religious sentiment of awe in other poets of the time, especially in Herbert and Crashaw. But of the less intellectual, more purely emotional, response of wonder there is much less. Here Vaughan is rather out of his time, not entirely, of course—there is always Sir Thomas Browne—but in degree and self-consciousness of feeling in this realm he tends to outstrip his fellow poets.

What is true of Vaughan's wonder is also, I think, true of his general perception of the reality beyond. It is a vague, diffused, often very imperfectly identified feeling. There is a certain aura-like character about it, quite foreign to the ecstasy of Crashaw, for instance, quite foreign to the substantiality of the whole baroque tradition and indeed to the metaphysical with its passion for precision and for compression of emotion as of thought. It is not highly articulated. Its points of reference are few; above all it is vague in direction. It is the sort of feeling that will make a man walk the ways of this world in wonder and delight rather than the passion that makes the mystic forsake all to concentrate on the spiritual labor of the mystic way.

Yet if there is such a thing as an emotional ground-work out of which more specialized passions and intensities spring, then Vaughan's discovery of God in his own feeling of nature is basically mystical. And no lover of the mystics will, I think, fail to add his "Amen" to what is Vaughan's final and most explicit prayer, the close to his poem "The Book":

> O knowing, glorious spirit! when
> Thou shalt restore trees, beasts and men,
> When thou shalt make all new again,
> Destroying onely death and pain,
> Give him amongst thy works a place,
> Who in them lov'd and sought thy face! [32]

As for the instrument which Vaughan had to hand for the expression of this experience of his, it was in itself, however imperfect, a rich one. There is none of his great predecessors in the field of devotional poetry whose influence cannot be found in his pages, Donne, Herbert, Crashaw. Particularly interesting is the influence of the latter, to be detected not only in specific phrases like "neast of nights" [33] but, still more important, in the general development of the emotional possibilities of his themes. It would be rash to say in view of the delicacy of some of Herbert's studies of his own states of mind that his influence would not be sufficient to account for almost any subjective elements in his disciple's work. But there is, as we have seen, a very real difference in degree of emotional self-consciousness between Herbert and Crashaw. There is a fullness of body to the emotional studies of Crashaw that beside the purposive analysis of Herbert must seem almost luxurious. There is something of this in Vaughan. The air is perhaps clearer, there is less of incense and more of the freshness of the free wind in it, but there is in it, too, the same seeing of all experience through the quickening but nonetheless veiling glass of personal sensitivity.

There is a very considerable range of feeling in Vaughan even in the religious verse alone, probably a greater range than in either Herbert or Crashaw. There is, as compared with Crashaw, not only a certain out-of-door freshness but also a certain modulation. There is less of fire in Vaughan and more of that diffused white light that was so dear to him and of which he speaks so often.[34] Sometimes, as he tells us in his poem on childhood, his eyes dazzle, but the "great *Ring* of pure and endless light" that is the height of his ecstasy remains, as he says, "All calm, as it was bright." [35] His perception of the world of his vision is flashing and intermittent, but there is about that world, however seen, the steadiness and the peace he could never find on earth in the troubled works of man. There is something other-worldly about Vaughan's visions that on the whole is not to be found in Herbert and Crashaw. That is the secret, I think, of that "mystical feeling" that is so common an impression of Vaughan's works.

No small amount of this impression is due, of course, to the character of his imagery. The modern reader who approaches Vaughan as a nature poet in the modern sense is likely to be disappointed. There is very little detail of nature in his verses. Very little of flower or tree or shrub. Those darkling gardens in which the lover of Keats revels, those verdant lanes into which Tennyson has brought now generations of readers, the daffodils that Wordsworth saw by Ullswater, all of these exquisite details which we owe to the romantic movement are not to be found in Vaughan. His flowers are the classical rose and myrtle and lily, and though he does mention juniper and oak, the primrose, and "the low violet" on occasion, there is no exploitation of their distinctive characters. Birds come in, but they are important chiefly for the voices they raise in the morning chorus. When they are named, the legendary phoenix comes in with the mystic dove. The remora and the ass and the bee and the silkworm receive their due share of notice, but it is to point a moral rather than to swell the treasures of poetic observation.

The truth is that it is the larger and more general aspects of nature that engage Vaughan's attention for their own sake. Yet there is nothing of landscape, nothing of wide views or sudden perspectives. Mountains or the movements of the hills do not interest Vaughan. But the flowing of a river, the dropping of a waterfall, the shifting of light across the hours of the day do very much engage his interest and his loving observation.

There are, too, in his verses a good many of those splendid openings of light and darkness with which the Elizabethans hailed the breaking of dawn and the coming of night. Indeed, there are passages where the sheer description takes on an unwonted precision, and the reader is wise to weigh every word and its implications carefully, as in the sixth stanza of "Regeneration":

> The unthrift Sunne shot vitall gold
>   A thousand peeces,
> And heaven its azure did unfold
>   Checqur'd with snowie fleeces,
>   The aire was all in spice
>   And every bush
> A garland wore; Thus fed my Eyes
> But all the Eare lay hush.[36]

But here again, the important thing is not the picture but the stimulus and the poet's reaction to it. Very seldom is any natural phenomenon, any moment of nature, viewed in its own literal light. Almost always nature comes suffused in feeling, with the light of its implications upon its calm surface. Sometimes this assimilation goes even to the extreme of the metaphysical absurdity, "the comely spacious Whale," [37] but that is very rare in Vaughan, for he lacks that preoccupation with the main advance of his thought that is responsible for most of the aberrations of the metaphysicals. There is usually in his imagery, as in his thought, less tension, greater flexibility and range than in that of his fellows. The result is that diffused magic so brilliantly illustrated by the opening lines of "The Timber":

Sure thou didst flourish once! and many Springs,
Many bright mornings, much dew, many showers
Past ore thy head: many light *Hearts* and *Wings*
Which now are dead, lodg'd in thy living bowers.

And still a new succession sings and flies;
Fresh Groves grow up, and their green branches shoot
Towards the old and still enduring skies,
While the low *Violet* thrives at their root.[38]

Indeed, in such a passage it is the poet's sensibility that clothes in fresh light an imagery as conventional as that of most of Shakespeare's sonnets.

But there is another type of imagery to be found in Vaughan which is probably more intimately related to his metaphysical heritage, which savors less of the classical movement from Jonson to Milton. That is to be found in those fascinating minglings of the lofty and the homely which add so much to the piquancy of metaphysical poetry as they did to that of the Middle Ages. In Vaughan the almost shocking audacity of Donne or Crashaw has been modulated, and the effect is charming rather than bizarre, giving intimacy rather than lightening to the passage as a whole. The opening of "The Bird" is one example and a very lovely one:

Hither thou com'st: the busie wind all night
Blew through thy lodging, where thy own warm wing
Thy pillow was. Many a sullen storm
(For which course man seems much the fitter born,)
    Rain'd on thy bed
    And harmless head.[39]

But for depth of significance the opening lines of "Buriall" are perhaps the finest of all:

O thou! the first fruits of the dead
    And their dark bed,

> When I am cast into that deep
>   And senseless sleep
> The wages of my sinne,
>   O then,
> Thou great Preserver of all men!
>   Watch o're that loose
>   And empty house,
> Which I sometimes liv'd in.

> It is (in truth!) a ruin'd peece
>   Not worth thy Eyes,
> And scarce a room but wind, and rain
>   Beat through, and stain
> The seats, and Cells within;
>   Yet thou
> Led by thy Love wouldst stoop thus low,
>   And in this Cott
>   All filth, and spott,
> Didst with thy servant Inne.[40]

But whatever the type of imagery Vaughan uses, it serves to express his predominant theme, the flash of that other world on the sight of this, the finding of God in the little things of the world he has made.

In the relations between style, in the sense of the general handling of resources, and the impulses which inspire that handling, it is dangerous to dogmatize as to which is cause and which effect. It is perhaps nearer to the truth to say that the same personal gifts and limitations that characterize Vaughan's mysticism are revealed in his verse as verse. There is that flashing quality that affords many brilliant beginnings and not a few brilliant endings, but that very seldom yields a fully sustained piece. This aspect of Vaughan's poetic power has been pretty generally recognized, indeed, perhaps over-emphasized. For there are more poems which carry through on a fairly sustained arc of feeling and imagination than most discussions of Vaughan's verse would lead one to suspect. But it is true that in a number of the better-known of his poems, there is a wonderful beginning which presently seems to fail completely. Especially is this true of what is perhaps Vaughan's best-known poem, "I saw Eternity the other night." Every student of Vaughan's poetry has been struck by the curious tameness and flatness of what follows that breath-taking opening. And most have sadly shaken their heads over the swift extinction of that wonderful jet of vision.

What has not been so generally recognized is that what follows is quite surprisingly coherent and logical and on its own level rather well-sustained picture of the world as seen from that vantage point of vision. It has been often said that Vaughan's mind, his faculty of sustained reflection and construction, is not of the same distinguished order as his sensibility. A great many of the world's poems begin in a jet of inspiration, and it is the business of the artist to take hold where inspiration fails and carry through the process of creation. So viewed, Vaughan's performance suggests two very different levels of intellectual capacity, very high on the level of sensibility, but much lower on the reflective level. There is a good deal of evidence in Vaughan's work to bear out that theory. Yet I am not sure that the real cause of this fall is not to be sought elsewhere, not so much in Vaughan's capacity as in his attitude. After all, if when he has eternity open before him, a man will look down upon time, it is not surprising if his verse looks down, too, and abashed marches along in much flatter and more conventional terms. Vaughan is not alone here. Most seventeenth-century poets seem to have some disinclination to remaining or trying to remain long at the white heat of ecstasy. It is not lack of faith in ecstasy; still less is it any failure of taste for the heights. But they have no passion for building castles in the lofty inane. Rather their taste is for keeping both heaven and home in sight. Vaughan is to some extent at least merely a rather dramatic example of a common tendency.

Less spectacular but no less characteristic is the general loose texture of his structure. Against the firm line of Herbert's structure, Vaughan's line seems often to fumble and waver. On the other hand, there are very few of his poems that can be fairly described in the terms with which Crashaw described some of his verses, as a descant on a certain theme. They do have beginning, middle, and end, but the articulation is often very easy, and there is no drive of logic to pull the elements more tightly together. In general, they are stronger in development than in form, and are copious rather than incisive. What is true of the whole poem tends to be true of the unit. Vaughan abounds in beautiful phrases but not in periods that shoot straight to their mark. Significantly, there is very little of the epigram or the emblem in Vaughan. For though the brief flight is his gift, he has little capacity for compression. One never feels of his verse that here is infinite riches in a little room, but on the other hand, there is an unmistakable power of radiance in it. It is always carrying the responsive reader beyond itself.

The same is true of Vaughan's vocabulary. That precision and variety of sub-surface implication that is one of the secrets of the perennial fascination of metaphysical poetry is rare in Vaughan. His vocabulary, like the vocabulary of Crashaw, is limited, and somewhat monotonous.[41] He has something of the same tendency to use words in a special, almost liturgical meaning, like "herb" and "star," but the emotional aura of his vocabulary is much more extensive. Very simple, often-repeated elements are charged with an emotion that gives them that constant air of freshness that is so characteristic of Vaughan's work.

And the emotion is much more direct in its operation than in Crashaw. Indeed, Crashaw's wonderful musical virtuosity sometimes makes it doubtful whether it is the feeling that charges the music or the music that generates the feeling. There is no such doubt in Vaughan. Of all these poets, with the exception of Traherne, he is the weakest in his command of the possibilities of sound and rhythm. Too much of his verse is monotonous in pitch, and loose-textured in its rhythm, and yet it is singularly responsive. One can never be sure that a poem of Vaughan's will not rise suddenly out of itself into something quick and beautiful. And he may well worry about that coldness and hardness of heart which seemed to Vaughan his own great defect, who can keep either heart or head when those great moments come. It is not a great mysticism or a developed mysticism this of Vaughan, but a very general and elemental and diffused mysticism, of swift insights and flashes of vision, quite out of the reach of most men, poets or devotees alike, in that white moment of full possession. The poetry is its fitting expression, in the perfection as in the transiency of its beauty.

Chapter XII

THOMAS TRAHERNE: THE PURSUIT
OF FELICITY

Romance would demand that the one of these poets whose work was most completely lost to sight and recovered almost by accident more than two hundred years later should be the best of the lot. Unhappily for romance, however, nobody but the enthusiastic discoverer in the first wonder of his good fortune has ever seriously advanced that claim for Traherne. Indeed, viewed simply as a poet, Traherne is almost certainly to be put below any of the men whom we have been studying. But there are other criteria. It may very fairly be claimed, for instance, that Traherne is the most original of the group, and in a good many ways as a man and a thinker, the most interesting. No one of the group except Donne has expressed himself so directly or at such length, and no one of them, with the same notable exception, suggests such diverse influences and such varied interests. Finally, in none but Donne is so much of his time summed up, with regard to both the prevailing tendencies of the present, and the as yet hardly discernible, and, in some cases, scarcely ever to be realized directions of the future.

Of the life of Traherne very little is known for certain, but that little is suggestive, though sometimes contradictory in its implications. Like almost all of this group he had some Welsh blood in his veins.[1] The place and the date of his birth are unknown, but Anthony à Wood in his *Athenae Oxoniensis* tells us that he was the son of a shoemaker of Hereford, and that he was entered commoner of Brasenose College, Oxford, on the first day of March, 1652.[2] Wood's statement is confirmed by the register of admissions for Brasenose which describes him as "plebis filii," and gives his age as fifteen. There is nothing improbable in that age for matriculation, but unfortunately, the date of his ordination is known, 1657. The law required that a candidate for ordination be twenty-four, and it is, though not impossible, very unlikely that it was infringed on this occasion.[3] Miss Wade, who has investigated the matter carefully, suggests that the fifteen is a copyist's error (the records were made in a very bad hand) for nineteen, and that he was really born in 1633.[4] Again that is not impossible, although here there is the difficulty of an age of admission to college somewhat more advanced than usual, but perhaps to be explained in the light of family circumstances.

Although an extensive search into the problem of Traherne's family has been made, by Miss Wade and others, at the present moment we still have nothing but possibilities. Indeed, the very abundance of possibilities makes it unwise to fasten on any one set of hypotheses. Anthony à Wood's statement about a shoemaker father seems to be borne out by the presence in Hereford in 1638 of a John Traherne, shoemaker, to whom Mistress Joyce Jefferies paid her ship money,[5] and by the discovery in the registers of St. John's Parish, Hereford, of the marriage of one John Traherne and Maria Adkins on the twenty-seventh day of April, 1628.[6] But it has also been pointed out that there is some evidence to connect Traherne with the ancient family of the same name that for three centuries owned Middle Court, at Lugwardine, a few miles from Hereford. The facts that Lugwardine is the only place named in Thomas Traherne's poems, and that his nephew, the son of Philip, on his entrance at Cambridge gave as his family arms the same arms which appear on a Traherne monument in Lugwardine Church, are suggestive as to the remoter connections of the family, at least.

But here, as always, the frequency of the name Traherne in this part of the world makes family identification more hazardous even than usual.[7] The same authority who made the above identification suggests that the tapestry-hung chamber noted at Middle Court as late as when it was sold in the nineteenth century may be the room that figures in one of the childhood poems. The suggestion, though as evidence distinctly circular, is interesting as to possibilities. Another hypothetical relative is that Philip Traherne who was twice mayor of Hereford.[8] But these identifications are all highly speculative.

What is more to the point as to the circumstances of the family is that Thomas Traherne was sent to Oxford and entered as a commoner, paying the customary fees, while Philip Traherne, his brother, though, not so far as there is any record, present at either university, received, as his later career demonstrates, a very good education.[9] Then, too, the subsequent careers of both brothers suggest influential connections, if not relations.[10] Both received substantial preferment, and though the later career of Philip suggests hope deferred, the career of Thomas for one of his age (and it must never be forgotten that at most he was barely past forty when he died) was prosperous, not to say distinctly promising. All these circumstances would indicate somewhat more propitious family circumstances than Wood's account indicates.

The first certain date in his life is that already noted, of his entrance at Brasenose College, Oxford, on the first of March, 1652–3. Brasenose was one of the most Puritan of colleges in a still very grave and godly Oxford.[11] There is in the British Museum a notebook, apparently in Thomas Traherne's hand, which may go back to these student days [12] (on the basis of handwriting Miss Wade suggests that he also used it later at Teddington).[13] If we can judge from this notebook, we may imagine him improving the years to follow in the study of Hermes Trismegistus (the note concerning Hermes is a bare introduction to that vast and fascinating subject), and like so many of his predecessors essaying the heights of Platonic speculation with the help of fifteenth-century Florentine enthusiasts.[14] Not the least remarkable thing about this notebook is its interest in the wisdom of the man Socrates, not usually the aspect of the Platonic writings to seize the interest of the English Platonist of the time. Some notes on the Stoic writers are evidence of Traherne's early interest in one of the great sources of moral influence in these years as well as in the period immediately before.

Traherne received his B.A. in 1657 and was presented by Annabella, the Dowager Countess of Kent, to the living of Credenhill.[15] One of "The Third Century of Meditations," in which he recounts how on his coming into the country he resolved to be content with ten pounds a year, leather clothes, and bread and water if only he might be free to devote his unimpeded efforts to the cultivation of his natural felicity [16] has suggested to some readers, among them his first editor, the parallel of Thoreau. Certainly, there is more than a little of the atmosphere of Walden about that passage, but nothing is more misleading than seventeenth- and nineteenth-century resemblances. However superficially identical the rue may seem, it is almost always worn with a difference, and from start to finish the contexts are certain to be quite unlike. The picture of the country clergyman resolutely clinging to his rural solitude is an attractive one, but one hardly compatible with certain facts. The Puritan authorities were, as is well known, hostile to absenteism, but it is almost certain that Traherne spent a good deal of the next ten years during which he held the Credenhill cure away from his parish.[17] Anthony à Wood says expressly of these ten years that Traherne was absent for some time from the University but received his master's degree from Oxford in 1661.[18] The "Advertisement to the Reader" of *Roman Forgeries* refers to life at Oxford in terms that suggest the mature student doing research there rather than the undergraduate. The degree of Master of Arts in 1661 and of Bachelor of Divinity in 1669 also indicate further university work. But still more does the reading revealed in Traherne's prose works make continued residence at the University almost certain. For the range and kind of scholarship displayed in the references and the quotations would require prolonged sojourn in a library not only of classics but of the current contributions of foreign and domestic learning.

A well-stocked parsonage library (it must never be forgotten, as has been pointed out before, that even George Herbert assumed that his country parson would have most of his professional reading done before he left the University) would, of course, account for his familiarity with the works of Thomas à Kempis, Bernard of Clairvaux, the Church Fathers, especially St. Gregory Nazianzen and St. Augustine, St. Anselm, St. Thomas Aquinas, and Luther. University days and possibly university notebooks might account for Seneca, Plato, Plutarch, Aristotle, Pico della Mirandola. The Hermetic writings in various forms were widely circulated, and the Bible was the staple of his daily meditation, even to that Song of Solomon that in general was not much cited in soberly Puritan circles. All of these books would lie along his daily way, so to speak. But the Roman controversy was a different matter. Bellarmine and Baronius came only in vast and costly tomes, and references to Surius and Merlin and Crabbe and Turrian must be made with precision and with a fresh grasp of context and implication, in a world where they were the commonplaces of probably the most exact science known to that time. Whatever may be thought of the man who wrote *A Serious and Pathetical Contemplation,* the man who wrote *Roman Forgeries* must have had the range of a university library for a very considerable length of time. The modern reader may feel regretful that the pursuit of felicity was so intermitted, but the inference that it was at least combined with some period of fairly strenuous library work seems inescapable.

To this period must also be attributed certain influential friendships. That with Sir Edward Harley of Brampton Brian, Herefordshire, is known, and this friendship may have given Traherne the privilege of an acquaintance with Henry Vaughan.[19] The relationship with Mrs. Hopton, a notable devotee and philanthropist of Hereford, is almost certain and opens interesting possibilities, for Mrs. Hopton was obviously something like the center, or at least the patron, of an early example of those pious confraternities that are so striking a feature of the religious life of the Restoration.[20] She may well have been the means of Traherne's acquaintance with his later patron, Sir Orlando Bridgman, for she was related to Bridgman by ties of marriage.[21] Moreover, her niece was the wife of Traherne's brother Philip, and for her Philip would seem to have made that adaptation known as *The Soul's Communion with her Savior*. It has also been suggested that she is the donor of the famous notebook in which Traherne wrote the *Centuries of Meditations*.[22] Certainly, there is every reason to believe that the Credenhill years were not only broken by extensive sojourn at Oxford, but also diverted with pleasant and congenial social relations.

Traherne's appointment as chaplain to Sir Orlando Bridgman some time before 1667 would be from every point of view a professional advancement and a personal enlargement. And his removal to London in 1667, when Bridgman became Keeper of the Seals, would bring Traherne into daily relations with stimulating and well-informed people.[23] The atmosphere surrounding the household of Bridgman and including its chaplain would be far different, it is true, from that of Whitehall and the various haunts of Charles II, but it would be also quite foreign to anything we are likely to envision if we take the Thoreau implications of some of the poems too literally.

And that Traherne was not unresponsive to that atmosphere may fairly be concluded from certain of the statements on wealth and position to be found in the *Christian Ethicks*, which indicate, not so much a change in point of view as a realization that some of the people to whom he is now talking of the problem of possessions are not simple folk to be reminded of the wealth to be found in freedom from possession but people of rank and position to whom the perquisites of their position seem inalienable, "Neither do I perswade you to renounce the Advantages of Wealth and Honor, any more than those of Beauty and Wit; so as a Man may be Happy without all these so may he make a Happy use of them when he has them." [24] Though slight, some of these signs of awareness of a particular audience in the *Christian Ethicks* are suggestive.

Still more impressive is the very fact of the *Roman Forgeries* itself. Miss Wade has pointed out that the appearance of *Roman Forgeries* in November of 1673 is to be related to those developments in the political and religious life of England that had led to Sir Orlando's dismissal from office and retirement a year before.[25] The line of interest indicated in that work cannot have been a new one, for, as suggested above, the amount of scholarship involved was too considerable for any sudden flurry of research. And the general position taken in that publication is about what one would expect from Traherne's past. Nor, viewed from the point of view of that time, is there anything in the mere fact of participation in controversy incompatible with Traherne's general character and philosophy. But the patness to the occasion suggests a responsiveness to environment and to the need of the moment as felt in the group about him that makes Traherne much more a man of the world than a perusal of the poems alone would suggest.[26] And this view of the *Roman Forgeries* is rather borne out by the timeliness of a good deal of the *Christian Ethicks*. The general effect of the latter work is certainly not that of the dreamer living in isolation, but rather that of a philosopher and critic immediately aware of and responsive to the intellectual currents of his day.

Bridgman retired to the country in 1672, and Traherne would seem to have accompanied him, for we find him at the deathbed of his patron early in 1674. In this fresh leisure he must have been hard at work on his *Christian Ethicks,* which was to appear in 1675, but he did not live to see its publication. For he was buried himself under the reading desk in the parish church at Teddington on the tenth of October of 1674.[27] One highly suggestive fact more is to be found in his will, in which he made disposal of an infinitesimal amount of property in little gifts to those immediately about him, even leaving his old hat to his brother, and said nothing of a row of five houses which some years later appear as his gift to the poor of one of the parishes of Hereford. Whether their disposition had been already determined on and so dismissed from his thoughts, or whether he had simply forgotten about them, we have no way of knowing, but the omission is interesting and picturesquely suggestive of a certain unworldliness which pervades everything he ever wrote.[28]

For one who died at not much past forty, Thomas Traherne left an impressive amount of finished work behind him. Three works were published in the seventeenth century, the *Roman Forgeries,* the only one of his works to appear in his lifetime, in 1673, the *Christian Ethicks* the year after his death in 1675, and *A Serious and Pathetical Contemplation of the Mercies of God,* in 1699. Ironically enough, the only one of these works that would seem to have enjoyed any popularity in its time is that one which to the present day seems least interesting and from any point of view is certainly the least distinctive of all his works, *Roman Forgeries.* The *Christian Ethicks,* which has long seemed to the present writer one of the most impressive examples of its kind in the seventeenth century, would appear to have made very little impression. And in all probability,

A Serious and Pathetical Contemplation was out of date and out of reach of any chance of popular appeal when it was published by the indefatigable Dr. Hickes at the end of the century. In view of these facts, it can hardly be lamented that the *Centuries of Meditations* and the poems had to wait for the sympathetic eye and hand of Bertram Dobell in the beginning of the present century.

The wait was expensive, however. It was only by chance that the long-neglected manuscripts fell into intelligent hands on the eve of almost certain destruction, and there is every reason to believe that another collection of verses, if not entirely lost, still eludes discovery.[29] Probably, Traherne's general reputation would have profited if he had been discovered earlier in the nineteenth century when the other poets of the period just before him were being revived, but it was good luck that he survived at all. Miss Gladys Wade has almost certainly extended the known Traherne material in her ascription of the notebook in the British Museum to Thomas Traherne the poet rather than to his nephew of the same name.[30] But her attempt to claim for Traherne the *Meditations on the Six Days of Creation* from *A Collection of Meditations and Devotions* which Nathaniel Spinckes published in 1717 as the work of Mrs. Hopton, seems to the present writer much less convincing.[31] The Hopton ascription is not, as Miss Wade suggests, to be taken too seriously, and so far as the known relations between Mrs. Hopton and the Trahernes are concerned, it seems not at all unreasonable to suppose that some of Thomas Traherne's manuscripts might have slipped into her papers.[32] But there is, with perhaps one possible exception, nothing to be found in the *Meditations on the Creation* of Thomas Traherne's distinctive ideas as to the Creation being made solely for me or the whole Creation being my glorious possession, and nothing, with again one exception, of the idea that my true felicity is to be found in the enjoyment of the Creation.[33] That the Heavens show forth the handiwork of God, and that the Creation is good seem to be the dominating ideas of the author of the meditations. Passages of such tenor are to be found in abundance in Traherne's work, of course, as well as in the work of a good many other writers of the time, but there is nothing distinctive in them. And the absence of Traherne's distinctive and peculiar notions from the sort of work in which one would expect to find them expressly set forth would be curious in view of the insistence and the iteration with which they are stated again and again in every certain work we have from Traherne's pen (with the exception of *Roman Forgeries* where, of course, there is no room for them). To the present writer this absence of evidence seems definitive. In manner the verses which Miss Wade prints are unquestionably like Traherne, but again the absence of his peculiar emphasis and passion in a context where, if anywhere, one would expect it, seems in default of more certain external evidence of authorship, conclusive. It is a pity, for Miss Wade's argument is a masterpiece of literary detection.

As for *The Soul's Communion with her Savior,* which Philip Traherne published as his own in 1685, the case seems again to the present writer to go against the Thomas Traherne ascription. The relation of that work to the second part of Spinckes' collection, which we have just been looking at, is quite clearly what Miss Wade says it is, the relation of a condensation and an adaptation to its original, but here the difficulty is that the original of the 1717 *Meditations and Devotions* is not to be sought in Hereford but abroad.[34] It is the same sort of thing which Mrs. Hopton professedly adapted from Continental sources in her *Daily Devotions and Thanksgivings.* Indeed, a complete check of the sources of either work would probably cover a considerable field of those Continental books of devotion that all through these years in various expurgations and adaptations were being made available to English devotion of the more contemplative type. In this connection it might be worth remembering that Traherne does in that highly personal and revealing fourth of the *Centuries of Meditations* make reference to a sort of master, "He from whom I received these things." [35] It may well be that this is just a modest indirection for himself, the sort of thing that Augustine Baker uses so effectively in his recounting of his personal experience in his *Confessions*.[36] And yet one cannot be certain, for modesty in general is not one of Traherne's peculiar qualities, and that particular type of modesty is rather incompatible with a certain directness and simplicity that do seem, on the whole, characteristic of him. Furthermore, the plain sense of the passages that follow as to the practises of that friend is certainly quite different from any fashion in which Traherne ever spoke of his adult self.[37] It is just possible that there is another master involved in the situation. The possibility is, however, interesting rather than important, because in spite of such references, there is no evidence in the meditations themselves that Traherne owed to anyone but himself his distinctive ideas. They must remain his own.

So much for the external record of Traherne's life. Fortunately, there is another. Of all these poets whom we have been studying, Traherne is the most fully and immediately personal. Not even John Donne is so direct and so constant in his self-revelation, nor so deliberately self-conscious. Indeed, in some of Donne's most intensely self-revealing passages, notably those in the *Devotions* and the sermons, one is aware of a tension between his self-consciousness and his desire to transcend himself. To Donne, this self-consciousness is a hurdle which he is forever trying to surmount and forever stumbling against. Seldom, except perhaps in that wonderful study of convalescence, *Devotions upon Emergent Occasions*, does he yield himself whole-heartedly to his self-awareness. For usually there is back of all the splendor of his introspection an uneasiness, a realization that this is a failure, as, indeed, from his point of view it is. But with Traherne the case is entirely different. He is not trying to transcend himself, but to reveal himself more fully. For he is a man of a revelation, and the heart of that revelation is his own experience. Alone, among all these poets, he is a prophet as well as a mystic, perhaps even more a prophet than a mystic. And if the text of his preaching be his revelation, the development of it is his own life story.

That story is behind everything he ever wrote. Even the impersonal *Roman Forgeries* in its vivid "Advertisement to the Reader" betrays the prophet's habit of discovering in the little incidents of his own day-to-day experience the manifestation of the central truth. And it is of course the inspiration of the great *Christian Ethicks* and of *A Serious and Pathetical Contemplation*. But twice at least he told the story immediately and directly, in his poems and in the *Centuries of Meditations*. And in both cases, alike in the straight-ahead narrative and in the incidental episodes and allusions, he told the same story with the same emphasis, the same direction, and the same implications. It is a remarkably consistent and sustained story. We have, of course, no way of telling just when Traherne composed any of his works, but the evidence of allusions in the poems would suggest that their composition extended over some years, perhaps over his whole short life. It is a story, like most stories of soul rather than of body history, that is easier to chart in general than in particular. Indeed, there is very little in it of time or place, but what there is is surprisingly definite and often in its suggestions startling enough. There is about the manner of the telling something of the immediacy, of that sharp reality independent of all specific location in time or place, that one finds in other prophetic writings, like those of Blake. He would be a rash man who would try to document a history from these revelations, but anyone who reads them through attentively can hardly help coming to feel that he knows their author as he knows few men, and that the experience expressed in Traherne's work has become in some degree a portion of his own. That is perhaps the final mark of their prophetic character.

In a certain sense, the story which Traherne tells begins before birth with the embryonic mind's first glimmer of a consciousness of the members of its own body.[38] But not even Traherne would, I think, expect this part of the story to be taken as more than a must-have-been, a reconstruction of an earlier stage from what is later apparent, something like that legendary history in which all peoples elaborate their dimly descried and passionately inferred beginnings. In a more normally autobiographic sense the story begins when the poet is four years old.[39] It begins in a moment of quite extraordinarily but not impossibly heightened awareness of self and of environment:

> As in the House I sate
> Alone and desolate,
> No Creature but the Fire and I,
> The Chimney and the Stool, I lift mine Ey
> Up to the Wall,
> And in the silent Hall
> Saw nothing mine
> But som few Cups and Dishes shine
> The Table and the wooden Stools
> Where Peeple us'd to dine:
> A painted Cloth there was
> Wherin some ancient Story wrought
> A little entertain'd my Thought
> Which Light discover'd throu the Glass.
>
> I wonder'd much to see
> That all my Wealth should be
> Confin'd in such a little Room,
> Yet hope for more I scarcely durst presume.
> It griev'd me sore
> That such a scanty Store
> Should be my All.[40]

That self-awareness is not so remarkable for its sharpness as for its fullness. It reveals a very definite character, the character, it should be added, that Traherne was to view as the normal human character for the rest of his life. It is, curiously enough for the common prejudice that sees the religious nature as deficient in self-assertiveness and fullness of passion, a nature extraordinarily ambitious and aggressive. Perhaps the most singular thing about the child's survey of his world is his sense of the poverty that surrounds him. It is, of course, always difficult to determine in any reminiscence of childhood how much is genuine remembrance and how much adult reconstruction. Indeed, if we accept Traherne's own theory of perception,[41] we may doubt if we ever have a child's picture of what happened so much as an adult picture of what the child thought happened. But whatever the basis in fact of Traherne's account, he seems to have been beset at once with a sense of poverty and of personal neglect. He could not believe that he was in the hands of a good God when that God left him so neglected and so poverty-stricken. The remarkableness of the experience is matched only by the candour and simplicity of the avowal. Something of the initial solipsism of the child, perhaps, it should be added, the persistent solipsism of the poet and the prophet, yet hangs about the avowal and gives it an incomparable immediacy and reality.

Then something happened. The story is told twice explicitly, and in fragments and implicitly a hundred times. Both the *Centuries of Meditations* and the poems agree as to its main lines. With the sharpness of vision of the child, the infant Traherne sees suddenly that he is really very rich, that everything the Creator has made is his, that all the treasures of the world are dross in comparison of the things which he has already, in his own body, in his own mind, in the splendor of the world of nature, in the beauty and the liveliness of activity of the other human beings he sees about him. He

sees that all this is his, because it was made for him, and for
him alone. Instead of being the poor neglected little creature
he had seen himself in his father's house, he is really the son of
God and the heir to all Creation:

> No more shall Walls, no more shall Walls confine
> That glorious Soul which in my Flesh doth shine:
>> No more shall Walls of Clay or Mud
>>> Nor Ceilings made of Wood,
>> Nor Crystal Windows, bound my Sight,
>> But rather shall admit Delight.
>>> The Skies that seem to bound
>>>> My Joys and Treasures,
>>> Of more endearing Pleasures
>>> Themselvs becom a Ground:
> While from the Center to the utmost Sphere
> My Goods are multiplied evry where.

> The Deity, the Deity to me
> Doth All things giv, and make me clearly see
>> The Moon and Stars, the Air and Sun
>>> Into my Chamber com:
>> The Seas and Rivers hither flow,
>> Yea, here the Trees of *Eden* grow,
>>> The Fowls and Fishes stand,
>>>> Kings and their Thrones,
>>> As 'twere, at my Command;
>>> God's Wealth, His Holy Ones,
> The Ages too, and Angels all conspire:
> While I, that I the Center am, admire.

. . . .

> For Me the World created was by Lov;
> For Me the Skies, the Seas, the Sun, do mov;
>> The Earth for Me doth stable stand;
>>> For Me each fruitful Land
>> For Me the very Angels God made *His*
>> And *my* Companions in Bliss:

His Laws command all Men
    That they lov Me,
  Under a Penalty
  Severe, in case they miss:
His Laws require His Creatures all to prais
His Name, and when they do't be most my Joys.[42]

Far from being abashed at the magnitude of this sudden wealth,
he sees that it is the very fact of his possession of all these things
that makes them so wonderful, that of all the things in the
world he is the most glorious.

It is an amazing revelation for anyone to have, four years
or forty. In spite of all the vicissitudes of his hold on this
revelation it remains the basis of Traherne's life-long thought,
the major premise of all his writing. In certain aspects, this
initial revelation was confirmed, or perhaps it would be closer
to the facts to say re-enforced, by another experience not so remarkable perhaps, because not so unique in its terms, an experience more akin to that of Vaughan and of Wordsworth.
It must have been about the same time that he found himself
alone in a field. The solitude awed him, and presently, as happens with children, the awe passed into terror. His own in-
significance and the vastness of the world oppressed him as
they have oppressed spirits much more seasoned than his.
Then suddenly he saw that God was here in nature, that all
those comforting reassurances of possession and of glorification
of himself were present in this scene that but a little before he
had found so burdensome. Again, he was sure and confident,
and filled with the delight of his possessions and of his own importance:

Another time in a lowering and sad evening, being alone in the
field, when all things were dead and quiet, a certain want and horror
fell upon me, beyond imagination. The unprofitableness and silence
of the place dissatisfied me; its wideness terrified me; from the utmost
ends of the earth fears surrounded me. How did I know but dan-

gers might suddenly arise from the East, and invade me from the unknown regions beyond the seas? I was a weak and little child, and had forgotten there was a man alive in the earth. Yet something also of hope and expectation comforted me from every border. This taught me that I was concerned in all the world: and that in the remotest borders the causes of peace delight me, and the beauties of the earth when seen were made to entertain me: that I was made to hold a communion with the secrets of Divine Providence in all the world: that a remembrance of all the joys I had from my birth ought always to be with me: that the presence of Cities, Temples, and Kingdoms ought to sustain me, and that to be alone in the world was to be desolate and miserable. The comfort of houses and friends, the clear assurance of treasures everywhere, God's care and love, His goodness, wisdom, and power, His presence and watchfulness in all the ends of the earth, were my strength and assurance for ever: and that these things being absent to my eye, were my joys and consolations, as present to my understanding as the wideness and emptiness of the Universe which I saw before me.[43]

In both experiences, certain basic human needs are dealt with in terms strikingly anticipatory of some of the main emphases of contemporary psychology. In both, certain elements of basic consciousness to be found in all religious experience can be discerned. Miss Holmes has called attention to the suggestiveness of Hudson's account of his boyish animism for the understanding of Vaughan's experience of nature.[44] Something of the same holds true for Traherne. But there are at least two striking differences between Hudson's account and either Vaughan's or Traherne's. In Hudson's experience, the occasion, the physical focus, is more definite and specific, while the reference, the interpretation, remains vague and unmediated.[45] In the case both of Vaughan and Traherne, the material of the experience is pretty general. The occasion of this intuition of the numinous remains general and diffused, but the reference, the interpretation, is much more definite. In other words, the basic ground of the experience would be in many respects the same, but the reassurance which the agnostic

Hudson would interpret as a disposition on the part of the other and the beyond not to interfere was interpreted by both Traherne and Vaughan as an active benevolence. In other words, if we can trust the accounts of Vaughan and Traherne, their reception of the raw experience was colored already by their Christianity, though still, especially in Traherne's case, only in very general terms. Even in his most elementary intuition of the immanence of divinity in the universe, Traherne was conscious of the presence of the seventeenth-century God of power and activity, the God who made the world and ordered it with his dominating providence.[46] Here was a characteristic mingling of the orthodox and the less conventional strains in seventeenth-century religious thought, a blending so important for an understanding of the mystical elements in the religious literature of the time.

But there is still another aspect of this early experience that is of the greatest importance for the later development of Traherne's thought. The child who saw these basic facts so clearly was not only an ambitious and self-conscious little creature, but his mind was to a very remarkable degree curious and speculative. Most children worry their elders with the why and the wherefore of things, but probably not very many exercise themselves for long with wondering about the limits and the bases of the world or what went before their appearance on the scene:

> When silent I,
> So many thousand thousand yeers,
> Beneath the Dust did in a Chaos lie.[47]

Eternity and infinity are spectres that have worried many a small brain, but such wrestling is usually brief, and the adult acceptances of what cannot be entirely understood are usually made early. In Traherne's case, the initial wonder and restlessness seem to have proved remarkably keen and lasting:

No Walls confine! Can nothing hold my Mind?
Can I no Rest nor Satisfaction find?
  Must I behold Eternity
    And See
What Things abov the Hev'ns bee?
  Will nothing serv the Turn?
  Nor Earth, nor Seas, nor Skies?
    Till I what lies
    In Time's beginning find;
  Must I till then for ever burn? [48]

And yet the curious thing is that the basic certainties would
seem to have come with the swift and the self-evident compulsion of intuition. The child simply saw these things. For one
as interested as Traherne was to prove himself in the problems
of epistemology, it is curious that he troubled himself little
about the nature of this childish vision. It was apparently its
own explanation and its own justification. That belief which
so many of the seventeenth century seem to have held, that
the child was closer to the secrets of things than the adult,[49]
may have been due to the light which certain episodes in the
Gospels had thrown on the innocence and the simplicity of
childhood. And that light may have been the more appreciated
because so many of the large hopes which the Renaissance
faith in knowledge had conceived for the nature and destiny
of man must have seemed in the middle years of the century to
have been completely disappointed. Another factor may well
be that widespread revolt against culture and learning that
plays so large a part in the "Enthusiastic" movements of the
century. It is hard to imagine a Donne or a Herbert looking
enviously at the innocence of the child. It may well be that
Donne, that darkened archangel, could not even imagine himself being as a child again. But it is interesting that both
Vaughan and Traherne, exposed as they were to influences that
could hardly have seriously affected their predecessors, take

far more seriously the traditional Christian respect for the child. Indeed, both go so far as to impute to the child types and degrees of insight that his elders as a rule have lost. And Traherne still further extends that faith in the child's insight when he wonders if, after all, the untutored may not keep this sensitiveness to reality longer than the educated, if, barring Christian learning, the naked savage is not closer to God's intention than all the Christians in civilization.[50] For a moment, a breath of the coming primitivism of a more exhausted and complacent time comes into the sophisticated civilization of the seventeenth century.

But the distinctive thing in what Traherne has to say of the child is his glorification of the child's undistracted and uncorrupted vision into the heart of things. The child sees because he is still in his innocence in touch with God and his activity in nature and the commonplaces of life. The beauty of the sun, the liveliness of the wind, the majesty of the sea, the comeliness of the earth, are not fictions for the child but the sole and immediate realities. In such matters there is no process of inquiry, no laborious business of learning, for him. These things burst in upon him, because he has no walls between them and himself. His infant eye is still clear as God intended it to be. He sees what is there. And being still in the state of innocence, his response to what he sees is the natural and unspoiled one of delight in its wonder and its beauty. Therefore, he appropriates it in the only way in which the wonder of the world can be appropriated, in spontaneous and immediate delight.

> How like an Angel came I down!
> How Bright are all Things here!
> When first among his Works I did appear
> O how their GLORY me did Crown?
> The World resembled his *Eternitie,*
> In which my Soul did Walk;

And evry Thing that I did see,
  Did with me talk.

The Skies in their Magnificence,
  The Lively, Lovely Air;
Oh how Divine, how Soft, how Sweet, how fair!
  The Stars did entertain my Sence,
And all the Works of GOD so Bright and pure,
  So Rich and Great did seem,
  As if they ever must endure,
    In my Esteem.

A Native Health and Innocence
  Within my Bones did grow,
And while my GOD did all his Glories shew,
  I felt a Vigour in my Sence
That was all SPIRIT. I within did flow
  With Seas of Life, like Wine;
  I nothing in the World did know,
    But 'twas Divine.[51]

Now, the glory of the world was one of the great themes of the Renaissance. On the whole, the seventeenth century had approached that wonder more soberly than had the sixteenth, with more regard for the manifestation of the glory of the Creator in the works of his hands and less absorption in the work itself. At least the religious poets had. And the same was true of that triumph of the Creator's hands, the soul and body and mind of man. The poets of the English Renaissance as of the Italian had been intoxicated by the wonder and beauty of man as they had been by the loveliness of the physical world. But the deepening of the shadows of the Reformation over the brilliance of Renaissance England had tended to replace that careless-hearted intoxication with a soberer scrutiny of man in his actual and literal state, and a calmer assessment of his liabilities in the light of the darker truths of sin and death.

So viewed, the dust from which he had come and into which he was destined to sink again dimmed that first radiance. And the varied spectacle of his blindness and his passion and his wilfulness, to which the Renaissance had made its due contributions, fell grimly on the eyes of those who awoke to a soberer morrow and a less exuberant reckoning. There is no reason to believe that Elizabethan human nature was any better than Jacobean, but the Jacobean eye was less confident, less well-pleased with itself, less warm with the glow of its own energies and its own high hopes.

We shall see that Traherne was quite aware of the shortcomings of his age, but his faith in the groundwork of human nature was stronger than that of most of his contemporaries. To begin with, his remembrance of the kind of child he had been pleased him. Of that first state he says himself that he was a thousand times more prone to good than evil, for seventeenth-century orthodoxy, a highly optimistic conclusion.[52] Likewise, when he had come to have a much more extensive acquaintance with his own evil possibilities and his neighbors', he made it his chief objection to the much execrated Hobbes that he gave so bad an account of human nature.[53] Human nature, at least in its beginnings, he found good, worthy of having the world made for it, and worthy of the delight in its own powers which he had himself known as a child. That first childish vision was, then, not so much a matter of insight as a matter of healthy response to and delight in the glorious world of which he found himself an as yet unestranged part. The only worship he could pay was the worship which the Creator had coveted and for which He had created the world and this wonderful creature in his own image, the worship of spontaneous and whole-hearted delight. The satisfaction which He had found in the world he had made was here intensified by the delight of his supreme creature, man, and so the ends to which He had proposed the Creation were accomplished.

> Am I a Glorious Spring
> Of Joys and Riches to my King?
> Are Men made Gods! And may they see
>   So Wonderfull a Thing
>   As GOD in me!
> And is my Soul a Mirror that must Shine
> Even like the Sun, and be far more Divine?
>
> Thy Soul, O GOD, doth prize
> The Seas, the Earth, our Souls, the Skies,
> As we return the same to Thee;
>   They more delight thine Eys,
>   And Sweeter be,
> As unto Thee we Offer up the same,
> Then as to us, from Thee at first they came.[54]

In a remarkable chapter in the *Christian Ethicks* Traherne
asks himself what would have been the condition of the world
and of man had man not fallen from this first state of innocence.
And he answers that question of his own in a very striking
passage that sweeps away most of the organized world of man
as it was known to his age and, indeed, to most civilized epochs.
For he declares that in Eden there would have been no need
of Church, or Society, or learning, or commerce, or industry, or
trade, or medicine. Apparently the only labor of Eden would
have been a little light work in the garden.[55] The farmer
would probably reply that it is easy to see that it is the poet
and the scholar who is painting this Eden, and it is undeniable
that many of the hardiest panegyrists of a uniformly agri-
cultural society have been knights of the pen rather than of
the plough. But the important thing is that for an obedient
Adam existence would have been one unbroken round of enjoyment of the wonders of the Creation and so, as Traherne
makes clear in another place, of unbroken communion with his
Creator. All the artifices and the burdens of society would have
remained undreamed of, and the only learning would have been

that of the exploration of the Creation, the only service that of delight.

> A quiet Silent Person may possess
> All that is Great or High in Blessedness.
> The Inward Work is the Supreme: for all
> The other were occasiond by the Fall.[56]

But neither for the individual nor for the race did this wonderful state last. Traherne is quite clear as to what happened and as to what was responsible for what happened. Apparently, the weak point in the radiant armor of man in the state of innocence is his educability. For it would seem that the child had no sooner taken stock of his delight, than those around him began to teach him to look in other directions for his satisfaction, to make him see that a hobby horse and a bit of tinsel were the things which he should prize.[57] The process of the world's corruption seems, then, to have been for Traherne essentially what later it was to be for Wordsworth, an inculcation of false values, and a distraction of attention from true. What followed was a gradual weaning-away from his true felicity to the noisy distraction and absorption of a completely misguided world. The result was that the growing boy of Traherne's history turned his face from the radiance of the natural world and became lost to everything but his own paltry sport, and, apparently, dead to every but the most shop-worn of the world's influences.

> But I,
> I know not why,
>   Did learn among them too
> At length; and when I once with blemisht Eys
> Began their Pence and Toys to view,
> Drown'd in their Customs, I became
> A Stranger to the Shining Skies,
>   Lost as a dying Flame;
> And Hobby-horses brought to prize.

> The Sun
> And Moon forgon,
> As if unmade, appear
> No more to me; to God and Heven dead
> I was, as tho they never were.[58]

Miss Wade has suggested that there may be some story of domestic discord and misfortune behind this account of Traherne's.[59] Certainly, he has some very sharp things to say of family and friends.[60] And he has some very sharp things to say of trade, which in view of the shoemaking and tavern-keeping propensities of the known Trahernes may have some substantial biographical foundation.[61] It may well be that we have a clue here as to where the world pinched him in his youth. But it should not be forgotten that the families of poets and prophets usually cut a poor figure in the accounts of their uncomfortable relatives, as perhaps may be expected of people who from the nature of things must now and then get in the way of those human types who seem to require rather more elbow room than most men. It would be rash to draw any very detailed conclusions from such passages, especially when we know that on the whole Traherne blamed not particular men but custom. Indeed, there are some passages on the tyranny of custom in the *Christian Ethicks* and in the poems that Rousseau [62] would not have scorned to own, nor would Blake.

> All that is Great and Stable stood
> Before thy Purer Eys at first:
> All that in Visibles is Good
> Or pure, or fair, or unaccurst.
>
> Whatever els thou now dost see
> In Custom, Action, or Desire,
> Tis but a Part of Miserie
> In which all Men at once conspire.[63]

This stage of his life was one that Traherne often alluded to with great vigor, never ceasing to inveigh against the blindness of men that was ultimately responsible for his loss of insight. But it does not seem to have been in his nature to dwell long on the darker side of things. Nor was it necessary, for he seems to have recovered from this state, and, especially, to have regained something of his first vision. He is not specific as to the process at this point, nor as to the time. But he makes the fact quite clear. It is possible that if we had the lost poems, we should be able to fill in the picture. After all, the collection which Philip Traherne prepared for publication was expressly called *"Divine Reflections* on the Native Objects of an Infant-Ey."* Certainly, no one familiar with the splendid models of the jeremiad and the inferno available in the seventeenth century will regret that Traherne, at least, chose to devote himself to the presentation of the positive side of the medal. But it is just possible, too, that there was not much in the way of a process about the recovery, that insight came with the swiftness and the undifferentiated immediacy of the first vision. There is more than one of the poems in which, after lamenting that he lost this first vision through the folly of his mentors and the blindness of the world's custom, he suddenly switches to a reassuring final line or two at the very end to the effect that now he sees things as they should be seen.[64]

In the third of the *Centuries of Meditations,* to which we are so heavily indebted for a picture of his life, we learn more as to the nature though little as to the time or place of this recovery.[65] He would seem to have been saved by the very insatiableness of his own temperament. Indeed, more than once in verse and prose he defends man's refusal to be content with little and his constant expansion of want on the ground that in itself it is a good thing, "Wants are the bands and cements between God and us." [66] The only fault is in the ends to which his hunger is directed.[67] It was the rebellion of his own nature

against the narrowness, meanness, and cheerlessness of the life
into which he had come that led him to seek for something
better.

> Let nothing satisfy me but all Eternity,
> And all within it.
> Since men upon earth live in darkness; and are infinitely
>   beneath thy glorious ways.
> Let me never be subject to their vain opinions, but ever
>   mindful of thee my God.[68]

Here in the direction which the seeking took we have an interesting evidence of Traherne's sensitiveness to forces in the
life of his time to which his predecessors would seem to have
been impervious. The years of Traherne's late boyhood and
adolescence were the great years of "seeking" in all directions
and in all fashions in English religious life. So far as we can
tell (some of the Trahernes of Hereford were prominent among
the Royalists of the country),[69] Thomas Traherne was brought
up in what was essentially the church of Herbert and Donne,
and in spite of certain vicissitudes which we shall look at in
more detail presently, that was the church which he was himself to serve. But probably in no period are the lines between
orthodoxy and heterodoxy drawn as firmly in practice as is
sometimes thought a priori, certainly not in the seventeenth
century when Hermetism and science, and Stoicism and
Christianity, could and did blend in strange and wonderful
fashions. And particularly would this be true of places somewhat off the beaten line in those troubled years of the Commonwealth when all the enthusiasms and the quests and the
cults on which the Laudian régime had borne so heavily came
out into the open and flourished as never before or since in
England.[70]

It would be a mistake to seek to identify the youthful
Traherne with any particular group of Seekers, but his psychol-

ogy as described in certain passages of the third of the *Centuries of Meditations* exhibits certain very characteristic elements of the Seeker psychology. Of these, easily the first is the desire for some direct, personal, immediate revelation. The young Traherne was conscious of certain needs and longings. He wanted an answer to them from heaven. More than that, he wanted a special revelation made to him that never had been made before, and he was quite clear as to the form in which he wanted that revelation. It was a form typical of that book-minded age. What Traherne craved was a new book not known hitherto, brought down to earth to him by an angel.[71] It was a type of aspiration not unknown among some of the more extreme of the English "Enthusiastic" groups like the Family of Love, that had been active in England since the days of Queen Elizabeth.

The psychology of the prophet is an interesting one, in some ways perhaps merely an exaggeration of tendencies found in all highly active and independent minds. Traherne made no secret of the fact that he knew what he wanted confirmed before he looked for it. This is best seen in the suggestions which he offered for the recovery of the vision of infancy. He believed that what the man should do was to use his reason to get hold again of that vision which the infant by virtue of the fact that he was an unclouded soul still in immediate contact with the light of God's presence in the world had possessed without any effort. In so far, then, as he was seeking confirmation of what he already believed, he differed from those among the Seekers who, dissatisfied with the Church as they knew it, took up the position that the world had not as yet received the perfect pattern of church life and government, and that their task was to wait until such a light should be vouchsafed. Their attitude may be most sympathetically described as one of an active and expectant vigilance.[72] Such at least was the theory of the answer they returned to the various types of pressure which the orthodoxies of their day tried to bring to bear upon them. Probably, in practice, many of these Seekers knew more of the secret than they prudently vouchsafed to their tormenters. Traherne, at any rate, did.

But like all the Seekers, he was looking for something esoteric, for something hidden from the beginning of the world till now, and to be made known to him and by him. The lure of the secret is one of the most ancient and most universal of all human motives, and seldom has it had freer sway than in the seventeenth century, when old methods of obtaining wisdom were not as yet wholly discredited, and new ones were just beginning to give some hints of the rich treasures they would yield. The yearning for something particular in the way of a revelation is a very common one, especially among the uneducated and the simple, and not unknown among their intellectual superiors. Here again, Traherne, whatever the peculiar influences to which he was exposed on the borders of England and Wales, was caught up in one of the strong tides of his time. He was looking for the sudden, personal revelation of things hidden from the foundations of the world that would confirm his deepest intuitions.

Chapter XIII

THOMAS TRAHERNE: POEMS AND MEDITATIONS

Not surprisingly for any student of the century, but apparently somewhat to his own surprise, Traherne found this revelation where most of his tribe found it in this period, in the Bible, read with his own eye of vision.[1] In reading a spiritual autobiography like Traherne's it is not always easy to tell whether an apparently chronological order is really chronological or genetic. The order may be of time or of logic, or sometimes in an age that still handled the categories with fluency, it may be of both. But the plain sense of what he says in "The Third Century" is that seeking for such a revelation, he found it in the Bible, found there that he was the son of God, in possession of all the wonders of the world, glorified as much as even his heart could desire.[2] Indeed, he found there more than he had dreamed. For he discovered that in the fact of the Redemption God had glorified him even more than he had thought possible.

This, it will be remembered, was the center of seventeenth-century Christianity, Christ's sacrifice and sufferings for the redemption of man. That fact which had filled a Donne with awe, which had moved a Herbert or a Crashaw to an ecstasy of pity and gratitude, which had focussed the more diffused feelings of a Vaughan into a deeper sense of mystery, meant something entirely different for Traherne. After a number of scattered but often highly realistic suggestions of the sufferings of Christ, he is moved to exclaim with wonder at the glory which

344

must be the portion of the creature for whom his Maker would undertake such sufferings:

How vile are they, and blind and ignorant, that will not see every one to be the heir of the world, for whose sake all this was done! He that spared not His own Son but gave Him up for us all, how shall He not with Him also freely give us all things? Is not he an object of infinite Love for whom our Saviour died? Shall not all things in Heaven and Earth serve him in splendour and glory, for whom the Son of God came down to minister in agonies and sufferings? O here contemplate the glory of man, and his high exaltation in the Throne of God. Here consider how you are beloved, and be transported with excess of joy at this wonderful mystery. Leave the trash and vanities of the world, to live here in communion with the blessed Trinity.[3]

This is an odd reversal of the traditional attitude of humility and self-abasement to which the contemplation of those sufferings has usually reduced the Christian, and one of the most original of Traherne's contributions to Christian feeling.

Yet although Traherne did again and again pick out in the Psalms[4] or in the Gospels, particularly, reënforcement for his favorite ideas, he does not seem, so far as we can tell, to have made any effort to do what most of the Seekers from the apocalyptic Henry Niclaes to the mystical Jacob Boehme had done, that is, rewrite the Scriptures in the light of this new revelation, from the point of view of truth "at last made clear and now fully declared," to borrow the optimistic seventeenth-century formula. This seeming respect for orthodoxy may in some measure be due to the fact that he was interested in wisdom made operative and passing over into action, and so found in the field of ethics his congenial opportunity for expression of what he was most concerned about. It may be that he was primarily a psychologist and a poet, and not an exegete or a metaphysician. But I am inclined to think that the determining factor in Traherne's development out of the general group of Seekers into that of the mystics is to be found in his educational opportunities. After all, the majority of the Seekers were simple men, without those advantages, and perhaps, also, those limitations or restrictions, which education brings.

It will be remembered that when Traherne in one of his few moments of despair asked if the naked savage had not a better, a more just and enlightened, attitude toward wealth than the so-called Christian world, he made an exception of learning.[5] Whatever elements of primitivism are to be found in Traherne, he never wavered in his conviction that in the present corrupt and fallen state of man, learning was one of his main instruments for the recovery of that primitive insight which the child had possessed in his infancy and which the man in his growth had lost.[6] True, in the unfallen glory of Eden, man would have had no need of the labors of learning or the toils of reason, for the fruits of both would have been present and apparent to him in the effortless vision of perfect felicity.[7] But in the world as it was, with men as they were, learning was one of the surest ways to a discovery of the universe which man had inherited. And not only was it a source of discovery, but in itself it was a delight, and as Traherne never tired of reiterating, as a delight, it was an instrument for the appreciation of God's work and so for communion with him in the enjoyment of his Creation:

Natural philosophy teaches us the causes and effects of all bodies simply and in themselves. But if you extend it a little further, to that indeed which its name imports, signifying the love of nature, it leads us into a diligent inquisition into all natures, their qualities, affections, relations, causes and ends, so far forth as by nature and reason they may be known. And this noble science, as such, is most sublime and perfect: it includes all Humanity and Divinity together. God, Angels, Men, Affections, Habits, Actions, Virtues, everything as it is a solid, entire object singly proposed, being a subject of it, as well as material and visible things. . . . It openeth the riches of God's Kingdom and the natures of His territories, works, and creatures in a wonderful manner, clearing and preparing the eye of the enjoyer.[8]

In two respects, Traherne was especially fitted for learning, two respects in which he sharply departs from the tradition of the unlearned seeker after hidden knowledge. The first is that he possesses something of the zest of an earlier age for the current excitement and drama of news of discovery and foreign travel:

> News from a forein Country came,
> As if my Treasures and my Joys lay there;
> So much it did my Heart enflame,
> 'Twas wont to call my Soul into mine Ear.[9]

His curiosity never slept, and since it heightened his awareness of his Creator's works, he made no apology for it. And the second impulse to a devotion to learning is to be found in his attitude toward history. The old sense of eternal contemporaneity was vanishing. The interest in the past as the past, an interest fostered, for one thing, by the directions which contemporary controversy had taken in church history, was coming to be one of the great interests of the time, at home and abroad. Traherne's participation in this historical interest is one of the striking things about his intellectual life. The past was for him not just an extension of the present, not just a happy hunting ground for relevant cases, but in itself a source of delight, as a treasure of revelation of the ways of God:

Men do mightily wrong themselves when they refuse to be present in all ages: and neglect to see the beauty of all kingdoms, and despise the resentments of every soul, and busy themselves only with pots and cups and things at home, or shops and trades and things in the street: but do not live to God manifesting Himself in all the world, nor care to see (and be present with Him in) all the glory of His Eternal Kingdom. By seeing the Saints of all Ages we are present with them: by being present with them become too great for our own age, and near to our Saviour.[10]

It afforded, moreover, a wider expanse for the roving mind than the confined present, and so in its very differences gave room and fresh life to the present-cramped soul.

Though Traherne would not have put it that way, it gave scope to the imagination and nourishment to it. One of the mysteries on which he never ceased to brood was the mystery of those faculties of the mind by which things long past and remote can be made present to the mind here and now. Indeed, there is probably no way in which Traherne better exhibits his peculiar blend of philosopher and poet than in his constant brooding over this aspect of the mystery of the imagination. And in a certain sense, when it is remembered that he believed that in such contemplations he entered into the mysterious life of God, such historical broodings may be described as in their degree mystical:

> The Thoughts of Men appear
> Freely to mov within a Sphere
>   Of Endless Reach; and run,
>   Tho in the Soul, beyond the Sun.
> The Ground on which they acted be
> Is unobserv'd Infinity.
>
> Traversing throu the Sky,
> Tho here, beyond it far they fly:
>   Abiding in the Mind
>   An endless Liberty they find:
> Throu-out all Spaces can extend,
> Nor ever meet or know an End.
>
> They, in their native Sphere,
> At boundless Distances appear:
>   Eternity can measure;
>   Its no Beginning see with Pleasure.
> Thus in the Mind an endless Space
> Doth nat'rally display its face.[11]

But it would be a mistake to view Traherne's passionate belief in learning solely or mainly from the angle of the imagination. For the growing rationalism of the age found no more enthusiastic supporter than Traherne. Something of the

Renaissance exultation of the power of the human mind blends with the surviving realism of the Middle Ages and the deepening rationalism of the coming scientific era. Traherne is moved almost to ecstasy when he contemplates the range and the power of the human mind. The swift, effortless intuition of the child's vision is left to infancy and the memory of the first Eden. For this life as we now face it, it is the reason of man that will save him, for it is his reason that will recover for him that lost scheme of values which the mind of man can no longer see in a flash. For this task all the ardors of faith and the resources of learning are needed, and the mightiest labors of the awakened and illuminated mind. Traherne never tires of wondering at the range and power of comprehension of the human mind, of inquiring into the ways of its working, and of exulting at the splendor of its conquests.

There is some foretaste of the age to come, too, not only in this exultation in reason, but also in the epistemological emphasis of Traherne's contemplation of the mind. The mystery of perception is ever with him, one of the themes that in verse and prose alike never fails to release a flood of wonder and speculation. It has been suggested that he comes pretty close to anticipating Berkeley and the whole idealist school in his insistence that unless an object is perceived by an eye that can appreciate it, it is for all value non-existent and meaningless.[12] His insistence that its character as an influence in the world depends upon the mind which beholds it is an important point, more important in our age even than in his or Berkeley's:

> Ten thousand thousand Things are dead;
> Ly round about me; yet are fled,
> Are absent, lost, and from me gon;
> And those few Things alone,
> Or griev my Soul, or gratify my Mind,
> Which I do find
> Within.[13]

But still more important for his thought in general and more strikingly original is his insistence that in perceiving an object the human mind takes it into itself, and in apprehending it re-creates it. It is in this sense that the mind of man enters into the Creation, and, fulfilling the function of an appreciative witness, for which God created him and intended him,[14] he as it were completes the work of the Creation.

> That all things should be mine;
> This makes his Bounty most Divine.
> But that they all more Rich should be,
> And far more Brightly shine,
> As usd by Me:
> It ravisheth my Soul to see the End,
> To which this Work so Wonderfull doth tend.
>
> That we should make the Skies
> More Glorious far before thine Eys,
> Then Thou didst make them, and even Thee
> Far more thy Works to prize,
> As usd they be,
> Then as they're made; is a Stupendious Work,
> Wherin thy Wisdom Mightily doth lurk.[15]

One of the most daring, it is also one of the most majestic of Traherne's conceptions, and one that he never wearies of expressing in any and all contexts. It may be doubted if higher claims for the glory of the human mind have ever been advanced than Traherne's, "Even so may we by the Reason discover all the mysteries of heaven." [16]

The problem of the relations of reason and faith, a problem that, as we have seen, did not, on the whole, much disturb the other metaphysical poets, was coming to be one of the major preoccupations of this later day. Traherne, characteristically, did not attack the problem directly. But he had his own

answer, and what it was, he made clear in a good many passages
on the action of the human mind. The solution he found in the
relation of the enlightened mind and its God, a relation best
described in terms of the action of "My Spirit":

> O Joy! O Wonder, and Delight!
>   O Sacred Mysterie!
>   My Soul a Spirit infinit!
>   An Image of the Deitie!
>   A pure Substantiall Light!
> That Being Greatest which doth Nothing seem!
> Why twas my All, I nothing did esteem
> But that alone. A Strange Mysterious Sphere!
>   A Deep Abyss
>   That sees and is
> The only Proper Place of Heavenly Bliss.
>   To its Creator tis so near
>   In Lov and Excellence
>   In Life and Sence,
> In Greatness Worth and Nature; And so Dear;
>   In it, without Hyperbole,
>   The Son and friend of God we see.
>
> A Strange Extended Orb of Joy,
>   Proceeding from within,
>   Which did on evry side convey
>   It self, and being nigh of Kin
>   To God did evry Way
>   Dilate it self even in an Instant, and
> Like an Indivisible Centre Stand
> At once Surrounding all Eternitie.
>   Twas not a Sphere
>   Yet did appear
> One infinit. Twas somwhat evry where.
>   And tho it had a Power to see
>   Far more, yet still it shind
>   And was a Mind

Exerted for it saw Infinitie
Twas not a Sphere, but twas a Might
Invisible, and gave Light.[17]

In the foregoing passage the emphasis is certainly more on process than on objective. And to that extent Traherne's mysticism differs from orthodox mysticism. But there is a character of "total-working" to this spontaneous activity of the spirit that is in its kind and degree to be described as "mystical." The resemblance of this spiritual activity to the "Divine Sagacity" of the Cambridge Platonists seems, as Mr. T. O. Beachcroft among others has pointed out, beyond question.[18] Indeed, the intellectual emphasis of the terms in which he expresses mystical experience is emphatically theirs.[19] And so, too, is the identification of thought and will and love as the inseparable constituents of one ineffable activity. An activity, it should be added, which in kind at least approaches the activity of God. This is on the philosophic side the most striking and the most important of Traherne's ideas. And, it should be added, the most mystical.

But beautiful as is this parallel between the activity of the contemplative and that of God, it is not without its hazards. There is at least one passage in the *Centuries of Meditations* where Traherne takes the promise of Revelation that man shall sit in the throne of God with a philosophic literalness that might well be viewed as perilous to the whole scheme of Christian value, and certainly dangerous to the store that most Christian thinkers have set by humility.[20] In general, however, the emphasis which Traherne observes in such discussions suggests the audacity of the mystic rather than the arrogance of the rationalist, and the distinction may be well insisted upon even if it must be granted that here, as elsewhere, Traherne is more concerned about the full statement of his doctrine than about its protection from misunderstanding.

At the same time it must never be forgotten that Traherne is a minister of his church, so far as we can tell, devoted sincerely to his work and his calling. If the lines between orthodoxy and heterodoxy are firmly drawn, then the question of how Traherne reconciled his intuitions and his religious traditions may arise. But, as suggested above, it is wise not to draw the lines too stringently, especially in the seventeenth century. Issues of temperament and of quality and cast of mind enter into the situation quite as much as issues of doctrine. Nor must it be forgotten that in any of the great areas of human experience, not all elements will be equally present or insistent in the same degree for all men. If one compares the position which Traherne took on some of the major issues of the time with that of his contemporary Vaughan, some rather striking differences emerge. Vaughan was a layman, and one would suppose that for him issues of church government would be much more remote than for one who might reasonably be supposed to take a professional interest in them. Yet Vaughan was moved to passionate protest at the Puritan lack of respect for the decent and reasonable order of the Established Church. We have no indication of any such feeling on the part of Traherne. Indeed, we have indirectly some pretty definite evidence to the contrary. Not only was Traherne ordained in the time of the Puritan domination of the Commonwealth, but Miss Wade has discovered that the necessary certificates of character and competence were signed by a group of divines of the neighborhood whose views were so Puritan that in 1662 four of them chose to surrender their livings rather than subscribe to the Book of Common Prayer and submit to episcopal reordination.[21] On the other hand, Traherne seems to have found no difficulty in submitting to the new order; indeed, the evidence is that he embraced it. Where Vaughan, staunchly royalist and High Church and passionately anti-Puritan, is yet moved to protest against what he considers the Pagan observance of the restored Christmas,[22] Traherne rejoices in the festal greens and the mirth-making.[23] And that this is no mere bowing to a new fashion is to be seen, I think, in the delight with which he writes of the music of the church bells. He even goes so far as to say that the beauty of the service and the decorations of the church is even more delightful than "Mines of Ore or Fields of Corn." It is hard to imagine Vaughan for all his sturdy churchmanship putting even the delight of the rites of the Church before his love of nature.

It would seem, then, that the questions of church government and order which had so tried his time were of little moment to Traherne. On the one hand, plain living and high thinking would appeal to him as to the Puritans, and, on the other, the same tastes and inclinations that made him delight in color and light and movement, that made him add to the great love of the seventeenth-century pious for music the less godly love of the theatre [24] and delight in the spectacle of happy people moving in a lively fashion,[25] would make the amenities of the new dispensation welcome. There is something of the temper of Crashaw in his taking of certain aspects of church life for granted and devoting his attention and his effort to the more congenial matters of the inner life, just as there is much of Donne in his preoccupation with the workings of his own consciousness. He has, too, something of Donne's disposition to be less certain of the metaphysical bases of institutional life. Only, for Traherne, with the tide setting in the direction of his inheritance and his traditions rather than against it, those questions of which is the right church never really arose. There can be no question that the Church of the Restoration was more congenial to Traherne than the Church of the Commonwealth, but I doubt if basically he would have been in any way different if the Restoration had never taken place.

But we must never forget that in the case of a man like Traherne with so specialized a poetic and philosophic body of writing as his, it is especially unsafe to argue from negative evidence. If we did not have *Roman Forgeries* actually in existence, every critic would agree that he had no interest in religious controversy, and the contemporary critic in particular would give thanks that here was at least one seventeenth-century religious poet who had escaped the restrictions and the distortions of the theological controversies of the time. We can therefore be sure only of that for which we have positive evidence. All the indications we have are that Traherne quite definitely accepted the religious orthodoxy of his day and found in it the vindication of his own insight. He believed in the importance of dogma, as did all men in that age to which ideas were of such great importance, and in general he accepted quite whole-heartedly the prevailing dogmas of his group and time.

What is perhaps an extreme example of this conformity is to be found in those passages on hell that so much distressed and disappointed Bertram Dobell, as they well might any nineteenth-century humanitarian. Most Christians of Traherne's day believed in hell and were not sparing in their consignments to that gloomy region. Traherne apparently accepts that belief without question. There are signs in his works that he believed that heaven was a spiritual state not to be deferred to another world but existent here and now:

> His Omnipresence is an Endless Sphere,
> Wherin all Worlds as his Delights appear.
> His Beauty is the Spring of all Delight,
> Our Blessedness, like his, is infinit.
> His Glory Endless is and doth Surround
> And fill all Worlds, without or End or Bound.
> What hinders then, but we in heav'n may be
> Even here on Earth did we but rightly see? [26]

But though he treated of the idea of a hell on earth,[27] there is no sign that he approached the hell of the after-life from the same

mystical point of view. Rather it would seem that he took the
fact of hell and asked himself how it would fit into his scheme
of felicity, that is, how it would promote the understanding and
the appreciation of the glory of the works of God. Accordingly, he found that place in a sort of contrast to the state of
felicity that set off its splendor the more brilliantly and filled
the heart of the fortunate man who had recovered the vision
of reality with a deeper sense of his own glory:

Hell itself is a part of God's Kingdom, to wit His prison. It is fitly
mentioned in the enjoyment of the world. And is itself by the happy
enjoyed, as a part of the world.[28]

This conclusion is the more striking in that Traherne seems
to have been free of that anxiety over the relations between
predestination and election and the innate sense of responsibility that had so troubled Donne and his generation. Traherne
more than once affirms his belief in the free will of man on
grounds similar to those on which Milton defended free will,
"All the Glory of the World depends on the Liberty of Men
and Angels." [29] And in the sequence of innocence, corruption,
redemption, and glory he recognizes the help which God has
freely offered to his sons:

> He courts our Lov with infinit Esteem,
> And seeks it so that it doth almost seem
> Even all his Blessedness.[30]

It is as if something of the old sentiment of election had remained when the rigor of the belief in God's choice had been
relaxed. But there is nothing unusual in that. One of the
characteristic tendencies of Christian tradition has been to keep
hold of both ends of a not always easy paradox. What is striking is that Traherne could bear the obvious diminution of the
sum-total of felicity that such an exclusion involved, for it was
one of his main tenets that the enjoyment by other people of
the wonders of the world enhanced his enjoyment as it en-

hanced God's.[31] The most reasonable explanation would seem to be simply that Traherne took hell for granted, but found it so little congenial or serviceable that he did not spend much time thinking about it.

Something of the same is true of his handling of sin. He is more interested in expounding the prevailing Christian theory in terms of his own scale of values than of searching out possible inconsistencies.[32] In other words, speculative as Traherne's mind unquestionably is, it is speculative in certain areas and not in others. His adjustment to the Christianity of his day is obviously sincere and easy, even if not always discriminating. And it is this because his central intuitions, those of the presence of God in the world he has made, of the out-going love of the Creator who cannot be content to rest alone in glory, of the mutual interdependence of all the creatures, especially of men, of the supreme power of love and worship, of the unique value of each man and his final end in the contemplation of God, all these things are the central values of Christian tradition. It is not over these conceived of as objectives that the historic strains of Christianity occur so much as over the ways and means by which these ends are to be achieved, and the practical consequences of their pursuit. At the same time these central aims are capable of a wide variety of interpretation and of emphasis, and of this variety Traherne has availed himself to the full.

How far is this revelation of Traherne's to be counted mystical? That initial overwhelming consciousness of the presence of God in his Creation, which Traherne shares with Vaughan, for instance, is unmistakably the basic intuition of the mystic. It rises above that state of undifferentiated awareness of something more than and behind sense phenomena that characterizes animism and is perhaps to be regarded as the bottom ground of mysticism. For it has definite and particular reference even in his reports of his earliest experiences, and there is in all his accounts that sense of immediacy, that warmth and glow of contact with reality, that are the distinguishing marks of the mystic's insight.

Traherne's insistence that in the fuller and deeper and more sustained experience of this contact is to be found the end and the satisfaction of the insatiable and restless nature of man is the mystic's, too. All the other aspects of human experience are, when in healthy relation to the whole, secondary, derivative, and ancillary, and, when broken off from their context, they become distracting and corrupting.[33] Traherne like Saint Francis, sees the problem as essentially one of value. The pathos of the worldling is in his blindness. He is taking dross for the true wealth and joy which are at hand, spread out, common and free and waiting for him. He is like that figure which Traherne's contemporary, Bunyan, drew so movingly. He persists in groping about amid the rubbish when above his blind head is a crown of glory waiting for him simply to look up and take.

And profoundly mystical, too, is his insight that the sum-total of true wealth and joy is to be increased by common sharing and not, as in the case of the goods of this world, to be diminished. Felicity is something to be shared because it is something to be enjoyed:

> The Light which on ten thousand faces Shines
> The Beams which crown ten thousand Vines
> With Glory and Delight, appear
>   As if they were,
> Reflected only from them all for me,
> That I a Greater Beauty there might see.
> Thus Stars do Beautifie
> The Azure Canopie
>   Gilded with Rayes
>   Ten thousand Ways
> They serv me, while the Sun that on them shines
> Adorns those Stars, and crowns those Bleeding Vines.[34]

That essential paradox of mysticism, the desire to devote all
of one's being to the sole and immediate contemplation of God
and at the same time the utter incapacity to stay within oneself, just because to look upon God is to become aware of all
the rest of Creation, is to be found in those sometimes awkward
and involved passages of the *Christian Ethicks* and the *Centuries of Meditations* in which Traherne wrestles for once with
a mystery that he cannot let alone. The world is mine, all
mine, made for me in particular, and yet there are all these
others. The end of that wrestling is what it seems always to
be for the mystic, the sharing, the helping, the spreading of
felicity, because it is of the nature of felicity to be communicated, and delight enhances delight:

Infinite Goodness loves to abound, and to overflow infinitely with
infinite treasures. Love loves to do somewhat for its object more
than to create it. It is always more stately being surrounded with
power, and more delightful being inaccessible in a multitude of treasures, and more honourable in the midst of admirers; and more
glorious when it reigneth over many attendants. Love therefore
hath prepared all these for itself and its object. And because it is
always more great by how much the greater they are that minister
unto it, it maketh its attendants the most Glorious that can be, and
infinitely delighteth in giving them all with all its treasures to its
beloved.[35]

Two of Traherne's preoccupations, however, tend rather to
carry him out of the circle of the mystics. The first is his
emphasis upon the personal character of his revelation. The
world is mine, the world was made for me, the glory of God
falls upon me—these are the constant themes of all his writing.
They are not, as we have seen, incompatible with a constant
awareness of the fact that all life is centered in God. And they
assume a very poignant degree of relevance if we remember
that the years in which Traherne was writing were years of
great material progress and self-aggrandizement on the part

of the middle class, from which Traherne came. Indeed, if we knew more of the immediate world of Traherne's youth, we might find that they spring very directly from his reaction to the main currents of that world. Nor must we forget that in all the writings of his that we have, even in the poems, we have not the communings of the mystic alone with his God, but the efforts of the priest and prophet to bring his misguided and blind age to reason and light. In short, this particular emphasis is due probably much more to the circumstances of Traherne's delivery of his revelation than to any basic egotism, even the egotism of the poet. But at the same time it must be recognized as something very different from the mystic's desire to lose himself in God, in its emphasis and direction quite different, say, from the aspiration of a Herbert or a Crashaw.

And the same thing must be said of Traherne's extraordinary subtlety and richness of self-consciousness. No one of these poets, except perhaps Donne, can approach him in this respect. It is one of the freshest, the most enduringly interesting things about his work. Scattered throughout his prose and verse are an astonishing number of shrewd and delicate observations of the processes of perception, of cognition, of understanding, of imagination, of memory, of dreams, of fancy. And these are almost all concerned simply with themselves. After all, Donne's careful observations of himself usually have some ulterior motive. He is struggling to bring his mind together for prayer. There is remorse and some desire for placation in his rueful enumeration of the distractions that have come between himself and his objective in this last half hour. Even in that wonderful study of convalescence in *Devotions upon Emergent Occasions,* the penitent and the schoolmaster are ever at the elbow of the poet. But in most of these observations of Traherne's, though the larger purpose of the glory of God is inscribed over the portals of his observation, the scrutiny is carried on for its own sake. And the prevailing mood is one of wonder. How strange

and surpassingly interesting are the processes of the mind that
comprehends all things absent and present, all times past and
present in its motions:

> My Naked Simple Life was I.
>   That Act so Strongly Shind
> Upon the Earth, the Sea, the Skie,
> It was the Substance of My Mind.
>   The Sence it self was I.
> I felt no Dross nor Matter in my Soul,
> No Brims nor Borders, such as in a Bowl
> We see, My Essence was Capacitie.
>   That felt all Things,
>   The Thought that Springs
> Therfrom's it self. It hath no other Wings
>   To Spread abroad, nor Eys to see,
>   Nor Hands Distinct to feel,
>   Nor Knees to Kneel:
> But being Simple like the Deitie
>   In its own Centre is a Sphere
>   Not shut up here, but evry Where.
>
>   .   .   .   .   .
>
> O Wondrous Self! O Sphere of Light,
>   O Sphere of Joy most fair;
> O Act, O Power infinit;
> O Subtile, and unbounded Air!
>   O Living Orb of Sight!
> Thou which within me art, yet Me! Thou Ey,
> And Temple of his Whole Infinitie!
> O what a World art Thou! a World within!
>   All Things appear,
>   All Objects are
> Alive in thee! Supersubstancial, Rare,
>   Abov them selvs, and nigh of Kin
>   To those pure Things we find
>   In his Great Mind

> Who made the World! tho now Ecclypsed by Sin.
>   There they are Usefull and Divine,
>   Exalted there they ought to Shine.[36]

In this observation there is a disengaged freedom in the play of his mind that is one of the most astonishing things about his work.

Indeed, here the poet that was kept in leash by the prophet, even in the survey of nature, slips away, and the result is a mood of wonder, a play of fancy and of observation that finally carries Traherne to the threshold of that rarest of all seventeenth-century religious activities, fantasy.[37] "On Leaping Over the Moon" affords a combination of matter-of-fact and absorbed observation with an almost freakish activity of the mind, a combination hardly to be equalled in the secular poetry of the day, and quite extraordinary in the religious:

> I saw new Worlds beneath the Water ly,
>   New Peeple; yea, another Sky,
>   And Sun, which seen by Day
>   Might things more clear display.
>   Just such another
>   Of late my Brother
> Did in his Travel see, and saw by Night,
>   A much more strange and wondrous Sight:
> Nor could the World exhibit such another,
>   So Great a Sight, but in a Brother.
>
>   .   .   .   .   .
>
> As he went tripping o'r the King's high-way,
>   A little pearly River lay
>   O'r which, without a Wing
>   Or Oar, he dar'd to swim,
>   Swim throu the Air
>   On Body fair;
> He would not use nor trust *Icarian* Wings
>   Lest they should prov deceitful things;

For had he faln, it had been wondrous high,
   Not from, but from abov, the Sky:

He might hav dropt throu that thin Element.
   Into a fathomless Descent;
     Unto the nether Sky
     That did beneath him ly,
       And there might tell
       What Wonders dwell
On Earth abov. Yet doth he briskly run,
   And bold the Danger overcom;
Who, as he leapt, with Joy related soon
How *happy he* o'r-leapt the Moon.

     .   .   .   .   .   .

As much as others thought themselvs to ly
   Beneath the Moon, so much more high
     Himself he thought to fly
     Above the starry Sky,
       As *that* he spy'd
       Below the Tide.
Thus did he yield me in the shady Night
   A wondrous and instructiv Light,
Which taught me that under our Feet there is,
   As o'r our Heads, a Place of Bliss.[38]

Clearly in such lines, the integration of the mystic has been somewhat dissipated, and the strenuous aspiration of his effort abandoned for a much lower level of consciousness. And yet, seldom have the riches of the masterpiece of God's Creation, the mind of man, been done more glowing justice. There is something of awe in the wonder that invests everything he writes on this congenial topic, but there is quite as much of sheer curiosity, and that has never been considered a mystical motive. Here at least the mystic folds his wings, but there is much beauty of the purely poetic kind in some of these passages, and much to delight the reader of the present, when the exploration of the intricacies of the human consciousness has been carried to heights of which even Traherne's self-conscious age never dreamed. It would be a different sort of stream-of-consciousness novel that Traherne would write from that of the contemporary writer, but it would have its own more recondite charm.

Original and arresting as Traherne is in what he has to say, the one among the poets of his group who may be said to have something like a revelation, and certainly after Donne the most interesting in his involvements with the life of his time, he is yet without question the least among them as a poet. Only in the first flush of his rescue from oblivion did Traherne seem to anyone the peer of the great religious poets of his tradition. The tendency of more recent criticism has been to recognize candidly his obvious shortcomings as a poet. There is no question that lovely as are some of the passages in his verse, and exquisite as are many of his phrases, he is sadly deficient in that sustained emotional glow of sound and movement that is the peculiar life of poetry. Indeed, the tendency at present is probably to rate him as a poet lower than he deserves. He is flat in sustained emotional pitch, heavy and aimless in movement, often in his phrasing singularly colorless. Too often the reader is conscious of prose motives in his verse. Yet there is no mistaking the reality and the intensity of his feeling. Even the almost obsessed repetition of a relatively narrow range of themes cannot blur the cumulative effect of conviction and of glow of feeling. That charge of "a poet in search of a subject" which has sometimes been levelled at Vaughan's flatter moments has never been made against Traherne, nor is it likely ever to be. The verses themselves even at their least successful carry their own conviction.

Quite as striking as are the deficiencies of the verse is the power of his prose. The *Christian Ethicks* contains an extraordinary variety of good and even remarkable prose. The range from the easy and the colloquial through the homely and the incisive to the stately and the splendid is such that had Traherne's book appeared at a more sympathetic time, it might well have taken its place among the notable monuments of seventeenth-century prose, for to a very remarkable degree it conserves many of the splendors of the involved style that was at that moment passing out of fashion, while anticipating the greater ease and perspicuity and simplicity of the new age. It is a great pity that this book has never been reprinted.[39] Its excellence would certainly raise the question of whether Traherne's real medium were not prose.

But that answer is too simple when the *Centuries of Meditations* are taken into account. For the most part, they are prose, clear, easy, within their short units often remarkably sustained. But every now and then, particularly in that wonderful "Third Century" to which reference has already been made so often, they break into a splendor that can only be regarded as something poised, and very successfully poised, halfway between prose and poetry. Indeed, some of these passages have just that fullness and integrity of movement that Traherne's poetry in general lacks.[40] They seem suddenly to roll up out of the depths of his consciousness with a power and volume that carries the reader quite out of the trough of his ordinary experience. So brilliant are some of these sudden waves of prose poetry that almost every critic who has studied Traherne's verse has included them in his consideration, and in the judgment of the present writer they should be so considered. The most famous is the third of "The Third Century":

The corn was orient and immortal wheat, which never should be reaped, nor was ever sown. I thought it had stood from everlasting to everlasting. The dust and stones of the street were as precious as gold: the gates were at first the end of the world. The green trees when I saw them first through one of the gates transported and ravished me, their sweetness and unusual beauty made my heart to leap, and almost mad with ecstasy, they were such strange and wonderful things. The Men! O what venerable and reverend creatures did the aged seem! Immortal Cherubims! And young men glittering and sparkling Angels, and maids strange seraphic pieces of life and beauty! Boys and girls tumbling in the street, and playing, were moving jewels. I knew not that they were born or should die; But all things abided eternally as they were in their proper places. Eternity was manifest in the Light of the Day, and something infinite behind everything appeared: which talked with my expectation and moved my desire. The city seemed to stand in Eden, or to be built in Heaven. The streets were mine, the temple was mine, the people were mine, their clothes and gold and silver were mine, as much as their sparkling eyes, fair skins and ruddy faces. The skies were mine, and so were the sun and moon and stars, and all the World was mine; and I the only spectator and enjoyer of it.[41]

A passage such as the foregoing makes quite clear that the flatness of much of Traherne's verse is due not to a defect in experience but in communication, in the choice and command of medium. And that raises the question of whether Traherne would not have done better to have chosen the medium of prose-poetry.

And yet granted, what is not too certain, that such a medium is possible, it is doubtful if Traherne would have gained much by such a choice. For the defect of his verse is not so much one of roughness or of awkwardness as of flatness of pitch and level. Traherne's difficulty is basically different in kind from Vaughan's. The *Christian Ethicks* shows a good deal of architectonic power, probably more than anything Vaughan ever wrote. But the power is essentially that of prose. As for the *Centuries of Meditations,* the passages of prose-poetry are essentially lyrical with the brevity, the suddenness, the fortuitousness, of the lyric. The finest of them are so perfect in themselves that they raise no question of genre. What they are they are, and the reader's own wonder and delight tell him that they are good. But the *Centuries of Meditations,* as a whole, move on a much lower level and with nothing like the firmness and accent of movement of the best of the poetic passages.

The difficulty with Traherne's verse is to be sought in much more fundamental circumstances than this of choice of medium. It is, of course, silly to say that a man might have been different if he had been born earlier or later, for obviously he would not then have been that man but a different one. But it is not without consequence that Traherne is found at his particular point in the century. It has even been suggested that it is an injustice to Traherne to range him at all with Donne and Herbert, since he belongs far more with Cowley's disciples, the philosophical lyrists, Flatman and Cotton.[42] There is a good deal to be said for that point of view, especially if Traherne is being considered as a poet, without much regard for his subject matter. But even then, it must not be forgotten that he is the contemporary of Vaughan, and only a little the junior of Crashaw. And in his material, in his fundamental impulses, and in his religious traditions, he is an inheritor of Herbert and of Donne. He is a more complicated figure, artistically speaking, than his writing of childhood suggests, and the variety of influences to which he was exposed must, I think, be kept in mind. He is a transitional figure, not in the sense that he is poised between two periods, but rather in the sense that certain aspects of the life of the past are very much alive in his work, while certain tendencies of the future are already shaping in his feeling and style.

To begin with the basic issue of motive and purpose in his verse, it should not be supposed on the strength of his exaltation of delight that he is a simple Elizabethan or Jacobean singer, singing with full-throated ease. He is, even in his hymns of praise, the most purely lyrical and, it may be added, mystical of his utterances, still the prophet of a new revelation. He is no Crashaw burning poetic incense in the inmost shrine of his God. He is rather the seer who is at once calling to his sleeping generation, and instructing them, and by his own life and experience bearing testimony to the truth of his message. The didacticism of his poetry is one of its premises, and just as any criticism of its tendency to solipsism must reckon with its social impulse, so we must take care not to let its often apocalyptic tone blind us to its essentially prophetic character. Even in the most directly personal of his narratives and the most delicately introspective of his analyses of sight or feeling he is bearing witness to a truth which he wishes his reader to feel and to embrace.

The philosophic control is one, therefore, never to be forgotten in reading his verse. It permits of a good deal of range in that ultimately it even gives range to fantasy. Traherne was never so much under the tyranny of the things that "are" as not to be able to mount the plunging steed of "as if." But when he came to define love in his most extensive and explicit handling of that key theme, he made all the mystery and vagary of love subject to the firm control of the will, enlightened by the reason. His ideal was "a regulated well-ordered Love, upon clear causes, and with a rational affection, guided to divine and celestial ends." [43] Where love is viewed as a matter of value, there is, obviously, clear reason for such an attitude. But there are several passages in which he considers more or less explicitly the problem of love for one individual, and in these he condemns the absorption of the lover in the beloved object, not for any defect in the nature of the passion but for its exclusiveness.[44] It is not that the lover loves his beloved too much, but that he does not love the rest of the creation enough, "To love one person with a private love is miserable: to love all is glorious." [45] The reasonableness of this comment is from his point of view and on his premises apparent, but the reader who smiles at that passage may be pardoned the wonder if Traherne had ever been in love in the romantic sense. And, to move, as the seventeenth century never wearied of doing, from

profane to sacred, is not Traherne's distrust of the absorption
of profane love perhaps the secret of a certain abstractness in
his expressions of divine love? Certainly, there is in Traherne's
praises of his God very little to match that accent of personal
human feeling that is responsible for so much of the charm of
Herbert's or of Crashaw's verse. There is perhaps less of the
stain of human inconsistency upon the white radiance of his
vision, but there is wanting, too, I think, for all Traherne's
charm, something of human tenderness and color.

To get at the same matter from a somewhat different angle,
there is much in Traherne's work to suggest that marvellously
as he grasped the cognitive powers of the mind, he was less
happy in his understanding of its creative capacities. The
mysteries of perception, of understanding, of memory, of
dreams, these fascinated him.[46] But the problem of images, so
central for the understanding of the imagination, receives but
scant notice.[47] The truth is that by and large the aspect of the
imagination that engaged Traherne's attention was its power
of comprehension, of re-creation.[48] He was much less interested
in all those problems that are involved in the operations of the
fancy.

The root of the difficulty is to be found, I think, in his theory
of perception, a theory of perception more favorable to the
aspirations of the mystic than to the necessities of the poet.
God was for him pure action. The soul was an active center, in
its beginning and in its state of recovered innocence in open
communication with the primary activity of God.[49] Indeed, in
spite of the enthusiastic praise he gives to the beauty and the
glory of the human body,[50] Traherne is inclined to be neglectful
of the instruments of communication. For all his loyalty to
the Established Church he is not much more of a sacramentalist
than Vaughan. And the same preference for the purity of the
unmediated "thing in itself" is to be found in his verse.

That would not be so serious if Traherne were writing in the full tide of the metaphysical movement, but by his time that has rather spent itself. Donne's power of speaking of abstractions with the fullness of passion possible for most men only in their relations to the concrete is a thing of the past. The expansiveness of energy Traherne still has. He can describe as mighty an arc as Donne, but that arc is entirely in the high empyrean. That jostling of earth and heaven that struck such brilliant sparks from the poetry of Donne is less possible in the more orderly universe of Traherne. The result is that while the latter can write a brilliant analysis of the concepts of eternity or infinity, one waits in vain for that sudden flash in the darkness with which Donne lighted a whole poem.

This does not mean that Traherne was in any sense indifferent to the physical impact of the world. He had a delight in color, in movement, in brilliance, that was keener than that of any of the other poets of this group, except perhaps Crashaw.[51] Indeed, in the frequency of his references to jewels, whether he is disprizing the vanities of wealth or enhancing the splendors of nature, he betrays what must have been a very real sense-delight in their splendor. Some of these passages suggest the passion of baroque art for the magnificences of gems, but Traherne's whole philosophy repudiated the artificial splendors of the baroque.[52] It would seem almost as if the strong middle-class bias for plainness of the time had overcome a personal taste for enhancement and adornment. And it may well be that that glory on which he laid such surprising stress was a sort of compensation for a love of splendor denied to him by his principles.

Yet even in his development of the theme of the wonders of the creation, there is very little in Traherne of detailed imagery. He had inculcated the glory of the creatures and he had vindicated the beauty and the wonders of the members of the body and the aptitudes of the senses, but there is very little of the sensual beauty of nature in his work. There is, of course,

THOMAS TRAHERNE   371

nothing surprising in the lack of vistas or prospects or scenes
in Traherne's verse. To note that lack is but to say that he belonged to his time. But there is also very little of that flash of
detail, of color, smell, light, shape, that from the early days of
Elizabeth had been one of the great glories of English poetry.
It is not that he could not give such detail. There are some
exquisite examples in his verse and his prose both. But in
general he turned away from the delights and the temptations
of imagery to put his trust in the bare relations of ideas.

Some of this austerity was due, doubtless, to his basic suspicion of the artificial, the extrinsic. He wanted to get at the
thing itself and to keep to that. Curiously enough both of the
dominating impulses of his mind confirmed this tendency. His
desire for a wider range than that of the immediate scene, his
urge to expand, expressed in his repeated injunction to his
reader to reach out to a wider life than that of the narrow
moment and the immediate environment, on the one hand, and
on the other, his love of analysis, of outlining a process of
thought, of plotting a reaction of the mind, both of these basic
impulses encouraged him to throw his great energy into the
elucidation of his ideas rather than into the suggestion of them
by picture or image. That is why there is more of the glory
than of the look of things in so much of his verse.

And that is why one finds in him a good deal of the passion
Wordsworth was later to show for expressing the simple things
of experience in language as simple and direct as possible. Some
of this is, probably, as suggested above, simply that enthusiasm
for plainness that seems every so often to fall upon large
sections of society under certain circumstances. The metaphysical poets had been anxious to establish contact with
everyday life, but on the whole they had not been disposed to
give up the magic of image and of sound that is the birthright
of poetry. But this zeal for realism had been succeeded by a
devotion to plain speech. With a man like Traherne, obviously

influenced by the popular movements of religious thought and feeling of the Commonwealth Period, it is quite possible that the desire for plainness that is to be seen in language, manner, dress, in these years, became more or less consciously one of his poetic tastes. It is also more than likely that the work of Cowley and his disciples with its emphasis on clearness, coolness, simplicity, was exerting its power on a poet who was for at least part of his life in closer touch with the great world than is always realized, and at all times more responsive to external influence than might be expected of one so original and so independent.

It is significant that it was in the couplet that Traherne was most successful, and that in the more spacious stanza he was feebler and flatter.[53] This skill with the couplet was an advantage for the relation of some simple memory of childhood, for a flash of wonder or delight. It was less happy for the development of the more expansive movements of his thought. For what he needed was the full surge of Donne's best lyrics to do justice to the character of his own thought and feeling. Unfortunately, there was little in the verse of the lyrists to whose influence he seems to have been most susceptible to help him here. The result is that the emotional body which the full and swelling movement of verses like Milton's gives to mighty themes very seldom was achieved in Traherne's verse. Consequently, like a speaker who is uneasily aware of the fact that he has never quite taken possession of his audience, he begins to repeat and to insist.

And this insistence becomes bald because of a deficiency that one can believe was perhaps equally compounded of infirmity and mistaken intention. And that is the lack of the one thing that had seemed to be the birthright of every Caroline poet but that seems to have failed to carry through the troubled years of the Commonwealth, the gift of singing. That sheer music that all but unfailingly breaks out of the most unpromising of Caroline lyrics is wanting here. Traherne is a much more accomplished singer within his limits than is commonly granted, smoother, easier than some of the comments of his critics would suggest, but of that happy sweetness of song that is never long absent from even the most desert of Caroline airs, there is very little in his work.

But this lack of music is not entirely to be ascribed to a natural defect in Traherne's equipment. There is a good deal of evidence to suggest that with all his acute awareness of the problems of the imagination he never quite grasped the essence of the artistic problem. It is not enough, as a man like Herbert well knew, to have something of great beauty and great value to say. There is also the problem of creation, with its own demands no less inexorable than those of experience. In some of the revisions of Traherne's work that still exist, and that we may be fairly sure are his own, there is evidence to suggest that he was not unaware of the problem, and that he made some effort to deal with it. But the limitations of his artistic outlook tended to reënforce rather than supplement the limitations of his native endowment.

However, it should not be forgotten that even with these limitations, Traherne's poetic achievements are, viewed purely as poetry, notable. There is a certain quiet, lucid simplicity about some of the poems in which he presents scenes from his childhood, notably his description of the room hung with painted cloth and of what happened therein, or of the time when he found himself appallingly alone in the field, that constitutes in itself a notable poetic grace. There is again an intensity of light and exultation in some of his paeans to the splendor of the world, or the wonder of his own mind, or the joy of felicity, that quite transfigures the grave literalness of the environing lines into poetic beauty. And through all is the fire and the light of a great enthusiasm and a great vision. If Traherne illustrates strikingly the thesis that mysticism and poetry are not the same thing, that spiritual insight is not enough for great religious poetry, he also demonstrates no less striikingly that religious insight and religious feeling can quicken and transform poetic gifts by no means of the first order.

Above all, one is conscious in reading Traherne of the privilege of entering into the experience of a man to whom God and the Creation have come home in a peculiarly intimate and direct fashion. There is something of the freshness of the beginning of the world about Traherne. For he has seen for himself the reality of which he is writing. Over his pages there is the light of something to which the troubled world has grown blind. And a promise of a felicity that will surpass its hungriest dreams, not afar off but here and now; and this not for a few, not for the great and the wise and the fortunate and the gifted, but for all, in the common simplicities of universal human experience. From any country, far or near, those are indeed tidings of felicity.

CHAPTER XIV

CONCLUSION

THE first of these poets whom we have been studying, John Donne, was born in 1572. The last to die, Henry Vaughan, died in 1695. In other words, the lives of these men cover a period of more than a century, and that one of the most disturbed and changing centuries in English history. One has only to try to imagine the difference between the England of 1572 and the England of 1695 to appreciate the magnitude of the changes which those years saw. As for the actual span of literary production covered by the work of these five men, the total effect is perhaps less dramatic but almost as impressive. In spite of the fact that Vaughan lived beyond the rest of the group, his poetic work was completed so many years before his death that it is more logical to take the last of these men to appear on the scene, Thomas Traherne, as our terminal figure. The earlier groups of the *Divine Poems* of John Donne can scarcely have been begun before 1607. It is harder to be sure of the dates of Traherne's poems, because we know less of his life, but though the terminal date of 1674 will have to stand, it is probable that most of them were written ten years before that. That will mean about fifty years to cover the dates of actual production. Even so, the lapse of time is impressive, and the contrasts involved stand hardly impaired.

When we try to view these men as a group, we must not forget this lapse of time with its attendant changes and developments in religious belief and mood and poetic fashion. For

375

both religion and poetry are peculiarly sensitive to changes in the prevailing weather of the mind. However impressive the continuing motifs of human impulse and feeling, it still remains true that whatever depends on emotion will, in expression at least, vary with the tastes and the techniques of cultivation of the time. For instance, John Donne and Thomas Traherne— to begin with, indeed, two very different men—are both of them at certain points in their lives visited with a very profound sense of dissatisfaction with themselves. For Donne that sense of inner lack of ease takes the form of a despair of his salvation, an overwhelming sense of the insuperable barrier that his sins have raised between his God and himself. For Thomas Traherne, the same inner restlessness assumes rather the form of a feeling of having taken the wrong turning, of being off his track, of having lost hold of his fundamental purposes. Again, both Herbert and Traherne are capable of rising to heights of genuine ecstasy. But it is interesting that where Herbert in such flights draws upon nature and church history for imagery and allusions to mediate between the naked feeling and the image-fettered mind of the reader, Traherne relies on the bare statement. Again, both Donne and Traherne are constantly interested in the human mind itself, and both show very considerable powers of introspection, but the way in which that interest finds expression is quite different. Donne is concerned about what the mind does, its operations. Traherne is interested rather in how it does it, in its processes rather than its operations. In all three instances there is a difference between individuals, it is true, but still more there is a difference in time, the difference between the first quarter of the century and the third.

There is a great difference, also, in the circumstances of these men's lives, especially in their basic points of orientation and of departure for their religious histories. And the important thing is that in each case, the circumstances of the poet in question are interesting not only for what they tell us about him but no less for their suggestiveness as to the varieties of religious alignment of the time. Donne, reared a Catholic yet conforming to the new order, represents the experience through which most of his countrymen had passed at a somewhat earlier time. But Herbert, born into the fully established and already traditional Church of England, knows nothing of those issues that had vexed an earlier generation, and is, consequently, free in the security and the emotional poise of the accepted and the taken-for-granted to reap the harvest of quiet beauty and unassuming realization possible to a more settled generation. In Crashaw the power of the Counter-Reformation, operative at a time when Puritan influence threatened the settled order, reaches its apogee, and so in many ways does the Continental influence which had in the work of Donne and his followers so enriched English poetry. At the same time the Puritan triumph disturbs that compromise that had made it possible for men like Crashaw to stay within the English Church, and seeing the end of the church in which he had lived, Crashaw crosses the sea, at first physically, and then spiritually. But for Vaughan, a man a little younger, it is the church of Herbert that holds his allegiance in the disturbances of the Civil War. The Continental influences which shaped Crashaw's course had never touched him.

It is another type of eclecticism which touches Vaughan, when in his medicine and in his Hermetism, he pays tribute to the advance of contemporary curiosity about the natural world. Perhaps, too, the retreat of the more imaginative and speculative aspects of religious thought and feeling before the advance of scientific positivism is to be discerned in his turning to nature for those mediations between the seen and the unseen which Donne and Herbert and Crashaw had found in scholastic speculation, or ecclesiastical commemoration, or the appeal for intercession to saint and angel. Traherne, on the other hand, receiving his theological education at the hands of Puritan masters in a college noted for the ardor of its Puritan sympathies, moves apparently without strain into the settled tradition of Donne and Herbert, as does the bulk of the nation. Yet he carries with him in the profoundest privacies of thought and feeling the influence of very different strains of religious sensitivity. In perhaps a superficial but none the less suggestive fashion the religious biographies of these men might be taken as an epitome of the religious history of the English people, certainly of that central portion that held by the varying fortunes of the Church of England during these succeeding decades.

Something of the same thing is to be seen in the succession of their verses. The themes of Traherne are not the themes of Donne. To some extent this is, of course, a personal matter, but there is a larger significance to these differences, quite as much of the time as of the individual. For it is not just a matter of a new type of theme or a changed handling of the same theme. It is rather a difference in basic preoccupations, in prevailing temper, in those matters of tacit assumption and incidental allusion that suggest the mood of a time. Donne's agonized wrestling with his own terror of damnation looks no stranger by Traherne's confidence than does Vaughan's absorption in the shifting of light and shadow with the hours of the day by Herbert's always purposeful scrutiny of a specifically humanized nature. Again, Herbert's not daring to salute the Virgin for fear of compromising his basic obediences, Crashaw's exuberant invocation of Saint Teresa, and Traherne's apparent unawareness of Virgin or saint alike, all mark basic differences in orientation, by no means peculiar to the men involved.

The same discriminations of value obtain in that much more subtle and difficult realm of temper. The passion of Donne, sombre, full in color and in volume alike, marked by energy quite as much as by intensity, is a very different thing from the diffused sensitivity of Vaughan, just as that persistent awareness of the mystery of life to be found in the recollections of childhood or the commemorations of death of Vaughan is in turn totally different from the quite unspeculative wonder of Traherne's contemplation of the world. Again, there is a tinge of the speculative, almost in the scientific sense, to Traherne's inquiry into the processes of cognition that is totally different from the emotional curiosity of Donne's self-observation. The one is reminiscent of the delicate self-observation of Saint Teresa, the other has felt the aura of the Royal Society.

Still more strikingly is this movement of time to be discerned in the changes in style of expression to be noted in the work of these men. Nothing is more sensitive to the expectation, the degree of permeability, of the possible hearer than the expression of emotion. One has only to compare the terms in which one generation voices its sense of the unique wonder of the beloved with those of the succeeding generation to appreciate the extent to which the surrounding atmosphere controls the range of utterance of even the most exuberant. Two of the most potent of the censors of humanity stand ever on guard, the laugh and the yawn, and he who unabashed would front heaven and hell falls back before the slightest glimmer of either—silent. Religious feeling, conscious of moral compulsions, and conservative of the accumulated intuitions and associations of the continuing ages, would seem at first sight immune to style, but, in fact, though its periods are probably longer, it is no less sensitive. Donne, Crashaw, and Traherne are, all three, not only men who feel more intensely than do the general run of their fellow men but poets who do not hesitate to use their resources of emotional expression to the limit; yet one has only to set any three of their more passionate utterances side by side to become aware of a difference in range that is something more than a matter of individual temper.

Such a difference is due quite as much to the emotional air

which the poet is breathing as to the inner impulse under which he is acting. There can be no question of the passion with which John Donne voices his terror, the candor with which he presents his pleading for divine mercy, nor the audacity with which he sweeps up the corners of the world in his contemplation of death and judgment, and yet there is a warmth of yearning, an intimacy of love, an ecstasy of the transcendent and the ineffable, which he never comes near, and which is the constant possession of his fellow in the baroque, Crashaw. It is true, as has already been pointed out in the chapter on Crashaw, that his great triumph is in an artistic spirit, an artistic idiom, that did not find in England anything like the permanent establishment it was to win on the Continent. The often-propounded thesis that the genius of Crashaw is, like certain aspects of the genius of Donne, something exotic, something alien, something not really English, finds some confirmation in the neglect from which the reputation of Crashaw has until recently suffered and the very frequent misunderstanding from which his memory cannot yet be said wholly to be delivered. Yet, as it cannot be insisted too often, the peculiar genius of Crashaw found a warm and lasting response in the men of his own time, as his reputation at Cambridge testifies, and as we may see from the way in which men like Beaumont and Cowley cherished his memory even though they could hardly approve of his latter course. After all, Crashaw spoke to something in his age, something which, as we can tell from the history of his friend Cowley, must have passed out of the picture pretty quickly but which was very potent in its time. In other words, the temper of Crashaw's age, or to be more precise of that portion of it which in university and poetic circles welcomed his verse, was hospitable to something and perhaps, it should be added, also stimulating to something which would have found little response a few years earlier or a few years later in the century.

An analogous though very different development is to be

seen in the temper and style of Traherne. In his own field, on his own themes, from his own approach, Traherne is quite as ecstatic as Crashaw. But there is something much cooler, much more abstract, in the expression of his ecstasy. It is as if the changing temper of English poetry in those years had carried on out of his native region one who in general had kept the orientation of an earlier tradition. That iterated flatness, that peculiar literalness, that mark the less happy moments of Traherne is something very different from the grotesquery of Donne's failures or the bathos of Crashaw's. It is rather that the intellectual diagram is washing out the colors of the naive immediacy of an earlier generation, and the passion for luminous completeness and tactile precision is giving even to awe and wonder a name and a local habitation. It probably is, on the whole, no loss for Traherne's reputation that his poetry was to be buried so long. For even as he wrote, his naive directness and individuality in what was fast becoming the enterprise of a past generation would have left his immediate successors cold. And the standards of a generation that was devoting to the cultivation of form the energies which its predecessors had given to metaphysics would have been less patient with his technical inadequacies than was the age which rediscovered him. Yet, though in so many ways he was not of his age, and though his poetry was to remain unknown to his own time, he was strikingly responsive to the impress of the changing movements of that time.

In a certain sense, one could write the history of English poetry for these years from the stylistic differences of these poets. It would not be a straight-ahead story, nor a logical or typical one. In some ways, each of these poets is unique and unrepresentative. And there are whole areas of the poetic life of their period which they do not touch. But even so, the movement of poetry for those fifty years is reflected to a striking degree in the succession of these men.

Yet, essentially, they are one. The elements of belief and purpose and value which they hold in common far outweigh those on which they differ. They all move into and away from and about and in the Church of England, and in spite of very considerable differences of emphasis and of temper, the area of their church experience is the same, that of the religious tradition of Hooker, of Andrewes, of Donne, and of Taylor. Practically all of them are open to, and even in some aspects of their work embrace, other influences, but, except for Crashaw, their allegiance to the Church of England remains the central point of their religious orientation. None of them is so thoroughly Anglican as Herbert, but that central influence is apparent as a check, a sort of counterbalance, for the Hermetic divagations of Vaughan or the unmistakable Inner Light yearning of Traherne. That restraint may be regretted by the Hermetist and the more thoroughgoing Protestant, but it is an integral part of their poetic character. Crashaw went to Rome, but it must not be forgotten that he had been one of a group which had hoped to realize the pattern of religious life which he loved within the Church of England.

Next to their continuing loyalty to the traditions of that Church, the most important single element in the religious orientation of these men is the fact that none of them was primarily interested in those questions of church order and church organization over which the great religious battles of the seventeenth century raged. Donne in his sermons did discuss them from time to time, taking a very definite stand on the key problems of discipline and church observance, but they hardly enter his poetry. When they do, it is more as a matter of personal allegiance than of social concern. The mighty issues of power involved do not touch him, and the prevailing psychology of the time, "This is the essential thing —without this nothing matters; with this all is secure," is foreign to his temperament, as it is to that of all these men, with the possible exception of Traherne. Like Donne, Herbert takes a very definite position on the issues of church order of the time, but that position he takes for granted rather than argues or maintains, and this is true of his prose work as well as of his poetry. In general, then, these poets have very definite convictions on the issues of the day, but they are not their primary interest. It is not the premises of the religious life which interest them. These they take for granted. What does interest them is the superstructure of feeling and imagination which can be reared on these premises. This is a very different matter from indifference to dogma or church order, but it is also very different from the fundamental preoccupation with those issues characteristic of their day.

This does not in any sense mean that they are devoid of social concern. John Donne, in all probability the most specifically egotistical of the group, has left in his sermons some very eloquent indictments of the forms in which the greed and arrogance of his time expressed themselves. One of the most attractive aspects of the Bemerton legend is the concern of the pastor for the physical as well as spiritual welfare of his flock. Traherne was even sweeping in his indictment of the false values of society, and Vaughan from first to last has some very vigorous passages of social criticism. But in general that is not the field of their poetry. It is with the relation of the individual to his God that they are mainly preoccupied, and this holds true of the hortatory passages in the preachers, Donne and Herbert, as of the more purely lyric ecstasies of Crashaw. Their field is primarily that of the inner life, and in general of the inner life conceived of in highly personal terms. This does not mean personal in the sense of personal preoccupation. There is very little of that, say, in the verse of Crashaw, but personal in the sense that it is the life of the individual spirit that primarily concerns them all. To that everything else, the proper pattern of church life, the shortcomings of society, the ageless woes of man, the treasures of legend and tradition, the occasions of rite and commemoration, all of these are subordinate and, on occasion, ancillary. Perhaps it would be more logical from the point of view of these men to say that all these other things come out of the central core of personal religion. And this is true for all the group, ranging from the diffused brooding of Vaughan to the tight-clenched meditation of Herbert, from the anxious psychologizing of Donne to the sure contemplation of Crashaw.

Closely bound up with this personal emphasis in religious orientation, is a very distinct if qualified other-worldliness, characteristic in varying degrees of the whole group. "The world" is a very general term, used with widely differing connotations according to the angle from which the problem is approached. Used in phrases like "a man of the world," "a wide knowledge of the world," "the ways of the world," the word suggests the general operations of secular human nature on a wide scale with connotations of scope and ease of familiarity with the conventions and the shifting impulses of human life as more or less organized in society. Used in the religious sense in a phrase like "the world, the flesh, and the devil," the implications are of secular society, primarily concerned with power and efficiency and delight on the natural level, the general operation of organized human nature without reference to supernatural criteria, without the leavening of grace, or the judgment of human activity by any standards other than its own purposes. In general, the world finds its criteria in results and its judgment in the present. Religion has been on the whole rather hard on the world. Some of this reprobation has been due to the idealist's age-long war with the actual order of things, a war never quite lost, never quite won. Some of it has been due to a fundamentally different standard of judgment. For the world, the rough and ready criteria of success or failure have been on the whole paramount, with

believe that the father of Traherne was a shoemaker in Hereford, he must have been a prosperous one, or there must have been some generous as well as wealthy relatives available to provide for his education. What we know of his personal connections suggests that he had at least influential friends, and during the years of his chaplaincy to Bridgman he must have seen something of the great world. All in all, then, these five poets had very considerable advantages from a worldly point of view, and there is much to suggest that they did not neglect them.

Another element in their relation to the world should be noted, especially in view of certain great examples of other-worldliness in the Middle Ages and of certain tendencies in the more radical sections of Protestant piety of their own time. All of these poets were men of education and even of learning. Although he must have gone pretty far with his university course, Donne did not stay to take his first degree, because of religious scruples. Vaughan would seem to have hardly begun his legal studies when they were interrupted. But in varying directions and under somewhat diverse circumstances both pushed on their studies beyond the range of most university men. Long before his ordination Donne's theological studies had attained proportions far beyond the reach of most theologians of his time, and we have plenty of evidence of Vaughan's readings in fields as far-extended as church history, devotion, natural science, Hermetic philosophy, to say nothing of the interrupted legal studies and the professional medical studies. Crashaw added to his professional equipment a wide-ranging knowledge of sacred and profane letters in several languages, ancient and modern, to say nothing of art and music. Herbert was, also, a learned man, at least in the fields of philosophy and theology, with the literary foundations of his time in classical letters and history, and a not inconsiderable degree of cultivation in poetry and music. Traherne, likewise a learned man, added a very considerable command of church history and contemporary controversy to his professional foundations, and we have important indications of a very impressive range of general curiosity in what we can determine of his reading. Moreover, there is even a certain self-conscious devotion to learning apparent in Traherne's poetry that is foreign to the matter-of-fact assumptions of his predecessors. Certainly, all of these men are educated men in every sense of the word, and in certain fields, even learned men. Whatever signs of primitivism are to be detected in some passages of Traherne's work, there is no question that all of these men took advantage of a very high degree of developed and self-conscious civilization, and that all were equipped in various fields and in various degrees to make the most of its resources and its amenities.

And yet all of them, each in his own fashion, repudiated the world which they were so well-equipped to appreciate. The reasons for each rejection varied from man to man. The end was basically the same. For Donne the world was associated with a past which his youthful bravado had paraded for its gay recklessness of the precepts of God and man, and his mature conscience repented of as sinful. For Herbert it was associated with a truancy from vocation, a postponement of calling, which had produced a deep schism in his consciousness at the time and which for most of the few years remaining to him seems to have haunted him with a sense of life wasted and time passed in futility. For Donne the revolt against the world seems to have taken mainly the form of devotion to repentance, of a firm repudiation of the man he was, and a renunciation of the ambitions which had entangled him. For Herbert a profound distaste for the world which had divided him led him to embrace the retirement of a country life and the obscurity of a country pastorate, which at the time he embraced it held no such romantic appeal to youthful idealism as that with which his noble example was to invest it. Vaughan, driven from the city by the events of the Civil War or disenchanted with his early love of it by the increasing violence and uncongeniality of the London of the time, gladly embraced the cares of a country doctor as a way of life which would give room and nourishment for his spirit. Traherne extends to all civilized society his indictment of the corruption which his early innocence had suffered from contact with his fellow men, and in the presence of nature, far from the distraction of the great world, he recovers his integrity and finds his peace. Crashaw alone seems to have been able to carry his own sphere with him in his progress through the troubled world of his day and to have suffered no lesion of the spirit from his contacts with it. But it must not be forgotten that there is much of the spirit of a flight from an intolerable environment in the letter from Leiden, and his passage through Paris and Rome to his final semimonastic seclusion at Loreto involves a very vigorous repudiation of several worlds. If he seems not to have suffered from the intrusion of the world into his own spirit as did Herbert, he certainly felt keenly the pressure of an uncongenial world from without and fled to the refuge of a very ancient pattern of religious sanctuary and seclusion.

This whole group of men, then, without exception, so far as we can tell from the not always abundant records of their lives, sociable men with rich capacities for the world, repudiated it. And they repudiated it, partly because it had made them strangers to themselves, partly because it pressed intolerably upon their dearest interests and devotions, but mainly because it threatened their scheme of values. Crashaw, who would seem with Traherne to have been the least touched of all the group with worldly ambition, saw the violence of the great contest for power of his time destroy the life of prayer and study and witty comradeship and rich delight in beauty and devotion which he had enjoyed at Little Gidding and

Cambridge. Traherne, looking back from re-enlightened maturity saw his boyish insight darkened by the solicitations of those of family and friends who had tried to make him value the tinsel of material and artificial things in defiance of the wonders of the universe which God had made for his delight. Vaughan, too, less secure in a sadder insight, looked back upon those days when the clear eyes of childhood had beheld the undistracted beauty of a life as yet free of the world. There was no looking back to innocence for Donne, but there was a constant struggle to free himself from the past that still limed his laboring spirit with the distractions and the despairs of its memory. And Herbert still strove to bring whole and entire to the present resolved contemplation of God the energies he had so dissipated. From whatever type of past they fronted eternity, all of these men repudiated either tacitly or explicitly the world which menaced their values, and, having learned by bitter experience that the kingdom they sought was not of this world, set their faces resolutely upon another.

For all five the arena of this choice was the field of poetry. All five (Traherne with the qualifications noted above) were poets. And they were self-consciously and deliberately and seriously poets. Donne was, it is true, a poet as he was a theologian or a soldier or a courtier, as he would have been a statesman or a diplomat had chance permitted. But he had written as he had done everything else, passionately and abundantly. And he had to his credit (Dean Donne tried to think to his discredit) a large body of brilliant achievement in a secular medium. He was a poet before he was a dévot. And when he was converted, his muse was converted with him. The poetry of the convert is the same type of poetry as that of the unconverted man with much of the same technique, the same strength and the same weakness, only now it is addressed to new themes and directed to new ends. It is not the lover or the cynic or the sensualist who writes this verse but the penitent and the aspirant to the sight of the unclouded face of God, and the result is religious verse.

The case is different with Herbert. He had never written secular verse. From the beginning, he had been concerned about the problem of the relation between poetry and religion, and he had resolved to do his part to restore the realm of poetry to religion. As he surveyed the poetry of his day, it seemed to him that it was wholly in the possession of worldly themes and worldly interests. It may be doubted if Herbert or his contemporaries saw the great movement of the Renaissance as a movement of secularization with the clarity or simplicity with which some modern historians have seen it. But Herbert was a man who saw religion in the specific sense of organized religious consciousness and institutions as the center of life. He was no Puritan in the narrower sense of a suspicion of the whole kingdom of the natural man, but he would probably not have given so much rein to the secular interests of man as, say, a Pope Julius. He is more rigorously theocratic and less tolerant of the expansive energy of the natural man. But he is too much the artist and the poet not to crave the satisfactions of beauty. So he will not be content to rest until he has restored the realm of poetry to the kingdom of grace.

The problem of the relation of religion and art is, as we have seen, by no means a simple one. It is not easy to determine, for instance, the precise degree or kind of influence which religion should exercise over art to serve best the interests of the life of grace. The seventeenth century was in general not the century for delicate discriminations of value and of relationship. The moods of the time were resolute and aggressive. The process of secularization had been a drastic one. The religious reaction was no less drastic. Herbert saw the field of poetry given over to the natural and the profane, and he resolved to atone for the profane poetry of his age with verse entirely devoted to religious purposes. In such a decision, he might seem to have solved one extreme by going to the other, were it not that he very definitely thought of himself not as legislating a new control but as helping to compensate for a prevailing neglect by a complete devotion of his own talents to divine poetry.

And in doing so he had set a fashion which other poets were quick to embrace. While it may be doubted if Vaughan was strictly accurate when he attributed his conversion to the reading of Herbert's poems, he probably owed the conversion of his muse to the inspiration and the fortification of Herbert's powerful example. He did write some secular verse after that conversion, but there is no question that the bulk of his poetic output is devoted to the service of divinity, that it was into that channel that he turned the current of his genius. And though some of his most famous poetry is religious only in a very general sense, still it remains true that he would probably not have thought of so addressing a world which had not been made ready by Herbert. Again, it should be noted that it was in this region that he touched depths of his own nature that his secular verse, however charming, never plumbed. It was here, that, as we have seen, he found himself. The influence of Herbert upon Traherne is, as we have seen, less easily demonstrable, but there can be no question, I think, that his example both directly and indirectly through Vaughan counted for the inspiration and the encouragement of Traherne. Certainly, Traherne quite as completely as Herbert devoted himself to religious themes and feelings. The number of his poems not to be counted specifically religious is so small that we may class him with Herbert as a poet who was moved to poetry only in the religious area of his experience, or, to be more exact, for whom the religious approach to experience alone led to poetry. Crashaw, upon whom the influence of Herbert must have been more direct because of his personal contacts, is a somewhat more complicated case. In certain directions the

world of the naturalistic man enters more sharply and confidently into his work than into that of any of his contemporaries after Donne. But it is also true that in his work
the assimilating power of religious motives is more thoroughly
vindicated. All of these poets are at one, therefore, in devoting
their poetry to the service of religion. It is not just an exploitation of religious themes and religious feelings. It is a
complete, spontaneous, and thoroughgoing devotion, spring-
ing out of the central interests and attachments of the whole
man.

The question that naturally occurs to anyone who contemplates that devotion side by side with the ranging curiosity and
versatility of Elizabethan poetry, in which the treasures of
life here and now are gathered as never before and probably
never since, is whether the claims of poetry have not been
sacrificed to the claims of religion. If that question means
a wonder as to whether these poets would not have written
better poetry if they had devoted more attention to the autonomous claims of poetry in and for itself, the answer would
seem clear. A fair case might be made out for saying that
John Donne in yielding to the overwhelming preoccupations of
his later years did make such a sacrifice, for brilliant as his
religious verse is on the whole, and in some cases profoundly
moving, it is probably true that it holds no such place in the
annals of religious verse as his love poetry holds in the field
of love poetry. But it should not be forgotten that the love
poetry represents a stage of his development that had been
left behind, and that it is by no means clear that anything was
sacrificed for the particular period which we are discussing.
As for the others, the answer is clear. Herbert wrote practically
no secular poetry and seems to have felt no particular impulse to write more. And the same is true of Traherne. As
for Crashaw, the nature of his poetry is such that it is not
easy to demonstrate what elements were sacrificed in his choice.

It might be possible to argue that a very great love poet of the more passionate variety was lost in his devotion to divine themes, but that would be to argue a basically different Crashaw.

A more important question to ask is whether these poets, granted they are the men they are, with the basic and overwhelming preoccupations we know them to have shared, whether in the verse they actually wrote, they have not sacrificed the claims of poetry to those of religion. Most people today would probably think of religious verse as involving some very definite narrowing and specializing of poetry, especially in the field of lyric poetry, where the large dramatic survey of religious motives coloring and inspiring human activity, such as we find in the epic of Dante, is not possible. But there are two considerations that we need to keep in mind in any effort to throw a bridge between the generally not very high conception of religious poetry current today and the work of these men. The first concerns the relations between learning and poetry, the intellectual side of the matter. The second concerns the cultivation and the expression of religious feeling. Too often the contemporary reader thinks of religious expression in terms of rather narrow and rigid exhortation or of rather vague and general expression of a narrow range of sentiment. And there is no question that there is all too much of short-viewed moralizing and of underdeveloped sentimentalizing in the field of religious verse. Probably, the minor religious poetry of the seventeen century erred too much on the side of the former as the inferior religious poetry of the nineteenth century tended to err on the side of the latter.

But these men whom we have been studying are of a different order. Their standards of thought were high, for religious thinking was a matter taken seriously in their time. Even the least philosophical like Crashaw was drawing for his ideas upon sources in which religious ideas were regarded as ideas to be defined and to be explored with scientific precision and epistemological as well as moral ardor. Crashaw was much more interested in feeling his religious experience than in analyzing it, but he would never have dreamed of offering feeling as a substitute for thought. And even less would he have dreamed of equating vagueness of thought with fullness of feeling. When Crashaw touches on an idea in his work, there is a precision in his references that shows that his grasp on the idea was sure and sharp. For all of these men were learned men in an age of learning, especially an age of theological learning. The result is that on the intellectual side, their poetry is richer in its convolutions and more developed in its implications than most of the religious poetry of later times. Where so often nineteenth-century poetry receives its intellectual content from moralistic generalizations and exhortations, this poetry proceeds upon the basis of a highly developed metaphysics. The result is an immeasurable gain in firmness of intellectual texture and breadth of intellectual involvement.

On the other hand, this intellectual interest does not necessarily imply abstraction or dryness. True, a good deal of seventeenth-century religious verse is dry and abstract, to no small extent because it is so strenuously and austerely occupied with ideas. But in these men we have been reading, the ideas are not operating in a moral vacuum. They give impulse to and are in turn colored by a very profound degree of religious passion. We today are so concerned with the cultivation of the mind that we sometimes tend to forget that the mind is not the only aspect of the human personality responsive to stimulus and amenable to discipline. The feelings and the imagination have their own capacity for improvement and enrichment. They can be starved and stunted, they can be quickened and enriched. There is probably a very definite ratio between complexity and energy of feeling and capacity for expression.

Feeling that never finds expression or that finds but meager opportunity in limited channels may be as intense and as sincere, but it will be neither as diverse nor as abundant as emotion that finds some form of expression. That does not mean necessarily that the volume of feeling will vary in any fixed ratio with opportunities for expression, for the stimulus of the environment is as important as the opportunities for expression, and there must be a continual fertilization and cross-fertilization of emotion as of thought, and a constant renewal of those springs of feeling that lie far below the surface in the depths of mind and will. But the character of any type of feeling will be profoundly affected by the possibilities of expression open to the individual and of stimulus of expression afforded by other people.

The seventeenth century was a time in which the rich possibilities of religious emotion were developed by attention and by expression. The love of God was not a tongueless passion locked in the devout breast. It found utterance, spacious and beautiful, in prose and in verse, in music and in ritual, in prayer and daily allusion and implication. Any emotion can be tarnished with cant and bleached and desiccated by conventional taking-for-granted. But it can be made rich and strong by widely shared appreciation and fresh and tender by the unceasing renewal of daily communion. With all that was conventional and fanatical at either extreme in seventeenth-century religious feeling, there was this power of feeling in "richest commonalty spread," and there was joy in its expression. Nor was it un-English to give voice to such feeling. It was a perfectly proper and normal thing in circles that made any pretense at being religious. Moreover, the English religious scene was not entirely immune, as we have seen, to influences from lands where traditions of warmer and even livelier emotional expression had long held sway, France and Spain and Italy. There was, therefore, a certain temperature in the religious life of the time not found perhaps in the England of later times.

Naturally, this warmth and intensity of feeling reached new levels in the work of men who, like these poets, not only felt with the energy and the completeness of religious genius but enjoyed the resources of poetic genius for the expression of their feeling. And that fact alone gives a richness and volume of emotional character not to be found in most poetry of so specialized a type. And, what is of still more importance for lyric poetry, it gives an immediacy to what so often in less intense speech remains remote and abstract. As for that great problem at the base of all religious poetry, the problem of the mediation between the other world and this, between conceptions and values primarily spiritual and a capacity for communication primarily sensuous, this very quickness and richness of feeling does something that no amount of imagery, that no grace of utterance, could effect. The man who reads Vaughan's "I saw Eternity the other night" is for a moment carried into another realm, regardless of where his habitual dwelling place may be. Without exception all of these poets have that peculiar richness and intensity of emotion that takes the reader into their own world. Like that other victim of the magic of poetry, Coleridge's famous wedding guest, he cannot, for that moment at least, choose but listen.

These gifts are shared by all these poets as a common heritage of their time and their particular group. But this does not mean that these men are by any means one type even of religious genius or religious poet. For in spite of the large number of common elements which they share, there is nothing stereotyped or monotonous about their performance. It is rather as if the different instruments of a well-tuned orchestra were taking up the common theme and discussing it, each with the peculiar grace and richness of expression of its own medium.

Perhaps the most fundamental and consequential of all these

personal differences is that to be found in the state of the individual consciousness, so far at least as one can conjecture it from the evidence of life and writings. Religious experience is peculiarly concerned with the building-up of wholes of experience, or perhaps rather of wholes of perception of experience. The extent to which this is true will vary, of course, with the kind and degree of religious experience involved, but we may be sure that any very extensive undertaking in that field will involve some degree of effort to integrate experience. Nothing more affects the success of that effort than the varying capacity of the individual spirit to pull itself together, or, perhaps the mystic would say, the capacity of being pulled together by religious experience. For there is from man to man, so far as one can tell, a very great difference in the initial character of consciousness. Some men are relatively at one with themselves. In general, their whole personal life flows into any particular channel without restraint or impediment. Others are divided within themselves. Some elements of their nature flow easily into some one groove, and then suddenly the movement is stopped not by any intrusion from the outside but by the very pull of other elements within the personality.

The present writer has often wondered if the real answer to the age-old argument between those who agree with Socrates and Luther that if a man really knows what he should do, he will do it, and Ovid and the medieval writers who lamented, "I see the better, I follow the worse" is not really to be found in this problem of divided consciousness. For the man with a unified consciousness, to know what he should do is to want to do it. There is no strain of conflicting motives, of incompatible values. For him the inner forces pull together, and the whole personality moves harmoniously as a whole. But the man with a divided consciousness is torn within himself by strong and sincerely conflicting motives. He would do this, but there is present also to his imagination other values no less potent. Even where he has been able to reach something like a reconciliation of these opposing forces, a fair degree of unanimity in the inner conclave, every so often there looms at least the shadow of a doubt, and the sensitive spirit looks aside from its seemingly fixed path. To the man whose inner life flows all in one direction, there seems nothing but weakness and vacillation in this hesitation, and where the violence of the conflicting motives vindicates at least their passional strength, nothing but a futile deadlock. Yet when the complexity takes the form of conflicting insights, of homage to values, none of which, it seems, can in justice be neglected, then the inner conflict assumes something of a tragic dignity, redeeming its inefficiency in some degree with the resultant suffering. At its sharpest, such a conflict may well challenge the easier securities of those for whom the issues of life resolve themselves with relative simplicity and clarity, and at its most wideranging may at least by implication raise the question of those fundamental incompatibles or, perhaps better, indismissibles, upon the reconciliation of which the race is still laboring in age-old tensions like those between liberty and order, personal autonomy and social coherence, or enthusiasm and reason.

But the basic human differences remain, and unless they are recognized, the man of unified consciousness will feel incredulously contemptuous of the wasteful distraction of the man of divided consciousness, and the latter will feel some condescension for the simpler fellow who makes his facile adjustments, untroubled by the misgivings of the more discerning. Some element of immunity will seem ever to qualify the enviable harmony of the former, some shadow of failure, worse still, of futility, to blunt the dramatic impact of the second. Yet here is one of the secrets of those qualities which we think of as most richly peculiar to each type. So much of the personal and intellectual fascination of a John Donne or a George

Herbert is due to this inner division, this never quite success-fully delimited awareness, this never securely resolved am-bivalence. On the other hand, it is precisely that steadiness of movement, that heightened authenticity, that neither Donne nor Herbert could long hold that constitutes the great charm of Crashaw and Traherne. For these latter the question of consistency does not arise. Very diverse elements go to their making, and in the course of their history they move through very diverse worlds; yet always they seem to carry their own world with them, for in a very profound way they are at one with themselves.

No less fundamental than this character of consciousness is the direction of the attention of the mind. There is a very great difference in the matter of the things to which a man will, as the expressive common phrase goes, "give his mind." There is a whole realm of speculative curiosity which John Donne, for instance, ranges, and which, on the other hand, Crashaw never enters. Vaughan, again, is deeply interested in the re-lations of the categories of experience without being especially concerned about the initial distinctions upon which those categories are built. He moves with freedom through the com-mon reaches between alchemy and Christianity without being disturbed by any inquietude about the metaphysical founda-tions of either. Traherne has something of Donne's speculative curiosity, but it operates in a much narrower, more abstract and specialized field. He is interested in the working of the processes of the mind, and that, as we have seen, in a very highly developed sense. The problem of the images which the memory presents to the mind engages his attention quite as much as the seemingly more urgent one of the machinery of knowledge. In certain areas, on the other hand, Traherne is quite as much absorbed as Crashaw in the exploration of values with as little uneasiness about the philosophic foundations on which those values are based, largely because, as in Crashaw's case, they are a matter of intuition and not of speculation at all. Again, Herbert is more like Crashaw than Donne in that his thought is for the most part reared on the foundations of settled acceptances. But, on the other hand, he is prone to explore intellectually his area of value where Crashaw takes possession of it in emotional and imaginative rather than philosophic terms. In other words, each of these acute and well-stocked and, for the time, highly trained, minds has its own characteristic foci and lines of operation.

The same is true of the preoccupations which every so often crop above the surface of the reflections of the poet. For Herbert the world of great affairs, for instance, had an appeal that it never had for Crashaw. Likewise, the contemporary movements of science and of philosophy had a relevance for Donne and Vaughan that they did not have for Crashaw. The concept of learning as distinct from ordinary human activity had no real existence for Donne, and it had for Traherne, partly because with the passage of time, a more specialized attitude to the life of the mind was emerging, and partly because however divided Donne's consciousness might be, there was no division between mind and feeling for him, and there was for Traherne. To take a simpler example, music was a common delight in varying degrees, of Herbert, Crashaw, Donne, and Traherne, but there is no comparison between what music meant for Herbert, who uses musical figures constantly, and for Traherne, who makes few and on the whole pretty general references to the entire field. Painting and drawing engaged Crashaw's interest and influenced the disposition of his material, as they seem to have influenced none of the others. In very different senses, Donne and Vaughan were both interested in natural science, and Crashaw and Traherne were not. Yet the latter shared Donne's enthusiasm for adventure and foreign travel, though it took more the form of a sentiment than of a persistent intellectual interest.

In the face of such basic differences in consciousness and in intellectual bent it is not surprising that the work of these men should reveal very profound differences even in the common sphere of religious thought and feeling. All of them are at one in finding their center in the inner life. As we have seen, it is not the political or the social aspects of religion that engage their attention, but the highly personal. And yet even within that field there is a very considerable difference in the aspects of religious thought and feeling on which they concentrate. Theology, to take the most obvious and most fundamental test, bulks very much larger in the thought of Donne and Herbert than of Crashaw and Vaughan. It is not a matter of time, for though the legalistic emphasis of the age of Donne on the account of the individual soul with his Maker and the legalistic stress on the action of the Redemption have pretty much disappeared or been mollified in the thought of Crashaw, still theological considerations, the precise and extensive rationalization of religious value, are to be discovered in full vigor in the thought of Traherne. Again, there is no question of the imaginative resources of Donne; yet the work of the imagination in throwing a bridge between this world and the next, or rather between the beings of this world and of the next, plays little part in his verse as compared, say, with the part it plays in Crashaw's. Or to take still another instance, there is no question of the force of passion in Donne's work. If it were possible to measure the intensity of feeling objectively, it would be found that there is quite as much intensity of feeling in Donne as in Crashaw and probably more volume, but the expression of religious feeling is incidental in Donne and central in Crashaw.

In other words, the centers of religious experience vary from man to man. The struggle of the distracted will, the puzzlement of the too perceptive mind, these are the centers of Donne's experience. But for Traherne the realization of a specific group of central values is the main thing, and so it is for Crashaw. Again, for Traherne these values are to be realized in his appreciation and in his remembrance, but for Crashaw they are to be re-created in the immediacy of his poetry, in the music of his prayer. In Vaughan certain insights are closely associated with his ethical aspirations, but if one compares him with Donne, the ethical side of religion is seen to play a much smaller part than that which concerns mood and feeling. For Herbert the tension between certain ideals of the mind and the facts of feeling, as interpreted in ethical terms of distraction and failure of will, gives a very composite character to his experience and makes it harder to find the center of attention. There is a sense in which Herbert is as complicated as Donne, though a certain firmness of emotional texture and restriction of intellectual range save him from being so distracted. Again, the character of this centering is profoundly affected by the relative purity or complication of the involvement of thought and feeling. But the essential point is that for each of these men religious experience finds a different center.

It is particularly important that we keep that fact in mind when we try to compare these men as mystical poets. As has been said before, but cannot be insisted upon too often, the value of such a discussion is dependent upon the definition of "mystical" which it takes for granted. If that word is used in its fullest sense, it means the successful effort of the individual spirit to get into direct and immediate relation with God. But here, as in any field of human activity, there are all degrees of endeavor and all degrees of success. It is not easy, therefore, to tell just where the line should be drawn, and that is why the term "mystical" is used so often for something that is only in a very elementary or a very partial or a very general sense "mystical" at all. For the present case, there is not one of these poets who has not been described as mystical. With the exception of Donne, there is not one of them who has not been acclaimed as the most genuinely mystical of the group, and, indeed, with the exception, again, of Donne, there is not one of them who has not been hailed on occasion as the one genuine mystic of the group. As has been made clear in the foregoing chapters, the present writer feels that there is a good deal of justification for all of these verdicts if the word is used in the more general sense of participation to some degree in the characteristic purpose and effort of the mystic. Even the least mystical, Donne, gives a good deal of evidence of sharing the interests and desires of the mystic. And this is so in spite of the fact that he had no sympathy for the mystic *per se*, sharing the common Protestant suspicion of his age of anything in which the miraculous and the supernatural might be involved. But the assurance which he craved passed the capacity of the usual enlightened and "rectified" conscience of the time, and the values which he invoked in the spirit and movement of not only his poetry but of much of his prose were of the emotional world of the mystics if not of the intellectual. It may seem a little sentimental, but it is certainly not inaccurate to describe Donne as a seeker who just fails to be a mystic in his seeking. Herbert is on his own showing to be described rather as a mystic distracted, or, perhaps more precisely, as a man who is intermittently a mystic. His aim is the mystic's, oneness with God, but the pinions on which he seeks that great height are not steady, and he knows they are not. Crashaw is steadier and surer, and the light of ecstasy is on his pages. His may not be the largest and the greatest of Christian mystical experiences—Crashaw is not an Augustine or a Bernard of Clairvaux, but he has the authentic accent, and he keeps it. Vaughan never rises to such heights, partly because his whole inspiration is more diffused, more fragmentary, partly because the sense of mystery is stronger in him than any specific insight, but on his level, with his limited references, he is genuinely mystical. And so, with different but similar qualifications, is Traherne.

Just as these poets vary in kind and degree with regard to the mystical elements in their religious experience, so do they differ in the ways in which they express those elements in their poetry. For purposes of analysis, of understanding of those ways, we may invoke that discrimination which was made in an earlier chapter between two major types of mystical poetry, the poetry of transcendence, that takes its reader out of his habitual world into another realm of value and of existence, and the poetry of immanence, that discovers that other realm here in the things of this world and opens our eyes to what is about us and within us. There are times when Donne manifests the whirlwind power of the first. He can take us off our feet and for a moment carry us to a vantage point far above this world from which we can hear the angels blow their trumpets at earth's imagined corners. But his habitat is not that lonely and lofty peak. Rather it is the battle-torn field of his own spirit, which he has made as familiar to generations of readers as the too familiar ground of their own soul's struggles. Herbert is distinctly the poet of the other type. It is along the roads of this earth that he goes to meet that immortal Easter, and the dust and the chambers of his world from which he wrings the secret of the peace of God.

Vaughan is of the transcendent. "I saw Eternity the other night," he begins, and we know that never again will that vast and to average humanity somewhat chilly realm seem quite so strange and remote, because for a minute we have been there. There is the light of another world in much of Traherne's poetry, too, but though it was orient and immortal wheat that he saw growing in the fields of his magical childhood, it was on this earth, in a specific part of Herefordshire that his vision was vouchsafed. Yet that vision, though like the insights of Donne, tethered to the consciousness of the poet, has its own vast implications that sometimes carry us quite out of the limitations of the moment into a wider and surer region. But most paradoxical of all, in this respect, is the poetry of Crashaw. For here, on the one hand, is a supreme example of the poetry of transcendence in some of those ecstatic contemplations of the newborn Babe of Bethlehem or the Crucified Christ. And, on the other, in some of the shepherds' choruses, for instance, or the hymn to Saint Teresa, are to be found exquisite instances of the sacramental approach, the use of the things of earth to naturalize divinity here among us.

Of course, these differences in effect are ultimately dependent on the use of the media of expression by each of these poets. However remote from earth be the feelings and the attitudes and the values which mystical poetry seeks to communicate, it still remains true that it is the material of this world and not of the next which offers the medium of communication. Each of these poets has with his own resources and his own purposes to meet this problem and to solve it in terms of his purposes, both poetic and religious. It is not, therefore, surprising that in spite of all these men have in common in fundamental purpose and feeling, the solution of each is very different, and that the mediating material chosen varies in kind and scope from man to man. Donne uses, as does none of the others, with the possible exception of Vaughan, ideas and their relations. Like Vaughan, he has a large and mature and well-organized body of ideas at his disposal. Indeed, he has much the advantage of Vaughan in the clarity and currency of the concepts which form the staple of the still most widely accepted philosophical system of his time, that of scholasticism. Vaughan in his dependence on Hermetic concepts does not enjoy anything like his advantage, for the very esoteric nature of his material favors more general and indistinct definition and more reliance on the aura of feeling which invests such concepts. They have not been worn so smooth with much handling in the places of the mind. Traherne is busy with ideas, but they are so few, so relatively uninvolved, that they count less as ideas than as the foci of attitudes. Ideas are for Herbert, intellectual as is his general method of procedure, the groundwork rather than the stuff of his poetic expression. And for Crashaw they may be said to be of very little importance, since that way of ordering experience is not his concern.

The same variety is to be found in the ways in which these men employ the other sources of mediating material of the religious poet. The dramatic symbols which Christian tradition and Christian legend afford were of course available to them in very different degrees. Two forces had combined to limit their resources to what could be regarded as sober and literal history. The first was the Protestant suspicion of the miraculous, the tendency to view any augmenting of Scriptural report, any continuing of the supernatural aspects of religious history beyond the apostolic days, as popish superstition. The second was the tendency of a growingly rationalistic temper to repudiate anything savoring of mythology in favor of a sober literalism. The operation of these two forces is to be seen most sharply in Vaughan and Traherne, in whom the use of nature affords that imaginative mediation that legend and saint's life gave to Crashaw's verse. The abundance with which the latter employs the imaginative interest of the Nativity traditions and the reports of the life of Saint Teresa may easily be traced to the influence on his whole culture of the contemporary Catholic life of the Counter-Reformation. In view of Donne's known sensitiveness to this influence, it is not surprising that there are a number of evidences of survival of the saints and angels of his youth in his later verses.

The same forces determine the warmth of human detail with which various aspects of Christ's life and personality are approached in the work of these poets. In general, Protestantism tended in that age to stress the rôle of the Saviour in the process of our redemption rather than the human life of the God-Man. There is, therefore, very little of the human Christ to be found in the verse of most of these men. Traherne hardly touches on the personality or the life on earth of Christ. Neither does Vaughan. Donne has more to say, or, to be more exact, his prayers suggest a more vivid sense of the person to whom they are addressed, and his references to Christ have sometimes a directness and a warmth that emotionally enrich his often rigorously legalistic conception of the Son's rôle in eternal history. But in such passages the reality comes from the poet's feeling, not from his presentation of the object of that feeling. Herbert is here in a very different category from Donne. His gift for realizing the things of the other world here and now in the homely passages of this life has led to some exquisite passages of address to Christ and of commemoration of his descent to earth and sufferings thereon. But that is a very limited element in his work as against the moral aspiration or the religious yearning that more commonly distinguish it. It is Crashaw who most lavishly avails himself of the dramatic possibilities of the human personality and life of Christ, and in this, of course, he moves, as do some of the less famous religious poets of the time, out of the prevailing atmosphere of contemporary Protestant England into that of contemporary Catholicism.

As for that other aspect of traditional Christian adornment, the commemoration of the life of Christ in the liturgical observances of the Christian Church, there is to be noted something of the same division. For Traherne, the Christian year, so important in his life as a minister of the Church of England, hardly comes into his poetry at all. Neither does it play much part beyond, for instance, suggesting some reflections on the Puritan objections to pagan observances of Christmas, in the verse of Vaughan. The use which Donne and Crashaw make of this liturgical material is characteristic. Donne is reminded by the thought that it is Good Friday that his sins still stand between his God and himself. As usual, it is the ethical aspects of the matter that excite his imagination, and as usual the beauty of the result lies not in any commemoration or re-creation but in the expression of his own feelings. On the other hand, Crashaw does lose himself in the theme of the commemoration and does succeed in re-creating the occasion commemorated in what, as we have already seen, is essentially a liturgical creation, but the fact of the commemoration, the ecclesiastical technique and spirit, is lost sight of in his absorption in the invocation of the original occasion. It is for this reason that the purely ecclesiastical elements in the expression of his religious feeling are so much less important in his work than they are in Herbert's. For Herbert the commemoration itself is important, carrying, as a commemoration should, the spirit of the original occasion into the context of the present situation.

Naturally, the use of the basic stuff of life, the data of the senses, is common to all of these men as it is to all poets, however remote from the day-to-day world, however rapt in a world of dreams they may at times seem. But nowhere is the factor of individual difference more apparent. Perhaps two extremes may be plotted in Traherne and Donne. Both abound in references to daily life, but those of the first are, on the whole, generalized and intellectual, closely tethered to the point, those of the second are distinguished for their intrinsic interest, for their engaging emotional quality. Herbert is, on the other hand, homelier, closer to the daily round, with a sense of its own flavor and a tenderness toward it that invests his simplest allusions with a charm of their own. There is no such tenderness in Donne. On the other hand, there is a fullness of sense-life in Crashaw's work beside which even the passionate energy of Donne assumes something of the ascetic character of an archaic piece of sculpture suddenly put beside a baroque. There is a luscious flowering in Crashaw that only the sincerity of his feeling and the unbroken innocence of his intention restrains. Beside that warmth and color of sense life, the imagery of Vaughan seems rarefied in that white light so dear to him. In the vast spaces of light and air and not too portentous shadow that constitute the sense world of Vaughan at his moments of intensest excitement, there is an impersonal peace not to be found in the man-centered abundance of Crashaw's. But in the less excited moments of both there is to be noticed, on the one hand, a more diffused luxury in Crashaw, and a simpler homeliness, reminiscent of Herbert, in Vaughan. Nowhere is the richness of discrimination within a common idiom more abundantly illustrated than in the varieties of imagery which these poets use for the expression of their experience.

Ultimately, the whole problem resolves itself into the question of what these men are trying to do. They are all writing lyric poetry of an intensely religious character. But within the common type their basic undertakings are radically different. In much of his religious verse John Donne is expressing to the ear of a supposedly attentive Heaven his religious yearnings, and his anxiety to placate outraged justice, and whatever comfort he can offer his own frightened soul out of his religious convictions. He is an undoubted master of the inner life but on the side of self-analysis and self-expression. It is perfectly possible to draw a very lively picture of his God from these poems, but God is the object of his prayers, the end to which he is reaching, rather than the theme of his contemplation. At the opposite extreme the verses of Crashaw have been described as a liturgical re-creation of the objects of his contemplation. In that contemplation the imaginative and the affective elements play a much larger part than do the intellectual and the ethical. The immediate presentment of the objects of his feeling, of his worship, is the triumph of his meditation on the crucifix, of his vision of Heaven in the hymn to Saint Teresa, of the choruses which his shepherds sang for the Nativity. Yet the poetic element of expression of personal feeling is no less important than the more purely mystical element of contemplation.

There is more of the purely contemplative in Herbert, certainly, than in Donne, but as against Crashaw's his verse still remains at its most intense, what he termed it, the history of his relations with his God, those things that had passed between his Maker and himself. There is a larger element perhaps, of the moralistic appeal in Herbert's verse than in Donne's, and there is a much wider range of personal feeling, of the affective elements so essential to mysticism, in his invocation of his God. Traherne, on the other hand, brings to the common biographical purpose of most of these lyrists a prophetic element not known to Donne or Crashaw and but little apparent in Herbert. For he has a message for his fellows, and a truth to which he wishes to bear his witness. Much of his delivery of that message takes the form of biography, but that is biography with a purpose, one may say, an effort to communicate his experience to the enrichment of his fellow Christians. And the fact that this communication is by infection quite as much as by exposition does not diminish its essentially prophetic aim or its essentially prophetic feeling. At the opposite extreme, Vaughan's motive is more purely lyrical, the effort to give the feeling of certain moments in which for an instant the veil between the next world and this wears thin, to recapture again the joy of vanished insights, to hold against the forgetfulness of time the treasure of the lost friend and the vanished self. Again, though all these men come from the same land and aspire to the same land, each has his own approach, his own method, his own objective. In a time such as ours, when the tendency is to deal with human feeling in larger units, it will not be irrelevant to recall the richness and delicacy of experience which a profounder cultivation of personal religious feeling gave to a generous tradition, and the treasures of lasting beauty and insight which individual genius wrested from some of the central preoccupations of a great age.

NOTES

INTRODUCTION

[1] *The Confessions of St. Augustine,* trans. E. B. Pusey (Everyman), I, 1, 1, p. 1.

[2] "The Rhodora."

[3] *Sayings of Rabi'a al-'Adawiyya,* trans. Edward G. Browne, quoted in *A Religious Anthology (The Augustan Books of English Poetry),* p. 6.

[4] Chesterton, G. K., *St. Thomas Aquinas,* New York, 1933, pp. 161–64.

[5] Psalms XIX. 1.

[6] *Life and Works of Saint Bernard,* ed. Dom John Mabillon; trans. and ed. Samuel J. Eales, London, 1896, IV, 457f.

[6a] Bergson, Henri, *Mind-Energy,* trans. H. Wildon Carr, New York, 1920, p. 94.

[7] *The Confessions of Saint Augustine,* IX, 10, 23, p. 194.

[8] Saint Bernard, *op. cit.,* IV, 457.

[9] Poincaré, H., *The Foundations of Science,* trans. George Bruce Halsted, New York, 1921, p. 387ff.

[10] *The Dialogue of the Seraphic Virgin Catherine of Siena,* etc., trans. Algar Thorold, London, 1907, p. 331.

[11] *The Confessions of St. Augustine,* VII, 10, 16, p. 134.

[12] Cf. Maritain, Jacques, *Art and Scholasticism,* trans. J. F. Scanlan, New York, 1930, "An Essay on Art," pp. 58–59 and 123–27.

[13] John III. 8.

[14] Cf. Maritain, *op. cit.,* p. 80.

[15] Eliot, T. S., *After Strange Gods: A Primer of Modern Heresy,* New York, 1934, pp. 30–31.

[16] "Auguries of Innocence."

[17] "The Kingdom of God."

[18] Chesterton, *op. cit.,* p. 172.

[19] Trans. from *Oeuvres,* V, *Exclamations,* II, 324, quoted in Etchegoyen, Gaston, *L'Amour Divin,* Bordeaux and Paris, 1923, pp. 203–4.

CHAPTER I

[1] From Glanvill's phrase, popularized by Professors Whitehead and Willey. See Willey, Basil, *The Seventeenth Century Background,* London, 1934, p. 170.

[2] *Paradise Lost,* II, l. 890ff.

[3] Burtt, Edwin Arthur, *The Metaphysical Foundation of Modern Physical Science,* London and New York, 1925, pp. 290–91.

[4] Grierson, H. J. C., *Cross Currents in English Literature of the XVIIth Century,* London, 1929, p. 7ff.

[5] Praz, Mario, *Machiavelli and the Elizabethans,* London, 1928, p. 9. Cf. Spens, Janet, "Chapman's Ethical Thought," *Essays and Studies by Members of the English Association,* XI, pp. 153–54.

[6] Cf. Liljegren, S. B., "The Fall of the Monasteries and the Social Changes in England Leading Up to the Great Revolution," *Lunds Universitets Arsskrift,* N. F. Ard I, Bd. 19, Nr. 10, Lund, 1924.

[7] Bacon, Francis, *The Advancement of Learning,* ed. William Aldis Wright, Oxford, 1900, I, 5, 11, pp. 42–43.

[8] Willey, *op. cit.,* p. 4.

[9] Clark, G. N., *The Seventeenth Century,* Oxford, 1929, p. 1.

[10] See Willey, *op. cit.,* pp. 42–43.

[11] *Ibid.,* pp. 1–12.

[12] *Ibid.,* pp. 54–55.

[13] Shafer, Robert, *Christianity and Naturalism,* New Haven, 1926, p. 5ff.

[14] Cf. Buckley, George T., *Atheism in the English Renaissance,* Chicago, 1932, pp. 2–4.

[15] Bredvold, Louis I., "The Naturalism of Donne in Relation to Some Renaissance Traditions," *Journal of English and Germanic Philology,* XXII, 478–79.

[16] Burtt, *op. cit.,* pp. 37–38.

[17] Notably Jacob Burckhardt in *The Civilization of the Renaissance in Italy,* trans. S. G. C. Middlemore, London, 1914, p. 275.

[18] Cf. Bredvold, Louis I., *The Intellectual Milieu of John Dryden,* Ann Arbor, 1934, Chap. II, "The Traditions of Skepticism."

[19] *Ibid.,* Chap. IV, "Roman Catholic Apologetics in England."

[20] The Thirty-nine Articles, Article XVII.

[21] Trevelyan, George Macaulay, *England under the Stuarts,* 1933, pp. 186–87.

[22] *Ibid.,* p. 256.

[23] Donne, "The Relique." Cf. Spencer, Theodore, "Donne and His Age," in *A Garland for John Donne, 1631–1931,* ed. Theodore Spencer, Cambridge, Massachusetts, 1931, p. 185.

CHAPTER II

[1] *Donne's Sermons, Selected Passages,* with an Essay by Logan Pearsall Smith, Oxford, 1920, pp. xxxv–xxxix.

[2] *A Sermon upon the XV Verse of the XX chapter of the Booke of Judges, etc.,* London: William Stansby for Thomas Jones, 1622, p. 52.

[3] *Fifty Sermons,* London: Ja. Flesher for M. F., J. Marriot and R. Royston, 1649, XXXIX, p. 363, A.

[4] *Fifty Sermons,* XVII, p. 141, C.

[5] *LXXX Sermons,* London: for Richard Royston and Richard Marriot, 1640, XIII, p. 130, C.

[6] *Fifty Sermons,* XV, p. 127, C.

[7] Gosse, Edmund, *The Life and Letters of John Donne,* London, 1899, II, 194.

[8] *LXXX Sermons,* V, p. 42, A.

[9] Fife, Robert Herndon, *Young Luther, the Intellectual and Religious Development of Martin Luther to 1518,* New York, 1928, pp. 159–82.

[10] *LXXX Sermons,* LXXX, p. 819, B.

[11] *Fifty Sermons,* XXII, p. 189, C.

[12] *LXXX Sermons,* LXIX, p. 702, C–D.

[13] *Ibid.,* VIII, p. 83, B–C.

[14] *Essayes in Divinity,* London: T. M. for Richard Marriot, 1651, p. 78.

[15] *LXXX Sermons,* XVI, p. 155, C–D.

[16] *Ibid.,* VIII, pp. 82, E–83, A.

[17] *Ibid.,* XXIII, p. 228, D.

[18] *Ibid.,* XIV, p. 143, C.

[19] *XXVI Sermons,* London: Thomas Newcomb, 1661, III, p. 40, A.

[20] *Essayes in Divinity,* p. 84.

[21] *Ibid.,* p. 82.

22 *Ibid.*, p. 21.
23 *Ibid.*
24 *LXXX Sermons*, VII, p. 63, E.
25 *Ibid.*, XXIII, p. 231, E.
26 *Ibid.*, I, p. 10, B.
27 *Essayes in Divinity*, p. 78.
28 *LXXX Sermons*, IX, p. 95, C–D.
29 *Ibid.*, XXI, p. 206, D.
30 *A Sermon of Commemoration of the Lady Danvers*, London: I. H. for Philemon Stephens, and Christopher Meredith, 1627, pp. 145–47.
31 *LXXX Sermons*, XLI, p. 403, D.
32 *Ibid.*, XXXVI, p. 361, A.
33 Elliott, George Roy, "John Donne: the Middle Phase," *Bookman* (London), LXXIII, 339, 346.

CHAPTER III

1 Leishman, J. B., *The Metaphysical Poets*, Oxford, 1934.
2 Johnson, Samuel, "Cowley," in *The Lives of the English Poets*, London, 1795, p. 19.
3 Eliot, T. S., "Andrew Marvell," in *Homage to John Dryden*, London, 1924, pp. 45–46.
4 Grierson, H. J. C., *The Background of English Literature and Other Collected Essays and Addresses*, London, 1925, p. 115.
5 *Ibid.*, p. 118. Cf. Praz, Mario, "Donne's Relation to the Poetry of His Time," in *A Garland for John Donne*," pp. 58–61.
6 Lea, Kathleen M., "Conceits," *Modern Language Review*, XX, 389–406.
7 Sharp, Robert Lathrop, "Observations on Metaphysical Imagery," *Sewanee Review*, XLIII, 467–69.
8 Ellis, Havelock, *Chapman*, Bloomsbury, 1934, p. 85. Cf. Croll, Morris W., "Muret and the History of Attic Prose," *PMLA*, XXXIX, 308.
9 Gosse, Edmund, *The Jacobean Poets*, London, 1894, p. 64.
10 "Un livido fiume sotterraneo di realismo macabro," Praz, Mario, *Secentismo è Marinismo in Inghilterra*, Firenze, 1925, p. 84. All the remaining Praz references in the book are to this work unless otherwise specified.
11 *The Poems of John Donne*, ed. Herbert J. C. Grierson, Oxford, 1912, I, 62. All the page references for Donne's verse are to this edition.
12 Johnson, *op. cit.*, p. 19.
13 Cf. "Loves Alchymie," I, 39; "The Flea," I, 40; and "Holy Sonnets," xix, I, 331.
14 Willey, *op. cit.*, p. 42.
15 Eliot, T. S., "The Metaphysical Poets," in *Homage to John Dryden*, p. 30.
16 *Ibid.*, pp. 28–29.
17 Read, Herbert, "The Nature of Metaphysical Poetry," *Criterion*, I, 249.
18 Leishman, *op. cit.*, p. 32.
19 "Upon the translation of the Psalmes by Sir Philip Sydney, and the Countesse of Pembroke his Sister," I, 348.
20 See Kane, Elisha K., *Gongorism and the Golden Age*, Chapel Hill, North Carolina, 1928, Plate XII.
21 Read, *op. cit.*, p. 264. Cf. Williamson, George, "Donne and the Poetry of Today," in *A Garland for John Donne*, pp. 158, 176.
22 Willey, *op. cit.*, pp. 2ff and 72.

[23] "Hymne to God my God, in my sicknesse," I, 368. For problem of date of composition see Sparrow, John, "On the Date of Donne's 'Hymne to God my God, in my Sicknesse,'" *Modern Language Review*, XIX, 462–66.

[24] Willey, *op. cit.*, p. 143.

[25] Cf. Eliot, T. S., "Donne in Our Time," in *A Garland for John Donne*, pp. 16–17.

[26] "Holy Sonnets," xiii, I, 328.

[27] *Ibid.*, I, 326.

CHAPTER IV

[1] "Holy Sonnets," xviii, I, 330, discussed by Professor Grierson, II, 235–36.

[1a] *The Poems of John Donne*, ed. Grierson, II, xv–xvii.

[2] Gosse, *The Life and Letters of John Donne*, I, 9, 13–14.

[3] Cf. *Ignatius his Conclave*, London: N. O. for Richard More, 1611; *Pseudo-martyr*, London: W. Stansby for Walter Burre, 1610, pp. 127–28, 142, 215; *LXXX Sermons*, XIV, p. 142, C–E; *Fifty Sermons*, XXXVII, p. 339, D–E.

[4] Gosse, *The Life and Letters of John Donne*, I, 14–19, 23–25; Simpson, Evelyn M., *A Study of the Prose Works of John Donne*, Oxford, 1924, p. 16.

[5] Praz, *op. cit.*, p. 38.

[6] *Pseudo-martyr*, pp. 43, 45; *LXXX Sermons*, LXXIX, p. 698, C–D; *Fifty Sermons*, XXIX, p. 256, C–D.

[7] Gosse, *The Life and Letters of John Donne*, I, 147–51; Simpson, *op. cit.*, pp. 23–25.

[8] Bredvold, L. I., "The Naturalism of Donne in Relation to Some Renaissance Traditions," pp. 471–502. Cf. Williamson, George, "The Libertine Donne," *Philological Quarterly*, XIII, 276–91.

[9] Cf. Eliot, "The Metaphysical Poets," pp. 28–29.

[10] *Devotions upon Emergent Occasions*, ed. John Sparrow, with a Bibliographical Note by Geoffrey Keynes, Cambridge, 1923, 5, "Meditation," p. 22.

[11] Mitchell, W. Fraser, *English Pulpit Oratory from Andrewes to Tillotson, A Study of its Literary Aspects*, London, 1932, pp. 3–4.

[12] "To Mr. Tilman after he had taken orders," I, 351–52.

[13] Gosse, *The Life and Letters of John Donne*, II, 59–60.

[14] Simpson, *op. cit.*, pp. 23–25.

[15] Gosse, *The Life and Letters of John Donne*, II, 58.

[16] *Ibid.*, II, 73.

[17] "To Mr. Tilman after he had taken orders," I, 351, ll. 13–14.

[18] Gosse, *The Life and Letters of John Donne*, II, 254–55.

[19] *Fifty Sermons*, XL, p. 371, D.

[20] Cf. Croll, Morris W., "Muret and the History of 'Attic' Prose," 309, and Knights, L. C., "17th Century Melancholy," *Criterion*, XIII, 111–12.

[21] *LXXX Sermons*, XXIII, p. 231, A–B.

[22] *XXVI Sermons*, XXIV, p. 324, D–E.

[23] *Fifty Sermons*, XXVII, p. 237, A.

[24] Walton, Izaak, "The Life of Dr. John Donne," in *The Lives of John Donne, Sir Henry Wotton, Richard Hooker, George Herbert & Robert Sanderson*, with an Introduction by George Saintsbury (World's Classics), Oxford, 1927, p. 78.

[25] More, Paul Elmer, "George Herbert," in *Shelburne Essays* (Fourth Series), New York and London, 1906, p. 96.

[26] Walton, "The Life of Dr. John Donne," p. 81.

CHAPTER V

¹ *LXXX Sermons,* VIII, p. 83, B–C; IX, p. 95, C–D; XXXVI, p. 361, A; LXVII, p. 674, A.
² Baker, Augustine, *Sancta Sophia,* "extracted . . . and digested" by Serenus Cressy, Douai, 1657, II, 2, Chaps. VIII–XIII.
³ John of Ruysbroeck, *The Adornment of the Spiritual Marriage,* etc., trans. Dom C. A. Wynschenk, London, 1916, pp. 155–56.
⁴ "Holy Sonnets," v, I, 324.
⁵ "Holy Sonnets," xix, I, 331.
⁶ Browning, "Abt Vogler," VII.
⁷ "A Hymne to God the Father," I, 369.
⁸ *Donne's Sermons, Selected Passages,* with an Essay by Logan Pearsall Smith, pp. xxv–xxvii.
⁹ "Holy Sonnets," xi, I, 327.
¹⁰ "The Litanie," I, 345.
¹¹ *Ibid.,* I, 338.
¹² *XXVI Sermons,* VII, p. 90, B–D.
¹³ "The Litanie," I, 346.
¹⁴ "A Hymne to Christ, at the Authors last going into Germany," I, 353.
¹⁵ Eliot, T. S., "Lancelot Andrewes," in *For Lancelot Andrewes,* London, 1928, pp. 28–32.
¹⁶ *Devotions upon Emergent Occasions,* 15, "Prayer," p. 91.
¹⁷ "Holy Sonnets," i, I, 322.
¹⁸ *Ibid.,* v, I, 324.
¹⁹ *Ibid.,* xiii, I, 328.
²⁰ "Ascension," I, 321.
²¹ Cf. Doggett, Frank A., "Donne's Platonism," *Sewanee Review,* XLII, 274–92.
²² *The Confessions of St. Augustine,* X, 27, 38, p. 227.
²³ "The Litanie," I, 338–39.
²⁴ "Upon the translation of the Psalmes by Sir Philip Sydney, and the Countesse of Pembroke his Sister," I, 348.
²⁵ "To Mr. R. W.," I, 210.
²⁶ Cf. "Holy Sonnets," ii, I, 322; xv, I, 329; "The Litanie," I, 338–39.
²⁷ "The Litanie," I, 346.
²⁸ "Holy Sonnets," i, I, 322.
²⁹ *Ibid.,* xvii, I, 330.
³⁰ "A Hymne to God the Father," I, 369.
³¹ Ramsay, Mary Paton, *Les Doctrines Médiévales chez Donne, le Poète Métaphysicien de l'Angleterre,* Oxford, 1917, p. 110.
³² *Ignatius his Conclave,* p. 14. For the effect of the "new astronomy" on Donne, see Nicholson, Marjorie, "The 'New Astronomy' and English Literary Imagination," *Studies in Philology,* XXXII, 449–61; and Williamson, George, "Mutability, Decay, and Seventeenth Century Melancholy," *ELH,* II, 140, 148–49.
³³ "To the Countesse of Bedford," I, 197.
³⁴ Ramsay, *op. cit.,* p. 246. Cf. Hughes, Merritt Y., "Kidnapping Donne," in *Essays in Criticism* (Second Series), by Members of the Department of English, University of California, Berkeley, 1934, p. 74.
³⁵ "The Progresse of the Soule," I, 300.
³⁶ "Holy Sonnets," xiv, I, 328.
³⁷ "The Litanie," I, 339.
³⁸ *Ibid.,* I, 340.

[39] *Ibid.*, I, 345. Cf. Moore, John F., "Scholasticism, Donne and the Metaphysical Conceit," *Revue anglo-américaine*, XIII, 292, 296.

[40] "The Litanie," I, 341.

[41] "The Progresse of the Soule," I, 298–99.

[42] *Devotions upon Emergent Occasions*, 4, "Expostulation," p. 18.

[43] *LXXX Sermons*, XXIII, p. 229, A–B.

[44] "Farewell to Love," I, 71.

[45] "Holy Sonnets," x, I, 326.

[46] "Death," I, 284.

[47] *LXXX Sermons*, XXIV, p. 239, D.

[48] "Holy Sonnets," vii, I, 325.

CHAPTER VI

[1] *The Compleat Angler or the Contemplative Man's Recreation*, London: T. M. for Rich. Marriot, etc., 1655, p. 156.

[2] Huxley, Aldous L., *Texts & Pretexts*, London, 1932, p. 86.

[3] *Ibid.*

[4] "George Herbert," *Times Literary Supplement*, March 2, 1933, p. 133.

[5] *The Autobiography of Edward Lord Herbert of Cherbury*, with an Introduction by C. H. Herford, Newtown, Montgomeryshire, 1928, pp. 6–7.

[6] Hutchinson, F. E., "George Herbert: a Tercentenary," *The Nineteenth Century*, CXIII, 360.

[7] Walton, "The Life of Mr. George Herbert," in *Lives*, p. 273.

[8] *Ibid.*

[9] "In honorem illustrissimi Domini Francisci de Verulamio, Vice-Comitis Sti Albani Post editam ab eo Instaur. Magnam," *The Poems of George Herbert*, with an Introduction by Arthur Waugh, Oxford, 1913, pp. 287–88. Until the Rev. Mr. F. E. Hutchinson shall have completed his projected edition of Herbert's verse, there is no standard critical text. The Oxford edition is at least as satisfactory as any and more accessible. All page references to Herbert's verse, unless otherwise specified, are to this edition. In this matter of the text as well as in the bibliography of the Herbert criticism I have had, thanks to the kindness of the author, the advantage of seeing the typescript of the valuable Master of Arts Thesis for the University of London of Miss Kathleen I. Barratt, B.A. King's College, *Studies in the Life and Writings of George Herbert*, 1934.

[10] Francis Lo. Verulam, Viscount St. Alban, *Translation of certaine psalmes into English Verse*, London: for Hanna Barret, and Richard Whittaker, etc., 1625.

[11] Cf. "Vanitie," pp. 85–86, and "Divinitie," pp. 137–38.

[12] [Oley, Barnabas,] "Of the Life of Mr. G. Herbert" etc., in *Herbert's Remains, Or, Sundry Pieces Of that Sweet Singer of the Temple, Mr. George Herbert*, London: for Timothy Garthwait, 1652, sigs. $a_{11}{}^{v}$–a_{12}.

[13] Walton, "The Life of Mr. George Herbert," pp. 262–63.

[14] "Affliction," p. 48.

[15] *George Herbert's Country Parson*, ed. H. C. Beeching, Oxford, 1916, pp. xvi–xvii.

[16] Donne, John, *A Sermon of Commemoration of the Lady Danvers*.

[17] Gosse, *The Life and Letters of John Donne*, II, 106.

[18] Daniell, John J., *The Life of George Herbert of Bemerton*, London, 1902, pp. 33–34.

[19] Palmer, George Herbert, *The Life and Works of George Herbert*, Boston and New York, 1905, I, 25.

[19a] Cf. Eliot, T. S., "George Herbert," *Spectator,* CXLVIII, 361.

[20] Letter to Sir John Danvers, Trin. Coll., March 18, 1617, Palmer, I, 394–96.

[21] To Sir John Danvers, Trin. Coll., October 6, 1619, Palmer, I, 401.

[22] To Sir John Danvers, printed by Palmer with letter from Trin. Coll., January 19, 1619, I, 398–400.

[23] Walton, "The Life of Mr. George Herbert," pp. 270–71.

[24] *Ibid.,* pp. 274–75.

[25] Daniell, *op. cit.,* p. 89.

[26] Hutchinson, "George Herbert: a Tercentenary," p. 363.

[27] Daniell, *op. cit.,* p. 103.

[28] Palmer, *op. cit.,* I, 37.

[29] Walton, "The Life of Mr. George Herbert," p. 279.

[30] *Ibid.,* p. 316.

[31] Trans. Richard Wilton and Alexander Grosart in *The Complete Works in Verse and Prose of George Herbert,* ed. Alexander B. Grosart (printed for private circulation), 1874, II, 55–84.

[32] Walton, "The Life of Mr. George Herbert," p. 284; Daniell, *op. cit.,* p. 147.

[33] *The Country Parson,* Palmer, I, 233–34.

[34] Walton, "The Life of Mr. George Herbert," pp. 285–86.

[35] *The Country Parson,* Palmer, I, 231–34.

[36] Walton, "The Life of Mr. George Herbert," p. 288.

[37] Daniell, *op. cit.,* p. 184.

[38] Walton, "The Life of Mr. George Herbert," p. 289.

[39] *Ibid.,* p. 302.

[40] *The Country Parson,* Palmer, I, 289.

[41] Walton, "The Life of Mr. George Herbert," pp. 316–18.

[42] Daniell, *op. cit.,* p. 239.

[43] Herbert's Will, Palmer, I, 415.

[44] Grosart, *op. cit.,* I, 234.

[45] *Ibid.,* I, 273.

[46] Catalogued in Dr. William's Library, London, as Jones MS., B, 62.

[47] Palmer, *op. cit.,* I, 185.

[48] *Ibid.,* I, 184.

[49] *Ibid.,* I, 188.

[50] *Ibid.,* I, 185–86.

[51] Walton, "The Life of Mr. George Herbert," p. 314.

[52] *Ibid.*

CHAPTER VII

[1] Valdesso, John, *Divine Considerations, the English Translation of Nicholas Ferrar with George Herbert's Prefatory Epistle,* London, 1905, pp. xxvii–xxviii.

[2] *Reliquiae Baxterianae: or, Mr. Richard Baxter's Narrative of the most Memorable Passages of his Life and Times,* ed. Matthew Sylvester, London: for T. Parkhurst, etc., 1696, Part I, pp. 2, 6.

[3] "The Church Porch," p. 11.

[4] "Judgment," p. 194.

[5] "To All Angels and Saints," p. 78.

[6] "Providence," p. 120.

[7] "Even-Song," p. 214.

[8] "The Song," p. 42.

[9] "The Sacrifice," p. 34.

[10] Huxley, *op. cit.,* p. 86.

[11] "The Collar," pp. 157–58.
[12] "Affliction," p. 48.
[13] "The Elixer," p. 191.
[14] Osmond, Percy H., *The Mystical Poets of the English Church*, London, New York, 1919, p. 73.
[15] "A Parodie," p. 190.
[16] "The Holy Communion," p. 53.
[17] "Church Musick," p. 66.
[18] "Perfection," Williams MS., pp. 74b–75a. In this and the following form all contractions have been expanded.
[19] *Ibid.*, "The Elixir," as revised by Herbert.
[20] "The Elixer," p. 191.
[21] "Bitter-Sweet," p. 177.
[22] "The Odour," p. 181.
[23] "Dialogue—Man," p. 116.
[24] "Decay," p. 99.
[25] "Vertue," p. 88.
[26] "Doom's-day," p. 193. Cf. Warren, Austin, "George Herbert," *American Review*, VII, 258, 261.
[27] "The Flower," p. 171.
[28] "Divinitie," p. 137.
[29] Lea, *op. cit.*, 405.
[30] "Whitsunday," p. 59.
[31] "The Thanksgiving," William MS., p. 22b; Oxford, p. 36.
[32] "Prayer," p. 52.
[33] "The Forerunners," p. 183.
[34] "Love," p. 195.

CHAPTER VIII

[1] *State Papers: Domestic James I*, LXI, No. 111, Feb. 26, 1611.
[2] Hutchinson, F. E., "The Sacred Poets," in *Cambridge History of English Literature*, Cambridge, 1911, VII, 33.
[3] *The Poems, English, Latin and Greek of Richard Crashaw*, ed. L. C. Martin, Oxford, 1927, pp. xvii-xviii. All page references for Crashaw's verse are to this edition. Cf. Gosse, Edmund, *Seventeenth-Century Studies*, London, 1883, p. 145.
[4] Sharland, E. Cruwys, "Richard Crashaw and Mary Collet," *Church Quarterly Review*, LXXIII, 359.
[5] Praz, *op. cit.*, p. 152.
[6] Confrey, Burton, "A Note on Richard Crashaw," *Modern Language Notes*, XXXVII, 250.
[7] Martin, *op. cit.*, p. xix.
[8] *Ibid.*, pp. xix-xx.
[9] Warren, Austin, "Crashaw's *Epigrammata Sacra*," *Journal of English and Germanic Philology*, XXXIII, 233–35.
[10] *Epigrammatum Sacrorum Liber*, Brit. Mus. Add. MS. 40176, Martin, *op. cit.*, pp. 2–3.
[11] Warren, "Crashaw's *Epigrammata Sacra*," pp. 234–35.
[12] Martin, *op. cit.*, p. xxi.
[13] *Ibid.*
[14] "Lectori," pp. 11–14.
[15] Acland, J. E., *Little Gidding and Its Inmates in the Time of King Charles I*, London, 1903, pp. 10–11.
[16] *Ibid.*, pp. 11–12.

[17] Peckard, P., *Memoirs of the Life of Mr. Nicholas Ferrar*, Cambridge, 1790, p. 243.

[18] Martin, *op. cit.*, pp. xxv–xxxii.

[19] Sharland, "Richard Crashaw and Mary Collet," p. 362.

[20] Cf. Beachcroft, T. O., "Nicholas Ferrar and George Herbert," *Criterion*, XII, 24–42.

[21] Carter, T. T., *Nicholas Ferrar, his Household and Friends*, London, 1892, p. 63.

[22] Oley, "Of the Life of Mr. G. Herbert," sig. b$_{11}$; Walton, "The Life of Mr. George Herbert," p. 312.

[23] Peckard, *op. cit.*, p. 315.

[24] *Ibid.*, pp. 288–89.

[25] Palmer, *op. cit.*, I, 77.

[26] Valdesso, *op. cit.*, pp. xxvii–xxviii.

[27] Praz, *op. cit.*, pp. 177, 185, Carter, *op. cit.*, pp. 31–41, 123.

[28] Peckard, *op. cit.*, p. 88.

[29] *The Arminian Nunnery: or, A Briefe Description and Relation of the late erected Monastical Place, called the Arminian Nunnery at little Gidding in Huntingdon-Shire, Humbly recommended to the wise consideration of this present Parliament*, etc., London: for Thomas Underhill, 1641, p. 2.

[30] Peckard, *op. cit.*, p. 289.

[31] *The Arminian Nunnery*, pp. 3–4.

[32] *Ibid.*, p. 9.

[33] Acland, *op. cit.*, p. 11.

[34] Skipton, H. P. K., "Little Gidding and the Nonjurors," *Church Quarterly Review*, XCIII, 62.

[35] Collett, Henry, *Little Gidding and Its Founder*, London, 1925, p. 33.

[36] Peckard, *op. cit.*, pp. 195–98.

[37] *Ibid.*, pp. 203–10.

[38] *The Story Books of Little Gidding, being the Religious Dialogues Recited in the Great Room, 1631-2*, with an Introduction by E. Cruwys Sharland, London, 1899, p. 2ff.

[39] Praz, *op. cit.*, p. 185.

[40] *The Story Books of Little Gidding*, Chap. XIII.

[41] Brémond, Henri, *Histoire Littéraire du Sentiment Religieux en France*, Paris, 1923, I, 2, Chap. V, "Le Roman Dévot."

[42] *The Story Books of Little Gidding*, p. 258.

[43] Peckard, *op. cit.*, pp. 178–79, 296.

[44] *Ibid.*, pp. 182, 289; Collett, *op. cit.*, p. 22; Carter, *op. cit.*, p. 113.

[45] Peckard, *op. cit.*, p. 242.

[46] Hutchinson, F. E., review of Martin's *Crashaw* in *Review of English Studies*, IV, 350.

[47] Martin, *op. cit.*, pp. xxii–xxiii.

[48] Chalmers, Robert, Lord, "Richard Crashaw: 'Poet and Saint,'" in *In Memoriam Adolphus William Ward, Master of Peterhouse (1900–1924)*, Cambridge, 1924, p. 47.

[49] Martin, *op. cit.*, p. xxii. Cf. Varley, F. J., *Cambridge during the Civil War, 1642–1646*, Cambridge, 1935, p. 30.

[50] Martin, *op. cit.*, p. xl; Confrey, *op. cit.*, pp. 250–51.

[51] Preface to 1646 edition of *Steps to the Temple*, p. 76.

[52] Warren, Austin, "Richard Crashaw, 'Catechist and Curate,'" *Modern Philology*, XXXII, 261–63.

[53] Martin, *op. cit.*, xxxiii.

[54] Warren, "Richard Crashaw, 'Catechist and Curate,'" pp. 264–67.

[55] Chalmers, *op. cit.*, p. 48.

[56] Quoted from Lloyd's *Memoires of the Lives, Actions, Sufferings, & Deaths of those Noble, Reverend, and Excellent Personages, That Suffered . . . for the Protestant Religion, And the great Principle thereof, Allegiance to their Soveraigne, In our late Intestine Wars,* London, 1668, in Martin, *op. cit.,* p. 416.

[57] "Reverendo admodum viro Benjamino Lany," pp. 6–8.

[58] Gosse, *Seventeenth-Century Studies,* p. 146.

[59] "Upon Bishop Andrewes his Picture before his Sermons," pp. 163–64.

[60] Martin, *op. cit.,* p. xxiii.

[61] "An Epitaph upon Mr. Ashton," p. 192.

[62] Chalmers, *op. cit.,* p. 51.

[63] "Luc. 18. 41.," p. 40.

[64] *The Complete Works of Richard Crashaw,* ed. Alexander B. Grosart (printed for private circulation), 1873, II, 100.

[65] "Upon the Bleeding Crucifix," pp. 288–89.

[66] Chalmers, *op. cit.,* pp. 56–57

[67] Praz, *op. cit.,* p. 229.

[68] "On the Gunpowder-Treason," etc., pp. 384–88.

[69] "Act. 5. 15.," p. 19.

[70] Trans. Grosart, *op. cit.,* II, 47.

[71] Trans. *ibid.,* II, 32.

[72] *Ibid.*

[73] "On a Treatise of Charity," pp. 137–39.

[74] Quoted from Elrington, *Works of Ussher,* XVI, in Martin, op, cit., p. 438.

[75] Shelford, Robert, *Five Pious and Learned Discourses,* Cambridge: the printers to the Universitie of Cambridge, 1635, pp. 96–97.

[76] *Ibid.,* p. 107.

[77] *Ibid.,* pp. 65–66.

[78] Warren, Austin, "Crashaw and St. Teresa," *Times Literary Supplement,* August 25, 1932, p. 593.

[79] Collett, *op. cit.,* p. 26.

[80] Martin, *op. cit.,* p. xxxii.

[81] *Ibid.,* pp. xxiv–xxv.

[82] Warren, Austin, "Crashaw's Residence at Peterhouse," *Times Literary Supplement,* Nov. 3, 1932, p. 815.

[83] *Ibid.*

[84] Martin, *op. cit.,* p. xxv.

[85] *Ibid.,* pp. xxvii–xxxi.

[86] *Ibid.,* pp. xxvi–xxvii.

[87] *Ibid.,* p. xxix.

[88] *Ibid.,* p. xxx.

[89] *Ibid.,* p. xxix.

[90] *Ibid.,* p. xxxi.

[91] *Ibid.,* p. xxxiii.

[92] "A Letter from Mr. Crashaw to the Countess of Denbigh," pp. 348–50. Cf. Warren, Austin, "The Mysticism of Richard Crashaw," *Church Quarterly Review,* CXVI, 82.

[93] "Prayer, An Ode, which was Praefixed to a little Prayer-book given to a young Gentle-Woman," pp. 328–31.

[94] Herbert, "To All Angels and Saints," p. 78.

[95] Martin, *op. cit.,* p. 234.

[96] Wallerstein, Ruth C., *Richard Crashaw, a Study in Style and Poetic Development,* Madison, 1935, p. 104ff.

[97] "An Apologie for the precedent Hymne," pp, 136–137. Cf. Warren, Austin, "Crashaw's 'Apologie,'" *Times Literary Supplement,* November 16, 1935, p. 746.

[98] Eliot, T. S., "A Note on Richard Crashaw," in *For Lancelot Andrewes,* p. 125.
[99] Martin, *op. cit.,* p. xxxiv.
[100] *Ibid.,* pp. xxxv–xxxviii.
[101] Eliot, "A Note on Richard Crashaw," pp. 119–20.

CHAPTER IX

[1] Chalmers, *op. cit.,* p. 55.
[2] Warren, "Crashaw's *Epigrammata Sacra,*" pp. 233–35.
[3] Chalmers, *op. cit.,* p. 55.
[4] Cf. Brémond, *op. cit.,* I, xix.
[5] "Our Lord in his Circumcision to his Father," p. 98.
[6] "Charitas Nimia, or the Dear Bargain," p. 280.
[7] *Ibid.,* p. 281.
[8] Cf. Praz, *op. cit.,* especially pp. 228–29 and 243–50; Wallerstein, *op. cit.,* Chap. IV, *passim.*
[9] "Sospetto d'Herode," pp. 114–15.
[10] St. John of the Cross, *Complete Works,* trans. David Lewis, London, 1864, I, 148.
[11] "A Letter from Mr. Crashaw to the Countess of Denbigh," pp. 349–50.
[12] St. Bernard, *op. cit.,* I, 360.
[13] "A Song," p. 327.
[14] "The Hymn of the Church, in Meditation of the Day of Judgment," p. 300.
[15] "Upon the Bleeding Crucifix," p. 288.
[16] "Crashaw the *Anagramme,* He was Car," pp. 233–34.
[17] "Pulchra non diuturna," p. 371.
[18] "Death's Lecture at the Funeral of a Young Gentleman," pp. 340–41.
[19] "Sospetto d'Herode," p. 116.
[20] "Death's Lecture at the Funeral of a Young Gentleman," p. 341.
[21] "An Apologie, for the Fore-going Hymne," p. 323.
[22] "The Flaming Heart upon the Book and Picture of the seraphicall saint Teresa," pp. 326–27.
[23] "Upon the Bleeding Crucifix," pp. 288–89.
[24] "A Song," p. 327.
[25] Mâle, Émile, *L'Art Religieux après le Concile de Trente,* Paris, 1932, Chap. IV.
[26] Praz, *op. cit.,* pp. 146–47; Mâle, *op. cit.,* pp. 148–49.
[27] "A Letter from Mr. Crashaw to the Countess of Denbigh," p. 348.
[28] "Prayer, An Ode," p. 330.
[29] "Description of a Religious House and Condition of Life (Out of Barclay)," p. 339.
[30] Falls, Cyril, "The Divine Poet" in *The Critic's Armoury,* London, 1924, p. 34.
[31] "In the Glorious Epiphanie of Our Lord God, A Hymn, Sung as by the Three Kings," pp. 259–60.
[32] Walton, "The Life of Mr. George Herbert," p. 314.
[33] Eliot, "A Note on Richard Crashaw," p. 124.
[34] "Un rosario di epigrammi o di madrigali malamente legati assieme," Praz, *op. cit.,* p. 231.
[35] Wallerstein, *op. cit.,* p. 97.
[36] "The Weeper," p. 309.
[37] *Ibid.,* p. 312.
[38] Cf. Wallerstein, *op. cit.,* p. 120ff, for a discussion of his use of emblems,

and for his symbolism in general, *ibid.*, p. 84ff.; Beachcroft, T. O., "Crashaw and the Baroque Style," *Criterion*, XIII, 420–21, 423; Praz, *op. cit.*, pp. 221, 230.

[39] Whitney, Geffrey, *A Choice of Emblemes, and other Devises*, Leiden: Christopher Plantyn, 1586, sig. **₄. Cf. Praz, Mario, "The English Emblem Literature," *English Studies* (Amsterdam), XVI, 129–40

[40] "Reverendo admodum viro Benjamino Lany," trans. Grosart, *op. cit.*, II, 12.

[41] Quoted in Beachcroft, "Crashaw and the Baroque Style," p. 421.

[42] *The Spiritual Exercises of Saint Ignatius of Loyola*, trans. Elder Mullan, S.J., New York, 1914, pp. 35–36.

[43] Cf. Grierson, H. J. C., *Metaphysical Lyrics and Poems of the Seventeenth Century*, Oxford, 1928, pp. xlvi–xlvii.

[44] Lea, *op. cit.*, p. 405.

[45] "A Hymne to the Name and Honor of the Admirable Sainte Teresa," p. 320.

[46] Cf. Beachcroft, "Crashaw and the Baroque Style," p. 420.

[47] Praz, *op. cit.*, pp. 146–47.

[48] Cf. Huxley, *op. cit.*, pp. 107–10.

[49] Cf. Empson, William, *Seven Types of Ambiguity*, London, 1930, p. 279.

[50] "A Hymne to the Name and Honor of the Admirable Sainte Teresa," p. 319.

[51] "The Weeper," p. 309.

[52] Wallerstein, *op. cit.*, p. 146.

[53] Cf. Read, Herbert, *Phases of English Poetry*, London, 1928, p. 73.

[54] Cf. Wallerstein, *op. cit.*, pp. 49–51 and her concluding chapter, *passim*.

[55] "The Flaming Heart," p. 327.

CHAPTER X

[1] *The Poems of Henry Vaughan, Silurist*, ed. E. K. Chambers, with an Introduction by H. C. Beeching, London, 1896, I, xvii.

[2] *"Brief Lives," chiefly of Contemporaries, set down by John Aubrey, between the Years 1669 & 1696*, ed. Andrew Clark, Oxford, 1898, II, 268–69.

[3] "Venerabili viro, praeceptori suo olim & semper Colendissimo Mᵒ. Mathaeo Herbert," *The Works of Henry Vaughan*, ed. Leonard Cyril Martin, Oxford, 1914, I, 93. All page references to Vaughan's work in this and the following chapters are to this edition.

[4] Judson, A. C., "Henry Vaughan as a Nature Poet," *PMLA*, XLII, 147.

[5] Waite, A. E., "Henry and Thos. Vaughan," *Bookman* (London), LXIII, 241.

[6] *The Works in Verse and Prose (Complete) of Henry Vaughan, Silurist*, ed. Alexander B. Grosart (printed for private circulation), 1871, II, xxxv–xxxvi.

[7] Letter to Aubrey, June 15, 1673, II, 667.

[8] *The Poems of Henry Vaughan*, ed. Chambers, II, xx.

[9] "Ad Posteros," II, 32.

[10] "Upon a Cloke lent him by Mr. J. Ridsley," I, 52.

[11] "An Elegie on the death of Mr. R. Hall," I, 58.

[12] Guiney, Louise Imogen, *A Little English Gallery*, New York, 1894, pp. 57–58, 69.

[13] Guiney, Louise Imogen, "Lovelace and Vaughan: a Speculation," *Catholic World*, XCV, 652.

[14] *The Poems of Henry Vaughan*, ed. Chambers, II, xxxi–xxxii.

[15] More, P. E., "Works of Henry Vaughan," *Nation*, CCII, 247.

[16] *Silex Scintillans*, "The Authors Preface to the following Hymns," II, 390.

[17] *Olor Iscanus*, "The Publisher to the Reader," I, 36.

[18] "To Etesia," etc., II, 623–27.

NOTES

445

[19] "The World," II, 466–67.

[20] "Henry Vaughan," *Times Literary Supplement,* April 20, 1922, p. 249.

[21] Cf. Hodgson, Geraldine, "Henry Vaughan," *Modern Language Quarterly,* IV, 80.

[22] Letter to Aubrey, June 15, 1673, II, 668.

[23] *Ibid.*

[24] Leishman, *op. cit.,* p. 151ff.; Holmes, Elizabeth, *Henry Vaughan and the Hermetic Philosophy,* Oxford, 1932, pp. 17–22.

[25] Clough, W. O., "Henry Vaughan and the Hermetic Philosophy, " *PMLA,* XLVIII, 1108–30.

[26] Waite, "Henry and Thos. Vaughan," p. 241.

[27] Letter to Aubrey, June 15, 1673, II, 667.

[28] *The Works of Thomas Vaughan: Eugenius Philalethes,* ed. Arthur Edward Waite, London, 1919, p. 449.

[29] Letter to Aubrey, June 15, 1673, II, 667; to the same, July 7, 1673, II, 671.

[30] Clough, *op. cit.,* 1119.

[31] "The importunate Fortune, written to Doctor Powel of Cantre," II, 616. See also "Vanity of Spirit," II, 418–19.

[32] Morgan, Gwenllian E. F., "Henry Vaughan, Silurist," *Times Literary Supplement,* November 3, 1932, p. 815.

[33] More, "Works of Henry Vaughan," p. 247.

[34] *Silex Scintillans,* II, 416–18, 420, 425–26, 478–79.

[35] "An Elegie on the death of Mr. R. W.," I, 49–51.

[36] "An Elegie on the death of Mr. R. Hall," I, 58–59.

[37] Vaughan, Thomas, "Memoriae Sacrum," *Works,* p. 449.

[38] Lathrop, Henry Burrowes, *Translations from the Classics into English from Caxton to Chapman, 1477–1620,* Madison, 1933, pp. 29–32, 182.

[39] Eliot, T. S., "The Silurist," *The Dial,* LXXXIII, 261.

[40] "An Elegie on the death of Mr. R. W.," I, 51.

[41] *Primitive Holiness, set forth in the Life of Blessed Paulinus,* I, 363; "Jacobs Pillow, and Pillar," II, 527–28.

[42] *Primitive Holiness,* I, 379.

[43] "The true Christmas," II, 646–47.

[44] "Upon Mr. Fletchers Playes," I, 55.

[45] "An Epitaph upon the Lady Elizabeth, Second Daughter to his late Majestie," I, 63, "Thalia Rediviva," II, 605–6.

[46] "Juvenals tenth Satyre Translated," I, 18–31.

[47] "To Amoret Weeping," I, 13–14; "To the pious memorie of C. W. Esquire," II, 609–10.

[48] Cf. *Primitive Holiness,* I, 371–72; "The Constellation," II, 469–70; "L'Envoy," II, 541–42.

[49] "The Nativity," II, 645–46.

[50] "Dressing," II, 455–56.

[51] "The Holy Communion," II, 457–58.

[52] *The Mount of Olives: or, Solitary Devotions,* I, 137–90.

[53] *Ibid.,* pp. 153–54.

[54] "Religion," II, 404.

[55] Herbert, "To All Angels and Saints," p. 78.

[56] "The Knot," II, 506.

[57] "Joy of my life!" II, 423.

CHAPTER XI

[1] Otto, Rudolph, *The Idea of the Holy*, trans. John W. Harvey, London, 1923, Chaps. II and III.

[2] Wordsworth, William, *The Prelude*, I, ll. 357–400.

[3] Brémond, *op. cit.*, I, xix.

[4] "I walkt the other day (to spend my hour,)" II, 479.

[5] "Resurrection and Immortality," II, 402; "The Bird," II, 497.

[6] "Distraction," II, 413; "The Morning-watch," II, 424–25; "Man," II, 477.

[7] "Corruption," II, 440; "Palm-Sunday," II, 501.

[8] Holmes, *op. cit.*; cf. Clough, *op. cit.*, Osmond, *op. cit.*, Chap. VI; Sencourt, Robert, *Outflying Philosophy*, London, n.d., p. 203ff.

[9] Holmes, *op. cit.*, p. 33.

[10] "Sure, there's a tye of Bodyes!" II, 429; "The Favour," II, 492. Cf. Holmes, *op. cit.*, pp. 24–25.

[11] "To Amoret Weeping," I, 12–13; "Cock-crowing," II, 488; "The Starre," II, 490.

[12] Letter to Aubrey, June 28, 1680, II, 672.

[13] Boehme, Jacob, *Mysterium Magnum*, quoted in Holmes, *op. cit.*, p. 41.

[14] Holmes, *op. cit.*, p. 28.

[15] "Cock-crowing," II, 488–89.

[16] "The Retreate," II, 419–20.

[17] "L'Envoy," II, 542.

[18] "The Request," II, 647–48.

[19] "Ascension-day," II, 482.

[20] *Ibid.*, II, 481; "Ascension-Hymn," II, 482–83.

[21] "Jesus weeping," II, 503–505.

[22] "Quickness," II, 538.

[23] "The Night," II, 522.

[24] "Come, come, what doe I here?" II, 420; "Silence, and stealth of dayes!" II, 425–26; "To the pious memorie of C. W. Esquire," II, 609–11.

[25] "They are all gone into the world of light!" II, 484.

[26] "The Water-fall," II, 538.

[27] Cf. Blunden, Edmund, *On the Poems of Henry Vaughan*, London, 1927, p. 48.

[28] Eliot, "The Silurist," p. 260.

[29] Warren, Henry C., *Buddhism in Translations* (Harvard Oriental Series), Cambridge, 1900, p. 56ff.

[30] "The Ass," II, 518–19.

[31] "The Constellation," II, 469.

[32] "The Book," II, 540.

[33] "Death," II, 399.

[34] Cf. Dowden, Edward, *Puritan and Anglican: Studies in Literature*, New York, 1910, p. 130.

[35] "The World," II, 466.

[36] "Regeneration," II, 398.

[37] "Psalme 104," II, 495.

[38] "The Timber," II, 497.

[39] "The Bird," II, 496.

[40] "Buriall," II, 427.

[41] Cf. Vaughan, Henry, *Silex Scintillans*, with an Introduction by W. A. Lewis Bettany, London, 1905, pp. v–vi.

NOTES

NOTES 427

CHAPTER XII

[1] Lewis-Jones, W., "Thomas Traherne and the Religious Poets of the Seventeenth Century," *Quarterly Review,* CC, 442.

[2] Quoted in Dobell's Introduction, reprinted in *The Poetical Works of Thomas Traherne,* ed. Gladys I. Wade, London, 1932, p. xxxviii.

[3] Hutchinson, F. E., "The Sacred Poets," p. 42.

[4] Wade, Gladys Irene, *Thomas Traherne and his Circle: a Literary and Biographical Study,* Thesis for the Degree of Ph.D. in English Literature, University College, University of London (deposited in Library of University of London, South Kensington, London), pp. 13–15. Miss Wade has made some of this material more accessible in the following papers: "Mrs. Susanna Hopton," *The English Review,* LXII, 41–47; "Traherne and the Spiritual Value of Nature Study," *London Quarterly,* CLIX, 243–45; "Thomas Traherne as Divine Philosopher," *Hibbert Journal,* XXXII, 400–408; but all Wade references in this book are to the thesis.

[5] Wade, *op. cit.,* p. 29.

[6] Hopkinson, Arthur W., Letter to *Times Literary Supplement,* October 6, 1927, p. 694.

[7] Dawson, M. L., "Thomas Traherne," *Times Literary Supplement,* September 29, 1927, p. 667.

[8] Hopkinson, *op. cit.*

[9] Wade, *op. cit.,* pp. 64–65.

[10] Dawson, *op. cit.*

[11] Wade, *op. cit.,* p. 66.

[12] Burney MS. 126 (British Museum).

[13] Wade, *op. cit.,* p. 84.

[14] *Ibid.,* pp. 83–84.

[15] Dawson, *op. cit.*

[16] *Centuries of Meditations,* ed. Bertram Dobell, London, 1927, III, 46, p. 186.

[17] Wade, *op. cit.,* p. 104.

[18] Quoted in Dobell's Introduction, *Poetical Works,* p. xxxviii.

[19] Dawson, *op. cit.*

[20] Wade, *op. cit.,* p. 194.

[21] *Ibid.,* p. 181ff.

[22] *Ibid.,* pp. 376–77.

[23] *Ibid.,* p. 219.

[24] *Christian Ethicks: or, Divine Morality,* London: for Jonathan Edwin, 1675, p. 10.

[25] Wade, *op. cit.,* pp. 328–29.

[26] *Ibid.,* p. 302.

[27] Dobell's Introduction, *Poetical Works,* p. li.

[28] Watkins, A., "Thos. Traherne," *Times Literary Supplement,* October 20, 1927, p. 742; Dawson, *op. cit.*

[29] *Poetical Works,* p. ix.

[30] Wade, *op. cit.,* p. 394ff.

[31] *Poetical Works,* p. xvff.

[32] *Ibid.,* pp. xiii–xv.

[33] *A Collection of Meditations and Devotions,* etc., published by N. Spinckes, London, 1717, p. 39.

[34] *Poetical Works,* p. xv.

[35] *Centuries of Meditations,* IV, 20, p. 243.

[36] *The Confessions of the Venerable Father Augustine Baker,* ed. Dom Justin McCann, London, 1922.

[37] *Centuries of Meditations,* IV, 30, p. 249 and IV, 39, pp. 252–53.

[38] "The Preparative," pp. 11–13. All page references to Traherne's verse are to Miss Wade's edition of *The Poetical Works.*

[39] *Centuries of Meditations,* III, 16, p. 163.

[40] "Poverty," pp. 126–27.

[41] "My Spirit," pp. 28–32; "The Inference," pp. 194–97.

[42] "Hosanna," pp. 204–6.

[43] *Centuries of Meditations,* III, 23, pp. 168–69.

[44] Holmes, *op. cit.,* pp. 17–18.

[45] Hudson, W. H., *Far Away and Long Ago,* London, etc., 1918, p. 227ff.

[46] "The Anticipation," pp. 56–60.

[47] "The Salutation," p. 3.

[48] "Insatiableness," pp. 200–1.

[49] Payne, Arthur, "A Prose Poet: Thomas Traherne," *Educational Times,* August 1922, p. 347.

[50] *Centuries of Meditations,* III, 12, p. 161. Cf. Whitney, Lois, *Primitivism and the Idea of Progress in English Popular Literature of the Eighteenth Century,* Baltimore, 1934, p. 51.

[51] "Wonder," p. 5.

[52] *Centuries of Meditations,* III, 8, p. 158.

[53] *Christian Ethicks,* pp. 519–21.

[54] "Amendment," p. 52.

[55] *Christian Ethicks,* pp. 46–47.

[56] "Silence," p. 26.

[57] *Centuries of Meditations,* III, 9, pp. 158–59.

[58] "The Apostacy," pp. 121–22.

[59] Wade, *op. cit.,* pp. 19–21.

[60] *Centuries of Meditations,* III, 7–11, pp. 157–60.

[61] "Right Apprehension," pp. 167–69.

[62] More, P. E., "Thomas Traherne," *Nation,* LXXXVIII, 162.

[63] "The Instruction," p. 14; cf. *Centuries of Meditations,* I, 7, p. 6.

[64] "Poverty," pp. 126–28.

[65] *Centuries of Meditations,* III, 15–46, pp. 162–86.

[66] *Ibid.,* I, 51, p. 33.

[67] "Misapprehension," pp. 144–46.

[68] *A Serious and Pathetical Contemplation of the Mercies of God,* published by the Reverend Dr. Hicks, London: for Samuel Keble, 1699, p. 131.

[69] Wade, *op. cit.,* pp. 23–24, 29, 98.

[70] Cf. Barclay, Robert, *The Inner Life of the Religious Societies of the Commonwealth,* London, 1876, and Waterhouse, Gilbert, *The Literary Relations of England and Germany in the Seventeenth Century,* Cambridge, 1914, Chap. VIII, "The Theologians."

[71] "Dissatisfaction," p. 130; *Centuries of Meditations,* III, 27–28, pp. 172–74.

[72] Jones, Rufus M., *Spiritual Reformers in the Sixteenth and Seventeenth Centuries,* London, 1914, p. 86.

CHAPTER XIII

[1] *Centuries of Meditations,* III, 27–31, pp. 172–75.

[2] "The Bible," pp. 131–32.

[3] *Centuries of Meditations,* II, 34, p. 103.

[4] *Ibid.,* III, 69–96, pp. 202–23.

[5] *Ibid.,* III, 12, p. 161.

[6] *Christian Ethicks,* p. 58.

[7] *Ibid.*, p. 46.

[8] *Centuries of Meditations,* III, 44, pp. 184–85.

[9] "News," p. 112.

[10] *Centuries of Meditations,* I, 85, p. 62.

[11] "Consummation," p. 202.

[12] See Dobell's Introduction, *Poetical Works,* pp. lxxxi–lxxxiii.

[13] "The Inference," p. 195.

[14] Cf. Thompson, Elbert N. S., "The Philosophy of Thomas Traherne," *Philological Quarterly,* VIII, 97–112.

[15] "Amendment," p. 51.

[16] *Centuries of Meditations,* IV, 81, p. 286.

[17] "My Spirit," pp. 30–31.

[18] Beachcroft, T. O., "Traherne and the Cambridge Platonists," *Dublin Review,* CLXXXVI, 279.

[19] *Ibid.*, p. 282.

[20] *Centuries of Meditations,* IV, 71–72, pp. 278–79.

[21] Wade, *op. cit.,* pp. 98 and 106.

[22] Vaughan, "The true Christmas," II, 646–47.

[23] "On Christmas Day," pp. 136–39.

[24] Cf. Wade, *op. cit.,* p. 322.

[25] "Christendom," p. 134; "The City," p. 198.

[26] "Thoughts. IV," p. 79.

[27] *Centuries of Meditations,* I, 47, p. 31.

[28] *Ibid.*, I, 48, p. 32.

[29] *Christian Ethicks,* p. 175.

[30] "Another," p. 63.

[31] "Ease," pp. 37–38; "Goodnesse," pp. 81–83.

[32] "Adam's Fall," pp. 115–16.

[33] "Blisse," pp. 69–70.

[34] "Goodnesse," p. 82.

[35] *Centuries of Meditations,* I, 68, pp. 48–49.

[36] "My Spirit," pp. 28–32; cf. "Thoughts. I," pp. 66–69.

[37] Cf. Christ, Ernst, *Studien zu Thomas Traherne,* Tübingen, 1932, pp. 44–45.

[38] "On Leaping over the Moon," pp. 183–85.

[39] Cf. Proud, J. W., "Thomas Traherne: A Divine Philosopher," *Friends' Quarterly Examiner,* LI, 74.

[40] Cf. *Felicities of Thomas Traherne,* ed. Sir Arthur Quiller-Couch, London, 1934, pp. xiv–xv; also Willett, Gladys E., *Traherne (an Essay),* Cambridge, 1919, pp. 38–57.

[41] *Centuries of Meditations,* III, 3, pp. 152–53.

[42] "A Newly-Discovered Poet," *Times Literary Supplement,* March 27, 1903, pp. 94–95.

[43] *Centuries of Meditations,* II, 69, p. 123.

[44] *Christian Ethicks,* p. 89.

[45] *Centuries of Meditations,* IV, 69, p. 276.

[46] "My Spirit," p. 28.

[47] "Consummation," pp. 202–4.

[48] *Centuries of Meditations,* II, 90, pp. 138–39.

[49] "My Spirit," pp. 30–31.

[50] "The Person," p. 42.

[51] "The World," pp. 116–19.

[52] "The Apostacy," pp. 120–22.

[53] Cf. "A Newly-Discovered Poet," p. 94.

INDEX

Acland, J. E., *Little Gidding and Its Inmates in the Time of King Charles I*, 205 *n.*, 206 *n.*, 212 *n.*

Adkins, Maria, 316.

Alchemy, 138, 400.

Allegory, 89.

Anabaptists, the, 55, 56.

Andrewes, Lancelot, 54, 61, 124, 132, 152, 154, 155, 158, 208, 218, 273, 278, 290, 382; *Devotions*, 124.

Anselm, St., 319.

Aphrodite (d'Erlanger), 84.

Aquinas, St. Thomas, 2, 26, 122, 227, 229, 247, 319.

Aristotle, 319.

Arminian, 59, 222.

Arminian Nunnery, The, 210, 211, 223.

Arnold, Matthew, 92.

Aubrey, John, *Brief Lives* (ed. Andrew Clark), 260.

Augustan poetry, 147.

Augustine, St., 108, 111, 116, 145, 319, 404; *The Confessions* (trans. E. B. Pusey), 1, 8, 15, 135.

Bacon, Francis, 98–99, 138, 152, 158; *The Advancement of Learning*, 36; *Translation of certaine psalmes into English Verse*, 152, 172.

Baker, Augustine, 126; *The Confessions*, 325; *Sancta Sophia*, "extracted . . . and digested" by Serenus Cressy, 126.

Barclay, Robert, *The Inner Life of the Religious Societies of the Commonwealth*, 242, 341 *n.*

Baronius, 319.

Baroque, the, 84, 198–99, 247, 254, 306, 370, 380.

Barratt, Kathleen I., *Studies in the Life and Writings of George Herbert*, 152 *n.*

Baxter, Richard, *Reliquiae Baxterianae*, 177.

Beachcroft, T. O., "Crashaw and the Baroque Style," 248 *n.*, 249 *n.*, 252 *n.*; "Nicholas Ferrar and George Herbert," 207 *n.*; "Traherne and the Cambridge Platonists," 352.

Beaumont, Charles, 222.

Beaumont, Joseph, 222, 380.

Bedford, Lucy, Countess of, 80, 108.

Beeching, H. C., ed., *George Herbert's Country Parson*, 154.

Bellarmine, 319.

Benlowes, Edward, "Theophila," 87.

Bennett, Joan, *Four Metaphysical Poets*, 71.

Bergson, Henri, *Mind-Energy*, trans. H. Wildon Carr, 6.

Berkeley, 349.

Bernard of Clairvaux, St., 16, 34, 111, 145, 319, 404; *Life and Works*, ed. Dom John Mabillon, trans. and ed. Samuel J. Eales, 6, 9, 17, 235.

Bettany, W. A. Lewis, Introduction to Henry Vaughan, *Silex Scintillans*, 313 *n.*

Bible, the, 44, 46, 271, 319, 344, 345; the Catholic view, 64; the Protestant, 64; emphasis on authoritarian values, 89; handling of, 219; and the Church, 284; and the Seekers, 345–46; Acts of the Apostles, 219; Gospels, 8, 219, 333, 345; New Testament, 89, 236; Old Testament, 89, 194; Psalms, 5, 89, 152, 345; Revelation, 352; Song of Solomon, 319.

Blake, 326, 339; "Auguries of Innocence," 23.

Blunden, Edmund, *On the Poems of Henry Vaughan*, 305 *n.*

Boehme, Jacob, 345; *Mysterium Magnum*, quoted in Holmes, *Henry Vaughan and the Hermetic Philosophy*, 295.

Book of Common Prayer, the, 353.

Book of Sports, 274–75.

lence," 338; "Thoughts. I," 362 *n.*;
"Thoughts. IV," 355; "Wonder,"
334–35; "World, The," 370 *n.*
Traherne, Thomas (nephew of poet),
323.
Transcendence, poetry of, 22–23, 405.
Trent, Council of, 43, 57.
Trevelyan, George Macaulay, *England under the Stuarts,* 45 *n.*
Turrian, Francis, 319.

Ussher, James, *Works of,* quoted in
Martin, ed., *The Poems of Richard
Crashaw,* 220.

Varley, F. J., *Cambridge during the
Civil War, 1642–1646,* 216 *n.*
Vaughan, Henry, 53, 70, 87, 88, 90,
93, 123, 148, 238, 320, 330, 331, 344,
353, 354, 357, 364, 366, 367, 369,
375, 377, 378, 379, 382, 384,
386, 387, 389, 390, 392, 400–411
passim; importance of his relation to
his group, 259–60; his family and
early environment, 260–61; his education, 261; and Bohemian life in
London, 261–62; uncertainty about
dates of his medical education and
marriage, 262; his return to Brecknockshire, 262; and the Civil War,
262–63; problem of his conversion,
264–65; the influence of Herbert,
266–67; unusual productiveness of
the following years, 267–69; possible causes of conversion, 269–72;
evidences of interest in the contemplative life, 272–73; his position on
contemporary ecclesiastical issues,
273–77; the devotional side of his
churchmanship, 277–79; influences
from other sources, 279–82; his relation to his tradition, 283–84; and to
the Seekers and the mystics, 285–
87; his preoccupation with the relations between life and death, 288;
his reminiscences of childhood, 288–
89; his feeling for nature, 288–89;
Hermetism and Christianity in, 289–
97; his "nature mysticism," 297–98;
his looking back to childhood and
Eden, 298–300; his mystical yearning, 301; his conception of God,
301–2; his contemplation of death,
303–4; his the desire of the mystic,
304–5; his experience of Reality in

nature, 305–7; the "mystical" feeling
in his work, 307–8; the effect of his
imagery, 308–11, and of his style,
311–14.
Letters to Aubrey: June 15, 1673,
260, 261, 262, 263, 268, 269–70,
386; June 28, 1680, 260, 295;
July 7, 1673, 260, 263, 270.
Translations: Anselm, *Man in
Glory,* 268, 272; Eucherius, *The
World Contemned,* 268, 273; Guevara, *The Praise and Happinesse of
the Countrie-Life,* 268, 272; Nierembergius, *Flores Solitudinis,* 268, 270,
272; Nollius, *Hermetical Physick,*
268, 270, 275; Plutarch, *Of the
Benefit We may get by our Enemies,*
268, 272, and *Of the Diseases of the
Mind and Body,* 268, 272.
Writings: "Ad Posteros," 262;
"Ascension-day," 299, 300; "Ascension-Hymn," 300; "Ass, The,"
306 *n*; "Bird, The," 291 *n.*, 310;
"Book, The," 306–7; "Buriall,"
310–11; "Cock-crowing," 294 *n.*, 295,
296–97; "Come, come, what doe I
here?" 271, 303 *n.*; "Constellation,
The," 276 *n.*, 306 *n.*; "Corruption,"
293 *n.*; "Death," 307 *n.*; "Distraction," 292 *n.*; "Dressing," 277;
"Elegie on the death of Mr. R. W.,
An," 271, 274; "Elegie on the death
of Mr. R. Hall, An," 262–63, 271;
"Epitaph upon the Lady Elizabeth,
Second Daughter to his late Majestie, An," 275 *n.*; "Favour, The,"
294 *n.*; "Holy Communion, The,"
277; "I walkt the other day (to
spend my hour)," 271, 291; "Importunate Fortune, written to Doctor
Powel of Cantre, The," 270; "Jacobs
Pillow, and Pillar," 274 *n.*; "Jesus
weeping," 301; "Joy of my life!"
280–81; "Juvenals tenth Satyre
Translated," 276; "Knot, The," 279–
80; "L'Envoy," 298 *n.*; "Man,"
292 *n.*; "Morning-watch, The,"
292 *n.*; *Mount of Olives: or, Solitary
Devotions, The,* 268, 273, 277–79;
"Nativity, The," 277; "Night, The,"
302; *Olor Iscanus,* 262, 264, 265 *n.*,
("The Publisher to the Reader"),
264; "Palm-Sunday," 293 *n.*; *Primitive Holiness, set forth in the Life
of Blessed Paulinus,* 268, 273, 274,